DOLLARS AND DOMINION

AMERICA IN THE WORLD

Sven Beckert and Jeremi Suri, Series Editors

Mary Bridges, *Dollars and Dominion: US Bankers and the Making of a Superpower*

Don H. Doyle, *Viva Lincoln: The Legacy of the Civil War and the New Birth of Freedom Abroad*

Edited by Jeffrey A. Engel, Mark Atwood Lawrence & Andrew Preston, *America in the World: A History in Documents since 1898, Revised and Updated*

Mark Atwood Lawrence, *The End of Ambition: The United States and the Third World in the Vietnam Era*

Roberto Saba, *American Mirror: The United States and Brazil in the Age of Emancipation*

Dorothy Sue Cobble, *For the Many: American Feminists and the Global Fight for Democratic Equality*

Stefan J. Link, *Forging Global Fordism: Nazi Germany, Soviet Russia, and the Contest over the Industrial Order*

Katy Hull, *The Machine Has a Soul: American Sympathy with Italian Fascism*

Sara Lorenzini, *Global Development: A Cold War History*

Michael Cotey Morgan, *The Final Act: The Helsinki Accords and the Transformation of the Cold War*

A. G. Hopkins, *American Empire: A Global History*

Tore C. Olsson, *Agrarian Crossings: Reformers and the Remaking of the US and Mexican Countryside*

Kiran Klaus Patel, *The New Deal: A Global History*

Adam Ewing, *The Age of Garvey: How a Jamaican Activist Created a Mass Movement and Changed Global Black Politics*

Jürgen Osterhammel and Patrick Camiller, *The Transformation of the World: A Global History of the Nineteenth Century*

Donna R. Gabaccia, *Foreign Relations: American Immigration in Global Perspective*

Thomas Borstelmann, *The 1970s: A New Global History from Civil Rights to Economic Inequality*

For a full list of titles in the series, go to: https://press.princeton.edu/catalogs/series/title/america-in-the-world.html

Dollars and Dominion

US BANKERS AND THE MAKING
OF A SUPERPOWER

MARY BRIDGES

PRINCETON UNIVERSITY PRESS

PRINCETON & OXFORD

Published by Princeton University Press
41 William Street, Princeton, New Jersey 08540
99 Banbury Road, Oxford OX2 6JX

press.princeton.edu

All Rights Reserved

Library of Congress Cataloging-in-Publication Data

Names: Bridges, Mary, 1979– author.
Title: Dollars and dominion : US bankers and the making of a superpower / Mary Bridges.
Description: Princeton : Princeton University Press, [2024] | Series: America in the world | Includes bibliographical references and index.
Identifiers: LCCN 2024005096 (print) | LCCN 2024005097 (ebook) | ISBN 9780691248134 (hardback) | ISBN 9780691248141 (ebook)
Subjects: LCSH: Banks and banking, International—United States—History—20th century. | International finance—History—20th century. | Financial institutions, International—History—20th century. | BISAC: BUSINESS & ECONOMICS / Banks & Banking | HISTORY / United States / 20th Century
Classification: LCC HG3903 .B75 2024 (print) | LCC HG3903 (ebook) | DDC 332.1/50973—dc23/eng/20240308
LC record available at https://lccn.loc.gov/2024005096
LC ebook record available at https://lccn.loc.gov/2024005097

British Library Cataloging-in-Publication Data is available

Editorial: Priya Nelson and Emma Wagh
Production Editorial: Natalie Baan
Jacket Design: Benjamin Higgins
Production: Danielle Amatucci
Publicity: William Pagdatoon
Copyeditor: Leah Caldwell

Jacket image: arenadesign / iStock

This book has been composed in Arno

Printed in the United States of America

10 9 8 7 6 5 4 3 2 1

CONTENTS

DOLLARS AND DOMINION

Introduction

THE HISTORY of the global financial power of the United States is often told from one of two perspectives. The first account leads with a person—perhaps a sweaty man in a wool suit. The man is a banker, and he steps off a steamer into a crowded port. We can imagine a version of his story animated in cinematic detail, the camera closely tracking his moves. Our fictionalized hero—let's call him Fred—weaves through Buenos Aires, Argentina, in the early days of World War I.

The city bustles. Carriages fill the tree-lined streets, and the man hears languages—Spanish, Italian, German, Russian, and more. He walks beyond the crowded port, and the architecture surprises him. The elegant buildings have columns, balustrades, and arched doorways. He squints and wonders if he has accidentally landed in Europe instead.

Fred's assignment is to serve as sub-accountant in a US bank branch in Buenos Aires. The job is a promotion from his last posting in Manila, where he helped open the first US bank in the Philippines. The work in Manila was a slog. His bank had rented space in the former horse stables of a Chinese merchant, and the branch flooded during monsoon season. When it rained, Fred had to find local men with wheelbarrows to move the bank's silver into the vaults of a European competitor.

Buenos Aires in 1916 is a different world. His new branch has hot water and an elevator. The situation in Europe—war, instability in London—has left everyone wanting dollars. His bosses in New York transferred him to Argentina to help the overwhelmed staff. New York should have sent a half-dozen men, but no more trained staff were available. Fred does what he can.

His colleagues organize a welcome dinner for him at the American Club. Next week, the Chamber of Commerce will host a luncheon for him and the new manager of US Steel, who just arrived from Panama. The dollar's star is rising, and Fred plans to follow its ascent. There are receptions to attend, credits to extend, and locals to meet.

In contrast to the character-driven approach, another vantage on the rise of US financial power in the early twentieth century emphasizes the role of institutions driving US imperial expansion. In this version, governments, the military, and banks claim center stage.

At the close of the nineteenth century, US politicians contemplate a new era of imperial expansion. The nation's tycoons are flush with the fortunes they amassed from westward expansion and industrialization. Now these financiers and industrialists search for new projects farther afield in Mexico, the Caribbean, and China.

Together with politicians in the Republican Party, the cluster of elites keeps a tight grip on political power. They rebuff populist calls for looser money, debt relief, and free silver. Instead, they advocate "sound money"—anchoring the US dollar to a specific quantity of gold—as well as Anglo-Saxon exceptionalism and spreading their civilizational gospel. The twin drives for political influence and commercial expansion help propel the US military into new territories overseas. In the early years of the twentieth century, US politicians advance their vision of US ascendence by claiming control over the Philippines, Puerto Rico, Cuba, and much of the Caribbean.

Some US leaders want to expand that authority over the Western Hemisphere and increase access to markets in Asia. To manage the nation's new colonial acquisitions, US officials create legal and social institutions to govern restive populations, secure access to raw materials, and ensure demand for US exports. In so doing, US leaders impose racialized social orders and collaborate with US financiers who operate from a shared playbook of white supremacist and patriarchal scripts.

A range of US institutions and actors—from the US Department of the Interior to banks to banana magnates to engineers—join in expanding US imperial power in the early twentieth century and accelerating the global rise of the US dollar. Their timing seems opportune: the nation is poised to surge to the top of the international political economy hierarchy, as war rages in Europe.

Both accounts—the sweaty-banker-in-a-suit and the imperial-institutions versions—offer key insights into a transformative moment in US history in the early twentieth century. During a few decades at the century's turn, the United States shifted from being a bit player in geopolitics to leading a new hierarchy of international political economy after World War I. Yet *Dollars and Dominion* argues that both frameworks—the individualist and the institutionalist—neglect important features of the emergence of US global power. They overlook the technologies, practices, information systems, and relationships that defined US global power. In other words, they overlook how the infrastructure of empire took shape.

Dollars and Dominion tells that story: it examines how US bankers worked overseas to develop relationships, gather information, and advance the US dollar. The book reveals the precarious origins of US overseas banking in the early 1900s and the durable foundation it established as the nation became a global leader after World War I. Many of the book's key moments happen not in DC boardrooms, diplomatic negotiations, or military planning sessions, but rather in the daily practices, relationships, and financial decisions that enabled a new financial infrastructure to support the empire of the US dollar.

The book's infrastructural account centers not on a single man, institution, or government, but rather the assemblage of financial practices, relationships, and systems that these entities created together. That assemblage emerged out of the interconnected structures of political economy—such as fiscal agent delegations, railroad contracts, and monetary policy—more than a monolithic master plan to promote US empire. Its interconnections made "Fred" more than just a lone banker working in a foreign port. Instead, he was a technician assembling a new financial apparatus that helped US banks pursue global profits, the Federal Reserve conduct monetary policy, and US empire reshape itself in new contexts.

Much of the infrastructure's power lay with the US government and its ability to back the payment promises of the US dollar. But the dollar meant little to the state or its citizens when it remained stagnant in government vaults. For the dollar to have an impact, it had to move. To do that, it needed banks. Specifically, in this early twentieth century moment, it needed banks to access new markets and broker new trading connections.

Thus, *Dollars and Dominion* finds an unexpected epicenter of US global power in the foreign branches of US banks and their New York records rooms. Bankers generated paperwork about foreign markets, and those records were compiled in thousands of reports and filed in manila folders. Named after "Manila hemp," or Philippine abaca fibers that made them stronger than traditional paper, the manila folders were woven from a colonial cash crop, while their insides contained facts about the commercial world beyond New York.[1] Credit dossiers, trade statistics, and customs protocols were centralized and organized in a single location. It was exactly the information that could help a US businessman send his wares to trading partners in Copenhagen, Calcutta, or Quito, or hundreds of places in between.

Indeed, the business*man* was nearly always that—a white, Anglo-Saxon, upper-class man. The pieces of paper he might encounter in New York filing cabinets were generated by similarly white, Anglo-Saxon, upper-class men, though women might have participated in the typing and filing.[2] The form's information was filtered through the men's worldviews about respectability, business etiquette, and the risks they associated with different parts of the world. The paper files and bank-brokered relationships offered a new commercial cartography to connect US businesses to overseas opportunities. And that cartography was shaped by the biases and belief systems of the people who made it. As of 1900, there was virtually no such thing as a US multinational bank. By mid-century, US banks dotted the globe, and the United States had become indispensable to the operation of the international financial system.

Dollars and Dominion's infrastructural approach reveals two important but often overlooked features of the rise of the United States in the early 1900s. First, the early pathways for expanding US influence, at least in the early decades of the twentieth century, had less to do with the innate savviness of US businesses and more to do with emulating British banking models and relying on the US government as a backstop. A retrospective account can obscure its wobbly beginnings, given that US multinational businesses became heavyweights in shaping international affairs in the post–World War II era. From today's vantage, it can be tempting to see the expansion of US managerial capitalism as a natural byproduct of its growing profitability and increasing efficiency. But from the perspective of the early 1900s, this outcome was far from assured. *Dollars and Dominion* reveals that the creation of the US financial infrastructure depended on imitating British predecessors, poaching European staff, and currying support from the US federal government.[3]

Second, the emerging infrastructure of US financial power reformatted and bureaucratized some of the more coercive displays of US imperialism that generated political resistance and became unpopular in the early twentieth century. US administrators and politicians struggled to preserve peace and govern populations in its overseas colonial possessions after 1898. These challenges helped strengthen anti-imperial pushback in the United States and rendered overt colonialism as an increasingly unpalatable political strategy for advancing its interests overseas. In this political climate, new expressions of US global power took shape. Creating a financial infrastructure anchored by multinational branch banks offered one way to expand the global reach of the US dollar and enlarge the nation's influence, profits, and domestic prosperity without the constant demands of colonial administration or the public visibility of using military force.

Certainly, the United States continued to send gunboats and deploy Marines in the Caribbean and Latin America to protect its self-declared interests.[4] These military incursions worked in tandem with US financiers to expand US imperial control in the Caribbean, as historian Peter Hudson has documented.[5] And the nation steadily amassed a network of overseas military bases.[6] But these strategies were unsuitable for expanding influence in many foreign locations.

Extending the reach of the US dollar through the private sector enabled a wider and more diffuse set of strategies for increasing international power.[7] Branch banks and the Federal Reserve System were foundational elements of the emerging infrastructure that undergirded the rise of the US dollar as a global currency and the influence of US commerce that accompanied this rise.

What kind of global power would the United States become? How engaged, how coercive, and how imperial? These questions were far from settled during the 1920s and 1930s. US politicians were eager to accelerate reconstruction in Europe after World War I, increase influence throughout Latin America, and expand trade with Asia, among other opportunities, but they equivocated about how much authority to exert over private banks, for example, or what type of leadership role to play in European peace negotiations. As politicians dithered, US banks forged new connections overseas, and their branches took root, built relationships with local clientele, and created new trade opportunities for US businesses.

The financial infrastructure that US banks helped establish offered a durable foundation for US power that could withstand the upheavals of the interwar period. The Great Depression caused global trade to collapse. It also fueled protectionist policies and impeded international cooperation. These changes could have hobbled US influence around the world, as nations defaulted on large debts to US private banks and anti-American sentiment surged in many regions.

Instead, in this fractured landscape, the financial infrastructure of US power proved malleable and enduring. US branch banks working overseas recruited local staff, shifted branding campaigns, and evaded regulations with innovative legal strategies. Their approaches maximized profits and avoided blowback throughout the turbulent 1930s. Branch banks pioneered many of the patterns of off-shoring, using tax havens, and creating subsidiaries to dodge oversight that came to characterize twentieth-century capitalism.[8]

Examining the origins of the financial infrastructure of US-driven globalization is particularly timely, given that it is once again in flux. Several recent trends suggest tectonic shifts in the foundation undergirding the last century of economic growth. The US economy is still the world's largest, but its share of global GDP has fallen to three-fifths of what it was in the 1960s.[9] Meanwhile, China's economic growth has become the headline story of macroeconomic change in recent decades.[10] Rising competition between the United States and China is one of several recent forces that seem to threaten the durability of dollar hegemony and highlight the tradeoffs of maintaining the dollar's preeminent global status.[11] The Federal Reserve's balance sheet expanded approximately tenfold in the fifteen years after the financial crisis, from less than $900 billion before the crisis to nearly $9 trillion in 2023.[12] How much balance-sheet ballooning is sustainable? How do political tensions between the United States and China affect the dollar's role as the world's leading currency?

In the absence of clear answers to these questions, China has invested in changing politics, economies, and ecosystems on the ground through its infrastructure construction and development projects around the world. The nation invested in building transportation, telecommunications, energy systems, and other large-scale projects in Asia, Africa, and Latin America through the Belt and Road Initiative.[13] And it has committed billions in development financing to help poor nations.[14] "Infrastructure statecraft" has become one of the central theaters of geopolitical competition in recent years, so the timing is particularly ripe to consider the politics and distributional impacts of the financial networks and economic patterns that guided political-economic change of the twentieth century.

Meanwhile, the financial infrastructure of trade and economic exchange is also in flux. New technologies, such as credit-rating algorithms that analyze terabytes of consumer data, or cryptocurrencies that bypass traditional clearinghouses, have challenged the centrality of traditional financial institutions. Distributed ledger technology, for example, offers ways to exchange money outside the traditional global payment systems governed by centralized banks and regulatory agencies. Finance is no stranger to innovating around geopolitical upheaval and technological disruption, but the convergence of these changes suggests that many of the bedrock systems and institutions supporting twentieth-century capitalism are now coming into question.[15]

One such institution in the crosshairs of public scrutiny is the US Federal Reserve System. The 2008 financial crisis and the COVID-19 pandemic profoundly reshaped how the Fed operates. Traditionally, the Fed has eased and tightened the supply of money in the United States by buying US Treasuries— short-term securities issued by the US government. Recent financial crises have broadened the Fed's power and expanded its toolkit for impacting the economy. Whereas the Federal Reserve Banks were once constrained to owning a narrow set of assets, quantitative easing reopened questions about what financial instruments were appropriate for a central bank to own. What investments and institutions get special protections in an economic crisis? What is the government's responsibility for stabilizing the financial system? How our society answers these questions affects which groups of people can access credit when, as well as what types of activities—from building schools to supporting electronic vehicles to buying homes—receive the greatest protections. The twin shocks of the 2008 financial crisis and the COVID-19 pandemic have reminded us that financial infrastructures are always freighted with social meaning and inherently connected to the politics of distribution.[16]

Dollars and Dominion contributes to debates about the politics of the Federal Reserve System by exploring the roots of this system. It examines the decades surrounding the passage of the Federal Reserve Act to understand how the nation's central banking system affected its financial status internationally and who benefited from the Fed's work. To preview the book's takeaways: the Fed's impacts on US finance internationally were tremendous, though not only for the most commonly cited reasons. Second, banks were among the most important beneficiaries of the Fed's early design, though again, not in all the ways that designers foresaw or that scholars have fully explored. Through new analysis of the impacts of an obscure credit instrument that was a cornerstone of the Fed's original design—the bankers' acceptance—*Dollars and Dominion* demonstrates that the Federal Reserve System depended on coordination with private-sector actors—namely, banks—for its monetary interventions to work. Moreover, banks had considerable leeway to shape the financial infrastructure as it unfolded.

Dollars and Dominion focuses on two institutions that had an outsized impact on the foreign branching activities of US banks. The nation's first broadly multinational bank—the International Banking Corporation—began operating branches in 1901. IBC was founded under a curious Connecticut charter by the owner of Remington Arms and a handful of Gilded Age tycoons. IBC originated in Connecticut, in part because larger national banks and most state banks at the time were not permitted to operate branches internationally. Thus, its Connecticut origins granted IBC privileges that few other US financial institutions could access. It built an international network of branches before the Federal Reserve Act was passed, at a time when national banks were prevented from such branching. IBC's initial operation piggybacked on the US overseas colonial empire. It was not oriented explicitly to promoting the US dollar but rather to supporting the military and commercial aspirations of a select handful of industrialist and financier-founders with robust ties to the Republican Party.

While other historians have unearthed pieces of IBC's peculiar history, *Dollars and Dominion* uses the bank's internal archives to map its inner workings and link its imperial aspirations to its on-the-ground operations and loan-making.[17] IBC was acquired by National City Bank, today's Citi, after the passage of the 1913 Federal Reserve Act, and National City—one of the nation's largest banks in the early 1900s and still today—becomes central to the second half of *Dollars and Dominion*. The bank emerged as the heavyweight in US multinational branching after World War I and the creation of the Federal Reserve System. With the new legal foundation of the Federal Reserve System, the operation of IBC branches—now operating under National City's purview—shifted, gradually reflecting the larger bureaucratic aspirations of its new corporate parent.

Hence, the Federal Reserve Act represents the narrative's turning point. The nation's central bank, created by Congress in 1913, changed the ground rules for US banks to operate overseas and also provided a backstop for banks' foreign work. Accordingly, the narrative explores how the Fed's decision-making and asset purchases influenced bankers' work. Federal Reserve bankers are not the story's protagonists, nor are the gritty mechanics of the Fed's governing board its central preoccupation. Nonetheless, the Fed looms large in the book's second half because its work had a foundational impact on how and where bankers operated and what they did once in place.

The book's geography spans multiple continents with several touchdowns, such as in China and the Philippines in the early 1900s and Argentina in the 1920s. Its goal is to map the coalescence of practices and relationships that created a financial infrastructure spanning multiple continents. Thus, the narrative hopscotches along with US bankers as they leave New York to work abroad. In the first part of the book, bankers prioritized sites of US colonial power, and *Dollars and Dominion* uses the Philippines as a case study for understanding US foreign banking in the pre–Federal Reserve era.

After the Federal Reserve Act and the start of World War I, the geography of US branch banking overseas shifted. National City Bank prioritized Latin America and Europe as new theaters for intensifying branch work. *Dollars and Dominion* draws out examples of work in Buenos Aires and other Latin American trading centers to exemplify different aspects of branches' work. The book also explores the integration of branching activities with other sovereign lending projects that preoccupied US bankers in the 1920s. Rather than approaching bankers' work with a preset geographic template, *Dollars and Dominion* follows geography as an evolving category to bankers themselves. Initially, National City executives envisioned branching in the "foreign field," as if the world beyond New York was a singular location, like a baseball field or a cotton field. Usage of the term "foreign field" fell out of fashion in the 1920s, however, as executives soon saw that different locations offered varying profit potentials, and regional demands required customized management strategies and oversight. Future studies will undoubtedly focus on the specific and nuanced dynamics that unfolded in discrete locations and assess how these patterns inform our understanding of US financial power.[18] The goal of *Dollars and Dominion* is less to focus on transnational dynamics of a single site than to map the extended topography of branching operations.

One location that rarely appears in the foreground of *Dollars and Dominion* action but nonetheless claimed a disproportionate mindshare for US bankers is London. As US banks embarked on their campaign to dot the globe with branches, their model for international banking excellence was Britain. London was the world's financial center in the nineteenth century. British money—the pound sterling—was the preeminent currency for denominating global trades. US reformers saw the British banking system as the apex of sound, conservative financial practices. US bankers viewed the vast networks of British branch banks as an enviable example for multinational finance. Given US bankers' preoccupation with British finance, the first three chapters of *Dollars and Dominion* explore how the long shadow of British banking provided the initial template for US bankers' work. As the United States emerged from World War I as the world's leading creditor, its political prominence, trade networks, and commercial influence expanded. *Dollars and Dominion* argues that branch banks offered foundational components of the infrastructure that enabled this expansion.

Why Banks?

Banks can seem at first like an inauspicious place to look for understanding the gritty texture of geopolitical transformation. In popular conceptions, banks function like black boxes that move money by issuing deposits and providing loans. They report earnings and losses, and their CEOs—often white men—use jargon to describe economic conditions and future risks.

This transactional view of banks misses much of their power, variability, and impact. For one thing, it ignores the hands-on role that banks play in shaping access to economic opportunity.[19] Banks provide funds to fight wars and build large-scale public works. They can change the money supply. Bankers create in-groups and out-groups by differentiating creditworthy applicants from the unworthy ones. What determines creditworthiness? What assets are "safe"? Who are "our customers"? These questions can, at first, seem like technocratic concerns, answerable through data analysis. But the history of banking reveals that determining what information counts as data was—and is—a process of creating categories, differentiating people, and extracting certain features of an ecosystem as relevant and quantifiable. Credit files are not preexisting artifacts that US bankers can collect from objectively accurate, predetermined sources. Information must get made.[20]

Dollars and Dominion argues that the process of making contacts, constructing credit information, and building a financial infrastructure in new places depended on how US bankers operated on the ground. The early cohorts of US foreign bankers worked to ingratiate themselves with local elites and adapt to new business norms. Leaving New York with racialized, gendered, and classist views of the world, bankers found that their views required adjusting to accommodate their new banking contexts, even though their biases often persisted. Once in place, they helped expand US global power on elitist, patriarchal, and racialized foundations. They did so not as part of a unified grand strategy or a monolithic conspiracy of US imperialism to perpetuate inequalities. Instead, the ad hoc, piecemeal accretion of business deals, British copycat strategies, and structural features of the US financial system created a flexible apparatus that, over time, conveyed financial opportunities to some more than others.

The conventional view of banks as black boxes ignores the fact that they have unique public duties that have given them a central role in mediating the expansion of US financial power around the world. Banks differ from everyday widget makers or merchants because they fulfill a public function—namely, they can expand and contract the money supply. Accordingly, they are regulated by different laws and require special government-issued charters or licenses to operate. Divisions of government exist to oversee their operations, and the government grants US national banks—banks that are members of the Federal Reserve System—a special license whereby private payment promises can be transformed into obligations of the state through banks' access to the Fed's unique instruments and facilities. Banks perform this remarkable alchemy through fractional reserves and their ability to access the Fed's discount window—a mechanism that allows banks access to short-term loans.[21] Banks are essential to the operation of the financial system in part because they can convert one type of payment promise—a bank deposit—into a different form of money—namely, liabilities of the central bank.[22] The 2008 financial crisis provided a reminder that banks' special powers carry risks and that their missteps can imperil public well-being.

Because of this special role, banks shape the social infrastructure that distributes access to wealth and economic opportunity. Instead of interpreting banks' impacts solely in terms of balance sheets, quantifiable metrics, and year-end reports, *Dollars and Dominion* sifts through the mezzanine layers of banking. It investigates training programs, middle management dynamics, and paperwork requirements to understand the richer, weirder, and more textured impacts US banks had within their communities. To understand US banking in the Philippines, the book investigates the loan portfolio of a branch to, quite literally, follow the money. To understand profitability, the book analyzes financial data alongside government documents, court cases, and bankers' memoirs to situate banks within the ecosystems where they operated. Thus, the book relies on qualitative and quantitative methods, political and business sources, and a distributed set of impacts to consider banking in a larger frame of reference. It draws on previously unanalyzed internal bank records, as well as government documents, bankers' papers, media reports, court filings, and other records from roughly two dozen state and international archives to piece together the fragmented origins of US branch banking around the world.

The focus on banks as infrastructure foregrounds several features of their work. For one thing, the perspective focuses our attention on the durability of branch banks' work.[23] An infrastructure need not be flashy, state-of-the-art, or headline-generating to impact people's lives. A special feature of infrastructure is, by contrast, that people tend to forget about it when it works properly. Sewage, electricity, access to clean water—these services represent the byproduct of civil engineering, major capital investments, and ongoing maintenance; nonetheless, they tend to operate in obscurity until something goes wrong.[24]

Even though infrastructures can operate underground or invisibly, they enable certain activities at the expense of others. As such, infrastructures have politics: they establish the "conditions of possibility" for how people exercise freedoms and what types of events can transpire within them.[25] For example, constructing an interstate system enabled greater connectivity and easier transportation across the continental United States. The system also prioritized the automobile industry and car ownership over bicycles, trains, and other modes of transport. Thus, the disposition of the US highway infrastructure was to enable automobiles and fossil fuel-based transportation. Moreover, this disposition continued even if operational control of the infrastructure changed hands. For example, ownership of a toll road could shift from a private company to a local government, but the change would not alter its path or preference for cars over trains and bicycles.

Branch banks have similar infrastructural capacities, in that they enable certain activities and benefit certain populations at the expense of others. And as brick-and-mortar outposts of US institutions, they have staying power, even when geopolitical conditions change. *Dollars and Dominion* reveals that US bankers working overseas did not have to be particularly good bankers to continue operating in the early decades of the twentieth century. Instead, they could rely on the US government for deposits and protection. Nor did they have to make great fortunes from new machinery established by the Federal Reserve System to make an impact. Instead, it was enough for them to be in the right places—major US trading centers around the world—at the right time, namely, when the United States emerged from World War I as a decisive power in international relationship. Thus, their orientation, modes of operation, and capacity to promote the dollar, when paired with the Federal Reserve System, had a lasting impact on the way US power took shape overseas.

The emphasis on the branch banks' durability and fixity sheds light on a perennial problem of economic analysis. In classical economics, lowering interest rates means that money is cheaper and easier to access. As anyone buying or paying college loans knows, it's better to borrow money at 1 percent interest than at 10 percent because lower interest rates mean that money is cheaper. In theory, cheaper money benefits the most productive economic actors—those best positioned to profit from the new financial calculus. However, seeing banks as infrastructure allows us to understand economic activity with greater nuance. In this framing, credit determinations are not black-and-white equations about the potential for productivity. Instead, credit moves through banking channels, and banks do not operate via frictionless networks, equally open to potential recipients. Banks have clientele, protocols, and points of connection that are shaped by history, relationships, paperwork practices, and other on-the-ground accidents. In other words, social and cultural histories matter to economic policy. When a central bank eases the money supply, its policies have different impacts on different populations, depending on those populations' historical relationship with banking infrastructures.

Context: Mapping the Existing Scholarship

Dollars and Dominion emphasizes the uneven foundations of US financial infrastructure in the early twentieth century. This view distinguishes its perspective from many accounts of dollar diplomacy, US empire, and banking in the early twentieth century. The existing historical scholarship has given us rich depictions of the rise of the United States in the early twentieth century. One recurring theme in the studies of US global power in the early 1900s involves a focus on the US government acting as the "promotional state" in advancing US business overseas.[26] The interconnection between business and state interests was no secret to US political leaders at the turn of the century. As President William Howard Taft told Congress in 1912, "Modern diplomacy is commercial."[27] In theory, Taft's vision for dollar diplomacy aspired to use commerce rather than military intervention to guide the nation's involvement overseas. In practice, attempts to implement the approach faltered regularly. The United States encroached on the sovereignties of other nations to protect its private-sector interests, but often those nations, as well as other great powers, pushed back. Opposition to "dollar dependency" policies became a rallying cry for groups to denounce US imperial influence, especially in the Caribbean and South America.[28] Subsequent presidential administrations backed away from Taft's foreign policy.

Nonetheless, the general formula—encouraging private-sector leadership with US government backing—persisted through the 1920s. One iteration of this partnership involved US government support for US economists to travel overseas and propose new monetary systems for its colonies and other Latin American countries. The reforms were designed to create a "gold-exchange bloc"—a network of nations and dependencies that pegged their currencies to the US dollar in hopes of one day rivaling the British pound.[29] Other iterations of public-private collaboration include policymakers' reliance on specific firms and business leaders to advance US interests abroad. For example, partners with JP Morgan and other US businessmen stood in for government actors in European summits to negotiate German war debt after World War I. In addition, the federal government created elaborate new bureaucracies to support US commerce overseas.[30] And during the 1920s, US foreign policy officials often deferred to US banks, which made ill-advised loans to governments around the world.[31] These examples reveal the centrality of public-private collaboration in expanding US influence in the early twentieth century.

Accounts of the "promotional state," as scholars have termed this mode of business-mediated diplomacy, provide powerful insights into state-directed efforts to shape US influence around the world. *Dollars and Dominion* adds a new vantage. It plumbs banking archives, bankers' papers, and ledgers to see this codependence not from the lens of foreign policy but rather in terms of the financial infrastructure it created. In doing so, it recasts the "promotional state" as one component of a larger apparatus of commercial power. Widening the analytical frame allows us to see the heavyweight role of another state-based institution that is often underappreciated in traditional accounts: the Federal Reserve System.[32] *Dollars and Dominion* positions the Federal Reserve Act of 1913 as a watershed event in US multinational banking and argues that the Fed's ongoing work provided a catalyzing and stabilizing force for US banking overseas.

This perspective sheds light on the middle layers of decision-making, management, and implementation that separated metropolitan dreams of US power from the messy, on-the-ground reality.[33] When US policymakers deputized bankers to do the state's bidding, bankers and other private-sector actors did not always share the state's vision for advancing US interests. Moreover, when US government priorities shifted, financial actors did not always move in lockstep. Focusing on how the infrastructure took shape demonstrates the inadequacy of seeing like a state or seeing like a bank if we want to understand how US global power unfolded over time.

Several historians, including Peter Hudson, Yoshiko Nagano, and Allan Lumba, have written pioneering studies about the racialized, imperial work of US bankers in expanding US financial power.[34] *Dollars and Dominion* builds on this groundbreaking work by positioning branch banks as part of an enduring financial infrastructure that acquired staying power, thanks in part to banks' ability to draw support from the Federal Reserve System and pivot based on local opportunities.

A second theme in the existing scholarship of US global power in the early 1900s emphasizes World War I and its aftermath as a watershed moment. In this view, the United States was relatively insignificant prior to the war and became a "super-state" in geopolitics in its aftermath.[35] Again, this account offers valuable insights into the political dynamics that emerged in the 1920s and 1930s, as new international institutions, such as the League of Nations, created alternative formats to a world order dominated by European empires.[36] However, the emphasis on change can obscure the continuities that predated it. Understanding the rise in US global power from the vantage of its financial scaffolding helps us see that US influence depended on a previous generation of financiers and diplomats who built a ramshackle network of business connections and financial institutions. This network emerged from Gilded Age fortunes and depended on British imperial power for know-how, staffing, and social hierarchies. *Dollars and Dominion* connects this earlier story to the nation's interwar transition by providing a new framework that identifies the inter-imperial continuities on which US global power was founded.

US historians have long debated the power and scope of US empire. What shape did US imperial power take, how punitive was it, and who designed it? These debates have, at times, spiraled into barbed exchanges about whether the United States was exceptional in its projection of global power. Claims to exceptionalism hinge on seeing the United States as a nation that differed from European precedent because it relied less on territorial colonial conquest than other methods of expanding influence.[37] At times, these debates have focused less on history and more on politicized debates about the nation's role in perpetuating and exacerbating injustice and inequality.[38]

Dollars and Dominion offers an alternative approach to these debates by shifting the "why" of imperial design to the "how" of its operation. What were the mechanics of extending the empire of the dollar on the ground? This recasting shifts the analytical emphasis from examining the intentions or hopes of the designers to the on-the-ground impacts of US power and the propensities of its financial infrastructure to empower some activities and actors over others. This approach reminds us that, regardless of where or why a system was conceived—a Washington conference room by imperialist politicians, a Manhattan board room by corrupt capitalists, or an academic summit focused on promoting economic progress—its operation rarely conformed to the blueprints of distant designers. Its forms depended on an interplay of economic and political pressures, as well as contestation, as it was being built. Charting the infrastructure of that power allows us to see what difference it made in practice.

Structure

The story spans the first three decades of US multinational branch banking. It begins in 1901, as the United States government found itself in the unusual position of managing an international empire without an international bank. Chapter 1 asks how the United States got into the business of international banking in the first place. Whereas British banks spanned the globe, only one US bank established a significant multinational network around the turn of the twentieth century: the International Banking Corporation. IBC was a bizarre mashup of Gilded Age wealth and British-banking aspirations. The first chapter explores its origin story. IBC opened more than a dozen branches on four continents at a time when not a single US national bank was permitted to operate foreign branches. Its international expansion was possible thanks to an unusual charter that IBC finagled from the Connecticut legislature, which allowed it to conduct almost any kind of banking business—collecting deposits, issuing notes, investing in infrastructure—so long as it did so outside the state of Connecticut.[39]

IBC was an imperial entity by design. Bank executives claimed to work "hand in hand with Uncle Sam."[40] It was the US government's fiscal agent in Panama and the Philippines and the collector of China's indemnity payment for the Boxer Rebellion. Several historians have examined IBC's imperial connections.[41] *Dollars and Dominion* expands the geography of those connections and deepens our understanding of state-bank relations: it argues that IBC's role as an imperial agent to the US government was not as linear or straightforward as executives claimed. In fact, the bank frequently worked at cross-purposes with US politicians about how to extend the nation's global influence.

The second chapter explores how US bankers made—and lost—money in new contexts. It examines the practices, from credit evaluations to penmanship, that IBC copied from European competitors to increase its business and assess would-be borrowers in new contexts. IBC executives regarded British banking protocols as the gold standard of international finance and sought to replicate numerous practices, from training junior staffers to relying on local go-betweens in China. Despite attempts to emulate British success, IBC struggled in its early years to gain a foothold in international markets and to develop the name recognition or capital base that would have granted it access to more lucrative syndicated loans and coveted business deals.

Chapter 3 delves a layer deeper into the core of bank operations by examining who benefited from IBC's presence overseas. Who could access IBC lending? The chapter analyzes the loan portfolio of IBC's Manila branch in the early 1900s. By tugging threads of bank-ledger entries, it unravels the connections and social positioning of borrowers. In doing so, the chapter maps more than 95 percent of the bank's loans and assesses the bank's broader social impacts. While IBC executives professed to extend the beachhead of commercial opportunity for US businesses in the Philippines, its loan portfolio suggests a different story. Much of IBC's lending in the early decade of its operation enriched existing elites, including Chinese merchants and European businesses. Moreover, the work of IBC bankers often undercut efforts of US colonial officials, who faced pressure from both Washington and Filipino communities to restore sovereignty in the archipelago to Filipinos.

The 1913 passage of the Federal Reserve Act represented a fulcrum for US multinational banking. Chapter 4 asks how the Federal Reserve System reconfigured the relationship between banks and the US state. It finds that an obscure credit instrument—the bankers' acceptance—became a conduit for channeling state support into private banks' internationalization.[42] Understanding the acceptance market requires a gritty detour into the mechanics of early-twentieth-century trade finance, but the payoff for delving into the seemingly arcane minutiae is large: acceptances meshed state power with banks' work overseas. Acceptances essentially turned a payment promise for overseas trade into a commodity. The secondary market for this commercial paper—the acceptance market—changed how US banks operated overseas, in terms of their capacity to finance trade and their risk calculations in expanding overseas.[43]

Moreover, the Fed imbued acceptances with special powers that privileged them over many other assets. The Federal Reserve Act allowed US banks to accept bills, and those bills were eligible for discount with the Federal Reserve—a special designation that made them more liquid than ineligible assets. Further, Federal Reserve Banks purchased acceptances to hold as assets in their own portfolios. Together, these powers expanded the way in which the US government supported the empire of the dollar without exerting military force, gunboat diplomacy, or overt coercion. Suddenly, the bureaucratized veneer of the Federal Reserve System offered a new mechanism to channel state backing for US global power in ways that did not resemble traditional imperial incursions—namely, by intermediating that influence through US banks. This legal framework transformed the way branch banks could and did operate. National City Bank acquired IBC and gradually refashioned its network of branches to promote new credit tools and shift operating modes to support larger corporate goals.

Chapter 5 asks how this new system related to both US banking and international financial norms. It argues that acquiring information—especially credit information about international markets—became a core feature of the new architecture of US international banking. National City Bank emerges as a protagonist in international branching. After the Federal Reserve Act removed a prohibition that barred national banks from opening branches abroad, National City Bank became the biggest and most aggressive in internationalization. Within a decade of the act's passage, roughly three-quarters of US overseas bank branches belonged to National City.[44] However, the practices that National City bankers sought to export overseas did not always mesh with business cultures where US bankers inserted themselves. Standards created by the Federal Reserve System pushed banks to systematize and standardize collection of credit information, among other data. US bankers working overseas struggled to adapt these demands to contexts where such disclosures were less common and, at times, caused resentment. US bankers overseas thus functioned as go-betweens who bridged new demands for standardized information with traditional practices of relationship banking and gentlemanly capitalism as they expanded their clientele.[45]

Chapter 6 analyzes the human infrastructure behind US branch banking overseas. If relationships and personal networks were integral to the operation of US banks overseas, who were the individuals cultivating those relationships, and what were their cultural expectations about "character" and "respectability"? The chapter explores the staffing pipeline of US overseas banking by examining the training program that National City Bank created to prepare young men to work as its junior staff overseas. The values, biases, and practices baked into the program reveal how US bankers constructed "us" and "them" overseas. Their training adopted the social hierarchies of Wall Street at the time and shared its racialized, elitist, and patriarchal foundations. However, US bankers were not mere carriers of racialized and gendered scripts that they imposed on overseas communities. Once abroad, US bankers' social hierarchies and practices proved amenable to adaptation and modification, depending on the opportunities for profit.

Finally, chapter 7 examines what happened when the Great Depression upended global trade and the multinational cooperation that followed World War I. Executives at National City Bank had designed their network of global branches based on their expectations of increasing US exports and international interconnection. The Depression challenged those expectations as trade declined and many nations turned inward. In this economic context, overseas branches surprised even the bank's executives with their resilience. Economic setbacks throughout the interwar period prompted bankers to realize that overseas markets were not a singular, undifferentiated expanse of a foreign field. Instead, each local community represented a distinct convergence of economic pressures, cultures, and politics. Further, greater profits could be made by getting local. Conducting thrift campaigns, selling securities, and downplaying ties to the United States were all strategies that US bankers used overseas to adapt in new economic conditions.

Through localization and regulatory adaptation, US multinational banking became an enduring feature of the international financial system and a cornerstone in expanding US commercial power in the early twentieth century. *Dollars and Dominion* ends on the eve of World War II, as the foundation of the Bretton Woods system was taking shape. This era cemented the dollar's role as the dominant global currency and offered a new foundation of postwar economic integration.[46] Nonetheless, in a testament to the durability of infrastructure, the branch network of the early twentieth century persevered and even provided a foundation for Citi's subsequent emergence as the bank that "never sleeps," because of its globalized, time-zone-spanning work.[47]

Dollars and Dominion demonstrates the risks of seeing our financial system as technocratic circuitry that enables the frictionless movement of money. Instead, the system was designed by politicians and advocates of specific commercial interests. It enabled some asset holders to gain power, and it created barriers that impeded others' access to opportunity or power. Understanding the system properly requires recasting the lore of swashbuckling US bankers abroad, on the one hand, and clinical, institutionalist accounts of ascendent US capitalism on the other. Instead, *Dollars and Dominion* explores the interstices and connective tissue of US global power by following the work of US banks overseas.

How we answer questions about the design of financial infrastructures—from how the Fed should operate to the US government's commitment to maintaining dollar hegemony—has long-term implications for society's winners and losers. Today, many of the pillars that undergirded the economic growth of the twentieth century have come into question. New technologies, like mobile payment systems and blockchain, give us a wide range of choices about how to redesign our financial system. And growing competition among great powers—the United States, China, and the European Union, for example—focuses not only on how those systems get built, but also who does the building, who owns their material underpinnings, and where its constituent pieces live. As we rethink many of the core tenets of how our financial system functions, understanding its rickety but enduring origins has become even more pressing.

1

The Empire Needs a Banker

BY THE TURN of the twentieth century, the United States had defeated Spain in the Spanish-American War and agreed to pay $20 million to purchase the Philippine Islands. The duty to oversee its new territorial possession, as well as its claims over the former Spanish territories of Cuba, Puerto Rico, and Guam, left the US government with a range of questions about executing its new colonial administration responsibilities abroad. What kind of imperial power would it be? How would it manage an overseas colonial empire? And, on a more mundane level, how would it pay soldiers, buy supplies, finance a colonial government, and handle cash flow in foreign locations?

In many ways, these questions represented routine challenges for colonial administrators. For centuries, governments had relied on private banks and other institutions to finance wars and move money overseas. And for decades, the US government had worked with foreign banks around the world to pay bills and purchase goods for consulates, diplomatic missions, and other activities. Before the twentieth century, the US government's foreign bankers of choice were British. At the time, British banks were the standard bearers for reliable, conservative international banking practices. The international expanse of the British empire cemented the importance of British financial institutions to service its trade, military, and administrative needs.

Whereas British imperial rule was deeply entangled with British international banking by 1900, the United States at the turn of the century was a relative newcomer to overseas empire-building. When it established a Philippine civilian government in the Philippines in 1901 under the leadership of William Howard Taft, the US government faced the challenge of supporting more than seventy thousand US troops, combatting a widespread Philippine insurgency movement, and overseeing the day-to-day logistics of archipelago governance, from collecting taxes to administering elections.[1] Suddenly, the nation found itself in a new position of needing to manage an overseas colonial empire without a US international bank.

An upstart firm emerged to capitalize on these new overseas opportunities: the International Banking Corporation. IBC emerged as a slapdash effort of US industrialists, railroad tycoons, and friends of President Theodore Roosevelt to create a financial institution that could support and profit from US imperial expansion. Much of IBC's early operation depended on providing banking services to US military and diplomatic missions overseas. IBC executives promised officials in Washington that the bank would create the financial circuitry for US colonial efforts to touch down, take root, and transmute metropolitan gold into local deposits that could expand US commercial interests. Its operation depended on a network of white male bankers who catered to the needs of—and profited from relationships to—imperialist politicians.

As this chapter demonstrates, dismissing IBC as a simplistic exemplar of gangster capitalism or huckster banking overlooks its deeper and more durable connections to the inner workings of US power overseas. Certainly, rogue bankers and gangsters of capitalism abounded in the early history of US international banking and helped shape the contours of finance capitalism.[2] But interpreting IBC as a fringe institution on the periphery of US politics and finance misses the deeper and more central ways in which the bank developed techniques, leveraged existing technologies, navigated political opportunities, and assembled durable systems that evolved and adapted overtime. Indeed, the story of IBC—the nation's first broadly multinational bank—was stranger, more circuitous, and more revealing of the eventual infrastructure of US financial power than just a one-off story of crony capitalists operating abroad.[3]

Due in part to the sturdiness of government support and the deep pockets of Gilded Age wealth from which it drew, IBC would endure, despite its faltering start and early missteps. What began as a side hustle by Gilded Age tycoons to dabble in international finance would evolve over the next three decades to become part of the financial substrate on which US commercial power was built. But until then, IBC would make its share of rookie mistakes even while expanding the beachhead for US businesses in foreign trade.

I. The British-Dominated Status Quo of Multinational Banking

In the late nineteenth century, only a few US banks had the reach and reputation to operate on a broadly international scale, and none did so through an extensive branch network. The field of multinational branching was instead dominated by British institutions, British technologies, and British norms. To gain staying power in this world, IBC sought to configure itself to fit the British banking mold by learning from and adapting to the landscape dominated by the gold standard and established British banks and international financiers.

In this world, several exceptional US banks, such as JP Morgan and the Brown Brothers and Company, maintained a strong international presence; however, they did so through London-based offices, family relationships, and intermediaries, rather than by maintaining an on-the-ground network of multinational branches. Such banks typically maintained offices in London and the United States. Partner offices handled international transactions with overseas agents, correspondents, and correspondent banks in locations beyond New York and London. The Morgan partners, for example, lent money to governments and financed trade all over the world in the nineteenth century. They participated in syndicates for projects ranging from India to Sweden to Costa Rica.[4] Likewise, Brown Brothers—another preeminent bank with Anglo-US origins—had been a leader throughout the nineteenth century in providing letters of credit and trade finance to support the movement of people and goods all over the world.[5] However, these institutions operated without an extensive network of international branches.

Such banks focused on providing financial services to an elite strata of US families and corporations, and they tended to be exclusive.[6] High barriers to entry limited the clientele they served. Both banks maintained their international reach through strong relationships, either family-based or through correspondents. They formalized relationships with agents in overseas locations or relied on trusted intermediaries in regions where they conducted regular business, such as Argentina or Chile.[7] If the US military wanted to pay a US soldier serving in the Philippines, or if a US missionary in China wanted to deposit money, however, neither JP Morgan banks nor Brown Brothers offered the optimal services, at least not without working through international partners.

The US banking system at the turn of the twentieth century focused primarily on domestic needs, and this inward focus had helped fuel decades of rapid infrastructure building to connect the United States—such as by expanding US railroads and transportation networks. The work produced great fortunes and generated vibrant economic opportunities in the 1800s, and it did so by using a fractured and locally oriented banking system. The system emerged from long-standing political opposition to the centralization of financial power in the nineteenth century. Rural communities throughout the nation tended to resist the emergence of large, metropolitan banks, and agrarian political groups blocked urban financiers from expanding their banking networks and amassing regional power.

This political landscape nurtured the development of small, local banks and deterred the emergence of strong, internationally connected banking houses. Instead, US financial institutions took shape as "unit banks," as the practice of establishing solitary offices or connected partnerships was known. In this system, the large, national banks—such as National City Bank and Chase National Bank, which had the resources to support extensive international operations—instead had to navigate a regulatory landscape that restricted international and domestic branching.[8] Given such terrain, US firms and individuals who needed international banking services often looked to British institutions or US banks that partnered with British banks to fulfill their international finance needs.

While the United States eschewed powerful, centralized banking networks, London thrived as an international hub where large banks could coordinate business. British sterling was the primary currency of international trade, and the global reach of the pound helped make London an efficient place to transact business. The tendrils of British banks expanded overseas, moving alongside the empire's growth. By 1913, British banks operated 1,286 branches around the world.[9] The reach of British banks was so extensive that *Bankers' Magazine* published a spoof prospectus to advertise a new bank in the only two places that seemed to lack British financial services: the North and South Poles.[10] Even within JP Morgan's banking partnerships, the London office was central to much of its overseas operation, and the balance of power between the London and New York offices began to favor the United States only toward the end of the nineteenth century. Throughout, the London office played a central role in foreign trade, currency exchange, and international loans.[11]

British financial dominance in global trade depended in part on the gold standard as a shared monetary framework that cemented trading relationships. Under the gold standard, a nation linked the value of its currency to a set value in gold and guaranteed the convertibility of its currency to that gold value—at least in principle. Adopting the gold standard conveyed advantages in both international trade and finance: foreign creditors were typically more willing to lend money to gold-standard nations, and gold-pegged currencies posed fewer risks of volatility to international traders. In practice, the nineteenth-century gold standard was less a monolithic system of global convergence than a variable set of practices, adopted and implemented differently depending on the political economy of a particular nation.[12]

Nonetheless, the gold standard became a proxy for judgments about the sophistication and stability of overseas markets, and the regime carried advantages for British intermediaries. US traders associated the British-led gold standard with norms about a society's level of advancement. As one US banking textbook instructed, "All the advanced nations of the world to-day have adopted the gold standard."[13] Moreover, the gold standard conveyed material advantages to the British, due to the importance of sterling as a global currency.[14] Throughout much of the British empire, operating on the gold standard meant that colonies pegged their currencies to sterling.[15] As a result, colonies had to keep sterling reserves to maintain the currency pegs, and they became more dependent on British monetary policy. Expansion-oriented US politicians viewed this sterling-exchange system with envy. Indeed, in the early 1900s, US colonial administrators developed a model for a competing currency bloc whereby US colonies and dependencies would denominate their currencies based on the US dollar, rather than sterling, as a foundation for the gold standard.[16]

As the gold standard became both a currency-management approach and a status symbol, Britain continued to represent the pinnacle of the geopolitical order. Before the outbreak of World War I, 60 percent of financing for global trade flowed through London's discount market.[17] Britain's dominance extended not only to financial systems, but also to the information and transportation infrastructures that accompanied it. British shipping companies transported more than half the global tonnage that traveled over oceans.[18] British firms operated 70 percent of the global infrastructure of telegraph networks.[19] This privileged position in international trade conveyed a competitive advantage to British businesses.[20]

For US businesses, the British dominance of global trade created costs—both real and perceived. Most obviously, trades were usually conducted in sterling, so US traders paid transaction fees and foreign exchange costs.[21] Another cost involved the loss of control over sensitive trade information. To secure British financing, US traders had to submit documentation that revealed prices of goods, shipping details, client information, and other facts that US manufacturers considered to be "trade secrets." In the early 1900s, US trade advocates accused European banks of sharing these secrets with their own business communities. Many US traders noted that European banks gave special treatment to clients of the same nationality and feared that their businesses suffered as a result.[22]

Not only did they give up control of proprietary information, but US traders also found that British banks did not participate in the information-exchange practices that were foundational to US credit evaluations. In the United States, banks frequently served as an information source about the creditworthiness of clients and associates. Banks exchanged information—such as merchants' reputations, payment histories, and general financial standing—with each other, mercantile agencies, and sometimes other firms. US sellers drew from these diverse sources to determine the credit terms they would offer to buyers. By contrast, British banks operated according to different information-sharing norms and practices. British banks did not customarily "answer inquiries coming from individuals or firms that do not keep an account with the bank," noted a US Commerce Department publication. "Information given out by

British banks in regard to firms' standings is usually of a general and non-committal character."[23] As a result, US traders saw asymmetries: they lost information they shared with British banks, and they failed to gain reciprocal information about buyers, competitors, and markets, which they were accustomed to receiving from US banks.

The overall landscape of international branch banking held British banks as a model to emulate for many US financiers. Several British banks, such as the Hongkong and Shanghai Banking Corporation, exemplified the power and status that an international network of branches could command. The Hongkong Bank was established by a group of British traders in Hong Kong in 1865.[24] Its founders rooted themselves in the financial worlds of China's treaty ports and London finance, due to its leaders' close connections to some of Britain's most respected financial institutions.[25] By the turn of the century, the Hongkong Bank operated branches throughout Asia and had established a formalized training program in London for preparing new hires for overseas work. Its staffing policies included an interview, entrance exam, and referral requirement.[26] Such structures offered a sharp contrast to the US banking system, which, at the time, had no established branch network—much less entry requirements, a training program, and human resources policies to guide it.

If not for several ruptures in geopolitics, British banking superiority might have simply been a matter of asymmetries in information and institutional experience. By the turn of the twentieth century, many US lawmakers and military advisers were searching for opportunities to expand the nation's economic and political profile.[27] In 1898, the outbreak of the Spanish-American War created new demands for the US state, as well as financial responsibilities, such as paying soldiers' salaries and buying supplies in Asia and the Caribbean. Subsequently, Secretary of State John Hay issued the first Open Door Note in 1899 to alert European powers that the United States sought greater access to trading with China. As US policymakers expanded their ambitions for trade, influence, and territorial control, a related question was how these broadened ambitions related to finance. US policymakers began envisioning different systems of financial exchange that could challenge sterling's preeminence as a global currency.[28] Some US officials sought to amass a network of trading partners that pegged their currencies to the US dollar, held their gold reserves in US banks, and relied on US financial institutions.[29]

This vision was aspirational rather than realized in the Philippines around the turn of the century. In 1900, even the US government relied on British banks for financial services. Like many US businesses before it, the US government ultimately decided that, for financial business in the Philippines, it would bank with the British as the most established, secure, and cost-effective option. The Department of War and the nascent insular government in the Philippines deposited funds in Manila with the two largest British banks in Philippines, the Hongkong and Shanghai Banking Corporation and the Chartered Bank of India, Australia, and China.[30] But how much more useful would it be for advancing US interests in Asia if a US, rather than British, bank handled the funds?

How timely that, around the turn of the century, a cluster of US investors sought new ways to expand their investing opportunities and international reach.

II. Chartering an Exceptional Upstart: The Creation of IBC

IBC entered this golden age of British multinational banking to provide US politicians and traders a US-headquartered alternative to institutions like the Hongkong and Chartered banks. The early push to create IBC came not from the highest echelon of US finance or from DC boardrooms, but rather from a manufacturer of munitions. Marcellus Hartley launched IBC toward the end of his business career, which had taken off after he earned handsome profits during the Civil War. The Union Army commissioned Hartley—based on his prior experience in the munitions industry and his international contacts—to travel to Europe and acquire weaponry, thereby thwarting Confederate arms buying. The profits Hartley amassed during the war allowed him to purchase Remington Arms and reorganize the company in the postwar financial downturn. In addition to becoming president of Remington Arms, Hartley also acquired several New England factories and combined them to form the Union Metallic Cartridge Company.[31]

Hartley climbed the ladder of industrialist affluence, and his influence grew during the late nineteenth century. He joined clubs with railroad magnates, industrial tycoons, and leaders of newly wealthy insurance firms. Hartley became close with the president of one of the nation's most powerful companies, the Equitable Life Assurance.[32] Hartley and Equitable president Henry Hyde had enough capital and enough political foresight to see that, by the turn of the century, the nation's status in the global economic hierarchy was changing. The investors and board members they enlisted to launch the International Banking Corporation represented a motley assortment of individuals with disparate financial goals. These individuals differed about their industrial pursuits and specific internationalist visions, but a throughline connecting their interests was to expand US commercial power overseas.

Curiously, realizing their expansionist vision required a detour through Connecticut. In 1901, the Connecticut legislature made an audacious move: it approved a charter for the International Banking Corporation that granted the bank sweeping powers—such as the ability to invest, issue bonds, accept deposits, and establish branches anywhere in the world—as long as it did so outside the state of Connecticut.[33] Hartley likely chose Connecticut as a state for incorporation because he had experience with the state's chartering practices: after the Civil War, he had reorganized several New England munitions factories under Connecticut law.[34] At the time, Connecticut's legislature was known for being susceptible to lobbyists' cajoling, but IBC's charter was noteworthy even by Connecticut's corporation-friendly standards.[35]

Several newspapers noted the unusual and broad scope of IBC's charter, and the *Hartford Courant* sharply criticized the move. It accused the state's legislature of giving the bank "gratuitous privileges" without benefiting Connecticut citizens. The charter did not require IBC to open its books to stockholders. Its directors did not have to live in Connecticut. The only real burden on IBC was the requirement to file annually with the state's bank commissioner and pay a state tax of 0.01 percent on the bank's capital.[36] Three decades after IBC's founding, its profile in Connecticut was so low that state officials notified IBC that they could not locate documentation certifying its registration to conduct financial business in the state. IBC bankers replied by citing the bank's 1901 charter and enclosing a duplicate of copy. The bankers also submitted an invoice that billed the state of Connecticut with costs for sending the documents.[37]

Why would the Connecticut legislature authorize a charter for an international bank from which Connecticut seemed to gain so little? At the time, the practice of special chartering had become the focus of political reform in many states. Anticorruption campaigners emphasized the opportunities for graft and abuse that accompanied the legislative requirements for issuing charters to start corporations and banks.[38] By the late nineteenth century, many states passed legislation to enable general incorporation—rather than special chartering—as the pathway to create new businesses, in part to reduce such corruption. As a result, many states adopted constitutional bans on the practice.[39]

Not so for Connecticut. Its system continued to allow special chartering, which left the legislature vulnerable to lobbying from industrial interests such as those of Marcellus Hartley. Further, the state's constitution allocated legislative power based on towns rather than population. The structure gave a three-hundred-person town as much influence as a city like New Haven, with a vastly larger population. In practical terms, the "rotten borough system," as some called it, left control of the General Assembly to a cluster of lobbyists and seasoned veterans who knew how to manipulate the system and woo inexperienced legislators for maximum political gain.[40]

Members of IBC's board had backgrounds and personal networks that would have had sway with Connecticut's legislature. In addition to Hartley, with his Connecticut-based operations, Connecticut legislator Allen Paige was among the first members of the IBC's board.[41] It is plausible that Paige played a role in lobbying for the bank's creation, though available archival evidence sheds little light on the dynamics of his support.[42] The precise spark for IBC's formation remains unclear, but it is clear that the bank's powerful board and early investors would have much to gain from a flexible international financing entity.

IBC's board of directors provided continuity between the nineteenth-century wealth and new forms of twentieth-century finance capitalism. Railroads, munitions, mining, and insurance industry featured prominently in the biographies of the bank's directors. Many of the initial board members had prior business interests in Mexico, the Caribbean, and the US West. For example, Jules Bache was a New York financier who founded a prominent investing firm, J. B. Bache. His firm invested in projects to develop Texas petroleum and Mexican railroads, among other ventures.[43] Juan Ceballos, a New York–born businessman of Spanish descent, had financial interests in a range of Caribbean and Mexican projects, such as the New York and Porto Rico Steamship Company and Cuban sugar exporting.[44] Industrialist and IBC board member Henry Manning owned a manufacturing firm that produced cranes, hoists, and other pneumatic tools.[45] An international bank would likely have been a cost-effective option to facilitate and enlarge Manning's export operations.

Board members also included the second generation of the titans of US rail construction. Indeed, the driving forces behind IBC were not necessarily the entrepreneurs and founders of the companies that built railroads and transportation networks to expand the boundaries of US settler colonialism; instead, IBC's leadership represented the heirs to such fortunes. Prominent names included Alfred Vanderbilt, son of Cornelius Vanderbilt, who inherited the bulk of his father's business in 1899. Isaac Guggenheim joined the IBC board, and with him came the family legacy of Guggenheim mining and its business connections. Other second-generation railroad names on IBC's board included Edwin Gould, son of railroad magnate Jay Gould, and Henry Huntington, nephew of Collis Huntington and founder of Huntington Library near Los Angeles, California.[46] General Thomas Hubbard, who became IBC president after the death of Marcellus Hartley, was a distinguished Manhattan attorney who specialized in railroad bankruptcies and reorganizations. Hubbard worked frequently with railroad executive Collis Huntington and became vice president of Huntington's Southern Pacific.[47] IBC's board was littered with names of families who had amassed wealth from over-constructing the US rail system and receiving government bailouts.[48] In IBC's flexible charter, these investors and industrialists would likely have seen the possibility of lowering transaction costs as compared to using British banks, as well as opportunities to expand their investments into new markets in Asia and the Americas (see figure 1.1[49]).

James W. Alexander

- Princeton-educated lawyer
- Won contentious succession battle to lead Equitable Life Assurance
- Became president of Equitable after founder's death

INTERNATIONAL BANKING
CORPORATION.

CAPITAL   ..   Gold $3 000,000.
RESERVE FUND   Gold $3,000,000.

Total Gold $6.000,000.
equivalent of £1,200,000
(Shortly to be increased to Gold
$10,000,(90.

Directors.

Thos. H. Hubbard,
(Chairman).   ⑤ James H. Hyde
① James W. Alexander   John B. Jackson.
Jules S. Bache.   Luther Kountze.
② Juan M. Ceballos   John Hubbard.
Ed F. Cragin.   John J. McCook.
George Crocker.   H. P. McIntosh.
Eugene Delano.   William H. McIntyre.
③ Henry C. Frick
Isaac Guggenheim,   Henry S. Manning.
④ Edwin Gould   Allen W. Paige.
Ed. H. Harriman.   Howard S. Rodgers.
Hippolyte Hardy.   Robert A. C. Smith.
Abram S. Hewitt.   Valentine P. Synder.
H. E. Huntington.   ⑥ Alfred G. Vanderbilt

Juan M. Ceballos
(1902–1906)

- New York banker of Spanish descent
- Invested heavily in Cuba after Spanish-American-Cuban War
- Defaulted in 1906, owing creditors $3 million

Henry Clay Frick (1902)

- Chairman of Carnegie Steel Company
- Known for railroad development and union busting
- Donated art to create New York's Frick museum

James Hazen Hyde
(1902–1904)

- President of Equitable Assurance Agency
- Son of Equitable founder Henry Hyde
- Threw decadent Louis XV-themed ball exemplifying Gilded Age excess

Edwin Gould (1902–1904)

- Railroad executive and son of Jay Gould
- Jekyll Island Club enthusiast
- Built Jekyll estate with bowling alley, indoor tennis court, and shooting range

Alfred Gwynne Vanderbilt
(1902–1904)

- Grandson of railroad magnate Cornelius Vanderbilt
- Known as sportsman millionaire
- Died in sinking of Lusitania in 1915

FIGURE 1.1. Prominent IBC Board Members, 1902. For data and image sources, see note 49.

The initial formation of the bank depended heavily on support from Equitable Life Assurance, the largest subscriber. Equitable held 17 percent of the initial issue of IBC stock, and eight of the firm's directors served on IBC's board.[50] Equitable did not hold the stake for long: Henry Hyde passed away shortly before the founding of IBC, and many of his successors believed that ownership of IBC constituted a conflict of interest with other banking investments that Equitable maintained. In 1902, the firm sold much of its stock to General Thomas Hubbard, who became president of IBC and a major driving force in the firm following Marcellus Hartley's death.[51]

Board members disagreed about the early vision for what kind of financial institution IBC would become. Should it serve as a holding company for amassing international and domestic assets? Should it become a vehicle for financing international railroad construction? Or should it open branches around the world, much like the Hongkong Bank model? Internal IBC records suggest that these options were far from settled when the bank was created. Several insurance-affiliated board members supported IBC not for the opportunity to operate international branches, but instead for its potential as a holding company to acquire stakes in other US banks and foreign firms.[52] During an executive committee meeting in 1903, the bank's leaders discussed different business strategies and ultimately decided against the diversified holding-company model. Instead, IBC would focus on multinational branching. Following the meeting, several directors associated with Equitable Life Assurance discontinued their involvement with the bank.[53]

IBC was forged in the crucible of Gilded Age affluence, and the wealth of its founders depended largely on the expansion of US power overseas.[54] Political connections were key to IBC's early success, and many IBC leaders were involved in Republican Party politics in the early 1900s. At the time, the Republican Party represented a powerful consortium of business and banking interests that rallied to support the gold standard, protectionism, and US foreign trade. The party's focus emerged partly in response to bitter contestation in the 1890s around financial panics, deflation, and the "free silver" movement associated with William Jennings Bryan. The Republican Party defined itself in contrast to Bryan's rural-leaning, populist stance. Republicans embraced "sound money," and the 1896 victory of Republican presidential candidate William McKinley cemented a leadership bloc that would hold the White House until President Woodrow Wilson's election in 1912.[55] Ideologically, the party supported a powerful US foreign policy agenda that included trade promotion to support US exports as well as high tariffs to protect domestic industries.

IBC's leaders typically moved in lockstep with the Republican Party agenda to expand US international influence. General Hubbard was well connected in the Republican Party, and he owned a large stake in the New York newspaper the *Globe and Commercial Advertiser*, which made his political views carry even greater weight.[56] Hubbard had close ties with prominent journalists, including editor Joseph Bucklin Bishop, who was also a friend of Theodore Roosevelt.[57] Hubbard leveraged these connections to lobby President Roosevelt about IBC. Hubbard asked for Bishop's help securing a role for IBC as the government's fiscal agent in Panama—a request that ultimately succeeded.[58] The bank also hired as its attorney Frederick W. Holls, a prominent international lawyer and US delegate to the Hague Convention of 1899. Holls was also a close friend and confidant of President Theodore Roosevelt and a frequent visitor to the White House.[59] According to the *Washington Post*, the US government likely selected IBC as the fiscal agent to collect China's indemnity payment following the Boxer Rebellion "due to the efforts of Mr. Frederick W. Holls."[60]

Numerous other IBC board members were also prominent Republican Party members and allies of President Roosevelt. Massachusetts Governor W. Murray Crane was Roosevelt's pick in 1901 for Treasury secretary, but Crane declined the position, citing illness in his family.[61] Crane continued to correspond and meet with the president periodically while holding a position on IBC's board.[62] Likewise, John J. McCook was a Roosevelt ally and confidant. Shortly after Roosevelt's 1901 inauguration, McCook wrote to Roosevelt about IBC board elections. McCook used a familiar tone suggesting Roosevelt's close knowledge of IBC and its activities. McCook referred to IBC simply as "the bank" and obliquely referenced internal debates about who should be selected to join IBC's board. The letter's tone suggested that Roosevelt had prior exposure to questions about the bank's leadership and was interested in the debate's outcome.[63] Letters from McCook to Roosevelt also suggest that the president wanted support and approval from the bank's leaders. Roosevelt sought an endorsement from the newspaper partially controlled by IBC President Thomas Hubbard. McCook wrote to assure Roosevelt that, if Hubbard retained control of the newspaper, Hubbard would surely "direct its policy aright, for he strongly favours your direction."[64] Similarly, IBC board member Allen Paige played a prominent role in Republican Party politics in Connecticut.[65] Given the levels of friendship and trust among multiple members of the IBC board and the Republican Party, it is not surprising that IBC received careful consideration for serving as the government's overseas banker.

Thus, the leadership of IBC represented a tightly entangled power network centered on railroad and insurance wealth and the Republican Party. The board maintained an insular and homogenous culture by handpicking its early investors. Shareholders were selected by "personal request," and if bank executives believed that an investor planned to sell off bank shares, the shareholder was refunded, in favor of someone interested in long-term ownership.[66] Equitable was the largest initial subscriber, and the second most important was the "Belgian Group," according to IBC's stockholder records—a consortium that represented the infamous King Leopold of Belgium, best known for genocidal exploitation of the Belgian Congo. The king invested in part because he wanted to secure Belgian participation in financing Chinese railroad construction between Beijing and Hankow.[67] While King Leopold played no direct leadership role in the bank, the Belgian interests maintained a seat on IBC's board through Pierre Mali, Belgian consul to the United States, and the consortium sought to use IBC to gain a foothold in a US-backed banking syndicate that could finance Chinese railroad construction.[68]

The bank's founders celebrated the possibilities of profiting from US colonialism overseas. As Thomas Hubbard told the *New York Times* in 1902, "Heretofore there has been no particular need in the United States for a banking institution doing an international business, but since the Spanish war and the tremendous trade of recent years with South America and the promise of constantly increasing commerce with China and the Orient, the necessity for just such an institution as this has developed."[69] IBC officials boasted that the bank was founded "closely in the wake of the Spanish-American war . . . for the purpose of developing American foreign trade, establishing branches in the Philippines, Panama and China working hand in hand with Uncle Sam."[70] The locations of IBC's early branches coincided with the US overseas colonial empire, such as in the Philippines and the Panama Canal Zone.[71] IBC considered expanding into Cuba, a key site of US imperial power in the Caribbean, but an adviser warned in 1902 that Cuba was already saturated with banks. IBC would be better served using correspondents on the island instead, the adviser noted.[72]

In broad contours, IBC served as a bridge between nineteenth-century modes of wealth accumulation—such as the over-construction of the US rail network—to new forms of multinational business that would later characterize US growth in the twentieth century. To IBC's founders, the vision was hazy at best when the bank was chartered. It was unclear if IBC would serve as an investing consortium to channel money into overseas infrastructure syndicates or whether the bank would become a traditional merchant bank, serving the foreign trade needs of a growing community of US exporters. Or, indeed, given IBC's flexible charter, the bank could dabble in a range of activities and find its purpose by trial and error. Amid the different visions of the bank's future, a ribbon of certainty connected the motivations of investors and leaders: that the growing international prominence of the United States would necessitate more overseas financial services. IBC's overseas presence could piggyback on US imperialism and use US government funds as working capital. Once in place, bankers would channel those deposits to advance a range of US business interests in Asia and the Americas.

An Inept Chosen Instrument

From IBC's perspective, working "hand in hand with Uncle Sam" had obvious upsides. The bank gained a healthy deposit base, as well as a revenue stream of guaranteed commissions and fees. But from the US government's perspective, downsides came from working "hand in hand" with IBC. At least in its early years, IBC operated less like a well-oiled capitalist machine and more like a bumbling, distractible sidekick that followed its own agenda and often faltered in its execution of government directives.

A brief tour of early state-bank relations reveals government ambivalence about IBC leaders' competency and questions about the bank's capacity to conduct the type of overseas banking that the government needed to execute. After all, venerable British banks were already capable of carrying out the functions that IBC purported to offer. One service the government needed was the protection of cash deposits. Without a financial intermediary, military personnel had to keep money in their possession, which exposed them to danger.[73] The government's financial needs grew as the US military expanded its international operations and long-term presence in more locations, and the government needed to pay an increasingly varied set of contractors and suppliers around the world.

British banks could execute these tasks adroitly, and the US government used British banks throughout the nineteenth century. Even after the formalization of IBC, the US government continued its practice of diversifying deposits among different institutions, including British banks. For example, in the Philippines, US government funds were entrusted to two British banks— the Hongkong and Shanghai Banking Corporation and the Chartered Bank of India, Australia, and China—in addition to IBC.[74] European international banks typically had more years of experience and greater capital at their disposal. For example, by 1903, the Manila branch of the Hongkong and Shanghai Banking Corporation had twice the deposits of IBC and five times its loan portfolio.[75] British colonial banks also had established track records of converting high rates of profit into large dividends for shareholders, as well as reputations for conservatism and safety.[76]

Why, then, would the US government want or need an upstart US bank to accomplish tasks already executed by British financiers? In practice, conducting Philippine financial work by using British banks in Manila also had disadvantages for the US government. British banks accepted US dollars as deposits from the US military, but they refused to denominate individual clients' accounts in US dollars. Instead, customers were required to use local currency. Thus, US soldiers could only access the spending power associated with their paychecks by converting US dollars to the local currency at whatever exchange rate the bank offered. In the Philippines, British banks faced accusations of conspiring "to rig their exchange rates at the expense of the [US] troops."[77] The system exposed the limits of the US dollar and the costs of US reliance on British institutions.

Moreover, on a strategic level, the broader agenda of Open Door–era politics involved creating more opportunities for US businesses overseas. With their domination of the White House around the turn of the century, Republican politicians advanced an imperial agenda to promote national economic interests.[78] In the eyes of these political leaders, a US bank could facilitate the expansion of US commerce and support the fiscal needs of colonial administrators.[79] However, IBC's failure to comply with guidelines for government fiscal agents complicated state-bank relations.

A running dispute centered on IBC's inability to provide sufficient security to accept government deposits—or at least its unwillingness to provide assets that the government deemed adequate. According to government stipulations, financial institutions needed to meet government eligibility requirements to hold state funds. One requirement was providing security—such as bonds or other assets—before qualifying as a fiscal agent.[80] However, government officials found that some of the bonds IBC provided did not meet government standards, and their market value was worth considerably less than their face value.[81] When government officials pressed IBC for better assets as security, IBC offered alternatives such as different railroad stocks, including one worth only 55 percent of its face value and another for a railroad partly controlled by IBC's Thomas Hubbard.[82] Some government officials lobbied for leniency in working with IBC. The chief of the Bureau of Insular Affairs argued that the government should be accommodating, given that IBC served the larger interests of promoting US trade. IBC should receive "special consideration" as a new bank finding its footing: the "withdrawal of the only American institution doing a banking business there would be a severe blow to that trade, in addition to the loss of banking competition."[83] Ultimately, the War Department concluded that supporting IBC was in the nation's best interest, but officials suggested capping deposits in the bank at $2 million to limit its risks.[84]

Additional tensions between US government officials and IBC bankers emerged in two aspects of IBC's work in China. The first involved IBC's desire to lead a railroad investing syndicate. Starting in 1907, IBC jockeyed to become the on-the-ground representative of an "American Group" to finance railroad building in China. The syndicate also included JP Morgan and National City Bank, among others. The State Department played an active role in the negotiations alongside US financiers who wanted to secure railroad construction contracts. Ultimately, the consortium chose JP Morgan rather than IBC as its loan agent, and Thomas Hubbard publicly denounced the State Department's endorsement of JP Morgan as an act of favoritism.[85] The government "ought not to countenance monopolies; it ought not to give special privileges,"

Hubbard admonished at a 1910 meeting of the American Asiatic Association.[86] Nonetheless, the State Department declined to rely on IBC due to its small resource base and lack of experience and preferred to work instead with more established financiers.[87]

A second sticking point in China involved IBC's handling of its fiscal-agent duties in transferring the US portion of Boxer Indemnity payments. The payment represented the financial settlement following an uprising of Chinese fighters to protest increasing Western influence and the growing power of Christian interests. The "boxers," as Western powers termed the resistance movement, objected to the legal exemptions granted to Christian missionaries and other concessions benefiting foreigners. Following an uprising of local fighters, a coalition of eight nations including Britain, Japan, and the United States combined forces to quell the rebellion. The coalition prevailed, and in the peace settlement, the victors required China to pay heavy reparations to compensate for property losses and damages. The US government named IBC as its fiscal agent to collect the nation's portion of China's payments due to IBC's ability to operate branches in China as well as the bank's connections in Washington. However, in 1913, a US government audit revealed that IBC owed the US government $111,956.30 in back payment. According to IBC attorneys, the discrepancy stemmed from disagreement about the proper exchange rate for the indemnity payment, which was a fraught topic under the terms of the peace negotiations.[88] The Protocol Treaty left ambiguity as to whether the indemnity payment was a gold or silver debt, in part because the reparations were structured as a loan against the collection of future import duties.[89] The exact nature of the US government's disagreement with IBC is unclear, but, ultimately, it was settled two years later with IBC paying $6,800 and an additional $5,000 to the special counsel—down from an initial claim of roughly $120,000.[90]

The disputes resulted in lengthy and sometimes tense exchanges between the bank and the federal government, but they never rose to the level of severing the state-bank connection. Moreover, the disputes were not severe enough to prevent future government reliance on IBC's financial services overseas. In 1917, the US government designated IBC's London branch as the depository and official banking institution for officers of the US Army and Navy.[91] That same year, IBC offered office space to the US consul in Manila.[92] Despite repeated questions about whether IBC could provide sufficient security to be trusted with state funds, key government leaders affirmed their support for the bank and their confidence in its leadership. An auditor commissioned by the War Department examined IBC's books in 1908 and raised concerns about the bank's management. The exchange between the two men—General Clarence Edwards, chief of the Bureau of Insular Affairs, and auditor Theodore

HEAD OFFICE: NEW YORK.

BRANCHES: LONDON, SAN FRANCISCO, MEXICO, MANILA, HONGKONG, YOKOHAMA, SHANGHAI, SINGAPORE.

FISCAL AGENT OF THE UNITED STATES IN CHINA AND THE PHILIPPINE ISLANDS.

International Banking Corporation,

1415 G. STREET, N.W.

CABLE ADDRESS
"INBANCOR"

WASHINGTON, D.C. *Dec. 23rd / 1903*

FIGURE 1.2. IBC Letterhead, "Fiscal Agent," 1903. *Image source:* James Morris Morgan Papers, #524, Southern Historical Collection, The Wilson Library, University of North Carolina at Chapel Hill.

Cocheau—was recorded in a "Confidential Office Memorandum" and provides insight on the rationale for the government's ongoing support of IBC:

> GENERAL EDWARDS: I have great confidence in General Hubbard and think he is a fine man.
> MR. COCHEAU: Yes, but he is not a practical banker, General.
> GENERAL EDWARDS: That is the trouble.
> MR. COCHEAU: . . . [IBC] might just as well speculate on Wall Street. That is not legitimate banking.[93]

Despite the concerns, War Department officials remained loyal to IBC and its president Hubbard, and IBC continued to benefit from the reputational associations of serving as fiscal agent—a designation that IBC emblazoned on its letterhead (see figure 1.2).[94] The bank leveraged the legitimacy conferred by being banker to the US government, all the while shape-shifting Gilded Age fortunes into a new era of economic development.

The International Banking Corporation emerged from the embers of overheated railroad construction and the expansion of settler colonialism toward the Pacific Ocean. It brought the wealth and legal savvy of second-generation Gilded Age tycoons into a new and malleable business form—the multinational bank. How it would use that power, where, and to what ends were open questions, even for the bank's directors. After all, settling those questions was not just a matter of centralized decision-making in New York committee meetings or dinners in Washington, DC. It also depended on the day-to-day actions of overseas bankers working in IBC's disparate branches.

After all, it was the on-the-ground workers in US banks who built the trackwork and trestles through which US dollars increasingly moved. Bankers' deftness in forging those connections and the sturdiness of the bonds they built would shape the durability of the infrastructure they helped create. The next chapter scrapes down a layer to examine the daily work of US international banking to understand how US imperial power was channeled, interpreted, contested, and reformulated in the hands of US private bankers.

2

Protocols and Penmanship

DANIEL DE MENOCAL's arrival in Hong Kong in the early 1900s marked a milestone in the history of US multinational banking, even though it hardly registered as newsworthy at the time. De Menocal became the first US trainee sent abroad to staff a branch of the first broadly multinational US bank.[1] Of all that might have impressed him—China's treaty ports, financing opium trade, the language barrier—one of the things that caught his attention was the hand-writing: "These young Britishers all had extremely good hand-writing," he later recalled.[2]

Early in his training, De Menocal had seen the importance of penmanship. The International Banking Corporation had sent him, along with several US colleagues, to London to learn about international banking. At the time, there was hardly such a thing as an international banker in the United States. In London, however, international finance was highly developed. IBC sent new hires like De Menocal to London to gain the experience that US bankers lacked. While there, several colleagues failed to master penmanship, which delayed their departure to new postings. "[T]heir handwriting was so bad," De Menocal recalled, "that the London office could make no use of their service and they were all sent to an English school to be taught how to write before they were permitted to touch pen to paper."[3]

As De Menocal learned, legible and accurate records were essential to financial institutions' success. Those institutions functioned as vital linkages connecting imperial metropoles to overseas markets, colonies, and territories around the world. Clean handwriting and rigorous bookkeeping constituted the prosaic foundations on which financial empires were built.[4] As US financial institutions sought to enter larger and more distant markets in the early twentieth century, US bankers modeled their handwriting and most other banking practices on the more established players in multinational banking: the British.

Much like De Menocal's early training in penmanship, the first wave of US multinational banking took shape in the shadow of European imperial domination, and US bankers looked to European—especially British—models for banking protocols and practices. A close study reveals that US banking overseas, at least in its early years, was a rickety enterprise that depended on British knowledge and US government backing for support.[5] This chapter tracks the way in which inexperienced US staffers learned the basics of foreign banking, from credit evaluations to branch management, in the early twentieth century. US banks modeled the practices of British colonial banks, from handwriting to foreign exchange, while following in the footsteps of US imperial expansion. Their ability to survive and win clients on the ground depended in part on their savvy in learning British strategies and adapting those strategies to their start-up work. Thus, the origins of US overseas financial power were deeply entangled with a prior generation of European empires. Tracing these origins reveals that a foundational layer for the future infrastructure of US financial power depended on a group of bewildered US bankers who poached the unwanted staff from European rivals, delegated vital banking business to local hires, and, when all else failed, looked to the US government for deposits and protection.

The Gold Standard in Multinational Banking: European Practices

Examining the roots of US branch banking overseas requires mapping the landscape established by a prior generation of British banks, which developed the practices and commanded the influence to which US competitors aspired.[6] The dominance of British foreign banking had its roots in British trade and imperial expansion. In the early nineteenth century, several British merchant houses gained international prestige by focusing on the global trade of commodities like cotton, tea, and sugar. The large firms opened branches overseas and contracted with agents across Europe and the Americas to broker deals throughout the British empire and beyond. Several merchant houses began to specialize in trade finance and other financial services. Merchant banks such as Barings, Rothschilds, and Brown Brothers had their origins largely in textile trading, and their financial connections gave rise to a sophisticated global network of contacts.[7] Likewise, starting in the 1860s, a second form of British overseas bank emerged: multinational British banks with overseas branches. These banks were organized as limited liability companies—rather than partnerships, as was the model for merchant banks—with headquarters in London. Unlike merchant banks, multinational branch banks accepted deposits overseas, in addition to providing trade finance, foreign exchange, and other financial services.[8]

In their overseas operations, British multinational banks developed several strategies and design features to offset the risks of global trade. A hazard for overseas branches involved extending too much credit to clients due to the risks associated with needing gold reserves from London. Should a branch find itself under liquidity strains, gold shipments from Europe would take weeks or months to arrive, so the risks of overextension could cause irreparable damage to the reputation of an overseas bank.[9] To mitigate these risks, branches developed protocols to safeguard their reserves. Many British banks were selective about what kind of security they accepted from would-be borrowers.[10] British multinational banks typically required liquid assets—assets that were readily resaleable—as security, rather than fixed assets such as land or heavy machinery, which might take weeks or months for the bank to recover losses.[11]

Because of their emphasis on liquidity, British multinational banks focused on serving European traders and elites, rather than financing the development of local businesses. Their disinclination to lend to upstart local businesses exposed British overseas banks to criticism for not supporting infant industries, particularly in Latin American and Asia.[12] Instead, the banks loaned money to their preferred clients, which were often British firms connected to British bankers through overlapping boards, business networks, and family relationships.[13] The branches frequently took deposits from foreign firms operating abroad, as well as deposits from individuals, and could remit the funds to London or other locations.[14] Due to their structure, banks such as the Hongkong and Shanghai Bank specialized in providing capital to more established firms rather than providing entrepreneurs' up-front costs or financing capital improvements. The Hongkong Bank made some exceptions, but still, less than 10 percent of its loan portfolio advanced funds to local companies.[15]

Such practices gave British banks a reputation for being cautious, conservative, and restrictive in their lending practices. Their modes of operation lent an insularity to British banking networks, whereby banks operated within circumscribed networks of traders and investors. These networks were themselves anchored by family relationships, interlocking ownership agreements, and historical connections.

In terms of their day-to-day work, British multinational banks could operate with greater flexibility and leniency than the lore of their conservative reputations suggested. British multinational banks worked with a close group of customers such that the technical requirements for security could be relaxed for the right client and right context, regardless of whether that client was local or European. British banks maintained an image of principled conservatism, though in practice they frequently made accommodations for long-term clients.[16] They often loosened requirements by providing longer credit terms, lending against mortgages, or even lending with only a client's signature to repay the loan as security.[17] Because these veteran institutions often had long-term experience and local knowledge, they could preserve their reputation for conservatism while still satisfying clients and generating returns for shareholders.

As the practices of British multinational banks became increasingly routinized, several Anglo-US and European firms developed systematic, paper-based rating systems to evaluate the creditworthiness of would-be borrowers. Brown Brothers, a prominent private bank involved in US-British trade finance, ranked borrowers according to standardized classifications as early as the 1820s. Agents and associates supplied information to their metropolitan partners using a numerical system from 1 to 4 and the designation of "A #1" for prime accounts.[18] British financiers often rated well-established firms according to similar ranking systems: "A1" constituted large merchant houses with strong reputations; "A2" referred to newer or smaller firms.[19] These rankings typically applied to large trading houses rather than broad swaths of local clients and potential clients, who received no systematic rankings.[20] And in many institutions, such credit records accompanied rather than displaced bankers' intuitions. Personal knowledge and long-term experience of managers and directors remained a cornerstone of the lending assessments of British overseas banks.[21]

Another strategy that contributed to the success of British banks involved their cultivation of long-term business relationships in their adopted communities.[22] Many British multinational banks provided financial services to a network of investors who were also clients of the banks in which they invested.[23] For example, in Argentina, Britain's London and River Plate Bank became one of the strongest foreign banks due to its connections with British railroads and utilities. The bank attracted deposits from the British firms and handled their financing needs.[24]

Further, once British bankers established themselves overseas, their connections to local businesses deepened. European bank managers of Argentine branches frequently formed and held important positions in Argentine companies throughout the early twentieth century.[25] British firms operating in Latin America often appointed local boards, hired political elites as advisers, and retained prominent local lawyers to embed themselves in their communities.[26] These dynamics helped ensure that British overseas bankers were closely enmeshed with the business communities they served. Their experience throughout the nineteenth century, combined with the global reach of British banks, helped make them the standard-bearer of multinational banking decades before US banks even opened their doors to international branching.

Emulating British Models: IBC's Early Work

In broad terms, IBC designed its branch network to replicate British models. Two areas in particular—IBC's training methods and hiring practices— demonstrate its attempts to emulate British rivals such as the Hongkong and

Shanghai Bank. IBC's training program depended on London as a place where new US hires could learn international banking. Around the turn of the century, formal education in banking and finance was relatively rare in the United States. Most US bankers entered the profession through family connections and personal networks rather than through formal training programs, which hardly existed for international banking in the United States.[27]

By contrast, Britain was home to multiple banks with formalized international training programs. The Hongkong and Shanghai Bank, for example, was founded in 1865 with offices in China, India, and Britain, and the bank's apprenticeship program became known for its extensive training. The program was even parodied in the 1910 P. G. Wodehouse novel *Psmith in the City*, as the protagonist Mike endures the mind-numbing, bureaucratic monotony of the "New Asiatic Bank" (see figure 2.1).[28] Mike joins the bank's London apprenticeship program to train for overseas service, and in London, he rotates through different departments to learn how the bank functioned.[29] Trainees would persist through the drudgery for several years to get the payoff: "You get your orders, and go to one of the branches in the East, where you're the dickens of a big pot straight away."[30] As Mike's experience reveals, bank protocols were so routinized and structured that they stripped any adventure, mystique, or sense of risk from the daily work: confined to the inside of a bank branch, Mike "worked away dismally at his letters till he had finished them. Then there was nothing to do except sit and wait for more."[31]

The hiring practices of British multinational banks ensured that the junior staff would conform to existing models of white male privilege and respectability. Applicants to the Hongkong Bank's London clerkship had to be personally introduced to bank leaders and have prior experience in banking. Applicants were also required to pass a written exam and undergo interviews. The requirements were more rigorous in principle than in practice. Interviews were often a formality, and written exams had less to do with evaluating skills and more with providing an excuse to reject applicants without offending their sponsors.[32] The interview questions elicited answers about whether an applicant's background, social standing, and upbringing would mesh with the bank's culture. For example, some interviewers asked applicants about their leisure interests and the sports they played; golf, rugby, cricket, and tennis were central to banking culture.[33] The result was an insular community that drew from the upper strata of society. From 1890–1914, roughly 98 percent of London bankers had fathers who belonged to the upper classes, and roughly 75 percent attended the same set of elite schools.[34]

IBC had no such formal entry requirements; instead, many US hires came from the alumni network of IBC's leader, Thomas Hubbard, who had graduated from Bowdoin College and remained an active booster of the Maine-based school. (A central building on Bowdoin's campus, Hubbard Hall, still

FIGURE 2.1. Banking at the "New Asiatic Bank." *Image source:* P. G. Wodehouse, *Psmith in the City,* London: A. & C. Black, 1910, 176.

FIGURE 2.2. IBC Staff in Yangon, 1920. *Image source:* "India an Increasing Market for American-Made Goods," *The Americas*, August 1920, 14.

carries his name.[35]) US hires were sent to IBC's London office for one year before their overseas work formally began. At least, that was the theory.[36] In practice, the training "actually ended when a call for help arrived from overseas," remembered one IBC veteran.[37] One IBC banker reported that his London training lasted only one month before he was sent to Yangon, Myanmar—then Rangoon, Burma (see figure 2.2). Two days after arriving, his supervisor went on furlough, and he was promoted to second in command of the bank branch. The only person available to teach him proper bookkeeping was "a small Hindu boy known as my chockra," or servant, the banker later recalled. The assistant "stood constantly beside my chair to hand me in turn each book, ledger, or other papers with which I had to deal." The "chockra" preserved institutional knowledge and shared banking know-how: "He saved me from infinite trouble and complications . . . such as posting a credit in the debit column of the cash book."[38]

Bank training was often ad hoc, piecemeal, and decentralized. Even when bankers could undergo a full apprenticeship in London, the preparation left major gaps. IBC's hires were given no systematic education about how to conduct credit evaluations or handle foreign exchange. Instead, credit and foreign exchange were two functions considered to be "mystiques sacred to management and seldom available to young officers for many years," according to an internal bank history.[39] The informality and unevenness of IBC's training for junior staff suggests bank executives either lacked the resources to design a more systematic program, or that they hoped exposure to London banking would allow US hires to glean enough to learn the rest on the ground.

Another strategy by which IBC sought to benefit from the prestige of established British multinational banks involved its on-the-ground hiring. IBC branches adopted a time-honored tradition to compensate for its deficiency of domestic expertise: they poached more experienced staff from their European rivals. "IBC's secret had been that it hired the British to compete with the British," recalled overseas banker George Moore.[40] The bank routinely hired the former staff of European banks in locations where it opened branches. British bankers held "all the positions of authority" in several IBC branches, according to one executive.[41] When Daniel De Menocal arrived in Hong Kong, he was the only US citizen among a staff of roughly twenty people.[42] That pattern continued through the first decades of IBC's operation.[43] Of course, the bank was only able to hire bankers amenable to quitting their existing posts, so IBC was often stuck with employees that European banks no longer wanted to retain—"the leavings from the other offices," noted an official with the US Bureau of Insular Affairs.[44] IBC records are littered with references to staffers' tendencies to "cocktail" excessively and falter in their banking work, after late nights spent at social clubs.[45]

IBC's pattern of hiring British-trained managers was so consistent that, in several overseas locations, locals perceived IBC to be more of a British institution than a US one.[46] While this disposition proved useful whenever anti-US sentiment surged, IBC executives grew concerned about its overseas reputation in the mid-1920s and launched a concerted campaign to "Americanize" the staff. Still, bank insiders observed that British and other European citizens often dominated overseas management positions.[47]

Hiring British managers helped compensate for some deficiencies in US staffing, but the practice was not enough to guarantee that IBC could sustain the same information networks that undergirded British banks' lending practices. British foreign banks often enjoyed connections to large British businesses operating in the same regions.[48] British firms commonly relied on the knowledge of London-based managers and advisers to gauge the credit standing of traders and would-be borrowers. They could assess a borrower's strength and reputation based on how London's money market valued the firm's payment promises—namely, by determining the discount at which the firm's bills were traded. And local managers could use London directors' information to ascertain larger commodity trends, price dynamics, and the international reputations of prominent firms.[49] These evaluations, combined with managers' relationships and the security being offered for a loan, became key inputs to British banks' credit evaluations.

In contrast, IBC's credit assessments tended to be opaque and somewhat haphazard. Like its British competitors, IBC could access information from London's money market, as IBC was authorized to trade acceptances in the British market.[50] Nonetheless, many of the prominent firms whose bills were traded in London already had long-term relationships with European banks and did not need IBC, an unknown US upstart, to conduct overseas business. To grow its client base, IBC needed to find depositors, creditworthy borrowers, and opportunities for trade finance. In doing so, IBC drew on the methods of New England banking in the late nineteenth century—specifically, it relied on the business connections and social networks of managers and directors. New England banks of the late nineteenth century operated more like investing clubs for their affluent directors than systematized businesses run by professional, salaried staff.[51] Directors typically entrusted the funds they controlled to friends, business associates, and themselves.[52]

"Insider lending" represented a common model for US banking throughout the nineteenth century, but by the turn of the twentieth century, US banks increasingly standardized their lending practices. Following several downturns and massive defaults in the late 1800s, many US East Coast banks looked to reform their credit practices, which bankers identified as contributing to economic instability and bankruptcies.[53] Domestic banks inside the United States began to move away from the insider-lending model by establishing systematized credit departments. Yet IBC bucked the modernizing trend that its peers embraced. IBC had no defined credit department or formalized hiring to recruit trained credit professionals. Instead, the networks and personal contacts of bank directors helped seed IBC branches with potential clients and credit information. After all, operating in new environments posed profound risks, from wars to natural disasters to information asymmetries. Leveraging personal networks and connections was a common strategy for international banks at the time to offset such risks.

The personal networks of the bank's New York leadership influenced the lending decisions of IBC branches. This strategy of relying on directorial prerogative was not explicitly codified as IBC's mode for assessing credit or seeking clients. Nonetheless, bank staff recognized that managers and executives would dictate the terms of bank lending.[54] The de facto approach resulted from a set of tacit assumptions, deference to British and US lending patterns, and the *absence* of more systematic, paper-based assessment practices. Executive committee meeting minutes lack reference to any consistent protocol about why some exporters received credit and others were denied. At times, the committee authorized loans without requesting security. In other cases, executives requested collateral to be held against loans.[55]

The basic formula for lending decisions seems to be that branch managers cabled or wrote to IBC executives in New York regarding requests for trade financing. Credit requests that fell beneath a predetermined threshold could be determined by local managers. Borrowing that exceeded the standard limit required New York's approval. In practice, managers often claimed more authority than New York directors wanted. As one IBC banker remembered, IBC's credit controls were "pretty casual. The managers had great latitude and they would commit the bank before New York started to gasp."[56] The bank's New York–based executive committee included at least four of the board's most active members, and the group met multiple times a week between 1902 and 1916. During these meetings, executives would authorize lending and determine clients' credit limits. After a spate of bad loans afflicted the Manila branch in 1907, New York executives tried to centralize control of lending decisions.[57] The executive committee notified all branches that accountants were required to report any suspicious activity to headquarters. Nonetheless, New York executives found themselves at the mercy of long lags in postal communication—after all, the sailing time from Manila to the US West Coast could take six weeks—and unreliable information flows from distant and sometimes unreliable managers in far-flung branches.[58]

The push to centralize decisions under New York's control gave IBC directors greater leeway to channel bank lending toward activities that enriched themselves and their associates. For example, the bank authorized a "liberal line of credit" for the Fearon Daniel Company in China in 1912. Not uncoincidentally, the firm's cofounder James Fearon was also an IBC director.[59] Board members would ask the executive committee for favorable financing terms to support their friends. Juan Ceballos, a board member during IBC's early days, requested in 1902 that the committee support "the banking business of my friends the Philippine Tobacco Company" by financing the firm's exports.[60] The committee did not simply greenlight all insider requests. Some were rejected or deferred, though bank minutes rarely provide a rationale for rejections. In 1909, an IBC officer in Mexico City requested a personal loan for the creation of a new life insurance company, but the executive committee denied the request.[61] Nonetheless, these references to personal connections, combined with the absence of other processes to mitigate credit risks, suggest that the personal connections of IBC directors were essential to vetting borrowers and developing new business opportunities.

IBC adopted another European strategy for assessing the creditworthiness of borrowers, particularly in its China-based operations: relying on compradors.

In China's treaty ports, a single, locally hired staff person—the comprador—shouldered the responsibility of building financial relationships between the foreign bank and the local Chinese business community. The comprador's role dated back to the opening of China's treaty ports in the 1840s.[62] The term came from the Portuguese word meaning "buyer" and referred to the Chinese intermediaries who helped European traders navigate business in China and in other major ports throughout Asia.[63] Compradors were instrumental to brokering cross-cultural deals: as a 1905 circular from the US Department of Commerce observed, "Practically all the business of foreigners with the Chinese is done through [compradors], whether it be in buying or selling, in loaning or in borrowing money. . . . There is no limit to what a comprador does not do under the present way of doing things in China."[64]

Compradors often occupied elite positions in local society and boasted strong connections to a range of local businesses. Many held influential roles inside foreign firms while simultaneously managing responsibilities within family trading businesses, such that comprador positions became a secondary occupation.[65] The comprador of the Hongkong Bank, for example, belonged to one of the city's most affluent families, which operated a domestic bank and an active import-export business.[66] A comprador for IBC, Wu Peichu, observed that nearly every bank comprador belonged to one of six prominent Chinese families.[67] Compradors' positions as go-betweens gave them numerous opportunities to profit from commissions and interest-rate arbitrage, as well as to earn salaries from banks and their work in local businesses. Foreign banks depended heavily on them to identify local clients, protect their investments, and sustain their businesses in China.[68]

Their essential work as intermediaries has made compradors a popular, albeit polarizing topic of scholarly debate in the history of China's treaty ports and economic development. Some scholarship has characterized compradors as handmaidens to European imperial expansion. Other works have cast compradors as empowered entrepreneurs who accelerated Chinese economic development.[69] More recent work on compradors' role in foreign banks has emphasized their hybrid roles in shaping the relationship between foreign and local firms and generating profits for themselves and their businesses. This characterization of compradors as nimble, self-interested intermediaries aligns with evidence about compradors' work in IBC's China branches.[70]

IBC carried on the tradition of relying on compradors to arrange local business, vouch for loans, and manage local staff in China. One of a comprador's biggest responsibilities was screening local borrowers and finding local investing opportunities. The comprador's approval was more than a friendly nod; instead, it represented a personal guarantee that a borrower would not default. The employment relationship between compradors and their European employers differed from a simple salaried hire. Instead, a comprador pledged security—often real estate or cash—before accepting the role of a foreign bank's intermediary.[71] The security provided a guarantee that protected European banks for the risks they took based on a comprador's assurance. If a borrower endorsed by the comprador failed to repay debts, the bank could rely on security from the comprador to offset its losses. "The comprador pledged to mortgage his house and his kids or anything else . . . and guaranteed all the loans," as one IBC banker remembered.[72] In exchange, a comprador received a salary and had a stake in some of the branch's deals and transactions.

Compradors' prominent role in the day-to-day work of foreign banks meant they shaped the local culture of the bank's office. One IBC banker in China recalled that the comprador determined how the bank engaged with local businesses: the comprador introduced a foreign bank to "the large, native clients that we didn't know very much. And he guaranteed them . . . He would tell us so-and-so was all right, and we did a reasonably good business if the comprador was competent."[73] Compradors also served as a source of stability and institutional knowledge. The turnover of US and European managers and staffers could be high, but compradors maintained continuity. IBC's Shanghai branch had twelve different managers in thirty-eight years, but only three compradors.[74]

The memoirs of IBC bankers typically focus on the quotidian roles of compradors, more so than their financial significance and business acumen, and the characterizations underscore the social segregation that US bankers perceived—and perpetuated—in their China-based work. Daniel De Menocal remembered that IBC's comprador would greet Chinese customers in his office by offering them "a drag on the [opium] pipe just as he might tender a highball, cocktail or glass of beer under similar circumstances."[75] The rituals for greeting Chinese clients differed from those of European customers, and US bankers tended to view local customs as primitive and culturally inferior. One impediment was "our different table manners. They ate with much slushing and shoveling," remembered one IBC banker.[76]

The assessment suggests that white, European elites differentiated their social networks from a perceived "other" of Chinese businesses. De Menocal moved in a Hong Kong network composed "almost entirely of cultivated Europeans who could have no place to climb but down as they were already sitting prettily on top and having a wonderful time."[77] While working in China, Europeans and US bankers often developed a sense of solidarity, and social institutions reinforced their interconnections. In nonbusiness hours, US bankers typically retreated to segregated social clubs—British clubs, polo clubs, and chambers of commerce (see figure 2.3).[78] In these spaces, IBC's European and US staff intermingled with leading business and political figures from the United States and Europe at dinners, parties, and holidays.[79] These social

FIGURE 2.3. Foreign Bankers' Residences in Hongkong, 1918. *Image source:* "The Currents of Merchandising in the Orient and the South Pacific," *The Americas*, December 1918, 15.

dynamics enabled the exchange of knowledge, impressions, and constructed racial solidarities among US and European elites living abroad.[80]

Cutting Corners: IBC's Deviation from European Scripts

As much as IBC sought to model the practices of established British multinational banks, it missed a few foundational pieces of the British banking systems that contributed to firms' longevity. First, elite British banks tended to move slowly when entering new markets. The Hongkong Bank typically operated through designated agents for years—sometimes more than a decade—before opening overseas branches. The relationships gave the bank experience and long-term connections with clients before it committed to the expense of maintaining offices. The Hongkong Bank opened an office in Manila in 1875 only after working through US merchant house Russell, Sturgis, and Company for ten years.[81] In Bangkok, it partnered with a German merchant house for more than a decade before opening a branch. In Sri Lanka, it did the same through a firm founded by former operators of a Mississippi River steamer line.[82] Likewise, the Deutsch-Asiatische Bank, a leading German bank operating in China, launched its network in 1889 after working for two decades as a German banking consortium to advance trade relationships and to lend to the Chinese government.[83] IBC opted instead to plunge into branching.

Some British and transatlantic banks used family relationships and prior business connections to manage the expansion of branches and extend business to new locations. Prominent banking families tended to intermarry and cement ties with other political and commercial elites through marriage.[84] For example, the Anglo-US bank Brown Brothers represented a family partnership in which brothers founded and managed offices in New York, Philadelphia, and Liverpool.[85] The Rothschild banking enterprise relied on a network of agents who provided information in exchange for payment and reputational benefits. Many of the agents were related to the inner circle of the Rothschild family or married into it, and Rothschilds tended to sustain relationships with trusted agents for decades.[86] IBC operated according to no such long-term timeline. Within five years of its chartering, the bank opened seventeen different branches in nine different countries or colonies.[87] In these locations, IBC bankers often found themselves lacking local networks and experience on which to draw.

Another strategy by which some European banks secured footholds overseas involved sovereign lending and financing major infrastructure projects. The Deutsch-Asiatische Bank became prominent in part because it helped the Chinese government finance its indemnity payment after the Sino-Japanese War of 1894–95. DAB's connections to large German banks helped it introduce a new scale of foreign borrowing in turn-of-the-century China. The relationships and prestige the bank developed from its sovereign lending facilitated its future role in Chinese infrastructure finance.[88] IBC, by contrast, aspired to such opportunities for infrastructure lending in China, but the bank's small capital base and relative inexperience left it sidelined.[89] Even though IBC served as one of the US government's fiscal agents for handling deposits in the Panama Canal Zone, such day-to-day dispensing of money did not garner the profits or prestige of large-scale bond deals for infrastructure construction. Instead, IBC's branches missed out on the high-profile financing opportunities that banks like DAB and JP Morgan were able to secure.[90]

Foreign exchange represented another potential profit source for foreign banks, and in that domain, IBC tended to hire European or Chinese expertise rather than cultivate those skills among US staff. De Menocal remembered that IBC's foreign exchange business in New York was dominated by two German bankers poached from Deutsche Bank of Berlin. The New York office provided a "stage for them to rush about, to shout commands, to battle over the telephone with brokers, dealers and competitors in the foreign exchange market. The speed, the fury of their attack on the days' problems was unlike anything I had seen before," he recalled.[91] Like credit assessments, foreign exchange operations were "mystiques" to IBC's junior staff trained in London, and expertise remained in the purview of more experienced European veterans.[92] US bankers often regarded foreign exchange as so complex that only a particular mindset and upbringing—"a studious 'Swiss or German type of mind,'" as one banker remembered—could master it.[93]

In China, local staff handled the complex work of foreign exchange. These staffers fell under the comprador's management and rarely appeared in New York banking records.[94] In markets such as China's treaty ports, multiple currencies circulated, and many were unfamiliar to US staff. In Hong Kong, for example, IBC bankers encountered Hong Kong dollars, Mexican silver, Spanish coins, coins from the British Straits Settlement, and eventually Chinese dollars. Daniel De Menocal remembered that a major duty for local staff involved testing the purity of silver coins because their values were not standardized. "[P]ractically every day some half dozen or more counterfeits would be returned to the sending bank," De Menocal remembered.[95] US bankers found the range of currencies disorienting and defined it as the domain for local workers. One US banker remembered that local debts were settled in taels, but taels' value depended on their province of origin. Banks would settle their debts by moving "lumps of silver contained in boxes," which were transported on wheelbarrows by the "coolie class." "If you owe ten banks you have to send one or more wheelbarrow loads of silver to each of them," the banker recalled.[96] China's treaty ports represented extreme examples for how complex currency calculations could be; nonetheless, US bankers throughout IBC's network deferred to more experienced Europeans and local staff in foreign exchange–related matters.

Another way in which IBC deviated from more established European models involved its profitability. Whereas British multinational banks had established records of paying high dividends, IBC's profitability proved a marked disappointment, particularly in its first decade. IBC's rate of profit fluctuated from zero to roughly 20 percent, prior to the passage of the Federal Reserve Act and National City Bank's acquisition of the bank. Between 1904 and 1910, IBC averaged less than 4 percent as a rate of profit. Profitability increased after 1910, averaging roughly 20 percent until 1913.[97] Thus its performance was highly variable in its early years of independent operation (see figure 2.4).

Assessing the bank's larger impact and lasting meaning, however, requires looking beyond profit analysis. Indeed, as any observer of contemporary markets can attest, if profit was a proxy for impact, then many of today's tech giants like Amazon and Uber would hardly warrant public attention.[98] Instead, the figures need to be situated within a larger context of financial, social, and political meaning. They must also be triangulated with other sources to evaluate the bank's performance. Accounting practices varied across banks and jurisdictions in the early twentieth century, and banks' year-to-year reports could range widely depending on different practices for writing off losses.[99] In addition to these inconsistencies, which characterized most

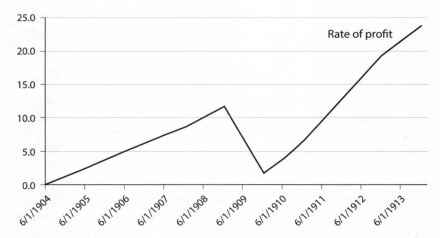

FIGURE 2.4. IBC's Rate of Profit, 1904–1913. *Data source:* International Banking Corporation. Semi-Annual Statement of International Banking Corporation, 1904–1913, RG 350, Box 418, Folder 5500, National Archives. Rate of profit calculated as profit divided by paid-up capital.

TABLE 2.1. IBC's Rate of Profit, 1904–1913

Date	Capital	Profit and Loss	Rate of Profit
6/30/1904	3,947,200	2,991	0.1
11/30/1904	3,947,200	40,000	1.0
6/30/1906	3,250,000	166,083	5.1
12/31/1907	3,250,000	278,720	8.6
12/31/1908	3,250,000	381,274	11.7
12/31/1909	3,250,000	55,710	1.7
6/30/1910	3,250,000	125,444	3.9
12/31/1910	3,250,000	210,398	6.5
12/30/1911	3,250,000	423,677	13.0
12/31/1912	3,250,000	627,772	19.3
6/30/1913	3,250,000	701,961	21.6
12/31/1913	3,250,000	773,688	23.8
Average, 1904–1913			**9.7**

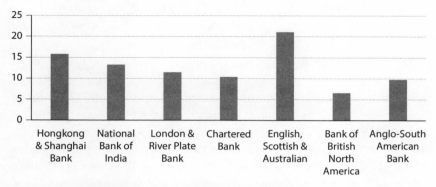

FIGURE 2.5. Profitability of British Multinational Banks, 1896–1913. *Data source:* Geoffrey Jones, *British Multinational Banking, 1830–1990*, Oxford: Oxford University Press, 1995, table A5.3. Appendix 5 examines performance and profitability measures, as well as challenges associated with banks' reporting from the period. See also Youssef Cassis, *City Bankers, 1890–1914*, Cambridge, UK: Cambridge University Press, 1994, 187–92.

turn-of-the-century financial institutions, IBC's data carries another challenge that IBC bankers' personal accounts are replete with stories of unbalanced books and questionable ledgers.[100] Nonetheless, tracking IBC's rate of profit for the early 1900s allows a baseline of comparison with British competitors (see figure 2.5). Sampling the profitability of several British multinational banks from 1896–1913 reveals that competitors' performance varied widely; nonetheless, British standouts such as the Hongkong and Shanghai Bank outperformed IBC. The Hongkong averaged a 15.8 percent ratio of net published profits to shareholder funds, as compared to IBC's average of 9.7 percent over a similar period.[101]

Anecdotal accounts from the early 1900s support the overall assessment that IBC's performance was lackluster. An auditor for the US War Department examined IBC's books and concluded that the bank's profits represented a "ridiculously" small showing, relative to $3.25 million in capital.[102] An internal history of IBC also suggests that the bank suffered from insufficient liquidity in its early years: the bank borrowed money when interest rates were high. IBC's contemporaries viewed its decision to borrow at 7 percent interest rates as evidence of its pressing need for capital.[103] In September 1904, the bank's executive committee responded to its weak profits by charging stockholders an additional $13 per share to raise funds.[104] Several months later, the committee voted to mortgage the bank's headquarters at 60 Wall Street to secure a $1.5 million loan.[105] Perhaps most tellingly, IBC paid no dividends for at least five of its first ten years.[106] When it did pay dividends in 1906, the amount was only

2 percent of its capital.[107] By contrast, the average dividend payments of British colonial banks were 20 percent in the same period.[108]

Indeed, without the consistent backing of the US government for its political support and deposit base, IBC might not have survived its early missteps. The reliability of state support sustained the bank in locations like Manila, which gave executives enough flexibility and stature to plot expansion in new locations. With its growth, the bank affected the flow of goods, the fates of businesses, and the economic opportunities of those who needed credit. The bank's profits paled in comparison to the financial behemoths of the day, such as JP Morgan or the Hongkong and Shanghai Banking Corporation. However, its improvised protocols and roster of connections took on outsized importance as IBC became folded into the larger, more powerful, and better capitalized international expansion of National City Bank after the passage of the Federal Reserve Act in 1913.

Moreover, because IBC hitched itself to the power of the US government, its network of brick-and-mortar branches took on outsized importance as the nation played an increasingly decisive role in international relations in the early twentieth century. IBC enmeshed itself in foreign markets, such as China's treaty ports and US imperial zones, where it could model more experienced European counterparts and root itself in a world of colonial privilege. It elbowed into that world by having the right connections in Washington and poaching already trained staff overseas. Once there, it parlayed government deposits and state-conferred legitimacy into economic opportunities for a handpicked set of borrowers, based in part on the personal connections of its elite board. While bankers like Daniel De Menocal working in Hong Kong might have looked to British models to emulate success, they could look in a different direction for support—the US government—when the bank's operations faced an existential threat.

De Menocal climbed the ranks of IBC's internal hierarchy and went on to manage other IBC branches in China. In 1911, revolutionary forces toppled China's ruling imperial dynasty, and the bank's Beijing branch faced peril. Who would arrive to bail out De Menocal, his colleagues, and the bank? The US Marines, of course, who rescued him and his staff and ensured the bankers' safety inside the city's foreign enclave.[109] Chapter 3 continues to examine IBC's entanglement with the US government by tracking the lending activities and daily work of IBC's branch in Manila. Pulling the threads of individual names in the bank's loan portfolio in the Philippines unravels the entangled components of US imperial power. With this approach, US empire no longer takes shape as a singular plot devised in Washington, DC, and projected overseas. Instead, this framing reveals the processes by which US power was constructed and enmeshed in overseas economic orders, through the decision-making and daily exchanges of bankers and their adopted communities.

3

Imperial Banking on the Ground

THE MANILA BRANCH of the International Banking Corporation opened its doors in June 1902, shortly before President Theodore Roosevelt proclaimed peace and an end to armed conflict in the Philippines.[1] From a number of vantages, the timing was inauspicious. Food shortages, an epidemic, and armed violence continued to ravage the islands, despite Roosevelt's assurances. The war had left hundreds of thousands of Filipinos dead. Sovereignty was still contested in parts of the archipelago.[2] And in the fall of 1902, locusts arrived.[3]

Nonetheless, the bank opened in Manila in the former horse stables of a Chinese merchant. The branch was sandwiched between a US import house on one side and, on the other, the Silver Dollar Saloon, a popular meeting place for local businessmen.[4] The branch had a financial cushion from the upheaval that surrounded it—namely, the assurance of US government deposits. The government named IBC as one of its fiscal agents in the archipelago and entrusted the bank with funds that constituted roughly more than 80 percent of its deposits in the branch's early months of operation.[5] The bank administered payments to soldiers and civilian officials, financed the purchasing of supplies, and exchanged currency as part of this work.[6] In return, IBC earned modest commissions. More importantly, it acquired a working base of capital. That capital could be used to finance exports, provide loans, and even build public works, according to the terms of the bank's expansive 1901 charter.[7]

This chapter tracks the junction points and touchdown sites of IBC's early influence in the Philippines by following its lending, investing, and social impacts.[8] In doing so, it offers a new vantage for understanding US power and how that power took shape when projected from meeting rooms in Washington, DC, to its intended colonial targets. Following IBC's convoluted path allows us to see how US power was extended, challenged, and reshaped in the day-to-day work of lending and money moving.

IBC's Banking Landscape in Manila

Monsoon season was just one challenge among many that beset IBC in its early years in the Philippines. The bank had opened its doors with one guaranteed customer: the US government. Prior to IBC's arrival, numerous financial institutions—European banks, church institutions, pawn brokers, and landowners—supplied the basic needs of different populations in the Philippines. In the late 1800s, the Philippine economy depended largely on agriculture. Local populations met many of their basic subsistence needs through small-scale farming, while large-scale, export-oriented agriculture was the domain of several large European or US-owned firms.[9] Rice, sugar, and abaca constituted its primary export crops. Manila served as a hub for European and Asian traders throughout the nineteenth century for exchanging Mexican silver for Chinese goods such as silk and porcelain.[10] Two prominent British banks—the Hongkong and Shanghai Banking Corporation and the Chartered Bank of India, Australia, and China—opened offices in the Philippines in the late 1800s to support these trading activities.[11]

Traditional banks with European connections emerged to meet the needs of foreign traders, while many Filipinos met their credit needs by using church institutions, landlords, and other less systematized financial entities. A church-affiliated financier—the Monte de Piedad y Caja de Ahorros—was the biggest credit provider for Filipino laborers and farmers. It granted loans in exchange for real estate and personal property.[12] Traditional pawn shops also provided credit, as did landlords and shopkeepers in rural areas where specie was scarce and people typically had little need for cash.[13] Tenant farmers and agricultural workers could mortgage future crops or receive advances on goods or farm equipment to meet their short-term credit needs, and these financial relationships created systems of debt-bondage that yoked farm laborers to dependency on landlords.[14]

Thus, prior to the Spanish-American War, different demographics in the Philippines relied on a range of financial institutions for banking services, and a web of intermediaries emerged to address these needs. Even the US government itself needed banking services prior to the arrival of IBC and found suitable options: in particular, the Hongkong and Chartered banks. Both British banks were well equipped to provide services such as foreign exchange, access to vaults, and payment of bills.[15] They also valued having the US government as a client, given the healthy deposits it provided. British bankers actively solicited the business of the US government. Before IBC's launch, its funds constituted roughly half of the total deposits of the Hongkong Bank in Manila.[16]

To some US policymakers, relying on British banks to move money in its new colonial possessions seemed worse than just missing an opportunity;

instead, US dependency on British finance actively strengthened the British empire by paying transaction fees, relinquishing trade secrets, and ceding sensitive data to British banks. These costs undercut the goal of imperialist politicians who wanted to secure opportunities to advance US business. This expansionist agenda took shape in turn-of-the-century policy doctrines such as Secretary of State John Hay's Open Door Notes and the Roosevelt Corollary, which asserted US authority to intervene in the affairs of nations in the Western Hemisphere. The policies celebrated US access to open markets, and the US government worked through diplomatic as well as bloodier and more coercive means, to promote US business.[17] Theodore Roosevelt's vision of making the world "safe for capitalism" involved the seizure of nations' customs and infringed on Dominican sovereignty, as Cyrus Veeser has described in the case of the Dominican Republic.[18] In cases such as Venezuela's debt crisis of 1902 or the pursuit of Panama Canal ambitions, the policy goals involved direct deployment of military force.

As the United States established a colonial government in the Philippines, the project of advancing US business largely fell into the hands of the Bureau of Insular Affairs, the division within the War Department created to oversee US territories. The BIA encouraged US businesspeople to invest in commercial ventures in the Philippines. BIA officials conducted outreach among New York financiers and traders so extensively that the BIA chief boasted in 1904 about being "on intimate terms now with all the hydra-headed capitalists in New York."[19] The bureau commissioned studies to evaluate business opportunities and pitched them to would-be investors in the United States. Government accounts typically described the Philippines as a blank slate of economic opportunity and natural resource wealth, primed for the infusion of US capital and management techniques. Coconut production was a prime example. BIA literature described the outdated, "peasant" methods of local production. Would be-investors would reap the "steady and assured returns from comparatively small investment," if modern harvesting and production methods were applied.[20]

In the eyes of many colonial officials, the presence of a US bank in the Philippines could provide the necessary financial infrastructure to expand opportunities for US business. "Our policy toward the Philippine Islands has been, naturally, to increase their trade . . . [and] to direct as much of their trade to our own merchants as possible," explained Clarence Edwards, chief of the Bureau of Insular Affairs.[21] US policymakers had noticed that British banks favored British clients. If US policy could rely on US financial operators rather than British ones, then the trackwork and trestles that conveyed US financial power would remain in nationally operated hands. The presence of a US bank suggested a greater likelihood that Philippine trade would strengthen the US

FIGURE 3.1. IBC Promotional Pamphlet, "The Philippine Islands" (1908). *Image source:* International Banking Corporation, "The Philippine Islands," New York: Brown, Lent & Pett, 1908, courtesy of the National Archives and Records Administration.

dollar, enrich US intermediaries, and create opportunities for the nation's businesses than the prevailing tendency to rely on British banks.

IBC shared the government's aim of fostering US investment in the Philippines. Lobbying investors in New York and touting Philippine financial opportunities represented a point of mutual self-interest for both state and bank, as IBC bankers expected to increase their business and commissions. IBC created publications advertising the Philippines' abundance of natural resources, and the materials echoed BIA reports about the blank slate of commercial opportunity in the archipelago. In 1908, IBC published a pamphlet promoting the Philippines for its raw, "undeveloped" resources and highlighting the need for US development: "There is probably no country of equal natural wealth where less has been done along modern lines to exploit it" (see figure 3.1).[22] Both the US government and IBC focused on the archipelago's inability to maximize its own commercial prospects and, as a corollary, the potential profits from US entrepreneurs' involvement.

IBC's goals aligned with those of the colonial administration in part because the individuals making policies within both the bank and the US government shared similar biographies, backgrounds, and worldviews. The social networks of IBC executives and US policymakers were enmeshed in the United States and on the ground in Manila. IBC's board included many former generals and military veterans. IBC President Thomas Hubbard had served in the Union Army as a Maine Volunteer and attained the rank of general.[23] BIA Chief Clarence Edwards respected and defended IBC's Hubbard, despite questions about the bank's performance. Edwards supported IBC management in the face of warnings about IBC's missteps and countered that the bank's management "in character and integrity leaves nothing to be desired."[24] Shared military backgrounds, in addition to collaboration as board members on projects such as the Philippine Railway, likely contributed to the government's ongoing support and willingness to accommodate.

Common military backgrounds created bonds between bankers and policymakers in both Washington and Manila, where US veterans played a large role in Philippine business.[25] Military experience was a hallmark feature in the biographies of many IBC bankers. General Charles Whittier joined IBC's board in early 1903. Previously, Whittier had been a member of the US military delegation that received the formal surrender of the Spanish in Manila. Whittier had also worked as the collector of the Port of Manila, a position that would have introduced him to leading traders and top colonial officials.[26] Captain Charles Palmer, a West Point graduate, became an adviser to IBC's Manila branch after working as the superintendent of transport for US forces in the Philippines.[27] An early manager of the Manila branch, Major PG Eastwick, had served as a US battalion commander in the Philippines and went on to hold board seats on several other Manila firms.[28]

Based on these common backgrounds, it is unsurprising that colonial officials saw IBC as an ally in promoting economic development in the Philippines. Indeed, the colonial government and IBC shared similar priorities about remaking the Philippines for US economic interests. Their ideas about growth and markets even shaped the way they designed education reforms imposed under US rule.[29] Throughout the 1900s and 1910s, the Bureau of Education developed new programs to mold young Filipino students into foot soldiers for the promotion of US-style capitalism. The bureau designed vocational training that taught students how to submit time cards and practice bookkeeping methods. A student's obligations in the market economy depended on gender: girls learned "cost accounting" associated with embroidery and sewing, while boys made work orders and kept time slips for their woodshop creations.[30]

The colonial government also taught students to become bank clients. It introduced US-style thrift and savings programs in conjunction with the state's creation of the Philippine Postal Savings Bank in 1906. Policymakers envisioned the Postal Savings Bank as an institution that would discipline Filipinos to become independent money managers. Through its offerings, Filipino savers could learn how to manage their money, thereby reducing their dependence on landlords, Chinese merchants, or pawnbrokers. Freed from their dependences that characterized Spanish imperialism, they would become enmeshed in US-oriented financial relationships and accustomed to US-style savings and consumption.[31] A program launched by the Bureau of Education organized contests that rewarded students and teachers for opening bank accounts.[32]

Monetary reform was another priority of colonial administrators. Some US policymakers regarded the Philippines as a laboratory for testing new currency schemes to expand the global influence of the US dollar. At the turn of the century, several different types of money circulated in the Philippines. Most Filipinos relied on copper coins for daily transactions; at least two types of silver pesos also circulated along with silver and gold coins, as well as multiple banknotes.[33] Policy leaders in Washington sought to streamline this currency system, which they perceived as backwards and unconducive to US business. In reforming the Philippine monetary system, Washington officials saw an opportunity to expand the gold standard—and not just any version of the gold standard, but a particular format that intermediated gold through the US dollar. The gold-exchange standard, popularized by financial "missionaries" such as Charles Conant and Edwin Kemmerer, would restructure the financial systems of US overseas colonies and dependent territories. Under the reforms, the dependent governments would issue new money denominated on the US dollar, which was itself a gold-backed currency, and the new currency would be supported by dollar deposits in New York.[34] This hybrid system offered an alternative to British colonial reforms that used sterling as the anchor currency for British colonies.[35] In the Philippines, the reforms culminated in the 1903 Philippine Coinage Act, which legalized the Philippine peso at a currency peg of two pesos to the US dollar.[36]

Monetary reform dovetailed with other reforms of the Philippine banking system, and these top-down political changes laid the foundation for IBC to expand its export-oriented business, without the encumbrance of onerous regulations. Whereas the colonial government established new financial institutions to serve unbanked Filipinos, its reforms allowed US and European banks to continue operating with minimal oversight. Regulatory minimalism had defined the Philippine banking system under Spanish rule, and a similarly hands-off approach characterized the US administration's attitude to US and European banks.[37] In 1900, the Philippine Commission deputized the insular treasurer as the supervising entity to oversee banks. Its requirements for banks such as IBC involved little more than enduring inspections by government auditors.[38]

While IBC and its European competitors served export-oriented traders, colonial administrators focused their economic reforms on creating new institutions—such as the Postal Savings Bank in 1906 and the Agricultural Bank in 1907, for example—to increase access to credit for Filipino populations. Each of the state-created banks was hamstrung by ideologies of the racial inferiority of Filipino people as well as shortsighted colonial policies. They ultimately failed to deliver on promises to improve economic opportunities to wide swaths of the population.[39]

The Agricultural Bank provides an emblematic example of the lackluster performance of colonial institutions. Founded in 1907 to help small farmers and tenants buy property, the bank's lending policies imposed stringent requirements for land titling. The rules prevented many of the intended loan recipients from accessing credit. In its first year of operation, the bank approved fewer than 6 percent of more than four hundred loan applications, largely because of inadequate titles.[40] The Bureau of Treasury concluded in 1910 that the low numbers were "disappointing" and that obstacles included the complexity and prohibitive costs of titling: "People possessed neither Royal nor Torrens titles and that the requirements for securing a Torrens title were so complicated and expensive that people would not attempt to secure them."[41]

The colonial project of converting tenant farmers into property-owning yeomanry got snarled in high fees, poor communication, and inept bureaucratic administration.[42] In the end, the reforms resulted in greater inequalities: small-scale farming became even less common, while large US corporations and existing landholders consolidated their ownership. The number of owner-cultivated farms declined by 9 percent and the number of squatter-cultivated farms increased from 1903 to 1918, according to census data, despite numerous colonial policies that, at least on the surface, sought the opposite outcome.[43]

IBC amplified economic inequalities that divided Philippine society. While bankers and colonial officials began the century ideologically aligned in their aspiration to advance US global interests, IBC's work on the ground at times undercut policies and reforms of the US colonial administration. After all, IBC did not have to answer to the US Congress, reelection cycles, or the vagaries of Washington politics. It operated from its own sense of self-interest, shaped by its New York-based board, an executive committee, and the dictates of management. Thus, as the infrastructure of US power evolved, IBC was not hamstrung to a Washington-dictated script for how that power should take shape. Instead, bankers operating in Manila could—and did—claim different parts of the emerging financial infrastructure of US power and co-opt it for the promotion of their own goals. Money that began as government deposits with

IBC could be reoriented to empower borrowers that IBC deemed worthy. The bank's influence and intermediation come to life by following the money that IBC managed. A deconstruction of IBC's loan portfolio sheds light on how the bank bolstered some elites, such as European traders and upstart US businesses, while contributing to the marginalization of other groups, such as Filipino tenant farmers.

Anatomy of a Loan Portfolio

As the US government sought to remake Philippine markets and communities in its business image, IBC was positioned to earn profits. Government deposits supplied a core part of the bank's available funds—more than 40 percent of the bank's total deposits between 1903 and 1915, based on analysis of bank balance sheets filed with colonial administrators (see figure 3.2). But even with this base of funds, the risks of operating in a recent warzone—and in a country still marked by violence and unrest—remained high. Casualties among Filipino soldiers amounted to 50,000 lives lost during the war, and civilian deaths due to war-related hunger and disease constituted between 250,000 and 750,000 people.[44]

IBC arrived in Manila against this backdrop, with few assurances of future business and little knowledge of local conditions. What the bank lacked in prior business relationships, it sought to hire in local staff by poaching expertise from more established British rivals. IBC's first manager in Manila was a British banker who formerly worked at the Chartered Bank, and its second manager was also British. IBC's systematic poaching might have allowed it to acquire European expertise, but newly hired managers declined to stay at the Manila branch for longer than a year or two. From 1901 to 1920, the branch averaged one new manager every two years.[45] At least one manager was fired for incompetence, and IBC lacked human-resources policies for staff retention or internal promotion that would have allowed it to develop talent internally.[46] By contrast, the first manager of the Hongkong Bank's Manila office held the post for a decade—not to mention that the manager brought prior experience and contacts from his work financing sugar trade between China and the Philippines.[47] Such turnover undoubtedly undercut IBC's long-term relationships with prominent members of the business community, given the central role that managers played in lending determinations.

Parsing IBC's loan portfolio shows the internal machinery of colonial bank operations at work. Loan portfolios were typically closely guarded secrets for most US banks. However, the operation of IBC's Manila branch was laid bare—in ledgers and auditors' reports—by the bureaucracy of US colonial rule in the Philippines, thanks to reports of the Bureau of Insular Affairs. The

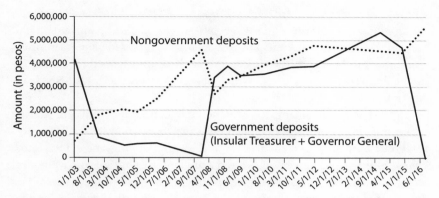

FIGURE 3.2. Government v. Nongovernment Deposits held by IBC Manila Branch, 1903–1916. *Data source:* "Comparative Statement of the Financial Condition of the Manila Branch of the International Banking Corporation," Various Years, RG 350, Box 585, Folder 550–250, National Archive. Nongovernment Deposits include: Individual deposits, time; Individual deposits, current accounts; and Savings Accounts. Government deposits include the categories: Deposits of Insular Treasurer, Deposits of disbursing officers (gov-general).

BIA's oversight of Philippines-based banks provides a paper trail of the bank's lending and credit allocation. How did IBC managers use its deposit base of colonial funds? How did its lending patterns impact people's access to economic opportunities in the Philippines?

The answer is surprisingly different from what IBC executives told BIA officials in Washington and New York. As much as IBC trumpeted its support for US business among US politicians, most of its loans in both 1903 and 1910 went to firms that were owned or dominated by European interests. Based on two snapshots of the bank's loan portfolios, in 1903 and 1910, I identified 97 percent of the recipients of IBC loans.[48] By investigating the line items listed in the bank's portfolio of secured lending, some patterns emerge. Borrowers belonged to several demographic categories. The dominant group of borrowers were European or European-associated merchants who worked in the Philippines prior to the US occupation. Chinese and Chinese-mestizo borrowers formed a significant constituency of IBC borrowers, as did US businesses and individuals who arrived in tandem with the US occupation. Finally, there was a cluster of borrowers with backgrounds I could not trace.[49]

These groupings—European, Chinese and Chinese mestizo, US, and "other"—emerge from the specifics of US rule over the Philippines. The designation of "Chinese" and "Chinese mestizo" arose in part from discriminatory legal status assigned to Chinese migrants under both Spanish and US rule.

Chinese merchants operated a range of businesses throughout the Philippines, but immigration controls under US rule restricted their free movement and contributed to the development of an insular and organized Chinese business community in Manila.[50] The US community in Manila tended to identify individuals and companies based on their nation of origin, such as British, Spanish, or German.[51]

The overwhelming majority of IBC lending in both 1903 and 1910 went to established European-affiliated businesses or European individuals. In 1903, this group claimed 86 percent of IBC's total secured lending, and in 1910, Europeans comprised 70 percent of secured loans and overdrafts. From a practical standpoint, the European bias is unsurprising, given that European businesses constituted the majority of established, export-oriented firms in Manila. Especially in 1903, IBC would have been hard pressed to identify a large enough client base of US businesses to sustain its operations. However, the practices ran counter to the messaging IBC executives provided to Washington officials about the promotion of US business interests on the ground.[52]

We can go further than just sorting borrowers into groups by peeling back one layer further and examining how IBC's clients put their loans to work. Reviewing the biographies and backstories of IBC loan recipients reveals the bank's dispersed impacts on the surrounding community (see figure 3.3[53]). IBC's two biggest borrowers in 1903 were a prominent British commodities firm, Smith, Bell & Company, and one of its subsidiaries.[54] Together, the businesses constituted over half of the bank's total loans. Smith, Bell was founded by a Scottish merchant to develop trade between China and the Philippines. The firm grew into a prominent, diversified commercial house. Smith, Bell also used banking services of the Hongkong and Chartered banks to distribute its borrowing across different financial institutions. Over time, the firm took both European and US partners, and by the early 1900s, it was involved in financing the mechanization and industrial processing of rice and sugar.[55] Smith, Bell was a major borrower from IBC in both 1903 and 1910.[56] The second largest borrower in 1910 was a hat maker from Zurich, Switzerland.[57] The third was a prominent merchant, Yu Biao Sontua, who was born in China and established a large shipping and trading conglomerate in the Philippines in the early 1900s.[58]

US citizens constituted only a tiny fraction—roughly 1 percent—of IBC's loans in 1903.[59] By 1910, IBC was lending to more US citizens and for higher amounts, and many of the loan recipients were US military veterans who originally came to the Philippines to fight. Upon leaving military service, many veterans opened businesses to serve the new colonial administration or capitalize on trading opportunities. Chicago native Walter Olsen, for example, arrived in the Philippines with the 20th US Infantry. After the war, Olsen borrowed money from IBC to finance his cigar business.[60] Another consortium

LOANS. (SECURED) (CONT.)

	AMOUNT	NAME	SECURITY
①	₱ 20,000.00	Sontua, Yu Biao	Loan Bond covering 55,000 arrobas rice and paddy stored in Sontua godown, market value ₱25,300.00. Insurance policy for ₱20,000 assigned to and held by Bank.
②	4,702.70	Olsen, & Co., Walter E.	Loan Bond covering Intnal Revenue bonded warehouse Receipts. Nos. 52-53 for 155 case tobacco valued at ₱6,726.64.
	1,000.00	Brown, S. R.	Loan Bond covering 50 cases... **⑨ Sanitary Steam Laundry**, per value ₱1,000.00, market value ₱2,000.00.
③	19,000.00	United States Shoe Company	Promissory Note dated M 7, 1910. Insurance policies for ₱19,000 assigned to and held by Bank.
	1,350.00	Melvie, C. B.	Promissory Note dated M 12, 1910.
④	10,000.00	Sellner, George C.	Property in Manila value at ₱24,000.00. Insurance policies for ₱24,000.00 assigned to and held by Bank. Torrens Titles.
⑤	10,000.00	Chay, S. C. & Limpangco, L.Y.	Promissory note dated M 19, 1910.
①	20,000.00	Sontua, Yu Biao	Loan Bond covering 5,000 sacks rice stored in Sontua's godown, warrant No. 2, valued ₱25,000. Insurance policy for ₱20,000 assigned to and held by Bank.
⑥	4,500.00	Carmen, D.M.	Promissory note dated M 26, 1910. See other loan.
⑦	3,500.00	Williams, D.R.	Promissory note dated M 28, 1910.
⑧	8,000.00	Artillery Exchange, Fort Mills, Corregidor Island	8 Promissory Notes dated May 21, 1910, signed by officers of the C.A.C. in charge of the Exchange.

① **Yu Biao Sontua**
- Prominent Chinese merchant
- Leader of Chinese General Chamber of Commerce in PI

② **Walter E. Olsen**
- Chicago-born veteran
- Traveled to Manila with US military
- Opened cigar business in 1904

③ **United States Shoe Company**
- US shoe-making company founded by US veterans

④ **George C. Sellner**
- Real estate investor
- On-again, off-again owner of *Manila Times* newspaper

⑤ **Lucio Ysabelo Limpangco**
- Native of Xiamen, China
- Converted to Catholicism
- Became regular client of Hongkong Bank

⑥ **D. M. Carmen**
- Vice-President of Chamber of Commerce
- Founded Moral Progress League to combat cockfighting and local "vice"

⑦ **Daniel Roderick Williams**
- Secretary for the Philippine Commission

⑧ **Fort Mills, Corregidor Island**
- US military installation to protect Manila Bay

⑨ **Sanitary Steam Laundry**
- Industrial-scale laundry facility
- Opened by US veterans in 1909
- Capacity to wash 10,000 pieces per day

FIGURE 3.3. Sample Page of IBC's Loan Portfolio, 1910. For data sources, see note 53.

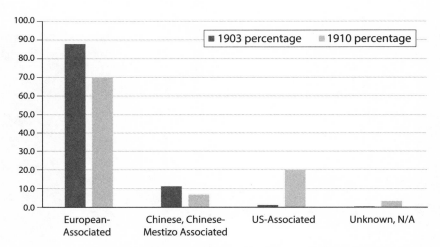

FIGURE 3.4. Recipients of IBC Lending in Manila, 1903 and 1910. *Data source:* H., B. H. Report of an Examination of the Financial Condition of the International Banking Corporation, Manila Branch, 1910, RG 350, Box 418, August 22, National Archives. Statement Showing the Condition of the Manila Branch, 1903, RG350, Box 419, November 21, National Archives.

of US military veterans founded the Sanitary Steam Laundry, an industrial facility built to handle the "rapid laundering needs" of arriving ships.[61] IBC lent to the laundry business and accepted the company's bonds as security for other loans. It also lent to Daniel Williams, secretary of the Philippine Commission, as well as the vice president of the US Chamber of Commerce, who cofounded the Moral Progress League to campaign against the local practice of cockfighting.[62] By 1910, lending to US-affiliated firms and individuals grew to comprise roughly 20 percent of the bank's total secured loans and overdrafts (see figure 3.4).[63]

IBC lending functioned much like the support beams undergirding the expanding apparatus of US commerce in the Philippines, as US veterans opened new businesses and existing merchants and traders adjusted to new conditions of US rule. The impacts of its financial activities were not defined simply by the nationality of its borrowers. Indeed, the category of national origin obscures the nuanced ways in which Philippines-based businesses were managed and operated. Several of IBC's European clients supplied goods and services to the US government and military. In addition, several European-owned firms took on US partners and employees.[64] For example, IBC borrower Adolfo Roensch & Co. was formed by German hat makers in the 1870s but refashioned its Manila business to supply US troops fighting Filipino forces (see figure 3.5).[65] Nonetheless, the breakdown of the bank's lending suggests that its initial

ADOLFO ROENSCH & CO.

The Oldest Military Supply House in Manila.

Regulation Caps, Helmets, Shoulder straps, and all kinds of embroidery for Army andNavy uniforms. Musical Instruments.

Large stock of: Hats, Caps, Shoes, Trunks, Valises, Mackintoshes, Rubber Coats and Boots, Slickers, etc.

71-73-Escolta, Old No. 21.   Branch House in Iloilo.

FIGURE 3.5. Alfredo Roensch & Co., Manila, c. 1914. *Image source:* Commercial Directory of Manila, Manila, 1901, 77.

operation strengthened well-established firms—mostly those founded and operated by Europeans—and individuals who already constituted Manila's elites.

The recurrence of Chinese merchants in IBC's loan portfolio is particularly striking given the discriminatory legal system that governed Philippine society under both the Spanish and US rule. Under Spanish rule in the nineteenth century, Chinese merchants and traders had developed strong business ties in importing textiles, for example, as well as rice milling and abaca trade.[66] Prominent Chinese merchants in Manila became increasingly insulated and interconnected due to immigration controls imposed by the colonial regime, and they established new business organizations and social clubs to support the community.[67] Several members of the community were IBC customers. Indeed, in 1903, 11 percent of the bank's loans went to individuals born in China or businesses founded by owners of Chinese descent.[68] In 1910, the figure was nearly 10 percent, although most of the loans related to a single individual and his associated firms.[69] IBC's records do not specify how these individuals became bank clients, but it follows that IBC's early British managers could have recommended them.

The prominence of Chinese and Chinese mestizo borrowers in IBC's loan portfolio suggests that the bank's lending was not dictated solely by the white supremacist rhetoric some US bankers espoused. In China, IBC bankers spoke in derogatory terms of locals and their uncouth habits, among other complaints. Moreover, they tended to delegate "local" work to a single Chinese intermediary, the comprador, as noted in chapter 2. But IBC's practices in Manila did not adhere to its China-based norms. Instead, managers in the different locations were free to develop policies that aligned with local customs and practices. In Manila, bank managers lent directly to Chinese clients without intermediating lending through compradors and without asking explicit permission or emphasizing the racialized dimensions of its lending with New York executives.[70]

Thus, IBC's lending in Manila influenced not only the sphere of European and US business, but also local social and economic hierarchies. Traditionally, scholars have seen US-European banking systems as operating independently from the financial institutions and credit circuits that served a broader range of Filipinos.[71] However, tracking IBC's lending patterns challenges this depiction by revealing the interconnections among credit networks. It was common practice for Chinese merchants in the Philippines to provide financial services for Filipino workers and other members of the community. Popular stereotypes cast Chinese merchants as usurers engaged in illegal financial activities, and the Philippine public could become suspicious of the Chinese business community in times of economic difficulty.[72] IBC lent to some of the Chinese and Chinese mestizo lenders who would have been the targets of this social prejudice. For example, Guillermo Cu Unjieng was known to provide financial services such as foreign exchange, loans, and remittances, though the terms of these loans are unclear, and his businesses borrowed from IBC.[73] In 1910, IBC lent to the Hongkong & Manila Yuen Sheng Company, a banking agency that managed branches throughout Asia.[74] By increasing the credit available to borrowers such as Cu Unjieng and the Hongkong & Manila Yuen Sheng Company, IBC affected the availability of funds to their clients.

IBC was involved in a lending scandal that underscores its interconnection with local circuits of credit. Shortly after opening its doors in Manila, IBC lent heavily to a local pawn shop, Casa Commission, which ensnared IBC in years of contentious litigation and substantial losses. When the pawn shop went bankrupt 1904, it owed IBC more than 440,000 pesos ($220,000) by one estimate—a significant sum that, if accurate, would have constituted roughly a fifth of the bank's total loans and overdrafts in 1904.[75] IBC's New York executives were incensed at the reckless lending and fired the Manila branch manager over the mishap. IBC became involved in a lawsuit to recover the losses, though ultimately the Manila branch wrote off the debt and asked headquarters to send additional gold from New York to maintain its reserves.[76] The deal—IBC's lending to a pawnbroker that served unbanked Filipinos—reveals the interconnections among banking spheres. The evidence suggests that IBC's work increased local lenders' capacity to provide credit to urban Filipino workers and farmers.

The bank's loans to large, export-oriented businesses—mostly owned by European and US citizens—also affected farmers' and tenant workers' access to credit. Foreign commercial houses served as stand-in financial institutions in some agricultural regions in the Philippines. Smith, Bell, for example, frequently lent funds to farmers by making advances on not-yet-harvested crops. The system allowed farmers to access short-term loans for sugarcane, hemp, rice, and tobacco.[77] While the lending helped meet the credit needs of larger farmers, it did not alleviate the plight of rural tenants, who had to negotiate credit extensions with landlords. In many regions, the terms of borrowing created escalating cycles of debt that caused tenants to be dependent on landlords for generations.[78] Interest rates could range from 20 percent to more than 100 percent, depending on the region, time of year, and local conditions.[79]

IBC's support for the providers of local credit by no means democratized or equalized access to financial opportunity in the archipelago. In fact, its work frequently exacerbated existing inequalities and strengthened the economic hierarchies of racialized capitalism. However, it did so not through flat, monolithic policies of white supremacy or dedication to nationalistic lending policies. Instead, the ideology governing IBC's work was guided by profit potential, more so than a singular conception of US power. Its lending benefited the European agricultural giant, Smith, Bell, and Company, as well as an upstart Spanish-Filipino clerk who pitched a business idea to IBC bankers in 1904. IBC extended a 10,000-peso ($5,000) loan to Vicente Madrigal and waived its requirement for collateral. At the time, Madrigal was a clerk in a British coal-importing firm, and an IBC manager was impressed with Madrigal's proposal to create a streamlined coal-delivery business, by purchasing coal in bulk, securing local warehouses, and using carabao-powered delivery. Madrigal went on to become a multimillionaire, business tycoon, and Philippine senator.[80]

IBC's lending patterns largely hewed to the predominant banking practices established by British institutions—patterns that benefited affluent incumbents. Nonetheless, the interconnections highlight how IBC's lending affected a broader swath of society by strengthening certain hierarchies and, at times, making space for the emergence of new ones.

Empire through Infrastructure: Railroads and Construction Finance

Lending to clients constituted a foundational piece of IBC's operation in Manila, but it was not the bank's only activity. At the time, the most elite banks of the day earned most of their profits and prestige not from such daily lending and trade finance, but through large infrastructure financing and sovereign lending deals. Banks such as JP Morgan and the Rothschilds became prominent names in the nineteenth century as they helped foreign governments finance wars, pay debts, and build infrastructure. Issuing bonds in international financial centers, such as London and Paris, became a popular way for governments to finance borrowing for public works in the nineteenth century.[81] The competition to underwrite and issue such bonds became a hierarchical and competitive business. Elite banks, such as Rothschilds and Barings, dominated the market in foreign lending. The elite banks' reputations for conservatism and stability allowed them to finance the most desirable projects and clients. Upstart banks, by contrast, were left with riskier options. "Good banks do what they want, bad banks do what they can," according to economic historians Marc Flandreau and Juan Flores.[82]

IBC ranked among the banks that did what they could—scrounging for pieces of deals and participation in loan syndicates. After all, the bank's size paled in comparison to the more prestigious financial institutions. IBC's paid-in capital in 1904, for example, represented just one-fourth of JP Morgan's annual profits.[83] While Morgan partners selected from among the most prized global lending opportunities—from financing Peruvian guano extraction to negotiating railway development in China—IBC struggled to access headline opportunities.[84]

Nonetheless, IBC tried to climb the ranks of the international banking hierarchy by partnering with more prestigious institutions on large deals. Outside of the Philippines, IBC followed this course by trying to access lucrative railway financing deals in China in the early 1900s. One case study of its failed attempts in China reveals the degree to which IBC remained marginal in large-scale international financing. IBC executives elbowed their way into negotiations over concessions for constructing an east-to-west rail line in China. The deal was contested terrain for international and domestic powers, with British, US, German, French, Belgian, and local Chinese investors competing to control negotiations and financing opportunities.[85] In 1909, IBC executives claimed to have won a special role for the United States, which guaranteed the employment of US engineers in constructing part of the line.[86]

IBC executives wanted to lead the US consortium of investors in negotiating the concession package with Chinese and European officials, but it lost out to bigger names, which dominated the syndicate. Prestigious banks such as JP Morgan and Company; Kuhn, Loeb, and Company; and the National City Bank of New York also partnered on the project. Ultimately, the State Department selected JP Morgan as the US representative on the loans.[87] IBC executives criticized the act as brazen favoritism toward Morgan. IBC President Thomas Hubbard denounced the State Department for doling out "special privileges" and ensuring Morgan's monopolization of such projects.[88] The sidelining underscored IBC's relatively lowly status in terms of large-scale financing in the early 1900s.

Within the Philippines, by contrast, IBC faced less competition for lower-profile colonial projects. Railroad construction was an obvious area of investing and development for IBC and its railroad-dominated board of directors. Of the thirty-eight names listed as members of IBC's board in 1903, more than half served on railway boards, led railroad reorganization trusts, or owned significant stakes in railroads.[89] It was only fitting, then, that IBC joined a syndicate for railroad construction in the Philippines in 1906.[90] The consortium, the Philippine Railway Corporation, won a contract to develop lines in the Visayas, a cluster of islands south of Manila. Partners in the syndicate included several New York investing houses—none of which carried the prominence of JP Morgan or National City Bank. Individual investors and the engineering firm JG White and Company also participated.[91] As an investor in the project, IBC President Thomas Hubbard sat on the Philippine Railway Corporation's board alongside both the chief and assistant chief of the BIA to oversee the line.[92]

US efforts to build railroads across its new colonial possessions showcased the continuity between US imperialism and the prior generation of European empire-building.[93] But in the case of the Philippine Railway Company, the construction effort took shape less as an omnipotent imperial behemoth rationalizing landscapes; instead, the venture looked more like a showcase of amateurism and mismanagement, despite attempts to deploy imperial best practices. The project faltered at nearly every juncture, as planners remained overconfident that the principles of scientific management and efficiency would eventually triumph over what they saw as the primitive tropics.[94]

Project managers, who lacked Philippine-specific experience, sampled widely from the imperial playbook of European and US techniques, and they outlined their ambitious construction plans to readers of US railway journals. The railway's designers mapped the line using statistical records from Spanish priests to identify the locations of natural resources. The planners calculated the potential balance of passenger versus freight by studying comparable British calculation techniques for building colonial railroads in Sudan and India. And they added a healthy infusion of US scientific management to optimize the diet of workers for maximum productivity. The caloric ratio—60 percent rice, 20 percent beef, 10 percent fish, and 10 percent vegetables—was "better calculated to forestall fatigue than anything to which the average of the men had hitherto been accustomed."[95] A celebratory article in the Railway Gazette in 1907 announced that railway builders made a bold choice in selecting workers: rather than importing Chinese laborers under deportation bonds, they hired Filipino workers (see figure 3.6).[96] The strategy presented challenges: managers had to convince workers to use tools instead of relying on the "native trait to use the hands and feet for working earth," but, the article ultimately concluded, "the use of Filipino labor is proving an unqualified success."[97]

FIGURE 3.6. Workers grading land for Philippine rail construction. *Image source:* Progress Reports, Philippine Railway Company, 1906–11. #192 of 280.

While enthusiasm marked the early years of railway construction, the project soon faltered. Neither freight nor passenger traffic increased as projected, and interest payments on the bonds came due.[98] The financial obligation to pay the railway's debt fell to the insular government because the Railway Company could not meet its payment obligations. The concession's terms specified that, in such a case, the government would become financially responsible. By 1913, the US government inherited the 4 percent interest payments.[99] The railway's owners encouraged the insular government to purchase all the company's stock and acquire full control.[100] Both the governor-general and BIA leaders balked at the proposal. Colonial officials resisted taking on the burden of the failing line due to its paltry revenues and the "moral responsibility" that would come with the regular operation of the line.[101] The administrators understood that managing a railway was not simply a matter of hiring engineers and laying tracks. Instead, it was an obligation to provide an ongoing service to ensure public access to transportation. US administrators in the Philippines abdicated that responsibility, at least in the case of the Visayas railway. The result was that the owners—including IBC—were saddled with the failing line.

Here again, IBC financiers sought creative ways to pass on the bank's financial mistakes to others. Rather than hold the underperforming railway bonds in their portfolio, IBC presented the bonds as security for getting more government work. The bank had been appointed as a government agent in financing construction in the Panama Canal Zone. In exchange, IBC had to submit security to protect the government's deposits, so bank executives offered the dubious Philippine railway bonds to meet the requirement. The bonds carried a face value of $151,000, but Washington officials observed that they traded at barely half the face value.[102] Government administrators challenged the valuation, and in response, IBC offered to provide more of the same railway bonds. The bank's negotiations delayed the need to give government officials more "secure" security until, three years later, the US government required Liberty Loans to replace the underperforming bonds.[103] Years later, after the bank had been acquired by the better capitalized National City Bank, IBC ultimately wrote down the Philippine bonds with a face value of $271,000 to $1 in 1926, and the railway went into receivership.[104]

To IBC, the importance of the railway was not solely in the returns it anticipated—returns that ultimately eluded the bank. Instead, the investment was an anchor of financial connections and board relationships. By participating in the syndicate, IBC enabled a revolving door of people and money moving between government and business—a revolving door that helped the bank ascend the hierarchy of international finance. Investments such as the Philippine Railway paled in comparison to the scale of deals that Morgan-level banks could conduct, but they provided a bedrock of social and professional connections that undergirded US power in the Philippines. Even the railway's board underscores these connections: the chief and the assistant chief of the BIA served on the railway's board alongside IBC President Thomas Hubbard and fellow IBC board member William Salomon, who was also chairman of the railway.[105] In addition, Cornelius Vanderbilt III served on the railway's board, and his brother Alfred was an early IBC board member. Though little remains in the way of records about the nature of those meetings, the structural connections would have provided a conduit for relationship building and information exchange. Such connections were essential to IBC for deepening its operations, gathering information, and expanding its networks overseas.

Another way that IBC became enmeshed in the operation of US colonial power was bankers' involvement in Manila social and business life. During nonbusiness hours, veterans, colonial administrators, and businessmen frequently retreated to private Manila social clubs. Institutions such as the Elks Club—the "most important of the pre-war American clubs"—enabled like-minded business and government leaders to relax, dine, drink, and converse in segregated spaces.[106] During the early years of US rule, racial exclusion was a hallmark of most social clubs. Several institutions admitted both Filipino and US members during World War I, but most continued to restrict membership to white US or European applicants, and some did so until the start of World War II.[107] Segregated social institutions were not an innovation of US colonial rule. British and other European clubs had catered to white elites in Manila long before the arrival of the US military. Under US administration, the clubs continued to function as sites for fostering imperial connections and Anglo-American solidarities based on whiteness.[108]

IBC supported these ventures implicitly, as the bank's Manila leadership played an active role in US social clubs. The bank also provided explicit financial support for the construction of additional segregated, pro-US social environments. And it did so in tandem with government officials. IBC helped finance the construction of the Manila Hotel in 1909, a project that exemplified the bank's work to expand US power. From the outset, the hotel construction involved a mix of private financing and public support. Investors provided $150,000, and the Philippine government committed to purchasing a bond issue of twice that amount.[109] The hotel's board brought IBC leaders in direct contact with powerful Manila business interests. IBC manager PG Eastwick served on it alongside cigar merchant Walter Olsen—also an IBC client—as well as some of the city's most prominent business leaders, such as directors of Smith, Bell & Company and lawyers for large US firms.[110] US Secretary of War Jacob Dickinson laid the cornerstone to celebrate the hotel's construction on his visit to Manila.[111]

Once completed in 1912, the Manila Hotel became a popular spot for wealthy, white Manila residents. Its roof terrace was a mainstay for the US community in Manila, on par with the popular Army and Navy Club.[112] The Manila Hotel provided exactly the sort of space where bankers and their clients could ensconce themselves, deepen connections, and confer about both business and nonbusiness matters. IBC helped finance the physical space, and it sustained the infrastructure that enabled both personal relationships and the brokering of business deals between politicians and executives in the secluded, sheltered spaces.

Friction in the Networks

Projects that fused public and private-sector power in the Philippines helped create an assemblage of interconnected, entrenched US interests. But the initiatives often encountered pushback, in both the United States and the Philippines. A scandal that came to be known as the Friar Lands controversy exemplifies how IBC's work complicated government objectives as US policy shifted. An early priority of US colonial officials in the Philippines was to undercut the power of Spanish imperial institutions, such as the Catholic friars who had amassed large estates under Spanish rule. In 1902, the US Congress authorized the Philippine government to issue bonds to purchase 400,000 acres of the friars' lands. The government planned to divvy the estates into smaller tracts, which owner-occupants could purchase. The deal was designed to be self-financing because, in theory, the land purchases by small farmers would have generated money to pay the interest on the bonds. In the meantime, the colonial government became the landlord to more than 150,000 Filipinos.[113] However, plans to sell the land to local tenants quickly faltered due to problems with surveying and land titling.[114] As interest payments on the bonds came due, the anticipated land sales were not forthcoming. By 1909, financial pressures mounted, and the colonial government increased the size of plots eligible for purchase to speed up the exchanges.

Not surprisingly, US companies emerged, ready to pounce on the opportunities to profit from US colonial politics. Investors associated with the "Sugar Trust"—the Havemeyer family's American Sugar Refining Company—purchased a vast swath of land in Mindoro known as the San José estate. The plot included fifteen miles of railway track, a hundred homes for workers, and ten homes for foremen.[115] News of the purchase incited a scandal in the United States because it came on the heels of newly favorable tariff policies for Philippine exports. US beet sugar interests had objected to the prospect of greater competition from Philippine sugar imports, and their campaigning helped to secure a colonial policy designed to exclude large corporations—businesses such as the Havemeyers'—from buying up large tracts of Philippine land.[116] Nonetheless, the Sugar Trust had exploited a loophole in regulations and was able to purchase the land, in part with IBC's help.

IBC's support for the transaction was twofold. First, in concrete terms, it served as the physical money mover for the US colonial government. The bank transferred the gold the War Department used to purchase the land from the Spanish friars.[117] The bank also lent to the consortium of US buyers to facilitate the sale. IBC borrowers included Horace Havemeyer, son of American Sugar Refining Company's founder; a Havemeyer cousin; and another US sugar planter. Moreover, when the buyers encountered financial difficulties, IBC was there to bail them out. The sugar consortium failed to turn profits on the land and became so indebted to IBC and other institutions that they mortgaged the property in exchange for a $300,000 line of credit from IBC.[118]

The upshot was that, in displacing a set of powerful Spanish friars as landlords, the US colonial government created space for US businesses to gain greater control of Philippine exports, and IBC provided the financial machinery to realize the consolidation. Meanwhile, disenfranchised Filipino farmers could not access credit facilities provided either by IBC or state banks, due to intractable colonial bureaucracies. Lack of access to credit meant that, when faced with economic downturns, tenant farmers often faced food shortages and crippling levels of debt. By contrast, IBC clients weathered economic downturns by taking out more loans. When the Havemeyers struggled to make the land profitable, IBC was there to grant flexibility and second chances in the form of greater access to credit and debt consolidation.

The Havemeyer purchase sparked opposition among both Filipino activists and anti-imperialists in the United States. The sale came following a 1909 overhaul of the tariff system in the Payne Aldrich Act. The legislation allowed Philippine exports, such as tobacco and sugar, to enter US markets tariff-free. Some Filipino politicians resented the tariff for its encroachment on Philippine sovereignty, even though it granted favorable terms for Philippine exports. The bill stipulated that US goods could enter Philippine markets for free—a provision that denied the archipelago needed revenue, as well as autonomy in determining its trade policy. Moreover, the tariff promised to reorient Philippine agriculture to the demands of US companies and consumers—a fate that would leave it dependent on the United States as an export market.[119] Politician Pablo Ocampo predicted that the bill would unleash an "avalanche of American monopolies" that would suffocate Philippine economic development.[120] The Havemeyer purchase seemed like a perfect realization of Ocampo's fears.

The controversy also sparked antagonism between pro- and anti-imperial factions in the United States. At the start of the US colonial rule, regulations of the Philippine Commission had barred US businesses from acquiring large tracts of land in the archipelago to minimize the power of large landholders and corporations.[121] When a 1909 news story exposed that the Sugar Trust had moved into the Philippines, US public outcry and political pressure prompted a lengthy congressional inquiry. The hearings revealed that US colonial officials had engaged in numerous questionable business deals in the Philippines.[122] At least seven colonial administrators had acquired significant land holdings or mining rights in the Philippines—all while crafting the official policies that governed access to those resources.[123]

It is unclear whether IBC played a role in financing the acquisitions of colonial officials outed during the congressional inquiry. However, the bank had friends in the US colonial administration and inside the Bureau of Insular Affairs in Washington that shielded it from critique. The governor-general of the Philippines, William Cameron Forbes, was himself an IBC client, and Forbes had communicated with the BIA about the Havemeyer sugar scandal.[124] Government officials noted that IBC was "anxious for business" related to the Havemeyer purchase, according to BIA correspondence with Forbes. And the BIA hoped that the US bank would continue to get such business in the Philippines, even if the dealings ensnarled officials in inquiries about dubious business dealings. The BIA chief expressed hope that US businesses investing in the Philippines would continue to "use American banking facilities."[125] At the time, IBC represented the only example of "American banking facilities" in the archipelago, thereby affirming the BIA's consistent support for IBC.

On the ground in Manila, IBC became a bulwark of pro-imperial interests of the US business community in the Philippines. Members of that community resisted calls for greater Philippine sovereignty, in part based on the fear that Filipino politicians would undermine their interests and jeopardize their investments.[126] The fears of the US business community regarding self-rule by Filipinos intensified after the 1912 election of Woodrow Wilson. The Wilson administration responded to escalating Filipino calls for independence by promising a gradual increase in self-rule. Wilson named a new governor-general of the Philippines, Francis Burton Harrison, who promised greater control for Filipinos. Harrison's promises ran in direct defiance to the imperial visions of many members of the US business community in Manila.[127]

IBC strengthened pro-imperial US business interests. It lent consistently to firms such as the American-Philippine Company, a bastion of US imperial interests. The company's prospectus reads like a manifesto for imperial business: it asserts a mission to secure "for Americans their rightful share of the trade of the Philippine Islands and of the Orient."[128] The firm was launched by disgruntled colonial officials, who resigned to defy the Wilson administration's plans for greater Filipino self-determination. The one-time director of the Philippine prison system, ML Stewart, joined the business, as did former Secretary of the Interior Dean Worcester.[129] IBC became a financial supporter of the firm and its affiliated businesses throughout the 1910s and 1920s. While these firms did not always generate steady profits, IBC lent dutifully to its inner circle of associates, even when business conditions and basic prudence suggested doing otherwise. Such flexible accommodations allowed a set of existing elites to enlarge control during booms and contractions, thereby deepening existing inequalities and creating new power imbalances in the archipelago.

As this chapter has demonstrated, IBC's mode of operation represented a new formula for US international banking that deviated from the traditional—and more profitable—script of JP Morgan-style investment banking. In a world where "bad banks do what they can," IBC did what it could by dabbling in a range of banking activities, from lending directly to European, US, and Chinese businesses and borrowers, to investing in archipelago infrastructure development. Moreover, the larger ripple of IBC's impacts in Philippine economic and social life amplified a range of existing inequalities and reoriented Philippine economic activities to the needs and priorities of US business. In doing so, IBC was not simply an agent for enacting Washington directives. The bank's work empowered existing European elites, supported Chinese merchants, and promoted aggressively imperial US business interests who opposed colonial administrators. Parsing these different activities takes us inside the machinery of imperial banking to see the mash-up of actors, activities, and agendas that converged to shape US power on the ground.

As IBC was constantly recalibrating its relationship to the US government, US foreign power was beginning to take new, less explicitly colonial shapes in the early twentieth century. Certainly, the deployment of Marines and the flexing of military power remained a go-to US strategy in the Caribbean and parts of Latin America. Simultaneously, a broader range of tools to project power, from economic advising to infrastructure building, became common avenues for US policymakers to advance national interests. For IBC to survive, it would have to hitch itself to new ways of expressing US international influence. Such changes arrived with the Federal Reserve Act in 1913 and the subsequent acquisition of IBC by the better capitalized, internationally oriented National City Bank.

4

US Imperial Power and the Fed

THE FEDERAL RESERVE Act of 1913 changed the ground rules for US banking. The legislation created a central banking system with a network of regional Reserve Banks and a board of governors. It also overhauled how US banks could operate internationally. Before its passage, when IBC sought to go overseas, the bank relied on the US government for deposits and legitimacy. After the Federal Reserve Act, US banks had new pathways for internationalizing, which left them less dependent on government deposits and more reliant on a financial market enabled by the Federal Reserve System.

National City Bank plunged headfirst into this landscape, opening nearly fifty international branches and subbranches within five years, as compared to only one other branch of a US national bank.[1] National City's strategy differed from that of IBC a decade prior. Some of the differences stemmed from size: National City was so well capitalized that it did not need the deposits of the insular government in the Philippines or Panama Canal Zone funds to underwrite its overseas operations. Instead, it needed a new legal framework. And that framework came with the Federal Reserve Act. After the act's passage, National City sought to dot the globe with its name-brand offices.

The legislation marked a watershed event in the internationalization of US banks and the emergence of a new infrastructure of US foreign power. By 1913, IBC had stitched together a ramshackle network of branches, which sustained themselves by profiting on the imperial aspirations of US politicians. After the Federal Reserve Act, National City Bank acquired IBC and folded its branches and staff into a more bureaucratized, centralized structure. More important than the insider story of what befell the individual banks is the larger question of how the nation's new central banking system altered the global power of US finance. This chapter pivots away from the innards of bank operations to assess the new topography of US banking and situate US branches within this international landscape.

The story hinges on the rise of a now-obscure credit instrument—the bankers' acceptance—which was a cornerstone of the original Federal Reserve System.

Acceptances lacked the blatant imperialist jangle of deploying Marines or building colonial railways. Their complexity and convoluted operation allowed acceptances to operate in technocratic shadows, shielded from debates about US interventionism, isolation, and imperial advancement. But their financialized veneer should not distract from the fact that acceptances created a new conduit to channel state support of imperial expansion and to alter the politics of distribution. "Paperwork favors the powerful," author Jennifer Pahlka has observed.[2] If so, then bankers' acceptances were an enabler of elite influence par excellence. The financial instrument sublimated imperial aspirations into financialized, routinized formats.

This chapter follows the strange life of bankers' acceptances in the United States. In many respects, they seem like an unlikely asset class to play a starring role in a story of the changing shape of US global power. Acceptances involved low margins and required high overhead. They generated few blockbuster fortunes. They were neither necessary nor sufficient for internationalization: US banks could open branches without a vibrant acceptance business, and they could trade acceptances without international branches. Why, then, are they at the core of a story about the creation of a new financial infrastructure of US global power?

Acceptances—and the Federal Reserve System's support for acceptances—changed the way in which US banks calculated risks of operating internationally and assessed their international work. The *possibility* of acceptance financing—even if the reality of acceptances proved lackluster in practice—shaped the staffing policies of overseas branches, banks' interactions with their adopted communities, and banks' ability to profit from trade finance and the promotion of the US dollar among US and international clients.

The interplay between the nation's new central banking system and private-sector banks shows how US infrastructural power took shape overseas.[3] The Federal Reserve Board relied on banks to generate and trade acceptances as part of fulfilling the board's congressional mandate to facilitate access to credit and provide an elastic currency for the United States. US banks, in turn, relied on Federal Reserve Banks to sustain demand for acceptances and reduce their risks in operating abroad. Moreover, once the infrastructure of acceptances, trade finance, and international branching took shape, the financial apparatus no longer operated under the thumb of either financiers or politicians working unilaterally. Instead, the network of bank branches and trading relationships were rooted in individual communities, which were themselves nested in a changing geopolitical context, as the United States emerged from World War I as both the world's banker and a heavyweight in international political economy.

This chapter investigates acceptances from two primary angles. First, it considers how acceptances functioned in the Federal Reserve System's toolkit.

Second, the chapter examines how acceptances impacted US banks' work overseas. In sum, this examination reveals that acceptances did not have to be lucrative, enduring, or wildly popular for them to have a lasting impact on the shape of US global power. Instead, they needed only fuse state priorities with the prospect of profits for private banks to shape how the US dollar expanded in the early twentieth century.

Bankers' Acceptances: Gritty Mechanics

The Federal Reserve Act authorized a new market in bankers' acceptances in the United States, but the act by no means invented acceptances as a financial instrument. Acceptances had, for centuries, been a popular mechanism for engaging in long-distance trade, and they served as the backbone of the British financial system.[4] Indeed, most of the world's trade was invoiced, financed, and settled in British pounds in the years preceding World War I.[5] "Bills on London," as sterling-denominated acceptances were often called, were considered one of the safest short-term financial assets that banks could hold.[6] By contrast, US national banks were not permitted to generate acceptances, and the United States lacked a similar market in acceptances until the Federal Reserve Act changed the rules for US banking.[7]

What is a bankers' acceptance exactly? It's tempting to explain acceptances by diagramming their hardwiring and mapping each step in their creation. However, even the most straightforward visualizations come with an inelegant number of vectors, transactions, and intermediaries (see figure 4.1[8]). A more intuitive way to understand acceptances is to consider the problems that they sought to solve and the communities that found them useful.[9]

Acceptances represented trade contracts between a buyer and a seller that a bank guaranteed to pay when the contract hit its maturity. Unlike traditional trade agreements between buyers and sellers, acceptances could be bought and sold by third parties, much in the same way that a home loan can undergo several additional steps of financial alchemy to become a mortgage-backed security, traded by third parties in financial markets.

Acceptances represented an improvement on traditional bills of exchange in that they contained an additional layer of security. A bank stamped its payment promise on the bill. The bank's "acceptance" of the bill transmuted it from a normal payment promise into a negotiable instrument that could be bought and sold on secondary markets. A bank's acceptance of a bill changed little about the terms of trade between buyers and sellers. In the case of both acceptances and more traditional payment promises, sellers in need of quick cash could take their agreements—whether accepted or unaccepted—to banks and receive immediate cash. Banks would offer sellers a discounted

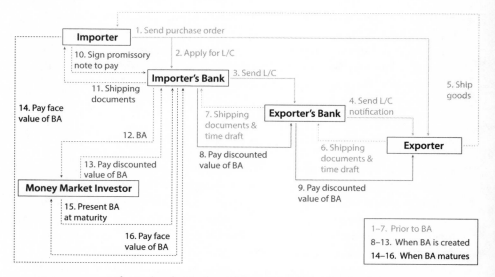

FIGURE 4.1. Life Cycle of a Bankers' Acceptance. BA = Bankers' Acceptance; L/C = Letter of Credit. For data sources, see note 8.

amount of the final payment—a process known as "discounting" the bill—so that the seller could access funds quickly. A major difference between acceptances and traditional bills is what happened next, once the discounted bill was in the hands of a financial intermediary. Traditional payment promises would typically remain in a bank's portfolio until the maturity of the contract. An acceptance, on the other hand, could be traded on secondary markets. In other words, the bank holding it did not need to wait until maturity to obtain cash for the contract, so its funds did not have to remain frozen until the buyer ultimately paid.

If that sounds complicated, it was. Documenting each step of an acceptance required a painstaking number of actors, documents, and intermediaries. One financial publication diagrammed the steps of using acceptances, and its description involved no fewer than ten steps and five different forms of financial documents, including a certified invoice, draft, letter of credit, insurance contract, and a bill of lading.[10]

But what seems like complexity in twenty-first-century terms was in fact directly responsive to the dynamics of international trade at the time—a risky and time-consuming enterprise. Goods, money, and correspondence moved on boats, and boats could take weeks or months to cross oceans. Why would a wool seller put wool on a ship without certainty that a buyer would pay on time, for example? Financial intermediaries—usually large merchant houses or banks—helped close the gaps in space, time, and trust. Acceptances allowed intermediaries to credit and debit each other's accounts without the laborious process of exchanging hard money, such as bullion or coins.

Acceptances were also financial abstractions. When a bank stamped its guarantee on a bill, its acceptance liberated the payment promise from its material origins. Suddenly, the slip of paper was peeled away from the goods to which it was originally tethered, whether cotton or cars or animal hides.[11] Instead, the paper itself became a commodity that could be bought and sold on secondary markets. The commodification of acceptances depended on an underlying legal system that granted the holder of an acceptance legal claims to collect payment upon its maturity.[12] The underlying legal architecture turned acceptances into more than just vehicles for executing international trades. Instead, they became financial instruments in themselves, whereby investors could earn profits by holding the future payment promises of borrowers.

The quality of an acceptance hinged on the reputation of the bank that accepted a bill. London investors might not know whether to trust the payment promise of a Chicago-based importer or a merchant in Buenos Aires, for example, but the guarantee of an internationally known bank like Barings or Brown Brothers instilled greater confidence. The bank's reputation assured other traders that the bill would be paid at maturity, and traders' confidence in that guarantee allowed acceptances to be bought and sold in open markets.[13]

The importance of reputation in acceptance trading was part of the reason that London acquired such a centralized role in global trade finance.[14] London banks and discount firms grew their businesses and established reputations throughout the nineteenth century by specializing in trades with specific commodities and in certain parts of the world.[15] The United States, by contrast, ranked as a second- or third-tier financial power. The US dollar was not terribly useful as a currency for international trade. The price of dollars was not typically quoted in major South American countries, for example, and the names of most US banks were too obscure to carry weight in many international markets.[16] Even the International Banking Corporation tended to use British pounds rather than US dollars in its ledgers and executive minutes.[17]

When US traders financed transactions with bills on London, they needed to utilize banks with either direct or indirect access to London's market; but relying on London trading, British pounds, and European intermediaries came at a cost for US businesses, both in terms of transaction fees and prestige. US firms had to pay commissions and exchange fees. US banks that were actively involved in trade finance held large balances of British pounds in London banks.[18] The net effect was that US traders paid a "tribute" to European intermediaries—often British financiers—to access the international circuitry of trade finance.[19] One executive estimated that US firms paid an aggregate of roughly $150 million each year in commissions to Britain for access to its bills market.[20] Such costs were not trivial, given that the average annual exports of US merchandise before World War I amounted to roughly $3 billion.[21] US trade lobbyists also complained that relying on European intermediaries diminished the competitiveness of US businesses. US companies had to disclose sensitive information to British banks when they secured financing. In turn, British banks could share this information with its long-standing British clients.[22] US traders regarded having to disclose such trade secrets as a competitive disadvantage.

Despite the costs, the lowly status of the United States in global trade troubled only a select handful of elites during the nineteenth century. After all, the expansion of settler colonialism across the US West consumed great fortunes and generated new wealth, and the prospects of financing such westward development preoccupied many US investors. By contrast, the United States possessed little control of the "sinews" of globalization around the turn of the century.[23] The circuitry that linked German bankers to Chinese silk traders, for example, or Argentine exporters to Liverpool buyers—shipping lines, foreign exchange trading, and banking relationships, among other networks—largely lay in the hands of more established European operators. Creating a bankers' acceptance market represented one effort to counter the nation's deficiency and boost the global status of the dollar.

The global status of a currency means more than just the denomination of money by which traders conduct their business. Currency domination conveys geopolitical and economic power to the country that produces it.[24] Indeed, the benefits of currency hegemony continue to shape international relations today, as commentators who debate about the future of dollar supremacy and "dedollarization" can attest.[25] Nations that issue global money have greater borrowing capacity, more leverage in international negotiations, and more flexibility on repaying debts. With the British pound as the prevailing global currency at the turn of the century, Britain deployed "currency statecraft" in ways unavailable to the United States, with its lesser-used dollar. US politicians sought to increase the global usage of the dollar in part to access these powers.[26]

Creating a new US market for bankers' acceptances provided one strategy to promote the dollar. At the time, the geopolitical status of the United States was changing rapidly. While the nation had lagged as a manufacturing power in the nineteenth century, by 1913, its manufacturing output was roughly the same as that of Germany, Britain, France, and the next three largest producers combined.[27] Yet economic crises in 1890, 1893, and 1907 hobbled the nation.[28] The rickety nature of the US financial system seemed increasingly mismatched to powering the global status that US manufacturers and politicians aspired to attain.

Calls for reforming the US financial system intensified after the Panic of 1907, and those calls would culminate in the 1913 passage of the Federal Reserve Act. But in the meantime, years of tumultuous debates would center on bankers' acceptances as a financial instrument, palatable to a broad range of political interests, that could stabilize US markets. After the 1907 panic, Congress authorized the creation of the National Monetary Commission to gather information about the organization of other nations' financial systems so that US policymakers could weigh options for reforming their own. A centerpiece of the commission's work involved investigating European models, which US reformers generally held up as superior and more stable.[29]

Britain's central banking system emerged from the commission's findings as an exemplar of financial stability, and the British system relied on acceptances as a primary mechanism for providing short-term credit. Paul Warburg, a prominent financier in New York with long-standing family connections to German banking, became one of the most articulate and influential champions of creating a US-based acceptance market to modernize the US financial system and bring it more in line with European competitors. Warburg advised the commission unofficially, and his support for acceptances, along with the commission's recommendations, helped frame debates about shaping the Federal Reserve Act.[30]

Bankers' Acceptances and the Fed's Toolkit

The Federal Reserve System took shape after several years of political contestation about how the nation's financial system should be organized. Policymakers and reformers considered questions like: How centralized should banking power be? What mechanisms could ensure that both agricultural producers and manufacturing interests had access to the right amount of credit when they needed it? Republicans, Democrats, progressive reformers, financiers, industrialists, and agrarian interests were among the interest groups that debated, splintered, and formed coalitions to answer a challenge that became increasingly urgent to all parties: the United States needed a more organized and stable financial system if the nation was to become a significant global power.

One of the most heated areas of debate focused on the centralization of banking power. After the Panic of 1907, Democratic politicians in particular expressed concern about the excessive power of the "Money Trust," as newspapers and investigators termed a consortium of powerful New York–based bankers. And they worried about ceding control of the financial system to Wall Street speculators. Acceptances became a politically viable tool for financial reform because they seemed to offer an alternative to Wall Street power. Inherently, acceptances financed the movement of "real" goods. They were not equipped to finance stock purchases or enable money market speculation, but as their underlying paperwork revealed, they provided credit for the international exchange of tangible goods. Following the Panic of 1907, many reformers agreed that the US economy needed exactly that kind of elasticity in its credit supply.[31]

In the economic thinking of the time, politicians on both sides of the aisle generally agreed that some types of credit were better than others. According to the real bills doctrine, acceptances represented good, "productive" credit because they enabled the short-term financing of production. Lobbyists differed about how the financial system should approach the more controversial, "speculative" credit, such as the financial activities that precipitated the 1907 collapse.[32] But bankers' acceptances allowed both Democrats and Republicans to find common ground in support for a financial instrument that, they believed, would not unleash rampant inflation.[33] To farming interests, acceptances were not the platonic ideal of a credit instrument because they tended to be too short-term—typically less than ninety days—to alleviate the pressures associated with crop cycles. Nonetheless, when combined with a broader portfolio of financial reforms, some of which addressed medium-term farm loans, acceptances ultimately proved amenable to agriculturally oriented lobbyists in debates about framing the Federal Reserve System.[34]

Bankers and investors such as international finance expert Paul Warburg saw acceptances as important for improving the competitiveness of the United States from an international perspective. After all, to financiers operating from New York, the weak position of the dollar as an international currency and the chaotic financial system were two deficiencies that a stronger central banking system could ameliorate. Organizing a central banking system with acceptances as a foundational credit instrument, US economic production could be better organized to promote the nation's exports and increase the nation's global prestige.[35] Such a modernizing step would address the "primitive" state of the US financial system, which ranked no better than Europe was "at the time of the Medicis, and by Asia, in all likelihood, in the time of Hammurabi," Warburg observed in an influential 1907 *New York Times* essay.[36]

Indeed, framers of the Federal Reserve System drafted legislation that organized the new US central banking system around acceptances. "Any member bank may accept drafts or bills of exchange drawn upon it and growing out of transactions involving the importation or exportation of goods not having more than six months sight to run," read Section 13 of the act.[37] Bankers' acceptances became the "most favored" of credit instruments of the Federal Reserve Act.[38] Rare are the moments in US history when international bankers, East Coast industrialists, and agrarian lobbyists rally around the same modality of financial reform, but the acceptance market was adopted as a matter of "curiously unanimous consent," recalled W. Randolph Burgess, a veteran of the Federal Reserve Bank of New York.[39]

It was not just the Federal Reserve Act that embraced bankers' acceptances. Importantly, the ongoing work of the Federal Reserve *System* depended on acceptances and, by extension, the US banks that generated and traded them. The Federal Reserve System imbued acceptances with two special powers. First, they were eligible for discount with Federal Reserve Banks. Second, Reserve Banks purchased acceptances and held them as assets in their portfolios. These privileges might sound like mundane, legalistic designations. However, they carry profound political and economic stakes because the US financial system granted acceptances special privileges that distinguished them from other types of economic activity.

First, the Federal Reserve Act designated acceptances as part of a privileged set of assets that could be discounted with Reserve Banks in exchange for cash reserves. That designation enabled an automatic upgrade: when discounted, an acceptance was transformed from a private-sector payment promise to a claim on the US gold supply, in the form of deposits at the Federal Reserve.[40] The upgrade made acceptances more attractive than assets that lacked discount eligibility. Acceptance holders could be confident that the instrument would remain liquid, even if money became tight and panic seized investors, because the Fed's policies assured banks that acceptances could be discounted.

Second, the ongoing work of the Federal Reserve System supported acceptances because Federal Reserve Banks participated heavily in the buying and selling of acceptances. Not only were acceptances eligible for discount, but Federal Reserve Banks held acceptances in their own portfolios such that acceptances constituted a significant part of their balance sheets. In particular, the Federal Reserve Bank of New York became the largest and most consistent buyer of acceptances (see figure 4.2[41]).

It is worth pausing to reflect briefly on how different this operation is from today's Federal Reserve System. In today's world, news headlines frequently announce the Fed's decisions to raise or lower interest rates, and the stories sometimes go into further depth about the financial mechanism for changing rates. Namely, the Fed operates primarily by buying and selling short-term payment promises of the US government. "Treasuries," as the Treasury-issued securities are called, are the most common financial instrument by which the Federal Reserve System eases or tightens the money supply. But it is a historical accident that the Federal Reserve operates in this manner at all. Indeed, in Warburg's day, such lending to the "crown" was seen as an unsuitable activity for a central bank.[42]

Instead, a central bank was supposed to operate as a backstop for the financial system and as a provider of liquidity by serving as a banker's bank. US

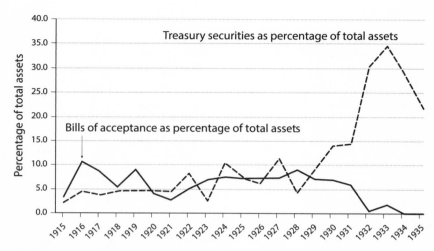

FIGURE 4.2. Federal Reserve's Balance Sheet: Treasuries and Acceptances as a Percentage of Total Assets, 1915–1935. For data sources, see note 40.

reformers envisioned that the Federal Reserve would function much like Britain's central bank, the Bank of England, by serving as the lender of last resort. In other words, it would provide liquidity and emergency funds to other banks, rather than facilitate government spending.[43] To fulfill this mission, Federal Reserve Banks were authorized to discount and hold specific categories of assets, and bankers' acceptances ranked among the most important of these financial tools.

The nation's entry into World War I quickly changed the calculations of politicians and central bankers, as the government needed to borrow roughly $25 billion to finance its participation in the war.[44] As the war effort escalated, the US Treasury pressured Federal Reserve officials to increase its support for government debt, and the Fed's portfolio shifted to holding a growing share of Treasury securities in the late 1910s and 1920s. But after World War I, both financial tools—acceptances and Treasury securities—played central roles in the Federal Reserve's portfolio.[45] The historical experiment in acceptance-driven central banking ended during the Great Depression, as the Federal Reserve's Open Market Operations narrowed almost exclusively to buying and selling Treasuries.[46] Moreover, the collapse in global trade caused the market for acceptances to contract sharply, and the Federal Reserve Board turned to other financial tools.

Nonetheless, in the late 1910s and 1920s, the Fed's support for acceptances boosted the global status of the US dollar and helped it overtake the British pound as the dominant global currency during the 1920s.[47] World War I severely disrupted London's centrality to international financial markets, and Britain emerged from the war with a weakened financial position. By the mid-1920s, the dollar had overtaken sterling as the world's leading currency, and the two currencies played a roughly equal role as the reserve currency of choice in the late 1920s and 1930s.[48]

Part of the reason that the dollar became so widely adopted was that Federal Reserve Banks purchased acceptances aggressively and did so at rates that lowered borrowing costs in New York as compared to London.[49] Economic historians have emphasized that the Federal Reserve System's support for acceptances accelerated the rise of the dollar; however, such analysis has overlooked the interplay between the Fed's work and its impact on US banks. This closer study of the infrastructural power of US banking tracks the way in which acceptances affected banks' balance sheets and international activities. Tracking this work helps complete a vital but heretofore missing piece in understanding how the infrastructure of US multinational finance expanded in the early twentieth century.

Branching

National City Bank was unique among US banks in its aggressive approach to international branching following the Federal Reserve Act. At the time, National City had existed for more than a century. Chartered in 1812, the bank was an early lender to the US government to fight the War of 1812 and became one of the largest banks in the nation in the nineteenth century.[50] Though banking regulations prevented national banks from opening overseas branches, National City used other strategies to develop international connections and profit from overseas financing opportunities. Around the turn of the century, its board of directors represented some of the nation's most internationally active companies, such as Amour & Company, General Electric, W. R. Grace, American Sugar Refining, and International Harvester.[51] To serve these clients, National City was among the first to develop an extensive foreign exchange business.[52] The bank kept millions of dollars in deposits with other banks around the world, from Deutsche Bank to the Hongkong and Shanghai Bank, so that it could work with correspondents to finance global transactions.[53]

Well before its acquisition of IBC, National City Bank experimented with other forms of internationalization. It invested in subsidiaries and affiliate banks throughout the Caribbean in the early 1900s, as historian Peter Hudson has shown. These ventures demonstrated that banks could benefit from advancing US imperial interests in countries such as Haiti and Cuba, in ways that perpetuated inequality and racial subordination on the ground.[54] National City Bank President Frank Vanderlip also helped create the international investing company American International Corporation to finance overseas infrastructure construction and global shipping.[55] And Vanderlip worked alongside Paul Warburg to champion acceptances as a central piece of the Federal Reserve Act.[56] Such activities allowed National City Bank to gain toeholds in international contexts even without branches.

National City Bank marked a new era of internationalization as it began its own branching campaign after passage of the Federal Reserve Act. One element of its strategy was acquiring IBC. As a state-chartered institution, IBC was governed by different rules than National City Bank, and the flexibility of IBC's legal structure appealed to National City executives. IBC was only a fraction of National City's size: its paid-in capital of $3.25 million was roughly one-eighth the size of National City's, as of 1912.[57] Nonetheless, IBC's international activities had caught Vanderlip's attention. He had explored the idea of joining forces with IBC as early as 1909.[58] That ambition would not be fully realized for nearly a decade: National City purchased a controlling share of IBC in 1915 and acquired the bank in full in 1918.[59]

A second dimension of its international work involved opening National City-branded offices overseas—a project that the bank pursued vigorously and one that dovetailed with its acceptance financing. Branching and acceptance financing were not inherently interconnected: banks could take up one activity without the other or, more commonly for most small-scale banks outside New York City, engage in neither branching nor acceptance trading.[60] However, when paired, the activities proved mutually reinforcing. Because acceptances were a credit facility anchored in international trade, the presence of US bank branches overseas facilitated access to credit information and increased US traders' access to new partners.

National City Bank designed its foreign branches to serve as a concierge service for US businessmen looking to expand trading opportunities overseas. A US salesman could hop off his steamer, head to a National City Bank, and find a warm, US-style welcome. National City bankers would help with luggage, translation services, train schedules, and recommendations for local barbers "with American chairs" so that business travelers could orient themselves.[61] Building such a network of branches was not cheap, and one of the reasons such a venture could be profitable lay in the new possibilities of acceptance financing and the rising global prominence of US exports.

The acceptance market changed banks' perceived risks in international branching and increased their willingness to open branches in more remote locations. An anecdote from National City Bank's internal meetings underscores this change. In a 1917 internal committee meeting, National City Bank executives discussed whether to open new branches beyond the major South

American capitals. Should they venture into smaller markets such as Peru, Ecuador, and Venezuela? One executive cited the risks associated with operating in highly agricultural regions. Crop financing would lock up the bank's funds in lengthy, eight- to ten-month harvest cycles. "Where are you going to get this money?" the executive asked an expansionist colleague. "On acceptances," replied the expansion booster.[62]

As the comment indicates, bankers knew that the Fed provided a backstop for acceptance trading: Federal Reserve Banks were always willing to discount bills that met the eligibility criteria.[63] As a result, branches could finance trades with acceptances and trust that the bills could be discounted in case they needed funds quickly. The policies meant that bankers could move into new markets, expand the balance sheets of their branches, and develop a client base with the confidence that financing trade with dollar acceptances would not lock up their funds or impair their liquidity.

US banks' ability to finance global trade in dollars became even more important as war consumed Europe. The outbreak of World War I upended daily life in Europe and trade patterns around the world. US exports surged, particularly in markets previously dominated by European business. The nation's exports to Latin America alone increased roughly 90 percent from 1915 to 1916, due in part to war-related upheavals.[64] Likewise, the war disrupted international traders' reliance on European intermediaries. Whereas sterling bills had traditionally served as one of the world's most reliable and liquid assets, the war jostled investors' confidence. Shortly after fighting began, London banks canceled credits abruptly so they could "conserve their resources for home requirements."[65] This interference caused the demand for dollar-denominated acceptances to surge, as the financial machinery of bills on London suddenly seemed precarious.[66] Thus the paired circumstances of a new Federal Reserve–approved financial machinery and the geopolitical disruption of World War I caused the acceptance market to become an increasingly important anchor of US-oriented finance and of the global uptake of the US dollar.

Despite the significance of the US acceptance market in 1920s finance, little attention has been paid to its impacts on bank's bottom lines. How much money could banks make from the new credit facility? Was the new acceptance market a windfall to banks? To answer this question, this chapter draws on newly compiled data sources—bank records, comptroller data, and bankers' correspondence—to consider questions that have previously gone understudied in the scholarly literature. These questions are at the heart of how the public and private sectors interacted with and benefited from the expansion of US global power between the wars.

Acceptances and Banks' Bottom Lines

Again, the story of the bankers' acceptance market is not one of jaw-dropping profits or crushing losses. Instead, acceptances were, at best, a tepid source of revenue for banks. Nonetheless, revenue generation is not the only axis worth considering to assess their overall importance. The acceptance market shaped how US banks branched, what markets they entered, and what risks they associated with internationalization. Banks' newfound ability to accept and trade bills made them indispensable cogs to the machinery that powered the rise of the US dollar and the new movement of US goods, workers, and firms overseas.

Historically, a barrier to analyzing the impact of acceptances on banks' bottom lines has been the wooly nature of accounting for acceptances on banks' balance sheets. The protocols for categorizing acceptances on banks' balance sheets were so messy and inchoate that the US Comptroller of the Currency used eight different accounting designations between 1920 and 1930 to describe banks' acceptance-related transactions.[67] Accounting for acceptances was so intricate that the 1929 forms printed by the Federal Reserve Board, for banks to report on their acceptance holdings, required 207 characters, as opposed to ten or fifteen characters for more straightforward financial categories, such as "overdrafts" or "circulating notes outstanding." The line item for acceptances used a uniquely tiny font to squeeze its description in two rows of text: "Customers' liability on account of acceptances executed by this bank and by other banks for account of this bank (exclusive of acceptances of this bank purchased or discounted, included in loans and discounts, and of anticipations by customers)."[68] Nonetheless, generalizing data based on banks' average commissions allows us to discern some trends and ballpark figures.[69]

For National City Bank in particular, the acceptance business represented a modest but not insignificant portion of its overall work. During the 1920s, commissions from acceptances constituted an estimated average of 5 percent of the bank's overall earnings. The following charts depict the bank's estimated commissions in comparison to overall earnings for a portion of the 1920s (see figures 4.3 and 4.4). This analysis, while coarse, suggests that acceptance generation was not a staggeringly lucrative business; nonetheless, as part of a larger portfolio of foreign trade, it played a nontrivial role in the bank's work in the 1920s.

Another way banks could profit from acceptances involved investing excess reserves in the acceptance market, but profits in this domain seem similarly lackluster. Acceptances were considered a useful tool for diversifying banks' reserves because they were highly liquid, short-term, and interest-generating.

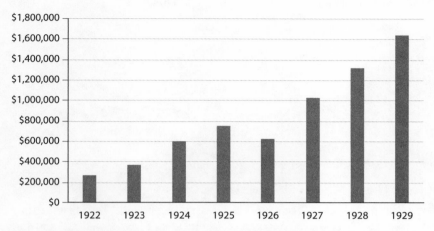

FIGURE 4.3. Estimated Commissions from National City Bank's Acceptance Generation. *Data sources:* National City Bank of New York, Statement of Condition, 1924–1930; "Editorial Comment: Commission Rates on Bankers' Acceptance Credits," *Acceptance Bulletin* 9, no. 5 (May 31, 1927): 3–5.

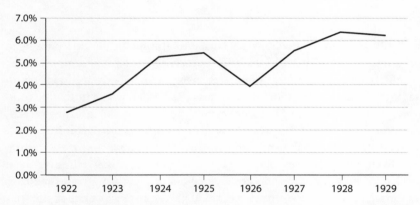

FIGURE 4.4. Acceptance Commissions as a Percentage of National City Bank's Earnings. *Data source:* National City Company, Memorandum to National City Company Managers and Representatives, 1930, RG 7, 2A, February 20, Citi.

National banks were not required to disclose the specific amounts held in acceptances; thus, acceptance-investing profits are difficult to calculate. Nonetheless, the existing evidence allows us to infer that the profits would have been relatively modest. The acceptance market had lower yields compared to average returns on the US call market throughout the 1920s. For investments in the call market, returns averaged 5.44 percent for paper with ninety days'

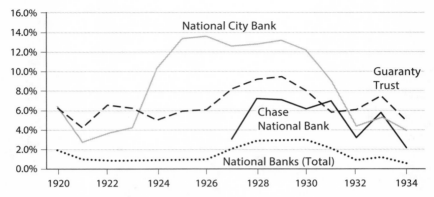

FIGURE 4.5. Bankers' Acceptances as a Percentage of Banks' Total Liabilities (1920–1934), *Data sources:* Acceptance liabilities taken from Proquest Annual Reports, Moody's Manual of Investments, and Harvard Baker Library Special Collections, as well as supplemental sources where needed. National bank data comes from Annual Reports of the Office of the Comptroller. See "Annual Report of the Comptroller of the Currency, Vol 1," edited by Office of the Comptroller of the Currency, Washington: Government Printing Office, 1914, and subsequent years.

maturity, a common time frame for such bills, during the period from 1919 to 1929. By contrast, New York's discount market averaged 4.15 percent in returns on ninety-day acceptances. Moreover, bankers' acceptances faced a tax disadvantage as compared to short-term Treasury securities, which further discouraged banks from investing in acceptances.[70] Therefore, as an investing vehicle, acceptances were useful more to diversify holdings than to maximize profits.

If great fortunes were to be made from acceptance financing, then presumably banks would have participated vigorously in the market. However, most US banks did not plunge into acceptance financing. Throughout the 1920s, acceptances constituted a relatively small part of banks' overall operations, even for banks heavily involved in the acceptance market (see figure 4.5). For National City, acceptances at their peak in the mid-1920s constituted less than 15 percent of the bank's liabilities, and the average for all national banks remained under 3 percent.[71] These calculations suggest that acceptance generation was not inconsequential, but that its profitability was not so great as to leave others clamoring to participate in the market.

What about banks that lacked an international branch network? How do we understand their impact on acceptances and the rise of the US dollar? While branching and the acceptance business were complementary parts of National City Bank's internationalization, not all banks took the combined approach of branching and acceptance financing. After all, launching a global network of branches with US-trained staff, real estate, deposits, and the ability to coordinate with headquarters was a resource-intensive proposition. Banks that lacked National City's broadly internationalized network could, and did, participate. Two rivals in acceptance generation—the Guaranty Trust Company of New York and the International Acceptance Bank—adopted strategies whereby branching played a lesser or nonexistent role. Far from undermining the importance of branching, the approaches of competitor banks reveal that family relationships and joint partnerships provided an alternative to branching. However, the strategies were ultimately more precarious and less enduring than National City's approach.

Guaranty Trust launched an internationalization push in the 1910s and 1920s, and acceptance financing was a pillar of its work. The bank's origins mirrored that of IBC in its early years. Both were founded in the crucible of Gilded Age fortunes, and both competed for the financial spoils of expanding US foreign power in Asia.[72] As the twentieth century progressed, both looked to larger banking institutions to support their international work. While IBC moved under the umbrella of National City Bank, Guaranty Trust relied on JP Morgan for financial support. Guaranty Trust, in 1897, was one of the first US banks to maintain a permanent office in London, but at the time its "foreign department" consisted of only a single employee.[73] After the Panic of 1907, JP Morgan acquired a majority interest in Guaranty Trust and consolidated several trusts underneath Guaranty Trust's name.[74] The consolidation produced a new, larger financial institution with diverse international interests.[75]

While JP Morgan and Company played a prominent role in financing World War I and postwar reconstruction, Guaranty Trust's work maintained a lower profile. JP Morgan grabbed headlines throughout the 1910s and 1920s for its large-scale lending. The bank played such an important role in financing US allies during World War I that, in 1916, JP Morgan's office became the headquarters for managing war procurement contracts for Allied powers.[76] After the war, the bank provided large loans to help European powers rebuild their economies. These sovereign loans differed from the type of financing that Guaranty Trust more commonly provided. Its acceptance financing was lower profile but nonetheless supported the movement of goods and the global uptake of the US dollar, as US financial institutions gained global prominence during postwar reconstruction.

After the Federal Reserve Act, Guaranty Trust opened several branches in Europe to support its commodity trading, particularly cotton financing. By 1921, Guaranty Trust operated eight European branches, as compared to National City's eighty-one global branches.[77] According to an internal bank history, Guaranty Trust financed as much as one-quarter of the nation's total

FIGURE 4.6. Cotton Shipment in US South (Guaranty Trust, 1921). *Image source:* Guaranty Trust Company of New York, *Our New Place in World Trade*, New York: Guaranty Trust Company of New York, 1921, 19.

cotton exports in the late 1910s and early 1920s (see figure 4.6).[78] In addition to a London office, its primary European branches were located in Liverpool, Paris, and Brussels.[79] Beyond Europe, the firm relied on connections with international correspondents and Morgan affiliates rather than operating its own branch network.[80] Guaranty Trust also promoted acceptance financing services by advertising and publishing pamphlets to explain the credit instrument to clients.[81]

Another useful contrast to the branch-focused strategy of internationalization pursued by National City involves the work of the International Acceptance Bank, or IAB, founded by Paul Warburg, champion of the Federal Reserve Act's adoption of the acceptance market.[82] Warburg helped shape the initial design of the Federal Reserve System through his advising and writing, and at the request of Woodrow Wilson, he served on the Federal Reserve Board from 1916 to 1918. After the war, Warburg created IAB to advance the twin goals of supporting the acceptance market and enabling the reconstruction of Germany. The bank did so without having any European branches.[83]

Instead, IAB drew on Warburg's extensive family connections and business ties in Europe. Warburg came from a prominent German banking family. His great-grandfather had founded one of the most prestigious banks in Germany in the 1790s. Warburg himself had been a partner in the Hamburg-based bank before coming to the United States, and his brothers continued to manage it.[84] Warburg stayed connected to developments with the family's business through regular meetings and correspondence with his Germany-based family before and after the war.[85] The family's bank served as IAB's German correspondent.

For business beyond Germany, IAB formalized relationships with several other prominent banking houses in France, the Netherlands, and Denmark, for example. In each country, IAB's partners were more than just distant correspondents. Instead, the banks were connected through joint stockholding arrangements.[86] These relationships drew on long-standing family networks and trusted trade relationships that had shaped European commerce for decades.

IAB's financial records show in concrete terms how acceptances made the US dollar easier for international traders to access in the 1920s. Paul Warburg drew on his professional and familial networks to use the strength of the US financial system to support European reconstruction and alleviate acute credit shortages in Germany. IAB directly financed the movement of goods to Germany through short-term, dollar-denominated debt. And it partnered with a range of European banks—including Warburg's brother's bank in Germany, MM Warburg—to enable financing. IAB granted credit lines and overdraft facilities to MM Warburg, which allowed the German bank to extend credit to European customers. These lines functioned much like rubber stamp agreements such that, when the German bank deemed a client creditworthy, IAB lent its financial strength to the same client. The agreements gave IAB "whatever position MM Warburg have with respect to their clients," as IAB meeting minutes from 1922 acknowledged.[87]

IAB's acceptance financing supported the movement of US goods to Germany and enabled trading for a wide range of products among numerous locations without crossing US ports. Coal moved from Germany to Buenos Aires; typewriters moved from the United States to Vienna; copper traveled from Chile to Italy.[88] Whereas in the nineteenth century, the trades might have been denominated in sterling and required settlement in London, a common denominator in IAB financing was that the trade credit occurred in US dollars.

As countries around the world struggled to adapt to postwar conditions, questions about whether nations should resume the gold standard loomed large. Many nations found their gold reserves depleted from wartime expenses and economic disruption. Resuming the gold standard amid an economic downturn risked imposing painful deflationary pressures. In 1922, European central bankers and policymakers convened at a postwar financial conference in Genoa. They agreed on the general goal of upholding the gold standard. To do so, they supported a gold-exchange standard whereby gold-based assets, such as the dollar and other gold-pegged currencies, could provide reserve assets for gold-exchange nations.[89] As a result, many central banks increased their foreign exchange holdings. The portion of such holdings in overall reserves doubled by 1927–28, as compared to prewar levels.[90] Amid this reconfiguration of central banks' strategies, the US dollar claimed a rival position to British sterling as countries' reserve currency of choice.

Acceptances became a mechanism by which central banks around the world could easily obtain reserves denominated in dollars. In the mid-1920s, the Federal Reserve Bank of New York, which had become a correspondent for a range of European central banks, developed the practice of investing its holdings of foreign banks' reserves in the US acceptance market. Within roughly three years, from 1925 to 1928, the Federal Reserve Bank of New York orchestrated an eightfold increase in the investment of foreign correspondents' funds in the US acceptance market.[91] Acceptance provided a liquid, easily accessible tool for foreign central banks to follow the recommendations of the 1922 Genoa convention and anchor their gold position in the US dollar.[92] And, as Federal Reserve officials were keenly aware, investing foreign banks' reserves in acceptances offered another means to nurture the fledging market—a goal many Federal Reserve System leaders embraced.[93]

The brief flourishing of the acceptance market helped enmesh many nations' trade in an expanding orbit of the US dollar, and US banks became critical intermediaries to manage this growing web of connections. The market didn't have to be wildly lucrative or terribly long-lasting to affect US global power. Indeed, the financial data suggests that many US banks found the acceptance market unenticing, based on national banks' underutilization of their accepting potential. In 1928 alone, if banks had maximized their acceptance financing capacity, they could have enabled over $3 billion in trade—a striking amount, given that annual exports in the 1920s averaged roughly $5 billion. In practice, national banks utilized only about 20 percent of that capacity.[94]

Even as the Federal Reserve Board tried to relax regulations to entice banks to enter the acceptance market, many banks resisted. The Federal Reserve Act initially authorized national banks to issue acceptances up to half of their total capital and surplus. In 1916, that restriction was lifted to allow banks to accept up to 100 percent of their paid-up capital and surplus.[95] The limits were so high in part because acceptances were seen as a safe financial instrument that would not encumber a bank's reserves. Acceptances did not require banks to advance their funds directly; instead, they guaranteed future payment of a trade contract as an extra layer of security on top of the original payment promises. Accepting a bill resulted in no short-term lock-up of funds. It simply created a contingent liability to pay if the underlying parties could not. "Acceptance credits may be extended even where the bank has *no funds* to loan," as a 1920s promotional bulletin about the acceptance market explained.[96] Because acceptances were considered a safe asset tethered to the production needs of the economy, regulators permitted banks to conduct extensive acceptance operations. Yet, banks' interest continued to be lukewarm.

A key takeaway from the US experiment in bankers' acceptances is the degree to which the US market failed to mimic the British system, despite the efforts of

US regulators and reformers to copy the British model. In the London market, intermediaries played a vital role as go-betweens and information brokers that sustained the market. Firms that specialized in buying and selling acceptances—known as discount houses—emerged throughout the nineteenth century to carry large portfolios of acceptances and to match sellers with buyers.

From a distance, the work of British discount houses seems like technocratic arbitrage. In practice, however, the firms depended on elaborate networks of person-to-person information gathering. As one US observer explained, discount houses operated through their salesmen. Brokers of discount houses held the key to understanding the British system: bills "are carried about through the streets by men in silk hats. Once you know that, your whole picture of the London discount market lights up and the place takes on an air of reality."[97] Brokers—the "men in silk hats"—knew the reputations and payment histories of merchants and financiers around the world. They made rounds each morning to "visit all the banks and merchant bankers to ascertain how much money they want to call or lend."[98] Banks paid them a premium for their services: brokers knew which bills and whose credit to trust, and they learned what commodities were desired where.[99] Information flowed both ways in the meetings: "Being a professional beggar, the bill broker must interest or amuse his patrons . . . by giving information as to the standing of a particular firm or trade or by supplying early news of any important financial business."[100]

The US market lacked Britain's ecosystem of established discount houses and information intermediaries. Instead, the beating heart of the US acceptance system was the Federal Reserve System itself—and especially the Federal Reserve Bank of New York. The Federal Reserve Bank of New York acted not only as an arbiter of the acceptance market ground rules, but it was also the largest and most important buyer of acceptances throughout the 1910s and 1920s. It channeled its own funds and deposits from foreign correspondents into the acceptance market. By the late 1920s, purchases of the Federal Reserve Bank of New York alone constituted 50 percent of the total volume of acceptances.[101] The resulting system was not a self-sustaining market, but one dependent on the Federal Reserve System. For much of the 1920s, the Federal Reserve System held, on average, a quarter to two-thirds of outstanding acceptances (see figure 4.7[102]).

When the Fed retreated from the market in the early 1930s, the market for bankers' acceptances largely faded. The onset of the Great Depression refocused the attention of Federal Reserve officials on different tools for affecting the US economy, such as US Treasuries, and the retreat of global trade in general caused the acceptance market to contract. References to the acceptance market largely disappeared from discussions of the Fed's open market operations by the 1930s.[103]

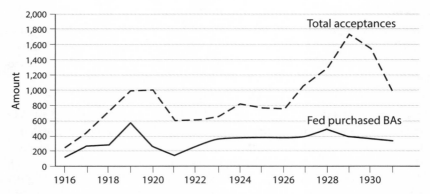

FIGURE 4.7. Federal Reserve's Acceptance Holding as Compared to Total Acceptances, 1916–1931. For data sources, see note 101. A similar graph appears in Barry Eichengreen and Marc Flandreau, "The Federal Reserve, the Bank of England, and the Rise of the Dollar as an International Currency, 1914–1939," *Open Economies Review* 23, no. 1 (2012): 65. Figure does not include acceptance held by the Fed on behalf of the accounts of foreign correspondents. Data represents annual figures only, reported in December, and does not account for seasonal variations.

Nevertheless, the Federal Reserve System's support for the acceptance market in the 1910s and 1920s provided a newly institutionalized channel for advancing US commercial power. Its work was mutually beneficial for US bankers and politicians. While acceptance trading was not as obvious as interlocking directorates or government contracting, the acceptance market provided a powerful, depersonalized mechanism to connect state power with US finance. Moreover, the system was less vulnerable to charges of unfair privileges. Whereas congressional committees following the Panic of 1907 denounced the shadowy power of New York financiers, the creation of the Federal Reserve System validated and institutionalized new pathways for such intermediaries to expand their work and earn profits internationally.

These practices were more amenable to depictions of a scientized, rationalized credit system and better contoured to support the shifting forms of US imperial power. This chapter has focused on structural shifts in the US financial system and particularly the creation of a new credit instrument—the bankers' acceptance. Acceptances empowered US banks to allocate billions of dollars toward trade finance. In practice, the uptake of acceptances proved more anemic than its original architects had hoped. Nonetheless, the structural changes associated with acceptances precipitated new dynamics in US overseas banking. International branching was not the only on-ramp to participating in the acceptance market; however, given the size and scale of National City Bank's operation, it was a key source of assurance in the creation of the bank's global network of branches.

In the next chapter, these structural changes in US finance come to life as we track how the new Federal Reserve System impacted banks' branching. Doing so reveals that *information* became the north star of branches' operation immediately following the Federal Reserve Act. What bankers meant by information, how it was gathered and encoded, and who benefited were stickier questions. Answering them requires us to drill down a layer deeper into the information practices that shaped National City Bank's overseas work.

5

Information and the
Routines of Empire

WHEN THE RUSSIAN Revolution broke out in 1917, the St. Petersburg branch of National City Bank had been open less than a year.[1] John Fuller was one of the first US staffers sent to the office. Before going to Russia, Fuller had completed a National City Bank program to prepare college graduates to become foreign bankers. Then he sailed for three weeks—a journey that lasted half as long as his entire training in banking. He arrived in Petrograd and found the city to be bustling and packed with foul streetcars. In October 1917, Fuller wrote in his journal: "The excitement seems to be coming at last. The latest rumor has it that the slaughter of the Americans is to begin tomorrow by the Bolshevicks."[2] Despite the rumors, Fuller's life continued relatively normally until late December. Then, several days after Christmas, Bolshevik soldiers stormed the bank with bayonets and "demanded that the bank be closed—or rather announced that the bank was closed," he wrote to his family in Indiana.[3] Soldiers arrested the bank's manager.

Following the armed takeover, Fuller's Petrograd office sent a message to New York. One of the central points was, strikingly, an apology: the branch would have to pause its work gathering credit information. "Due to conditions prevailing, it is quite impossible for us to obtain any credit information, as the Banks are not answering any of our letters. . . . It is impossible to gauge the credit standing of any firm or individual under the present conditions." The branch advised New York to "[t]emporarily discontinue accepting from outsiders names for investigation in Russia."[4] At first glance, it seems curious that, during the tumult of revolution, forced shutdown, and managers' imprisonment, the branch would prioritize telling headquarters that it had paused its collection of credit information. Weren't there more important messages to share— about the safety of staff or the status of deposits, for example?

A closer look at the bank's work reveals that its emphasis on credit information was not just a throwaway remark in a Petrograd memo; instead, it was a pillar of the bank's international expansion. Why information? What did information-gathering have to do with the expansion of US power overseas? This chapter investigates how National City Bank plotted its international expansion—its organization, foundational logic, and source of profits—around access to information and, further, how this information shaped US financial power around the world.

Overseas bankers gathered, codified, and shared credit information and business contacts with the bank's US clients. This work connected to larger changes in geopolitics and global finance, which were themselves in flux after World War I. Filling the pipeline of financing bankers' acceptances depended on information: banks needed data about international markets, the credit-worthiness of firms, and trade conditions to fuel the new machinery of US trade finance. That machinery supported the dollar's rise as a dominant global currency in the 1920s and the expansion of US monetary sovereignty beyond its territorial borders.

Acquiring information had long motivated multinational enterprises to expand into new locations. In the nineteenth century, European multinational banking opened offices or acquired competitors overseas in part to overcome "information asymmetries," as banking historians have noted.[5] From National City Bank's perspective, the challenge was not only that information about foreign markets was asymmetrical—namely, that European competitors had it, and US financial institutions did not. The thornier problem was that US banks had to create the information in the first place. US bankers couldn't simply open foreign offices and take credit information from a competitor's filing cabinet. The reports, rating scales, and collection apparatus needed to be created. Making the information required building a base layer of institutional relationships, communication patterns, and staff that could transform the risks of international trading into legible categories and portable paper formats.[6]

Branching abroad for the sake of information might sound at first like a middling goal when compared to more lucrative projects, like underwriting securities or loaning to governments. However, the ambition was compelling enough to early-twentieth-century US bankers to power the initial design of National City Bank's expansion. The bank's plans for overseas branches had little to do with attracting international customers; instead, foreign branches were meant to support *domestic* clients. Executives believed that collecting information to provide trade support would distinguish National City Bank from competing US banks, which lacked such services for foreign trade. This goal also distinguished National City's aspiration from the previous generation of internationally oriented financiers that banded together to form IBC. For Marcellus Hartley, Thomas Hubbard, and the consortium of Gilded Age elites who led IBC's board, IBC represented an enticing investment because it offered a toehold in new markets where the US government made imperial advances. And it provided a usefully ambiguous mechanism to finance trade and hold a diversified set of international investments. National City Bank acquired IBC over the course of World War I, but the parent bank's ambitions for its own branches focused more centrally on systematic information-gathering and expanding access than the diffuse, individual profit-oriented aspirations that characterized IBC founders.

New York executives saw the passage of the Federal Reserve Act as an opportunity for National City Bank to strengthen its comparative advantage as an internationally connected bank. The bank could offer credit information, financing, and on-the-ground support for clients' trade needs: "We could offer [US businesses] credit information and represent them in other ways which I am certain would attract a large number of accounts to us," National City Bank President Frank Vanderlip explained to the bank's chairman, James Stillman.[7] Branches were designed to facilitate those services.

Thus, information, rather than overseas profits, was the cornerstone of National City's foreign branching project. Each foreign branch mattered less for its revenue generation or loan portfolio than for the information and services it offered the bank's US clients, executives believed. "I do not expect much profit out of it," Vanderlip wrote to Stillman about overseas branching—as if to manage his boss's expectations. "[B]ut I hope to get a very considerable return by offering facilities that other banks cannot offer to exporters, and thus attract their attention to the City Bank."[8]

The "foreign field," as Vanderlip called it, lacked the contours of specific locations or markets; instead, US bankers saw it as a vast, undifferentiated expanse where they could gain a competitive edge and offer services that would attract new US customers. "Many of the branches now operated by American banks in foreign countries make little or no profit," echoed bank Vice President Charles Schwedtman in a speech to the National Association of Manufacturers in 1922. "Their function is largely to establish and maintain a local connection in such countries for American merchants. . . . The collection of dependable credit information that has been secured by means of them is of incalculable value."[9] In the mental geography that organized bank executives' expansion plans, the United States reigned supreme as the location that ultimately warranted serving.

Building Information Systems

The locations where National City opened its first branches were selected in part as a credit-information play. Frank Vanderlip had discussed with James Farrell, the president of the US Steel Corporation, the idea of National City opening a network of international branches. Farrell encouraged National City's expansion and, to help, offered to give the bank access to his company's credit files in Buenos Aires and Rio de Janeiro if National City would open branches there.[10] Indeed, National City selected Buenos Aires as the site of its first overseas branch. A branch in Rio followed shortly after.[11] It is unclear if US Steel ever transferred its credit files to the bank; nonetheless, once National City was operational in Buenos Aires, US bankers quickly assembled credit dossiers and information systems of their own.

These information systems were designed to help US clients rather than expand branches' in-house lending. After all, the mechanics of bankers' acceptances largely shielded banks from the financial risks of lending directly to clients. Instead, with acceptances, banks' profits depended more on commissions and fees than on careful assessments of the creditworthiness of parties involved in the underlying transactions. In using an acceptance, sellers bore ultimate responsibility for determining the creditworthiness of their trading partners. Exporters could discount their trade bill with a bank and obtain cash before the contract's maturity; however, the bank held legal recourse to reclaiming the advanced funds should the buyer fail to pay. As the fine print of acceptance paperwork revealed, the bank provided credit information as "a matter of courtesy" to customers rather than to endorse or vouch for a would-be borrower. If the buyer refused to pay for the goods once they arrived at their destination, the bank would simply reclaim the funds that had been advanced to the seller.[12] Paperwork required clients to agree that banks carried no responsibility for problems associated with the trade, and clients had to accept the obligation to pay upon "non-performance" of the agreement.[13]

Some US manufacturers resented the way that acceptances insulated banks from financial risks. At the 1919 Foreign Trade Convention in Chicago, a locomotive manufacturer complained: "A bank charges you for discounting a draft and then has the hardihood to say to you that if the foreigner whose credit it has recommended does not pay you must return the money."[14] National City Bank defended its policy by arguing that, in providing credit information, it did not take "even an implied moral responsibility for the foreign consignee's taking, and paying for, whatever an exporter ships."[15] Further, bank officials downplayed the risks of such problems by assuring US manufacturers that most disputes arose from misunderstandings. Moreover, resolving such misunderstandings was one such service National City overseas bankers were uniquely positioned to offer. Bankers could troubleshoot any problems that might arise. Thus, the credit information gathered by branches served more as a support service to help US clients gain insight on potential trading partners, rather than an internal mechanism for safeguarding bank loans.

FIGURE 5.1. Uruguay Branch, Commercial Representative (right) with Branch Manager. *Image source:* W. F. Voorhies, "The Wool Industry in Uruguay," *No. 8,* 11, no. 1 (January 1916): 26.

Staffing practices at the branches also reflected the bank's emphasis on information. National City created a new job description for its foreign branches, the "commercial representative." The job involved gathering information about "reputable and responsible" local merchants and compiling local and regional statistics (see figure 5.1).[16] National City also created a new executive position to oversee the bank's massive increase in data acquisition: the statistician. To fill the post, the bank poached Oscar Austin from the Bureau of Statistics of the US Department of Commerce.[17] Austin had previously authored government reports about trade expansion and global commerce, including a nearly five-hundred-page book comparing the practices of colonial administrations.[18] For National City, Austin compiled reports and published essays in the bank's newsletters and other publications.[19] Bank executives envisioned that this staffing structure would allow it to amass data about the world, organize the sources into legible categories, and make the risks of overseas trading quantifiable and manageable to US businesses.

The bank showcased its foreign information machinery in a range of publications. It created new formats of reports and updates—weekly and bimonthly—and a monthly magazine, *The Americas*, to provide statistics and commentary about international trade, ranging from export data to new customs regulations.[20] By early 1916, roughly two years into its branching project, the bank's Foreign Trade Department boasted that it had connected three hundred US firms to South American trading opportunities, in addition to attracting "a surprisingly large number of new accounts."[21] Executives monitored the bank's information services internally: staff tallied new subscriptions, inquiries, and connections the bank made among trading partners.[22] They even considered publishing credit-rating books, much like those of Dun and Bradstreet and other mercantile agencies, to make its internal reports available to clients—though the bank ultimately opted not to do so.[23] Credit information was the flagship of the bank's international services. Executives boasted of the bank's credit library with reports on seven thousand "leading South American concerns."[24]

Having an overseas branch was not the only path for a bank to gain credit information about overseas firms or support an acceptance business, as chapter 4 noted. US banks that lacked National City's overseas network could— and did—engage extensively in trade finance and acceptance generation by relying on correspondents. The Guaranty Trust Company also launched an internationalization push in the 1910s and 1920s, and acceptance financing was a pillar of its efforts.

To support its clients' international trade needs, Guaranty Trust shared National City Bank's emphasis on providing credit information to clients, even though it lacked National City's broadly global network. A 1919 article in *Bankers Home Magazine* boasted that Guaranty Trust maintained a library of sixty thousand records on overseas firms in its Foreign Credit Division. Much of the information—said to contain both the "moral and financial rating" of firms— came from the bank's international correspondents, but a portion came from Guaranty Trust's own international branches.[25] The firm encouraged customers to use its information services, such as "very complete files on most of the important firms in the Latin-American countries," by working with the bank's International Trade Service and Publicity Department.[26] It also sought to demystify the mechanics of bankers' acceptances for clients by publishing pamphlets about how to use acceptances.[27] The materials included samples of acceptances and anecdotal examples of how an exporter like "John Doe" in Galveston, Texas, might use an acceptance to move his merchandise (see figure 5.2).[28]

Nevertheless, in the quest for information acquisition, National City Bank had an edge over Guaranty Trust, given that National City could obtain information directly from its branches. At the time, many US traders viewed credit information created by US banks as more accurate than non-US sources. The Department of Commerce noted in the 1920s that "credit information obtained from foreign correspondents is often incomplete and in many cases

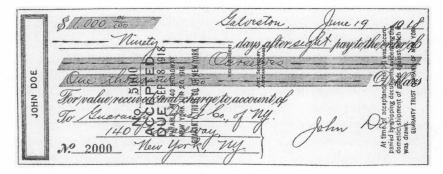

FIGURE 5.2. Sample Acceptance from Guaranty Trust's *Acceptances* (1919).
Image source: Guaranty Trust Company of New York, *Acceptances*, New York:
Guaranty Trust Company of New York, 1920, 25.

unreliable."[29] The Federal Reserve Board agreed and concluded that there was a "general belief that credit data given by American banks are by far more reliable and valuable than information furnished by foreign banks."[30] National City Bank claimed a competitive advantage over other banks for the quality of its information and its ability to provide on-the-ground support.

Shifting US Credit Standards

As US banks created new information systems overseas, norms about credit information and lending were also changing in the United States. Throughout the 1800s, bankers relied on a shorthand formula for evaluating credit. Known as the "three C's," the approach emphasized character, capital, and capacity as the foundations of credit evaluations. Directors' personal networks often played a central role in a financial institution's evaluation of a borrower's three C's: reputation (character), worth (capital), and business prospects (capacity). However, financial upheaval in the late nineteenth century prompted many banks to reorganize their credit operations. After the Panic of 1893, many East Coast US banks restructured their loan-making practices to rely less on directors' personal networks and more on the input of salaried staff. Banks increasingly established credit departments, which collected information about borrowers and monitored lending across larger and more dispersed customer bases.[31]

Alongside these changes, a new category of professional worker—the "credit man"—was emerging in the United States.[32] In 1896, a group of bankers, manufacturers, and distributors organized the National Association of Credit Men. NACM created guidelines to standardize credit evaluation practices and differentiate worthy borrowers from those they deemed unworthy.

Its approach blended moralistic ideals about vice and weakness with efforts to scientize business.[33] Thanks to NACM lobbying and advocacy, the position of credit manager became common in banks and commercial credit reporting agencies as well as in retail businesses and manufacturing firms.[34]

In this landscape, a range of institutions and services emerged to popularize credit information and introduce financial tools that ranked borrowers, as well as investments. Ratings for bonds became a particularly lucrative format popularized by new financial publications. *Moody's Analyses of Railroad Investments* published its first ratings book for railroad bonds in 1909, and the service expanded to include industrial and utility bonds in 1914.[35] Ratings publications from Fitch, Poor, and Standard Statistics followed soon after.[36] Many of the information systems adopted analogous models to the ratings schemes popularized by Lloyd's registry from the 1830s.[37] Common characterizations and terms emerged across the different systems. "A1" designated top borrowers; "A2" and lower categories raised questions about borrowers' repayment prospects.[38] Credit ratings became so common that the terminology seeped into the London and New York vernacular, such that a reliable, affluent person might be called "A1."[39] The categories suggested that borrowers could be measured against common standards and that local idiosyncrasies could be compressed to "calculable risks."[40]

Credit reporting agencies such as Dun and Bradstreet expanded their international services in the early twentieth century. R. G. Dun & Company, as the firm was known before its merger with Bradstreet in 1933, began operating international offices as early as the 1860s. Throughout the nineteenth century, Dun's subscribers in the United States wrote frequently to request information about international firms, and Dun employees responded by querying international contacts and compiling information about overseas firms.[41] The firm's leaders expressed wariness about the costs and operational challenges of reporting on overseas firms.[42] Throughout the nineteenth century, Dun limited the services offered with subscriptions to domestic reports, and executives advised its staff to minimize reporting on foreign concerns. As one Dun executive advised the New Orleans office in 1897, "We always tell them in New York that it is very difficult to procure such information, and that such information when procured is more or less of a doubtful character."[43]

Demand for information on foreign firms grew in the early 1900s as US exports increased, and in response, R. G. Dun expanded its international coverage by hiring agents and enlarging its network of correspondents.[44] By 1916, R. G. Dun had agents working in eighty-three locations outside the United States.[45] The firm promised it could provide "detailed information on almost any company in the world within 48 hours."[46] Nonetheless, provision of international information constituted only a small piece of the firm's business through the

1930s. Like National City Bank's expansion strategy, R. G. Dun used foreign branches more for enhancing its reputation among US clients than for serving overseas markets: "Our interests outside of this country give us prestige here and have a broadening effect in many ways which are intangible."[47] Both National City and R. G. Dun sought prestige and domestic market advantages by positioning themselves as clearinghouses of international information.

The creation of the Federal Reserve System further strengthened efforts to scientize rating practices by emphasizing financial statements as a key tool in credit determinations. Shortly after the Federal Reserve Board was created, it issued lending guidelines that encouraged banks to evaluate borrowers' creditworthiness based on a review of their financial statements. Financial statements were a relatively new technology: they emerged in the 1880s and 1890s as a tool for summarizing a firm's assets and liabilities, but their usage was relatively uncommon until the economic upheavals of the 1890s. By the 1910s, creditors, such as banks and sellers, frequently requested financial statements from borrowers to assess their cash on hand, existing inventories of goods, and receipts due from customers, among other categories. However, accounting standards varied across industries and cities, and independent auditing was rare.[48] According to studies of the National Association of Credit Men, in 1897, the overwhelming majority—more than 80 percent—of credit reports contained no financial information whatsoever. Roughly twenty years later, in 1919, 40 to 60 percent of credit decisions were based on the study of financial information.[49] It was the creation of the Federal Reserve System, one credit study noted, that cemented the financial statement as the cornerstone of US credit evaluations.[50]

The Federal Reserve System helped standardize accounting and reporting practices so that financial statements could become more reliable tools in credit assessments. One challenge involved creating common guidelines across a range of different businesses. In 1916, the Federal Reserve Bank of St. Louis published three different formats of financial statements because it regarded the financial needs of farmers, merchants, and manufacturers as sufficiently distinct to warrant different types of paperwork.[51] The Federal Reserve Board also commissioned the creation of elaborate ratio calculations— "credit barometrics"—to guide credit practitioners in interpreting financial statements. The *Federal Reserve Bulletin* and other credit publications printed guidelines to help credit men interpret and evaluate financial statements in different industries. Calculating ratios could allow a credit man to determine whether a business followed general industry practices regarding the volume of sales as compared to receivables, for example.[52]

As an information technology, financial statements did not necessarily represent a superior, more reliable tool than other traditional, reputation-based ways to evaluate borrowers—particularly in international contexts. After all, financial statements relied on borrowers to self-report their financial standing, and there were no consistent guidelines about reporting practices or independent auditing. Credit men acknowledged that statements were vulnerable to misrepresentations. Dishonest borrowers could easily falsify financial statements. Even more dangerous, according to credit men, was "the deceived borrower—the one who is himself misinformed as to his condition," observed one text.[53]

Given the lack of consistency, relying on a financial statement meant taking a leap of faith in trusting a would-be borrower.[54] British businesses in the early 1910s tended not to collect financial statements because prevailing business norms rejected relying on unaudited personal statements. Relying on statements created "suspicion to the British trained business man," according to a British author, writing in the *Bulletin of the National Association of Credit Men*, because it created a double standard of trust.[55] If a would-be lender was doubtful about a firm's capacity to repay debts, why would that lender trust its financial reports? As a Liverpool firm wrote to a New York credit agency: "If you do not trust us sufficiently to accept our agreement to pay on a certain date, we cannot see how you are justified in taking our bare word as to our financial condition."[56] As such resistance indicates, the shifting landscape of credit information lacked consensus about what criteria or information standards were necessary and sufficient to vet would-be borrowers.

Credit Standards and the Federal Reserve

US credit norms were not changing in a vacuum: as US traders expanded their global reach in the early 1900s, they encountered alternative European and Latin American approaches to credit information. In both Britain and Germany, traders established credit cooperatives in the nineteenth century to pool information about problematic borrowers. These mutual aid societies focused on flagging risky debtors and creating blacklists rather than exchanging information and payment histories of more reliable businesses.[57] In the late eighteenth century, for example, a British credit society named itself the "Society of Guardians for the Protection of Trade against Swindlers and Sharpers" and sought to safeguard members against bad actors and unreliable borrowers.[58] By the late nineteenth century, British and German credit cooperatives increasingly exchanged information with each other, and they alerted members about borrowers who were slow or negligent in repayment. By contrast, US subscription services, like R. G. Dun and the Bradstreet agency, offered more comprehensive information about the reputation, financial standing, and history of a broad range of firms, rather than just providing warnings about delinquent ones.

Historians have offered several explanations for the different credit information ecologies in the United States as compared to Europe. Some accounts emphasize US exceptionalism as the "land of immigrants." In this account, the rapid emergence of new businesses and relative dearth of personal and familial connections created challenges for establishing trust.[59] Mobility, territorial expanse, and a constant influx of new people increased demand for systematized credit information. Private firms could generate profits by gathering and distributing reliable information because that information helped lenders minimize their losses. By contrast, countries with more stable populations, such as Germany and England, did not experience the same market pressures.[60]

Other explanations of the different credit landscapes in the United States and Europe have focused on their contrasting legal practices. Lenient bankruptcy regulations in the United States favored debtors, unlike the more stringent policies in Europe. As a result, lenders in the United States had stronger incentives to gather information prior to extending credit rather than relying on the court system to collect debts from delinquent borrowers.[61]

The different architectures of US and European credit systems also stemmed from different banking practices.[62] Many British banks maintained "character books," or account books, with notes on clients' creditworthiness; however, lending was not routinely correlated to specific criteria contained in the books, and there was little consistency in categories or traits recorded. Instead, lending practices typically depended on trust built from long-term relationships and institutional continuities.[63] Managers had extensive flexibility regarding the terms offered to borrowers.[64] Moreover, when character books did comment on personality or reputation, nineteenth-century British bankers typically assessed "character" in terms of property ownership rather than morality or social virtue. Reliability in repaying debts, instead of habits like churchgoing or treatment of neighbors, were characteristics that mattered to banks' recordkeeping.[65]

The information ecology of British banking encouraged financial institutions to keep credit information proprietary and fragmented, as opposed to adopting the centralized model that shaped US mercantile agencies. As a British banker observed in his 1922 comparison of the two nations' systems, "No centralized credit department exists in the English bank . . . [C]redit information is carried exclusively in the head of the local manager and the bank's records."[66] Banks' information collection depended largely on familial connections and long-term relationships in specific regions.[67] British colonial banks also relied on well-connected local boards of directors. The branches worked with a regular set of clients, many of whom were investors in the bank.[68] As banking historian Geoffrey Jones notes, British banks "made very effective use of socialization strategies to control their overseas branches."[69]

Another feature of British banking involved constraining credit assessments within specific financial limits established for each client. Rating books advised appropriate boundaries regarding a borrower's capacity to repay, unlike the ledger systems of many US mercantile agencies.[70] The International Banking Corporation, in its emulation of British banking, adopted a similar model in its executive committee meetings of linking borrowers to specific limits.[71] These limits reduced the lenders' exposure to risks and limited the need for additional information about overall financial capacity or character of a borrower.

Likewise, British banks' information-gathering practices supported their involvement in buying and selling sterling acceptances—or trading on the London money market, as the practice was known. The London market for bills incentivized different credit information practices, such as developing long-term relationships with discount houses or acquiring expertise in specific commodities. The US financial system, by contrast, had no comparable trade in acceptances prior to the Federal Reserve Act.[72] Instead, US banking was composed of fractured, decentralized banks that were barred from building branch networks. Lenders often looked outside the "unit banking system," as the model of decentralized banking was known, to source information from private firms such as R. G. Dun. By contrast, British banks managed information collection internally, through relationship networks with intermediaries such as discount houses.[73]

In both British and US cases, credit information was commodified, but the structure of the commodification differed.[74] British banks internalized information-gathering practices by maintaining ratings books and setting credit limits for clients.[75] These procedures alleviated some of the pressure to evaluate the ultimate trustworthiness of borrowers by relativizing the assessment: Was the borrower good for the sum in question? Britain's commodification of credit information was, in some ways, less visible than the emergence of mercantile agencies and centralized credit-information services in the United States; nonetheless, both systems used information about borrowers to generate profits.[76]

The Federal Reserve Act pushed US credit standards more into the foreign-trade mainstream by establishing centralized guidelines about the content and format of credit information necessary for discounting bankers' acceptances. Before a bank could discount an acceptance with a Federal Reserve Bank, the paper needed to meet specific standards of eligibility. The Federal Reserve Board established and frequently revised those standards in the early decades of its operation. Indeed, one of the early tasks for the board was to issue eligibility standards for the paper it would discount.[77] In April 1915, the Federal Reserve Board set a high bar: it required banks to obtain signed financial statements for borrowers before an acceptance could be discounted with Federal

Reserve Banks. Private banks had to certify to Fed officials in application letters for discounting bills that the banks kept financial statements on file.[78]
These guidelines were not specific to bankers' acceptances; they applied to
larger categories of commercial paper, and they represented a marked change
in orientation to credit information.

The Fed's purpose in requesting financial statements had little to do with
monitoring individual transactions or second-guessing banks' credit alloca-
tions. Instead, it was a procedural requirement that helped ensure that the
underlying transactions facilitated commercial activities rather than speculation. When bankers sought clarification about the information requirements,
the board explained that "satisfactory" information was a question of format
more than substance: "Ultimate responsibility in purchasing these acceptances
must rest with the banks."[79] The Federal Reserve wanted no role in evaluating
the quality of credit decisions; instead, its duty was to safeguard against risks
to the financial system by ensuring that banks took "adequate precaution" in
their credit practices.[80]

Even though the Federal Reserve did not meddle directly in credit evaluations,
the board's emphasis on financial statements did not sit well with banks, which
had long maintained their own lending and record-keeping practices. The Fed's
initial requirement of financial statements met a "great storm of protest" from
bankers, according to a finance expert at the time, and within a matter of
months, the board relaxed the guidelines.[81] The revision backtracked by no
longer *requiring* statements; instead, it merely *requested* that member banks
"maintain a file which shall contain original signed statements of the financial
condition of borrowers."[82] The board also published different templates of
credit information forms to encourage banks to standardize their records.[83]

Maintaining consistency around financial statements was a thorny enough
problem in domestic business; collecting such information on an international
scale raised a host of additional problems. In many parts of the world, requests
for financial reports ran counter to prevailing norms about the confidentiality
of a business's finances. Instead, lenders opted for relationship-based information gathering or other indirect ways to learn about borrowers.[84] Some businesses overseas interpreted demands for financial statements as an affront to
their reputations and indicative of mistrust. The Federal Reserve Board acknowledged this difficulty and accepted that, at times, banks would be unable
to obtain financial statements from international trading partners. In those
cases, the financial statement of the bank guaranteeing payment, rather than
the parties involved in the underlying trade, could satisfy the documentary
requirements.[85]

Even though its standards were piecemeal and fragmentary in nature, the
Federal Reserve Board's emphasis on financial statements pushed consolidation

and greater consistency in banks' lending practices. Its guidelines and recommendations nudged banks working domestically and overseas to place greater emphasis on financial statements and gather them where possible. With the hundreds of millions of dollars that Federal Reserve Banks could commit to acceptances, its standards around recordkeeping could and did move markets.

Promoting the Dollar

The changes in credit information formats constituted more than just window dressing of financial recordkeeping. They shaped the way in which US financial institutions expanded overseas and developed trade with US partners. Moreover, they occurred in the context of larger changes in the geopolitical and economic status of the United States after World War I. In the pivotal postwar period, the United States emerged as both the world's largest economy and largest creditor.[86] New York City became the financial epicenter for credit, as the United States lent more than $10 billion to foreigners between 1919 and 1930.[87] Within this time, US bankers working overseeas formalized the new information architecture that structured the nation's financial power.

Two major macroeconomic shifts accompanied the rise in the nation's status as an international financial power. First, the US dollar overtook British sterling as the leading reserve currency in the mid-1920s.[88] Second, US banks began massive lending campaigns to soveriegn governments in the 1920s. The US government played an ambivalent role in fueling these changes. While policymakers worked to expand US influence and secure opportunities for US business, government officials and lawmakers equivocated about the degree of responsibility and international obligation the state would undertake in global leadership.[89]

Amid top-level equivocation among policymakers, a new infrastructure of US foreign power was taking shape on the ground. US investment banks like JP Morgan and Dillon Read lent hundreds of millions to foreign governments. US households fueled the investing dynamics by using their savings to buy foreign bonds and finance European reconstruction.[90] The US Department of Commerce organized conferences, published pamphlets, and brokered introductions between US exporters and foreign buyers. The Federal Trade Commission gathered data and publicized foreign trade opportunities. Niche trade-oriented publications, such as the magazine *Export Advertiser*, emerged to take advantage of the unique moment of US ascendence in the postwar order.[91] Following the work of US bank branches helps us understand how these shifts in geopolitics took shape, as US overseas banks sold Liberty bonds, promoted dollar-denominated trade, and collected financial statements across their international branches. This new infrastructure of US financial power relied less on the US government's pursuit of overseas colonial expansion than it had in IBC's era and more on the growing prominence of US business norms and expanding the dollar.

The US government was an ambivalent partner to the work of US banks in the interwar financial order. Some government departments, bureaus, and officials actively facilitated banks' efforts. The State Department, for example, promoted the work of US foreign branches. State Department officials encouraged their consular offices to promote the use of bankers' acceptances in overseas markets. They sent letters, surveys, and promotional material to help US banks gain traction overseas. In 1916, the director of consular service wrote to all US consuls to explain how bankers' acceptances worked and to encourage their usage: "Consular officers [should] employ suitable means to bring these facts, informally and as convenient opportunity presents, to the attention of the local bankers and business men in their districts."[92] The following year, the department mailed surveys to all consulate-generals to gather data about the viability of opening new US bank branches. The surveys solicited information about local banking laws, practices for handling bills of exchange, "public opinion toward Americans," and the prospects for US bank branches, among other questions.[93] The State Department coordinated with the Commerce Department's Bureau of Foreign and Domestic Commerce to evaluate opportunities and notify banks about places in need of US financial services.[94] In 1924, the US consul in Karachi determined that the city held promise for a US bank, so the Commerce Department contacted IBC—then owned by National City Bank—about the opportunity. IBC politely declined, citing "insufficient business" between the US and Karachi.[95] Nonetheless, the exchange demonstrates the mutually enabling relationship between state and bank.

Meanwhile, some branches of the US government raised concerns about how the nation's trade promotion conveyed benefits to some actors over others. As they noted, the government's trade boosterism did not just open new opportunities for US businesses to operate internationally; it also changed firms' domestic competitiveness, depending on which businesses were positioned to benefit from working abroad.[96] Some government officials worried that National City Bank acquired unfair advantages over its US competitors in operating its foreign branch network. Federal Trade Commissioner Edward Hurley expressed concerns in the late 1910s that elite East Coast banks were increasingly dominating US trade finance, to the detriment of US competitors. Hurley noted that National City Bank possessed outsized advantages over western and southern banks, due to its international branch network. "Western manufacturers now realize that the one who is carrying a balance in the National City Bank had a decided advantage over the one who is not a customer of that bank," he noted to Treasury Secretary William McAdoo.[97]

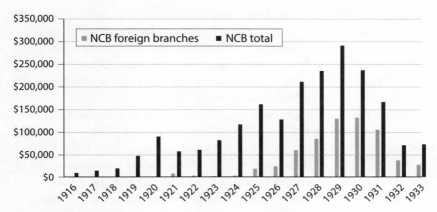

FIGURE 5.3. Acceptance Liability of NCB Foreign Branches versus Headquarters, 1916–1933. *Data source:* "Annual Report of the Comptroller of the Currency, Vol 1," edited by Office of the Comptroller of the Currency, Washington: Government Printing Office, 1914 and subsequent years to 1933.

National City Bank used this advantage in part to advance trade and the uptake of dollar-denominated acceptances. As bank president Frank Vanderlip had suggested, the bank's early internationalization strategy hinged less on generating profits from foreign branches and more on enabling new trade-promotion services to support the New York office. Financial analysis about the bank's acceptances underscores that branches played a subordinate role to headquarters. While branches generated some acceptances with clients overseas, that activity paled in comparison to New York's work. Prior to 1927, overseas branches generated less than one-fifth of the bank's total acceptance liability (see figure 5.3).[98] Meanwhile, the bank's total acceptance activity grew steadily in the 1920s.

As the US acceptance market grew from nonexistent to a multimillion-dollar market, these financial activities required paperwork, relationships, and institutional capacity. Financial statements needed recording. Coordination among banks needed processing. Each trade transaction needed points of touchdown for the acceptance to be realized in terms of the movement of goods and money. In this landscape, bankers like John Fuller served as the frontline workers who fused the metropolitan machinery for moving US dollars into on-the-ground opportunities, as conveyed through acquiring international information.

Bankers' focus on paper-bound recordkeeping loomed so large among National City Bank trainees that, even as Petrograd teetered on the brink of war in January 1918, Fuller's sights remained trained on his ledgers. Food shortages became commonplace. Foreigners left in droves. Bolshevik leaders met to discuss workers' rights. Throughout this, Fuller journaled nearly as much about the bank's disorganized books as he did about the shortages of jam and other quotidian challenges that accompanied the political upheaval.[99] If auditors were to arrive to inspect the branch, "our books would be in a terrible shape to turn over to the home office," he wrote.[100]

As this chapter has demonstrated, the emergence of a new architecture of trade finance pushed bankers to streamline information practices and create commensurability among businesses across the world.[101] Working in Manila in the early 1900s, IBC had accepted household furniture and warehouse receipts for gin as security to ensure that borrowers would repay debts. The machinery of the acceptance market necessitated new forms of systematizing and transmitting information about foreign businesses. The changes did not necessarily prevent bankers from accepting warehouse receipts for liquor as collateral, for example, but they did change the way borrowers, clients, and local businesses were encoded as paperwork and shared among far-flung locations. The new information formats depended on the connections, impressions, and understandings of the bankers who created them.

Understanding how the world of US trade finance was populated with new trading contacts and financial statements requires parsing the worldviews and biases of the worker bees like Fuller who built the information architecture. How did they see the new business communities they entered? Who was encoded in bankers' information systems, and who was excluded? The answers to these questions depended as much on the seer as the seen.

6

The Human Infrastructure
of Foreign Finance

IN 1916, a group of young, white men from elite US colleges enrolled in a program to prepare them for the work of international banking. The course was part of a six-week bootcamp to train staff for National City Bank's burgeoning network of overseas branches. The students' introduction to the world beyond New York was a class titled "Commercial Geography." Most of the curriculum focused on mundane banking skills like arithmetic, business English, and proper usage of pneumatic tubes, among other topics.[1] But Oscar Austin's course was different: his class taught the forty-two young men about business beyond the confines of a US bank. Austin had previously worked for the Treasury Department, until National City Bank lured him away to lead a new banking division dedicated to compiling and analyzing statistics.[2] Austin lectured the students about the global economy they would encounter in their new overseas lives.

What did the curriculum for commercial geography entail? On the first day, Austin gave the students a thumbnail sketch of the "History of World Commerce." It compressed four thousand years of economic activity into a one-hour lecture. Students learned that global commerce had more than doubled since the turn of the twentieth century and that banks were among the drivers of growth. Trade had helped the world become more integrated and productive. Modern transportation, communication technologies, and investing were among the main enablers of this progress. Subsequent lectures depicted a world ready for more—more commerce, more communication, more shipping, and more banking.

Religion, skin color, language barriers, and cultural practices received virtually no mention in Austin's commercial geography. Instead, he described the world as an expanse of economic potential with regions that varied by climate, terrain, and commodity production. Because of environmental differences, some regions produced agricultural goods while others specialized in manufacturing, for example. Environmental differences explained the variety in regional production. From this instruction, students learned a commodity-oriented approach to foreign banking. The people who inhabited the commodity zones warranted only passing mention.[3]

The curriculum points to a paradox in the early years of US overseas banking. The creation of information systems was a central component of overseas branches' work, but what constituted "information"? Who gathered it, and who benefited from systematizing it? One way to understand the predispositions and blind spots built into the emerging architecture of US finance is to understand the way its builders were taught to understand the world through categories such as creditworthiness and business respectability.

National City Bank created an education program in international banking because, at the time, the professional category of "international banker" barely existed in the United States. There was no ready-made cohort of US professionals to work in the new branches, so National City Bank designed a training program to prepare staff to become the front lines of US commercial expansion. Executives described the "College Training Program" as an immersive experience—a "régime which might make even West Point cadets turn pale," noted a *New York Times* article in 1915.[4]

As the outbreak of war consumed Europe, references to military service, patriotic duty, and masculinity abounded in banking literature. One article called upon "men of blood and iron . . . men sired by a bull-dog parent and steeled in the furnace heat" to join the program.[5] Another described the training as a "furnace in which the fire of patriotism, loyalty, co-operation and organization is brought to bear on the quartz of common tasks, to draw from it the pure gold of service."[6] What the comments lacked in rhetorical finesse, they compensated for with insistence on the rugged intensity of the training.

The training program coincided with a moment of transformation in US global power. Amid the upheaval of World War I, the United States shifted from a debtor nation to becoming effectively the world's financier of postwar reconstruction. In that time, National City Bank created a training program to produce a pipeline of young men to leave New York and serve as the foot soldiers for expanding US trade and access to the US dollar. The men set sail with a template for evaluating what a respectable borrower looked like and how an honorable business operated, as well as what to expect from local populations.

The training and early experiences of US bankers shed light on the biases and power dynamics that accompanied the growing prominence of the United States in the world. Their preconceptions stemmed in part from the bank's training program, which relied on an implied us-them binary. The program imprinted staff with a framework for understanding trust, respectability, and proper business etiquette. Further, the framework solidified and became more durable as the program strengthened solidarities among its imagined "us"—a cohort of young, privileged white men who commuted to the Manhattan bank from their Brooklyn clubhouse—in contrast to the "them," the populations they would encounter abroad.

At the time, US credit professionals sought to scientize ratings systems and develop systematic standards for evaluating borrowers. But these practices were less monolithic in practice than in principle, as the work of US bankers overseas demonstrates. For US bankers working abroad, evaluating the creditworthiness of would-be borrowers in new contexts depended heavily on long-standing practices of gentlemanly, relationship banking. The financialization of credit did not displace peer-to-peer knowledge, intuition, or deference to existing social hierarchies. Instead, the information practices that had for decades sustained relationship banking and European firms' multinational operations served to strengthen a new, New York–based financial architecture anchored by the Federal Reserve System, as the two ways of knowing were interconnected in US bankers' overseas work.

Scholars have emphasized the importance of racial differentiation in strengthening white elites' hold on capital and social power. Historians such as Destin Jenkins, Peter Hudson, and Susie Pak have demonstrated that notions of white supremacy, Anglo-Saxon superiority, and anti-Semitism shaped twentieth-century banking.[7] Recent work has also shown that Westerners working abroad often reconfigured their white supremacist and Orientalist beliefs as they navigated social hierarchies overseas.[8] National City Bank's training program offers a new entry point for understanding the mechanics of racialized capitalism by investigating a site where those beliefs were constructed: the training program that shaped bankers' understanding of "them" and fortified a sense of belonging to their imagined "us."[9]

Further, as graduates of the training program moved overseas, their New York–based worldviews informed their pursuit of profits but did not necessarily result in a rigid imposition of Manhattan social hierarchies. Instead, bankers applied their training as they accommodated and adapted to the new social orders they encountered. US bankers working overseas began to articulate new approaches to credit that married the social hierarchies and business customs in their adopted communities with US-friendly business logics that would appeal to domestic clients. Thus, the foundations of US financial power around the world were built on these racialized, gendered, and profit-maximizing practices.

Credit's Classroom: Creating an International Banker

National City Bank's College training program represented a novel turn in business education in the United States in terms of prestige and internationalist orientation. The program was the first formalized curriculum for training international bankers in the United States, and it emerged just as business schools and commercial training programs were becoming more popular on the East Coast. Private colleges for business instruction had existed throughout the nineteenth century, but the programs tended to train lower-paid clerical workers rather than executives or managers.[10] In the mid- to late-nineteenth century, advanced training requirements and education prerequisites elevated the status of fields such as engineering and medicine, due in part to the entry restrictions they imposed on the professions. Some business leaders looked to these fields as models for raising the status of business careers.[11]

Overhauling business education also aligned with the ambitions of Progressive Era reformers who sought to eradicate the outdated, inefficient, and vice-prone spoils system. Under that system, businesses were rewarded for cronyism rather than merit and honesty. Scientizing business training could, according to reformers, modernize US commerce by developing a standardized curriculum and guidelines for professional advancement. Such reforms promised to increase efficiency and reduce corruption, as Marion Fourcade and Rakesh Khurana have argued.[12] National City Bank brought elements of the broader reform agenda into its in-house training efforts. In the early 1900s, the bank introduced courses and lectures series. By the 1910s, training expanded to include classes in French, German, and Spanish, as well as penmanship, "business English," and mathematics.[13]

The opportunity to open foreign branches presented the bank with a new education problem: how to make an international banker. What were the skills and traits necessary for the future staff of its multinational branches? To answer these questions, bank executives organized a meeting of business faculty from several elite universities such as Harvard, Princeton, and Yale. Their discussions focused on the relative deficiency of the United States in foreign trade as compared to European powers like Britain and Germany, as well as how the nation could rectify that deficiency.[14] Following the discussions, executives formalized the bank's college training program to create a specialized cadre of young bankers for overseas work. The program required applicants to be male, unmarried, born in the United States, and enrolled in a participating college. Participating schools included much of the Ivy League, some state universities, and several private, East Coast colleges, and professors at participating institutions helped select and screen applicants.[15]

The program's selection criteria virtually guaranteed that participants would be white men with backgrounds that mirrored the biographies of existing bank leaders. Executives screened for candidates who had "good character": "Personality is the chief asset," explained bank president Frank Vanderlip in a 1916 interview about the training. "By this I don't mean a dominant spirit, but charm—the quality that makes people like a person and feel that he is frank, honest, and friendly."[16] In a letter to National City Bank Chairman

FIGURE 6.1. National City Bank's College Class. *Image source:* "The 1916 College Class [Photograph]," *No. 8* 11, no. 3 (September 1916): 113.

James Stillman, Vanderlip assured his boss that all students came from "good families."[17] Another executive told a 1919 meeting of bankers that it hired "clean-cut" trainees.[18]

The traits that executives emphasized—personable, coming from good families, and charming—have a reflexive, self-validating quality. Prioritizing these traits helped ensure that New York banking remained an insular social world in the early twentieth century. Its epicenter spanned several blocks of lower Manhattan and depended on connections to a set of elite social clubs and universities.[19] Bankers' views about what constituted "good families" were shaped by their experiences of privilege and exclusiveness. In class photographs, a homogenous group of young white men wore suits, ties, and stoic expressions—a picture that resembled the bank's leaders, minus twenty-five years of aging (see figure 6.1).[20]

The prestigious universities from which the bank recruited already mirrored the social hierarchies of New York finance. Harvard, Princeton, and Yale, for example, used admissions criteria such as language exams that blocked most students of color and those with underprivileged backgrounds from admittance. The colleges required exams in Latin and, in some cases, Greek— languages that were taught by only a few selective high schools.[21] High tuition costs created another barrier that ensured that the student bodies of Harvard, Princeton, and Yale reflected the "most privileged strata of society"—almost entirely white, Anglo-Saxon, Protestant graduates of expensive, private high schools.[22] Many elite universities imposed quotas to limit the number of Jewish students, and a number of prominent university presidents espoused strongly anti-immigrant views in the early 1900s.[23] A handful of Black students attended Harvard, and the university sought to increase representation of poor students in the 1910s. Nonetheless, at all three schools, white, Anglo-Saxon Protestant men dominated social life.[24]

Systems of privilege affected the distribution of job opportunities for graduates of those schools and other prestigious colleges. Business executives often filled job openings by consulting with professors to identify talented students. In 1917, less than 1 percent of corporate leaders were born to manual-laboring fathers; instead, most were US-born white men who often hired applicants with similar backgrounds.[25] As late as the 1930s, employers frequently requested that Harvard's career placement office provide photographs of applicants and information about the applicant's father because "family background" was thought to affect students' capacity.[26] In other words, the program's guidelines did not have to explicitly require whiteness or affluence because nearly all the criteria that guarded applicants' entry already ensured that Anglo-Saxon privilege was baked into the selection process.

The formal curriculum of National City Bank's college training program had little to say directly about cultural difference, racial categories, or gender. In fact, most of the courses in the bank's six-week training program focused on the skills of day-to-day banking such as arithmetic and business English (see figure 6.2).[27] However, white supremacist ideas and visions of Anglo-Saxon solidarity suffused the program, and students absorbed these lessons via formal and informal aspects of the curriculum. Numerous lessons and activities relied on implied distinctions between "us" and "them." The imagined category of "us" referred to white, Western Europeans, while "them" gestured toward dark-skinned people colonized by Europeans. Many of the program's cultural assumptions borrowed from European imperial hierarchies of a ruling class and subordinate, colonized populations.

The us-them binary is clearest in one of the few courses that focused on the world beyond New York banking: commercial geography. Professor Oscar Austin, formerly of the US Bureau of Statistics, organized his lectures around commodities. After the first lecture that distilled the history of global commerce into an hour, he led the students through a tour of the world's most important raw materials, with each lecture focusing on a commodity, such as forest products and hides.[28] Each presentation depicted a world ready for capitalist advancement—more technology, better infrastructure, and modernized resource extraction. Investment was the way to reach that potential, and banks were key to unlocking investments. Austin outlined a global economic order in which the "great manufacturing nations of the world" enlarged their markets "by increasing the purchasing power of the undeveloped areas of the world."[29]

FIGURE 6.2. Banking Lecture in National City Bank's Training Program.
Image source: "The Banking 'A' Lectures," *No. 8* 11, no. 3 (September 1916): 79.

Austin's conception of commerce rested on racialized ideas about how different climates created different capabilities and aptitudes in the populations that inhabited them.[30] "Tropical man is not a manufacturer," he noted. Instead, "temperate zone man" used the natural resources extracted by tropical man to develop manufactured goods.[31] Ideas about the inferiority of "tropical" people had helped sustain European imperialism for centuries, and it informed US colonial governance in the Philippines.[32] European and US scientists, doctors, and even insurance professionals had developed the concept of "tropicality" to characterize parts of the world they regarded as abundant, exotic, and destructive for "white health."[33]

Austin's work and the discipline of commercial geography adopted the widespread and racialized ideology of the "tropics" and applied it to commodity production and global commerce.[34] The approach became popular in US commercial education in the early twentieth century. In this framing, the rest of the world represented an "opportunity for economic exchange, profitability, and civilizational 'progress.'"[35] The logic imposed a duty on the United States to share its more advanced systems with the world and enlighten communities at lower stages of "civilizational progress."

Language training was one area that required more customization with regard to populations and cultural differences. Executives envisioned training overseas bankers in the languages of their future branches. The bank offered courses in Spanish, French, Portuguese, and Russian. Trainees attended two classes a week and participated in language tables at lunch.[36] Little information exists as to whether these courses taught students about culture, etiquette, or any content beyond grammar and vocabulary. One promotional article claimed that students learned about the "customs, habits and manners of foreign people."[37] However, educational records indicate that such lessons—if they existed—would have been piecemeal and offered outside the regular banking curriculum.

Further, language training did not determine where trainees would be assigned. College training program graduates were sent to China and Japan in 1916, but the bank offered no language training for either location. The omission suggests that executives believed language preparation was unnecessary for these positions, or they assumed that overseas staff could rely on local translators in China and Japan.[38] In addition, the bank often mismatched a trainee's language education with the foreign assignment. For example, a Portuguese-trained graduate was sent to Spanish-speaking Chile. A Spanish-language trainee was assigned to Hong Kong. And a French speaker went to Buenos Aires.[39] Trainees' assignments could be changed with little notice: one banker set sail for Manila only to learn that his ultimate destination would be Kolkata, known to the banker as Calcutta.[40] Of those with training in a geographically appropriate language, many found their preparation inadequate. A Spanish-language trainee sent to Buenos Aires noted that his lack of language expertise was a barrier. "I must learn Spanish. It is almost essential to the work that I am doing," but he confessed a lack of know-how.[41]

While the formal curriculum rarely focused on racial, cultural, or national differentiation as an explicit topic, trainees became attuned to social hierarchies through a range of extracurricular channels. Minstrel shows and enactments of racialized stereotypes helped create the system of bankers' white racial dominance in New York finance, as Peter Hudson has shown.[42] That framework shaped students' preparation for overseas work. National City Bank had commissioned minstrel shows to be performed at holiday parties and other official bank functions since the early 1900s.[43] The shows rendered differences in skin color as the source of comedy and other-ing.

Racialized differences were also on display during annual parties at President Frank Vanderlip's home. A 1914 article in the bank's internal magazine described entertainment ranging from a dog-and-monkey show to a German comedian with a false mustache. Performers included a "Mexican looking individual" who shot "ashes of a lighted cigar in [a] young woman's mouth . . .

Another attraction was a troupe of tumbling Arabs. They did every kind of thrilling stunt imaginable."[44] Minstrel shows and other theatrics highlighting cultural and racialized stereotypes were not unique to National City Bank.[45] They were one of the conduits for the bank to assert social hierarchies to trainees and strengthen connections within a constructed in-group.

Films offered another technology for training bank staff to see racialized and class-based differences. The program's curriculum included regular film screenings, which brought the insights of commercial geography to life.[46] Students watched a documentary about cotton production and another about transforming yarn into garments. The ostensible focus of the films lay on commodity production; however, students' accounts suggest that the footage projected a range of racial and cultural messages.[47] For example, a film about Peruvian mining taught one student to distinguish "sluggish, dirty and dense Indians of the hot climate" from "fine, cleanly cut Indians of the North," as the student wrote in his exam.[48] One film came directly from Vanderlip's personal library and showcased an "Iroquois Indian pageant." Vanderlip had purchased the movie "so his own children could see what they might do when 'playing Indians.'"[49]

The clubhouse for trainees also strengthened their sense of solidarity, which persisted after they were sent overseas. During their New York education, many members of the college training program lived in a house in Brooklyn Heights owned by the bank (see figure 6.3).[50] The dormitory-style housing created strong bonds among the trainees, and the ties continued after graduation as trainees dispersed to overseas posts. According to National City Bank's internal magazine, students who lived in the clubhouse "felt a decided need of keeping in close touch with one another while so widely separated."[51] Once overseas, the men created their own club, and they established their own magazine. The publication, *Aspersions*, printed "letters from the boys at the front and . . . the general news of the home office" to stay connected.[52]

The "boys at the front," as bankers called the cohort, often described their new contexts by using the United States as a reference point. One man wrote about his surprise at finding Petrograd to be a modern city with "tall smokestacks of some factory belching smoke exactly like a train-yard in New York."[53] Another commented on Japan's shoddy infrastructure, as compared to the United States': "Japan has a long distance to go before she reaches our plane in development."[54] The magazine also allowed the men to reminisce about New York instructors and share mundane concerns. In a 1917 article, one banker complained that his monthly stipend did not cover the purchases recommended on the bank's packing list, which included twenty-four collars, twelve handkerchiefs, and five pairs of shoes.[55] The reports strengthened a sense of unity and fraternity among "us"—the kind of men who bought twenty-four white collars before boarding a transatlantic steamer.

FIGURE 6.3. Room of National City Bank's Club House. *Image source:* "City Bank Club House," *No. 8* 11, no. 3 (September 1916): 117.

Bankers also learned to see finance as a world in which women played only a peripheral role and added little, if any, value. At a time when women's share of banking and clerical jobs was growing, the training program barred women from applying, and it eschewed traits associated with femininity. Members of the program were expected to be single, and the bank barred overseas staff from marrying until employees' salaries reached a threshold that executives deemed adequate for providing for a family.

The bank was not alone in regulating the marriage practices of its staff. Marriage bans were common among clerks' employment contracts during the time—so much so that newspaper columnists debated the "vexed question: should a man marry on less than a thousand a year?"[56] A 1904 headline in the *Brooklyn Daily Eagle* asked: "Shall Bank Clerks Marry?"[57] The answer for college training program enrollees was: decidedly not. A lecturer for National City Bank explained that, overseas, "it is essential that a man have no family responsibilities unless he is in a position to meet them suitably."[58] As the remark suggests, executives understood a man's "family responsibilities" as consisting primarily of the salary he earned. Living "suitably" meant earning enough money that a young banker could provide for dependents and model affluence within his community. Bank executives regarded overseas employees' social standing as a reflection on the bank, and they expected young staff to conform to New York social norms about men as husbands and providers.

Such marriage bans also carried a practical advantage for the bank: single staffers were easy to transfer. British multinational banks often imposed marriage restrictions on recent hires. The Hongkong and Shanghai Banking Corporation famously had a "ten-year rule," which held that a banker had to work for the bank for ten years before obtaining executives' permission to marry. British bankers reasoned that unmarried staff were more dedicated and mobile: "Marriages too early are detrimental to the service," observed one veteran of the Hongkong Bank.[59] For National City, the policy eased transfers of single staffers among its foreign branches. A bank executive advised trainees in 1918: "You will do well to keep yourselves foot-loose . . . [A young banker] is likely to be shifted frequently from branch to branch, and this with a family is a difficult and expensive matter."[60] Another executive claimed that the success rate of young bankers in new foreign posts was two and a half times greater for single men than married ones, though he offered no evidence to substantiate his calculations.[61] Flexibility and portability conflicted with executives' understandings of married life and of the bank's overseas needs.

Additionally, the "foreign field" represented a place of adventure for men, which complicated traditional gender roles for bankers' personal and professional lives. One executive believed that wives ought not accompany their banker husbands overseas because of the cheapness of domestic labor. The lack of housework would create marital problems, he reasoned: "In plain words, she hasn't enough dishes to wash! Idleness of hand and mind quickly leads to discontent and querulousness."[62] In their overseas posts, US bankers often employed numerous local workers in their homes. A US banker in Beijing, China, in the early 1900s employed a staff of eleven, including two rickshaw coolies and a "Japanese nursemaid."[63] A US manager in Buenos Aires in the 1920s kept five domestic staff, including a chauffeur and a cook.[64] The wives of senior bank executives played a crucial role in entertaining and hosting events, but the wives of junior staff would lack this focus. Better to spare young bankers the encumbrance overseas, bank executives reasoned.

The training program and its acculturation shaped the way the new cohort of US overseas bankers understood social hierarchies and community relations in foreign posts. The program animated subjective categories, such as respectability and "good character," with real-life examples and role models. The preparation calibrated bankers' expectations about their new social worlds and shaped their determinations about who they would later inscribe in credit files—and who they chose not to see. Just because the training program lacked an explicit course that focused on cultural differences, racial typologies, or lending practices for women does not mean that bankers were oblivious to racial difference, gender, or class. Instead, silences about gender and race in the formal training placed greater emphasis on extracurricular channels as a way for bankers to learn social norms and business conventions.

On the Ground: Bridging Cultures and Credit Systems

An interesting pivot happened as US bankers immersed themselves in their new overseas communities: many became advocates of alternative approaches to credit information and trust. Traders working overseas championed more flexible and fluid epistemologies of credit. Instead of adamant insistence on financial statements, they became champions of less formalized, paper-bound information, such as family networks and face-to-face experience. Family relationships represented a different foundation on which Latin American businesses operated, they noted.[65] It was not necessarily an inferior approach to assessing creditworthiness, they argued; instead, it simply relied on a different foundation of knowledge. As one report explained, "Social contact means more to the Latin American than it means to the busy, hustling merchant of the states."[66] As a National City Bank lecturer explained to a class of trainees in 1917, South American merchants did not need to exchange credit information because "native business men are well known to each other through social relations, and consequently a great deal is learned about them through personal contact."[67]

US bankers' descriptions of local credit systems often ignored more systematized information networks that predated their arrival. For example, in Buenos Aires, bankers and traders relied on a combination of credit information sources, including general stores that brokered the exchange of credit information among lenders and local merchants. In addition, local credit businesses offered subscription services for accessing credit information, much like US mercantile agencies such as Dun and Bradstreet.[68] Yet US bankers tended to overlook such systems in their reports back to New York. To those working overseas, the most striking consideration about foreign credit systems was the resistance to disclosing financial statements and the importance of family and social networks in verifying trust.

US bankers working overseas became spokespeople advocating greater flexibility and understanding from US businesses. They positioned themselves as cultural go-betweens, translating credit information from foreign contexts to US standards. Many of their accounts insisted on the equivalence of different credit information systems, rather than the superiority of one over the other. US bankers overseas warned exporters at home against looking down on the customs of other nations, even if the practices seemed, on the surface, primitive or counterintuitive. One article noted the tendency of Mexican merchants to "falsify their statements"; however, that tendency stemmed from the particulars of the local taxation system, not from dishonesty. "Comparatively speaking, there is more honesty among the native merchants of Mexico than any Latin-American country in the world," the author noted.[69] Another article echoed that "the Mexican is often a much keener trader than the American," despite different traditions of information disclosures.[70] Another report affirmed that the merchants of South America "have just as high a sense of business honor as the merchants of any other country."[71]

The different customs associated with credit information often aligned with bankers' characterizations of racial "types." National City published travelogue-style essays from bankers traveling or posted around the world in its new magazine, *The Americas*. Some essays were commodity-oriented accounts of exports and imports for a given region, such as the forestry and fishing industries in Norway, for example. Others referenced superficial differences among "types" of populations, such as orientalist accounts of primitive "native" populations in Guangzhou, China.[72] A frequent trope in bankers' accounts and business literature from the time characterized South American businessmen as volatile, impulsive, and easily angered: "Latins are so sensitive that one frequently offends," one noted.[73] Another cautioned that the "extreme sensitiveness of the Spanish merchant has not yet been fully overcome."[74] Such characterizations aligned with beliefs in the social sciences that different races were predisposed to particular traits and occupations.[75] These writings sought to translate foreign trade to US audiences by appealing to readers' understanding of both economic principles and racialized traits of foreign populations.

Some bankers argued that differences in business cultures should not give rise to celebrating US superiority, but instead to demonstrating flexibility, understanding, and humility. Authors urged US businesses to broaden their ways of operating and accommodate different international norms. They depicted parochialism, egotism, and aggressiveness as challenges that US businesses needed to overcome to engage more widely with overseas trading partners. In 1917, a National City Bank executive noted that collecting credit information in South America required diplomacy: one couldn't simply ask a merchant for a financial statement. Instead, one needed to "cultivate friendship and confidence, to approach the merchant with proper credentials."[76] The Guaranty Trust Company of New York encouraged US customers to develop better firsthand relationships with overseas partners to gain "personal knowledge and closer contact."[77]

Some trade experts went a step further by arguing that US businesses needed to show even greater accommodation to foreign social hierarchies. Executives should be mindful of the social status of the US agent tasked with representing a business overseas. US firms couldn't simply put *any* salesman on a ship to pitch wares to foreign merchants: they needed to send the "right type of man," noted the vice president of National City Bank in 1915—again invoking racially coded and class-oriented rhetoric.[78] Another National City banker reported that, to make headway in Argentina, US businesses needed to send "gentlemen" who had generous expense accounts and could stay at "first class hotels."[79] Similarly, one veteran of Latin American trade noted that overseas US sales- men needed to display the right markers of class and respectability: they needed to have "elegance of dress and courtliness of manner," and to seek ac- commodations at the right type of social clubs.[80] These characterizations echoed the criteria for the college training program in terms of mirroring and valorizing attributes of those already in power.

US banks overseas accommodated foreign social hierarchies in their staff- ing policies. Hiring local elites was one strategy by which US banks showed attunement to patterns of elitism and local class dynamics. National City Bank employed the daughter of Panama's president as a clerk in the Panama branch, and the Panama branch manager "prided himself on being [the] confidant and advisor" of the president and finance secretary of Panama.[81] The Bank of Boston opened a branch in Buenos Aires in 1919, and to have local legal representation, the bank retained the minister of the interior of Argentina himself.[82] At the minister's request, the bank also employed a teller rumored to be one of his henchmen.[83] In China, US bankers continued to rely on compradors to navi- gate local social hierarchies and business opportunities. IBC's branches in China retained this practice even as many of the branches were rebranded as National City Bank offices.[84]

Bank managers overseas were also expected to be social figures in the inter- national club scene in the various cities where branches operated. Elite clubs in China's treaty ports were cornerstones of expat social life in the early twen- tieth century, but simply being a US banker in a treaty port was not enough to guarantee acceptance into elite society. Overseas staff found they often had to earn their way into social acceptance. The Peking Club represented the pin- nacle of foreigners' social order in 1919 Beijing; so, a US banker noted, "it is necessary for us to belong as representatives."[85] Acceptance to local social clubs was not always guaranteed for US bankers. The Shanghai Club was a "very exclusive outfit," a US banker described to his parents in Texas. Its opu- lent building was larger than the "court house in Nacogdoches," with modern elevators, steam heat, and exquisite food.[86] Residents were eligible to apply for membership after six months in Shanghai, and the club's admissions standards were high but opaque: "If you are not known, or known too well, you are not elected," the US banker observed.[87]

Likewise, in South America, US bankers frequently commented on the need to organize their lives and networking around social clubs. Upon their initial arrival in South American posts, some US bankers were struck by the elitism and difficulty of gaining access to local social clubs.[88] Yet, opting out of club life was not an option if a foreign business wanted to succeed. As the US consul general in Brazil observed, National City Bank's Brazilian operations faltered in the bank's early attempts to court local businesses. One of the staff's missteps involved lunching at local restaurants—especially German restaurants—"instead of at the Club where most Englishmen and Americans, and some Brazilians congregate daily at lunchtime."[89] In Buenos Aires, US bankers sought to ingratiate themselves in preestablished social clubs, such as the Jockey Club, and to build US and Anglo-American club connections. One US banker noted that an implicit duty of a US bank manager in Buenos Aires was "to sacrifice himself" to the chamber of commerce and American Club.[90] The clubs held regular Friday luncheons, lectures, roundtables, and receptions for visiting dignitaries. They also represented a mainstay in bankers' dining routines. Kermit Roosevelt, son of President Theodore Roosevelt, became a staffer in National City Bank's Buenos Aires office, and meals at the American Club feature as prominently in his journal as do tennis matches with the Tornquists, a prominent Argentine business family.[91]

Bankers' acute awareness of social class and status gives context and depth to the information architecture they helped construct. Commercial experts depicted the Federal Reserve System and practices like "credit barometrics" as markers of the improved efficiency and modernization of US markets. And indeed, new graphs, financial metrics, and calculations became commonplace within the field of credit evaluations. On the surface, the changes seem to affirm a narrative of "modernization" in which an accretion of bureaucratic processes moved in lockstep with changes in US political economy to rationalize and streamline national markets.[92] But a closer look at the information architecture that underlay this evolution suggests a more nuanced story—namely, that its foundational logic depended on class differences, imagined racial solidarities, and preformulated conceptions about elitism and privilege.

Thus, at least two worldviews about credit information coexisted peacefully in the minds of US foreign bankers: in one, reputation and personal relationships provided the foundation for assessing risk. In the other, financial statements and hard facts were the cornerstones of the efficient operation of markets. These worldviews—or epistemologies of credit—might seem incompatible or even contradictory from a contemporary perspective. However, to foreign bankers and credit experts, they were merely different approaches to understanding an expanding geography of commercial opportunity. Person-to-person knowledge and quantitative data were not conflicting modalities; instead, the different approaches underscored the complexity of credit operations and justified the hiring of trained professionals in the field. No matter how sophisticated credit algorithms could be, only a trained credit expert could balance these assessments with a reading of a borrower's character.[93]

This dualism—a reliance on both personal and quantitative information—underscores the fact that foundational changes in the operation of the US economy were built on continuities with nineteenth-century business norms and European imperial practices. The new systems and processes enabled by the Federal Reserve System shifted the way credit was encoded, and it changed the way that information traveled from gatherer to decision-maker. In so doing, it did not vanquish long-standing practices of relationship banking so much as create new channels that helped them endure.

Deepening Roots: Human Intermediaries of Information

A great challenge for US businesses seeking to expand their international trade involved developing trust with new foreign partners—particularly for firms that did not operate overseas branch networks. Many of the customary channels for verifying creditworthiness in the United States, such as mercantile reports and references from peers, were unavailable for overseas customers. Businesses generally agreed that information from US foreign banks was one of the few safe sources of foreign credit information: "We consider the most reliable information received is that secured from American overseas banks or foreign branches of American banks," said one respondent to a survey commissioned by the Federal Reserve Board.[94] The survey found that financial statements were rarely available for foreign firms. Without this, what information was necessary and sufficient for a US business to conduct business with a new international partner? According to the *Bulletin*, an ideal dossier would include a customer's name, address, and standing, as well as information about its duration, business contacts, and estimated worth.[95]

The dearth of archival sources about banks' credit reports makes it difficult to assess the thoroughness of paper-based records. However, a sample credit report from National City Bank sheds a bit of light on these questions. The report provided a credit profile of a Buenos Aires–based importer, Casteran Hermanos & Co, the first South American firm to sell Caterpillar tractors.[96] Categories on its credit report included location, description of business, lines of goods handled, and "other lines they would be interested in." None of the categories necessitated quantitative financial information. In fact, the report on Casteran Hermanos contained no valuations whatsoever. In the "remarks" section, a National City Bank employee commented: "Business seems to be well managed. They are said to be very strong with several branches of Government, particularly with the City Fire Department."[97]

Could the observation that a business "seems to be well managed" have been enough to engender trust with a US trading partner? The cursory nature of the information and the lack of quantification suggests that a US business would need to cross-reference the reports with other sources. Credit evaluations, in other words, rarely involved comparing statistics to yield definitive calculations; instead, credit evaluations were, and always had been, human-powered assessments of a shifting matrix of considerations. On-the-ground staffers at US bank branches added dimension to thin, paper-based records by offering the potential—both real and imagined—of connection and dispute resolution with business partners.

US bankers overseas offered a diverse range of services to normalize and offset perceived risk associated with foreign trade. Dispute resolution was one such service. National City bankers offered to intervene on behalf of US clients to help settle local disagreements—a service that distinguished the bank from many of its competitors. The service was particularly useful for resolving shipping-related disputes, which plagued foreign trade. Broken boxes, dented cans, leaky barrels, and other damages to inventory provided grounds for importers to reject shipments upon arrival. As one US banker in Buenos Aires noted, an importer "can always refuse the goods on some technical grounds and threaten suit for non performance," due to the numerous technicalities in shipping documents.[98] The latitude to reject shipments posed even greater risks when commodity prices changed abruptly and the price of goods dropped or spiked in the time separating a trade agreement and the goods' arrival at their final destination. National City Bank's branches promised to help clients resolve such challenges (see figure 6.4). *The Americas* magazine published frequent articles about how US exporters could mitigate disputes, such as minding detailed instructions about packing protocols.[99]

Moreover, if conflicts escalated, US bankers could become the human face representing US businesses overseas. The bank advised clients that, in South America, the high price of retaining lawyers meant that exporters should waive protest for items worth less than a thousand dollars.[100] In Buenos Aires, the bank boasted about its role mediating a conflict between local importers and US businesses. The Argentine Industrial Union filed an objection with the US consul-general about the shoddy practices of US exporters in 1916. Among the grievances, the union flagged that a shipment of stockings contained twelve mismatched shades of black, and that delays in an order of drills had cost the importer thousands of dollars.[101]

National City Bank intervened to negotiate remedies and defend well-intentioned US companies. According to the US consul-general in Buenos

FIGURE 6.4. Canned Meat Shipped to Chile and Dented due to Bad Packaging. *Image source:* "Why Exports to South America's West Coast Must Be Well Packed," *The Americas* 6, no. 8 (May 1920): 24.

Aires, the bank advocated on behalf of "the large class of honest and careful merchants and shippers, whose reputation is unfairly affected by the ill-deeds of other members of the commercial brotherhood."[102] In its trade journal, *The Americas,* National City scolded US businesses for an "unpardonable aggregate of slip-shod export work."[103] The bank's role in smoothing relations between US traders and their overseas partners offered assurance that the bank's paper files on potential buyers were connected to real people, known by and accessible to US bankers.

The bank's trade support overseas was so extensive that overseas branches acted almost like welcoming committees for traveling US businessmen to ease their entry to foreign ports. Bank branch staff would broker introductions with important local businesses.[104] The executives in the bank's Brazil branches even proposed that US bankers could meet traveling businessmen on board their steamers. By sailing in launch boats to greet arriving ships from New York, bankers could maximize "the period of about one hour, from the time the steamer anchors in the outside harbor to the moment when it comes alongside the quay" to orient newcomers from the United States. "Great service can also be rendered to travelers by the Bank's representative in helping travelers to take their baggage out of the Customs House," the memo proposed.[105] Such services helped routinize and render mundane the risks and unknowns associated with overseas trade. Having a US banker on the ground made the great geographic distances involved in such trade seem cozier, more ordinary, and knowable.

As Oscar Austin's students became enmeshed in new communities, their roles as mediators, go-betweens, and information-gatherers thickened. Their New York social and racial hierarchies had to be adjusted and reconfigured to understand new contexts. While the trainees fed the accumulation of foreign credit information, they also championed a broader range of approaches to credit information and called on US businesses to become more flexible and less parochial. The systems they built provided a bridge between the increasingly bureaucratized and scientized modes of US business with the varieties of capitalism that bankers encountered overseas. Their adaptations, network-building, and interpretations on the ground deepened and broadened the staying power for US business.

While the shape of bankers' activities—from recommending barbers to collecting financial statements—might not have carried the overt trappings of imperial expansion, their actions were nonetheless deeply entangled with expanding the reach of the US dollar and increasing US power overseas. US bankers offered translation services that made foreign businesses knowable, legible, and commensurable from the convenience of a New York records room. The standardization of credit information knitted the system together, but, as the next chapter considers, uniformity on paper masked regional differences and the underlying precariousness of the credit system itself.

7

Getting Local

THE QUESTION of place mattered greatly to the aspiring bankers enrolled in National City Bank's foreign training program, but selecting the place where they would eventually work was a decision over which they had little control. Executives doled out their overseas assignments like lottery tickets: Hong Kong, Panama, London, Valparaiso. "Lucky" trainees were sent to Rio de Janeiro, while others were sent to less prized destinations.[1] John Fuller, the US banker who waited for Bolshevik soldiers on the eve of the Russian Revolution, learned about his Petrograd assignment two weeks into his six-week banking education.[2] Another student learned that his assignment had changed—from the Philippines to India—while sailing to his original posting.[3] According to their instructors, a world of adventure lay in wait no matter where they were posted: "We must pave the way for the United States exporter," a lecturer told the students.[4]

The trainees set sail ready to create foreign markets, but once in place, some were surprised to discover that markets already existed. A banker sent to Buenos Aires observed to colleagues in New York that European and Argentine banks were already operating in his city and that these banks conducted sophisticated work. "Most of us have been surprised at the size of many of the banks here in the Argentine," observed Ralph Kellogg. "[M]any of them have branches all over the Argentine that have been established for years."[5] The fact that a commercial world predated the arrival of US financiers came as news to the young trainees, who had expected to find a blank slate of economic opportunity, ready to absorb US commerce. Yet the longer they operated abroad, the more their views diverged from the templates that New York had imprinted on them. Each place required local customization, adaptation, and improvisation before bankers could lay the foundation to expand US business and to chart the circuitry by which the US dollar would move.

As US overseas bankers adjusted to their contexts, new realities of postwar commerce changed the landscape on which National City Bank operated. One vector of change was the new geopolitical status of the United States: the nation had emerged from the war as a leader in the postwar order. In Europe, this power took shape in the form of providing loans and organizing reconstruction efforts. In Latin America and the Caribbean, US economic power manifested in terms of lending, imperial control, and commercial influence. Between 1915 and 1916 alone, US exports to the Americas grew by more than 150 percent.[6]

National City Bank organized its international expansion to capitalize on the ascendance of the United States geopolitically. Ninety percent of the foreign branches that the bank opened by the end of World War I were in the Caribbean or South America. The bank opened sixteen branches and subbranches in South America and twenty-six in the Caribbean.[7] In addition, the bank had taken a controlling interest in IBC's twenty-three foreign branches, most of which were located throughout Asia.[8] The postwar boom-and-bust economic cycle shaped how National City organized its international operations and how the foundation of US financial power took shape overseas.

This chapter pushes beyond the first wave of banks' internationalization to examine how US branches became a routinized part of US global power. By hopscotching to different locations, it covers a wide geography in which local conditions varied dramatically. Rather than focus on the nuanced conditions of any single branch or community, its goal is to survey the broader landscape of US global influence.[9] By considering practices of adaptation as well as resistance in China, Europe, South America, and the Caribbean, for example, it identifies common threads in how bankers shaped their work based on the demands of different locations.

Moreover, it tracks how the overarching bank—National City Bank as it incorporated IBC branches into a centralized management structure—used a lava lamp of legal formulations to maximize profit potential and overcome legal challenges. These combined strategies allowed US bank branches to build a sufficiently enduring foundation that they could weather the Great Depression and nations' inward turns in the 1930s. What was left was a malleable network that could ground and sustain US financial influence through the early twentieth century.

Tectonic Changes in US Foreign Banking: Overextension and Reorganization

World War I caused US exports to surge and commodity prices to increase, but a sharp recession in the early 1920s whiplashed global economies. The contraction changed US banks' approach to internationalization and reconfigured the foundation for US global power during the interwar period. Amid the wartime boom, US foreign branches had proliferated. At the 1920 peak, US banks operated 181 branches and affiliates around the world.[10] "American manufacturers got writers' cramp taking down orders, and the foreign departments of all the banks were working overtime," recalled a veteran of US foreign banking of the early years.[11] But by 1921, demand had collapsed "like a punctured balloon."[12] Amid the volatility, bank executives adjusted their internationalization strategies. Their new approaches focused less on serving the needs of US exporters—a goal that defined the bank's original strategy—and more on responding to the economic opportunities of communities where National City inserted itself.

The proximate cause for overhauling the bank's international operations involved a series of bad loans in the early 1920s—especially losses linked to Caribbean sugar exports. National City Bank expanded feverishly in the late 1910s, and the prices of many commodities soared during the war. In less than two years, the bank opened twenty-three new offices in Cuba alone, and its operations became heavily invested in sugar, Cuba's major export. At first, the expansion seemed like a windfall: sugar prices increased more than fourfold during the war and its immediate aftermath.[13] The boom became known in Cuba as the "Dance of Millions" for the prosperity that accompanied the spike. National City Bank became a major lender to sugar producers, and its involvement helped reshape Cuba's export economy in the years that followed the late 1920 collapse.[14] By the end of 1921, National City Bank had acquired vast sugar estates and mills due to defaults. As sugar prices fell by more than 80 percent in late 1920, National City Bank held more than $60 million in bad loans.[15] The bank's total sugar exposure amounted to control of roughly one-fifth of Cuba's sugar production, according to one account.[16]

The International Banking Corporation also faced heavy losses associated with sugar loans amid the postwar downturn. At the time, National City Bank had acquired IBC, but its overhaul of IBC practices and the bulk of its rebranding of branches did not take place until the late 1920s and early 1930s. In the interim, National City changed IBC's board, but many branches continued to operate with existing staff and semiautonomous management practices.[17] In 1917, IBC purchased a bank in Santo Domingo, the Michelena Bank, which served as a depository for the US government's collection of Dominican customs revenue.[18] The arrangement stemmed from a long history of US imperial dominance in the Dominican Republic whereby the US government seized control of key functions of the Dominican state as part of debt repayment agreements.[19] IBC purchased Michelena Bank, which was a financial intermediary to US domination, and, according to banking veteran Joseph Durrell, it overpaid for rotten assets. After IBC took over, the Dominican bank's problems worsened still, as IBC appointed a string of inept managers.[20] The bank had taken risky loans to profit from booming sugar prices in the late 1910s. As the price of sugar fell, borrowers defaulted, and, ultimately, IBC wrote off nearly $6 million in losses.

Accounting for Caribbean sugar losses in the early 1920s served as an object lesson in the insight that assets bankers deemed as "security" for a loan were only as secure as the economic context in which it was valued. In one case, IBC held the mortgage on a Dominican sugar mill as security for a $250,000 loan.[21] The borrower had valued the property at $313,000—more than enough to cover the bank in case of default. Subsequently, an auditor found the estimate to be a "gross over valuation, the property in question being worth approximately $100,000."[22] Another borrower, a dealer in men's furnishings, had provided security that could not even cover the costs of liquidating the business.[23] IBC's Dominican loan portfolio was riddled with such overvalued accounts. As borrowers defaulted on their loans, the bank was left with little in the way of assets to offset the defaults.

IBC and National City Bank were not the only US banks to experience overseas losses in the early 1920s. The Mercantile Bank of the Americas, another upstart that expanded internationally in the late 1910s and early 1920s, also found itself overextended with the collapse of Caribbean exports. The Mercantile Bank was a short-lived experiment in US multinational banking.[24] The bank represented a consortium of powerful banking interests, including JP Morgan and Brown Brothers and Company.[25] By 1918, the Mercantile Bank had established eight affiliates in Latin America, as well as several European branches, but the bank struggled both to turn profits and establish its reputation for legitimacy.[26] Many of its branches and affiliates in Latin America were linked to unpopular authoritarian governments supported by the United States.[27] Even officials in the US State Department worried about the bank's public relations problems, as the bank often "aroused the dislike of local commercial interests."[28]

The Mercantile Bank's missteps showcase the risks of US banks' quick international expansion and inexperience. The bank lost heavily when the Cuban sugar market collapsed in the early 1920s, and it folded after less than five years of overseas branch operations.[29] Following the 1920 crash of sugar prices, JP Morgan announced a $55 million infusion of new capital for the bank in 1921, but not even assurance from Morgan could overcome the Mercantile Bank's problems.[30] A few years later, executives sold off different Mercantile Bank branches to banks such as National City Bank and the Royal Bank of Canada.[31] Of its $27 million assets, only $5 million was collectable.[32]

National City Bank ultimately avoided the losses that brought down the Mercantile Bank; however, the early 1920s contraction prompted executives to change the bank's approach to foreign branching. The timing coincided with a larger overhaul of the bank leadership in the late 1910s, following the death of longtime chairman James Stillman and the ousting of President Frank Vanderlip. Vanderlip had driven much of the bank's early internationalization, but his enthusiasm for international expansion left him vulnerable to critique when the bank fumbled overseas. National City suffered heavy losses after its Russian branches were nationalized during the revolution, and Vanderlip resigned amid the infighting that followed.[33] The new president, Charles Mitchell, instituted new accounting procedures and changed the reporting structure of overseas branches. The restructuring moved operational control away from the bank's powerful board of directors and into the hands of salaried managers. The bank also changed how it compensated managers: the new policies linked managers' pay to the performance of branches. The restructuring incentivized managers to focus more attention on improving the quality of loans and safeguarding the bank against losses.[34]

Prior to the restructuring, New York executives had managed foreign branches through a single committee—the Bank Branch Committee.[35] The committee distributed information to branches, and it hired and assigned overseas staff, much like arranging Tetris pieces in a video gaming screen. The committee, which guided the first wave of foreign branching, transferred Argentina-based bankers to Russia or Italy.[36] Staff in Brazil were relocated to Europe.[37] The haphazard distribution of assignments suggested executives believed that, to work abroad, bankers needed only the generalized skills of international banking and that the "foreign field" required no place-specific training.[38]

However, after the bank's heavy losses in the early 1920s, executives reconfigured oversight of its overseas branches and restructured the operation of the Bank Branch Committee. The new organization defined geographic zones, such as the "Far East" and "the Caribbean District." All regional divisions reported to a single Overseas Division. The overhaul was prompted by executives' alarm about "the numerous foreign loans that were going sour, particularly in Cuba," recalled banker Joseph Durrell.[39] The new structure resembled the organization of international sections of the US Department of Commerce, which also created geographic departments for its Bureau of Foreign and Domestic Commerce (BFDC) in the early 1920s. BFDC divisions oversaw work in the Far East, Near East, and Western Europe, for example.[40]

The geographic structure represented one approach to organizing foreign operations, but it was not the only format for foreign branch oversight. The Guaranty Trust opted for a different strategy: it managed overseas divisions according to zones of imperial power. In 1920, Guaranty Trust created research sections for the British Empire, as well as divisions for "non-Britain Europe," Asia, and Latin America.[41] The different logics that banks used to organize their international expansion—imperial versus geographic—reflected the commodity-specific or global aspirations of each institution as well as their past connections.

For National City Bank, restructuring came with centralized, streamlined oversight processes for foreign lending. Loan authorizations were routed through a single, New York–based "Committee for Foreign Loans," which supervised credit and lending overseas.[42] Prior to the centralization, branches often quibbled with headquarters about loan limits and protocols for information collection.[43] New York officials frequently complained about branches' inconsistent reporting and lending practices. One New York executive found that financial statements submitted by a Brazilian branch were in fact mismatched pages of account books and ledgers. One form, submitted under the guise of a financial statement, showed disparate entries for assets, liabilities, and "unintelligible" categories, "many of which mean nothing to us."[44]

New York executives reorganized the work of branches such that the foreign information provided by branches would be intelligible and also commensurable with other branches and with the standards and sensibilities of US commerce. In 1933, the bank published a handbook that codified new protocols for loans and expectations of bank managers. The guide, which was particularly directed at Cuban branches, required managers to vet the security that clients offered for loans. In response to losses such as those in Santo Domingo, the new protocols required branch managers to inspect firsthand any property used to secure a loan and determine personally that the "condition is satisfactory and that it amply covers the loan with an adequate margin."[45]

The policies departed from prior practices at the branches and from the general tone of relationship banking that had dominated the bank's expansion in the early twentieth century. In the new regime of transaction-oriented international branching, the bank's protocols required staff to become more routinized in their interactions with local communities—following real estate trends, inspecting properties, and soliciting financial statements. Branch managers had to complete standardized questionnaires—in the case of National City branches, it was "Form F.565"—to comply with requirements from the New York review committee. Forms were color-coded based on lending thresholds, and once sent to headquarters, they were presumably filed in the bank's records room.[46] The new systems created a bureaucratic infrastructure that pushed control to New York City, where executives could systematize the work of disparate branches.

The changes in commercial lending practices took place alongside a reconfiguration of foreign lending practices of US banks in the 1920s. Increasingly, large US private banks provided massive loans to governments around the world to finance postwar reconstruction and new infrastructure building.

Whereas the United States began World War I with nearly $4 billion in debt, by the 1920s, the nation had cemented its status as a global creditor, lending more than $10 billion internationally from 1919 to 1930.[47] JP Morgan played an especially prominent role in lending to European governments for postwar reconstruction in Europe. Morgan partners and allies helped devise the 1924 Dawes Plan to offer a $200 million loan to cover German debts, with $110 million of the loan floated in New York.[48]

Lending by US banks was deeply entangled with the US federal government, though administrators and politicians expressed ambivalence about what role—if any—the federal government should have in private-bank lending to foreign governments. On the one hand, some US policymakers saw an essential role for the nation's banks to play in financing European reconstruction and sought to encourage the leadership of the US private sector. On the other hand, many officials were wary of committing formalized state support to private banks' foreign lending.[49] The ambivalence created space for Morgan partners and other US business leaders—self-fashioned "financial diplomats"—to guide the movement of US dollars overseas.[50]

Throughout the 1920s, US government officials regularly coordinated with private bankers to provide "stabilization loans" to governments in need of funds for reconstruction and development. The approach contributed to financial problems and popular resentment throughout Latin America, as denouncements of the US "dollar dependency" approach became a rallying cry for groups to denounce US imperial influence.[51]

Even though the policies consistently failed to yield the intended political and economic effects overseas, they led to a broader formula of collaboration and exchange between the US government and private US banks. For example, in 1922, the US State Department issued a policy whereby private banks needed to submit foreign loans for government review. The policy did not mandate a formal vetting process; nonetheless, the State Department's review of applications, which involved collaboration with the departments of treasury and commerce, implied that the federal government authorized and supported private banks' foreign lending.[52]

Even as US officials sought to avoid being seen as officially endorsing or guaranteeing the loans, the government's policy required both direct and indirect partnerships with private banks.[53] Within four years of issuing the policy, $3 billion in foreign securities were issued in the United States.[54] The pace of lending intensified in the second half of the 1920s as a broader range of US banks entered sovereign lending and international infrastructure financing.[55]

In many respects, US banks' lending to sovereign governments operated as a parallel workstream, rather than an intersecting one, with the work of brick-and-mortar overseas branches. Large investment banks, such as JP Morgan and Kuhn, Loeb & Company, often conducted high-level diplomacy in metropolitan centers like Paris, London, and New York. The negotiations produced underwriting agreements and divvied banks' responsibilities for selling securities in different markets. JP Morgan partners such as Tom Lamont and Dwight Morrow participated in overseas conferences, in part as representatives of US interests but also to advance their own economic agendas.[56]

Meanwhile, the commercial operations of brick-and-mortar foreign branches relied on relationships with local clientele and support for merchants' importing and exporting activities. Even when the geography of bankers' activities aligned—such as with sovereign lending in Brazil alongside the operation of US bank branches in Rio and beyond—the large-scale model of underwriting did not necessarily intersect in operational terms. Bankers operating on the ground rarely played a formalized role in the high-level negotiations that shaped sovereign lending. And just because a US bank lent to a foreign government did not mean that a branch office would follow. Nonetheless, as the 1920s progressed these banking trajectories—large-scale sovereign lending and commercial banking—intermingled and blurred in the day-to-day work of foreign branches. Together, the two workstreams created a foundation for increasing the US dollar's access and utility in global markets, as well as creating new entry points and openings for US businesses.

Retail-ification and Localization

Initially, executives of National City Bank had assumed that the greatest benefit of overseas branches would be the services they enabled for US-based clients. National City Bank prized foreign branches for their collection of credit information, promotion of acceptances, and assistance for traveling US businesspeople. However, in the upheaval of the 1920s, branch banks expanded into other activities—from soliciting local deposits to selling securities. These services gradually overshadowed and eventually replaced the emphasis on foreign information collection as the north star of branch banks' activities. Particularly as other information providers—from the Commerce Department to the National Association for Credit Men—expanded their collection of foreign credit information, bank branches shouldered less responsibility for collecting credit dossiers, and they began discovering the profit potential of capitalizing on local markets.[57]

For the most part, these services constituted a different type of financial interaction than the sovereign lending activities that preoccupied some US banks in the 1920s.[58] Foreign branches were by no means a prerequisite to sovereign lending. Banks such as JP Morgan and Dillon Read conducted extensive international lending with no formal international branch network. Even for National City Bank, which issued some foreign loans in locations where it operated branches, the involvement of branch staff in lending operations was more happenstance than formalized or premeditated. As one bank executive noted, outsiders often assumed that a major responsibility of "American banks overseas is to take an active part in negotiating bond issues for foreign governments." In practice, however, overseas branches did not have a structured role in sovereign lending. "Branch banks abroad were primarily established to facilitate commercial business based on the export and import of raw materials and manufactured goods," the executive noted.[59]

Nonetheless, National City bankers working overseas could and did play an informal role in facilitating shuttle diplomacy for large-scale lending. Boies Hart, a National City banker working in Brazil, described late-night message relays between his New York bosses and the residences of Brazilian state governors. In one case, a negotiation stretched late into the night, after an 11 p.m. banquet, and "involved rather a delicate matter of future policy."[60] He was on the ground relaying messages from New York and developing workarounds to resistance on each side. Hart also organized social events that provided a cover for conducting financial negotiations, such as a performance by a French opera singer, beloved by the Brazilian president's secretary. The singer's private performance provided an excuse to conduct talks between US bankers and the president's staff.[61] These functions were not codified parts of bank operations, nor were they prerequisites to the expansion of US banks' foreign lending. Nonetheless, the connections and personal networks that branch banks enabled helped deepen financial ties and interdependent lending relationships between US bankers and foreign borrowers during the interwar period.

As US dollars financed an increasing number of overseas projects, US foreign bankers stood ready to find entrepreneurial routes to take advantage of the nation's growing prominence. For many, entrepreneurship meant resigning from their bank posts to open new businesses (see figure 7.1[62]). Of the first class of bank trainees that National City Bank shipped overseas, more than a dozen went on to play a foundational role in structuring and marketing Latin American bonds to the US public. In the first cohort of eight National City Bank trainees to sail to Buenos Aires, Franklin Baker and Ralph Kellogg were among the pioneering group of trainees to become the first US staffers in the bank's new South American branches.[63] A few years later, Baker and Kellogg partnered to create Baker, Kellogg & Company, an investment bank that helped finance hundreds of millions of dollars in loans in South America and Europe in the 1920s, from construction projects in Colombia to provincial loans in Austria.[64] Other graduates of the program went on to work in acceptance houses that supported US foreign trade. Still others went into government service to promote foreign lending, in addition to launching their

① Stephen Danforth
- Led US Chamber of Commerce in Rio in 1930s
- Joined multiple US–Brazil trade delegations to promote bilateral trade
- Served as manager of large appliance importer in Rio

② Franklin H. Baker
- Cofounded bond brokerage Baker, Kellogg & Co with NCB peer Ralph Kellogg (#8)
- Brokered hundreds of millions of bond deals in Latin America
- Floated $30 m in bonds to Colombia between 1926 and 1928 alone

③ Douglas F. Allen
- Became manager of National City Bank's Buenos Aires branch
- Represented bank on US Chamber of Commerce in Argentina

④ E. L. Sylvester
- Joined board of Foreign Credit Corporation in 1919
- Promoted acceptance market

⑤ John J. Lynch
- Subsequent work unknown

⑥ George E. Devendorf
- Became investment leader for American Founders Company
- Firm invested in and promoted foreign bonds to US public
- Served on board of Cuba Company and other foreign utilities firms

⑦ Richard O'Toole
- Became Latin American representative for Bureau of Foreign and Domestic Commerce
- Later led Division of Brazilian Affairs, US State Department

⑧ Ralph DeWitt Kellogg
- Cofounded bond brokerage house Baker, Kellogg with NCB peer Franklin Baker (#2)
- Deemed a "specialist on South American financing" by *New York Times*

⑨ Kenneth Apollonio
- Harvard graduate and son of prominent Boston banker
- Founded export-import firm in Buenos Aires in 1920s
- Married heiress to Argentine ranch and remained in Buenos Aires

FIGURE 7.1. The "First South American Contingent" and Their Career Pivots. *Image source: "College Men in Foreign Service," No. 8 11, no. 3 (September 1916):* 109. For data sources, see note 62.

own trade-related businesses.[65] The biographies of the early cohorts of US international bankers demonstrate how branches served as a foundational piece of the international infrastructure of US financial power.

As individual bankers helped expand business connections overseas, domestic US banking in the 1920s underwent dramatic changes in marketing and retailing, which reverberated across National City's overseas branches. In the nineteenth century, private banking had traditionally remained the province of affluent investors and traders, rather than middle- and lower-class workers. By the 1920s, new marketing techniques and investing trends increased the uptake of retail banking. Under the retailing model, bankers catered to the needs of small-scale savers and borrowers and actively solicited new business. Many of the changes stemmed from wartime economic upheavals and advertising campaigns to sell US government debt to small savers. Liberty Bond drives to finance the nation's war effort prompted many US savers to exchange their cash for paper-based financial abstractions for the first time. In 1899, less than 1 percent of the population owned stock or bonds. By the end of World War I, approximately one-third of the population had purchased a federal bond.[66] Consistent with finance's embrace of retail savers and marketing trends, the New York Stock Exchange reoriented itself to focus on small-scale investors rather than just an elite slice of financiers.[67]

One of the architects of this transformation was none other than Frank Vanderlip, onetime president of National City Bank and a driving force of the bank's early internationalization. Vanderlip pioneered new techniques in mass marketing securities while working with the Treasury Department in 1917.[68] Vanderlip helped create the war savings program, which targeted low-income savers as investors in Liberty Loan campaigns to support the nation's wartime spending. The programs that Vanderlip helped design allowed people to buy stamps in twenty-five-cent increments—rather than having to purchase an entire fifty-dollar Liberty Loan—as an entry point to bond buying.[69] The campaign aimed to transform the US public into habitual savers and investors and to cast bond-buying as a basic expression of patriotism.[70] Vanderlip had resigned from National City before the bank launched the bulk of its mass-retailing campaigns overseas. However, his approach to mainstreaming finance became part of the institution's culture and endured long after his departure.

Within the United States, savings drives and thrift campaigns acquired nationalistic overtones to "Americanize" immigrant communities in the 1910s and 1920s. During the period, commentators and politicians expressed concern about rising Bolshevism and the social "menace" posed by communism, socialism, and anarchism within US borders. Critics focused on immigrants as propagators of destabilizing ideologies. Finance, according to some US bankers, offered a potential solution to stabilize restive populations. In late

1919, the American Bankers' Association established a committee on "Americanization" in response to the threats of social unrest.[71] "By whatever they are known—Socialists, Anarchists, Industrial Workers of the World, Bolshevists— all are animated by a common purpose to destroy existing methods and standards in politics, economics, and morals," noted a Guaranty Trust executive in 1919.[72] Bankers worried that immigrants' remittances to their countries of origin constituted a drain on US finances and impeded the development of patriotic connections in their communities. Bankers could staunch this "drain upon the nation's capital" by encouraging immigrants to open bank accounts in the United States, according to the American Bankers Association. Banks could refocus foreign-born workers on financial goals, thereby making them invested, literally and figuratively, in "our social and economic system," noted an article in the association's journal.[73] "If he puts his money into good American investments, and a piece of land he can use, he likes America," said one US banker of recent US immigrants.[74]

"Americanization" was not the only messaging campaign that thrift promoters in the United States grafted onto banking products. The campaigns grew out of a longer history of progressive era reforms to expand access to savings banks, such as establishing postal savings banks in the United States.[75] They took on a diverse range of social scripts and meanings. For example, marketing campaigns emphasized the roles of women and women's management of household finances.[76] Banks created "home economics" departments and "women's departments" in the early 1920s to reframe finance as a domestic issue amenable to women's input.[77] The services were designed to welcome a broader swath of clientele to open bank accounts, borrow money, and invest in securities. National City Bank created special reception areas and dedicated staff to serve women's interests and train women in household budgeting and saving (see figure 7.2).[78] The ideological expansiveness of the saving and thrift campaigns made them convenient candidates for National City Bank to export overseas. Bankers could adapt the branding of savings drives with locally relevant scripts—stories that linked family, patriotism, and even civic pride with enrollment in US banking services.

In the mid-1920s, National City Bank began to push its savings campaigns outward to international branches. National City Bank opened a division for interest-bearing accounts for small savers, known as the "Compound Interest Department," in 1921 in New York. Bankers touted the department as a way for retail depositors to enlarge their savings and provide for their families.[79] After the program's early success in New York, executives expanded the campaigns to the Caribbean, where they surpassed executives' expectations, as historian Peter Hudson has noted.[80] The bank expanded the campaigns across its international network. National City's in-house magazine celebrated employees'

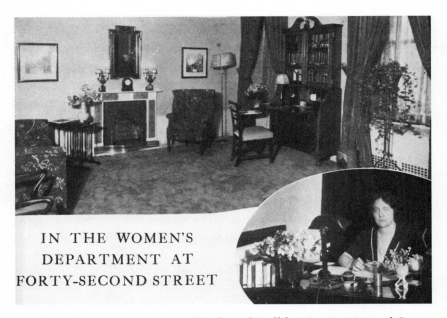

IN THE WOMEN'S
DEPARTMENT AT
FORTY-SECOND STREET

FIGURE 7.2. Reception Room and Dedicated Staff for Women, National City
Bank. *Image source:* "In the Women's Department at Forty-Second Street,"
No. 8 20, no. 4 (April 1925): 13.

heroic efforts to popularize savings accounts.[81] In 1926, National City bankers
visited Cuban sugar mills to encourage unbanked workers to open savings
accounts. One strategy to enlist new savers would have been petitioning workers individually, but instead, US bankers approached the mill owner and tried
to convince him to deduct five dollars from employees' paychecks and invest
the funds automatically in savings accounts. After the owner declined, bankers
approached the manager of the company store, who handled workers' paychecks, and found greater success. The bankers celebrated their hard-sell techniques: at first, "every one, known or unknown, refused us! They would object
at first, but fall in the end. And they liked it!"[82]

Bankers adopted different pitches and marketing tactics, depending on the
region and community where they sought new clients. In Yangon, Myanmar,
which US bankers knew as Rangoon, the strategy focused on thrift and savings
drives. An article in the bank's newsletter praised the US bankers for disproving
Europeans' belief that "the Burmese are not a thrifty race."[83] But US bankers
defied the skepticism of foreign competitors by "teaching the Burmese" about
the benefits of US banking services.[84] Sometimes US bankers appealed to
"civic pride" by staging competitions between cities or countries. Branches

FIGURE 7.3. "Scoreboard of Thrift," Nuevitas, Cuba branch. *Image source:* "Cuba's Brilliant Record," *No. 8* 23, no. 8 (August 1928): 27.

displayed scorecards and savings meters to highlight how many accounts had been opened in competitions (see figure 7.3).[85] Other campaigns emphasized family norms by focusing on how interest-earning accounts could increase children's long-term savings: bankers explained "what a small initial deposit of $1.00 a week would amount to in five or ten years, and how their little baby would come into a small capital upon reaching manhood or womanhood!"[86]

Retail savings drives and thrift campaigns brought US banking in contact with different demographics and into spaces that European banks typically had not accessed. In Cuba, bankers made inroads in "cement factories, tobacco fields, coffee plantations, sugar cane colonies, cattle ranches, copper and iron mines" and other places by using "high pressure salesmanship and oratory" to urge workers to open bank accounts.[87] Competitions in Asia included thrift campaigns, newspaper advertisements, and contests for student essays.[88] In India, National City Bank embraced retail banking by opening branches in high-traffic, mainstream locations such as bazaars and pearl markets to increase access to local clientele—a practice that US bankers interpreted as challenging European competitors: "Managers of the long-established British banks were considerably annoyed at the aggressiveness of our boys."[89]

Cumulatively, the bank's intake from the savings drives did little to change National City's overall financial position, but the programs represented a break from its original model for interacting with surrounding communities. In less than three years, the campaign increased overseas deposits to more than $10 million.[90] The amount constituted only a small fraction of the bank's total overseas deposits. It comprised 2 percent of the total deposits of the overseas division in 1929 and roughly a fifth of the total deposits generated by comparable New York-based drives that year.[91] Nonetheless, the campaigns broadened the bank's focus overseas beyond the interests of elite US businessmen.[92] Only a few years earlier, National City Bank executives hewed to the more traditional British banking practices, whereby foreign banks did not poach the clientele of local banks in their own communities. Foreign branches were not designed to "seek local deposits in competition with local banks"; instead, the purpose of a US bank was "to serve as the handmaiden of American commerce," said a National City Bank executive in 1922.[93] The savings drives marked a departure from that ethos. Suddenly, National City banks became peddlers of mass-marketed ideas about thrift and consumption in the foreign communities where they operated.

Overseas branches were also sites of experimentation for different kinds of retail banking projects, from utilizing multilingual staff to selling securities. In Buenos Aires, the bank expanded small-scale lending programs to include consumer and household loans. The bank's Buenos Aires branch opened its "Personal Loan Department" in 1928, modeled on a New York version of the department created the previous year. Both departments offered small loans to middle-class borrowers to finance expenses such as medical bills and college tuition.[94] Another innovation tested in Buenos Aires was the opening of a branch oriented to the needs of newcomers to Argentina. Services at the branch were designed "expressly for the convenience of immigrants in Buenos Aires." Employees spoke twenty-one languages to serve clients from Polish, Ukrainian, Yugoslav, Czechoslovakian, Greek, and Armenian communities, among others.[95]

The banking services it touted were not just a bastion of white, Anglo-Saxon privilege, though the realities of US overseas banking had never adhered exclusively to the racist scripts that bankers often espoused. Even as staffers made derogatory comments and nationalist generalizations about their overseas communities, their white supremacist beliefs could make room for recruiting nonwhite, non-Anglo-Saxon clients to rely on US financial services.[96] With local savings drives and the retail banking turn of the 1920s, US bankers overseas expanded their vision and identified potential customers in places previously invisible to them, from sugar mills to women's retail stores.

As US investment banks increased their sovereign lending activities, National City Bank's overseas branches also marketed securities among international clients. The bank's experience in Argentina and Chile offer two different case studies as to the potential for marketing national bonds to the populations of each nation. In Argentina, the bank found anemic interest for Argentine savers to invest in its government bonds. In 1915, National City financed a $25 million loan to the Argentine government. Demand in the United States for the bonds was high, but interest in Buenos Aires proved lackluster.[97]

The bank's experience in Chile offered a counterexample of local interest in bond purchasing. The bank opened its first Chilean branch in Valparaiso in 1915, almost immediately following the passage of the Federal Reserve Act.[98] Initially, the branch served US businesses engaged in Chilean nitrate and copper mining—especially Du Pont, which had opened a major nitrate facility in the region the previous year.[99] The bank opened a second branch in Santiago shortly after.[100] As National City expanded its branches and lending in Chile, branches sought to sell Chilean government bonds to Chilean savers. Throughout the early 1920s, the indebtedness of the Chilean government grew and created volatility in the nation's currency, as well as political resistance.[101] By 1927, the government had borrowed so extensively that it consolidated the debts and appointed National City Bank as its exclusive fiscal agent for future loans.[102] In 1929, National City Bank's Chilean branches launched a competition to sell that debt to the Chilean public. Staffers created an installment plan—much like the war savings program that Vanderlip led during World War I—to encourage Chilean depositors to buy government bonds through a series of installment payments. Staff could win prizes for selling the most bonds, including a week of extra vacation.[103] The competitions and savings programs highlight the improvisation that helped enmesh US branches in the financial dynamics of the economies in which bankers inserted themselves.

The Great Depression abruptly ended the easy money of the late 1920s, as prices for copper and nitrate—the backbone of Chilean exports—fell nearly 90 percent amid the economic collapse.[104] The Chilean government eventually suspended payment on foreign debts, and the country defaulted on the

FIGURE 7.4. Example of Spanish-language Promotion of National City products. *Image source:* "Cuba and Porto Rico Set a World Record in Savings Contest," *No. 8* 21, no. 1 (January 1926): 11.

National City Bank loan. National City ultimately wrote down more than $16 million in Chilean government bonds.[105] Nonetheless, the bank's work in Chile highlights the pairing of its sovereign lending with its attempts to recruit local customers.

Overseas, National City Bank branches worked in parallel with the bank's investment-oriented subsidiary, the National City Company, to sell a wide range of bonds and financial products to international customers. National City Bank created pamphlets and educational material for its Spanish-speaking clients to highlight the range of investing products clients could access through its South American branches.[106] One such pamphlet in Spanish from 1927 advised clients that savvy investors relied on dollar-denominated securities because US issues "are many of the most desirable securities on the international market" (see figure 7.4)[107] Where could a Latin American investor access such products? At a National City Bank branch, of course. Branches could supply clients with assets ranging from the municipal bonds of Milwaukee, Wisconsin, to foreign bonds issued by the government of Switzerland.[108]

Certainly, foreign branches were not essential to sovereign lending, as the cases of JP Morgan, Dillon Read, and other branchless institutions demonstrate. Nonetheless, foreign branches offered feedback loops that muddy the traditional depictions of 1920s sovereign lending as a one-way movement of funds from the United States outward. Evidence of the multidirectional movement of lending, investing, and marketing also appears in the earlier history of US foreign branching. One of the early experiments in selling US securities overseas involved pushing Liberty Loan drives to foreign branches. From Shanghai to Petrograd, National City Bank and IBC branches aggressively sold Liberty Loan bonds in the late 1910s.[109] IBC alone sold $3 million in subscriptions to the Third Liberty Loan, enacted in 1917.[110]

This smattering of international efforts demonstrates the improvisation and local adaptation that National City Bank branches initiated as they established themselves in different international contexts. Whereas the push to create a foreign-branch network originated from an inward-looking project to recruit US clients, the shifting economic, geopolitical, and local contexts of the 1920s allowed and even encouraged deviations from that inward-looking plan. As new norms of rationalized credit and retail banking dominated US finance, a wide range of context-dependent practices overseas recalibrated bankers' relationships to their local contexts and the personalized ways US bankers meted out access to financial opportunities.

Regulatory Navigation

Looking back on the 1920s from the perspective of the Great Depression that followed, it is tempting to see the frothiness of the late 1920s as a harbinger of the collapse that lay ahead. Indeed, scholars have repeatedly—and often rightly—looked to 1920s finance to understand the dynamics of economic collapse and the missed opportunities to avert and manage it.[111] A fixation on the Depression is partially warranted, given how much of the previous decade's growth it upended. The bonds of sovereign and subsovereign international governments defaulted at a rate of nearly 40 percent.[112] The US Congress pilloried bankers' recklessness, and new regulations such as the 1933 Glass-Steagall Act reined in the freewheeling capitalism of the 1920s. However, the foreign branch–level view offers a more diverse perspective on the overall impacts of the Depression. The financial upheaval prompted retrenchment, certainly, but overseas branches also served as a source of continuity from the 1920s frothiness to the 1930s collapse. Branches provided an enduring instrument for US banks to evade regulation, expand business opportunities, and preserve long-term international connections through economic restructuring.

Many nations turned inward during the Depression era, as nationalist sentiment caused countries to enact protectionist tariffs. This political climate presented National City Bank's overseas division with a financial and existential threat. In many parts of the world, antagonism toward the United States was rising, and resistance to US power often took shape as retaliation against US bankers and corporations.

The resistance was particularly pronounced in the Caribbean, where the United States had imposed violent, racialized, and destabilizing forms of imperial power. In these contexts, local leaders often equated National City Bank with US exploitation. A 1929 Salvadoran writer warned that inviting US bankers into local markets was essentially the same as surrendering to conquest by US business: "Nothing can make the path of American business so smooth,— and the conquest of our country so easy—as can the pre-existence of a great North-American bank in the Republic,—the National City Bank."[113] Political activists across the Caribbean also saw National City Bank's record in Haiti— of perpetuating US imperialism and reproducing white supremacy—as a warning of the perils of partnering with US finance.[114]

National City Bank tempered its relationship to surrounding communities by downplaying or amplifying its "Americanness," depending on the local political climate. One strategy was to diversify its hiring practices at its branches to put local staff in leadership positions. Local staff had long powered the day-to-day operations of foreign banks, whether through reliance on compradors in China or hiring of local clerical workers and assistants in other contexts. Indeed, when the wartime draft in the United States contracted National City Bank's overseas staff, the Branch Committee cabled its branches: "Suggest you strengthen local staff all branches as required in view of prevailing conditions."[115] In 1919, IBC's Beijing branch depended on more than forty local workers to support three European and US staff.[116] As one US banker in China noted, his job was less about doing work firsthand and more about overseeing others as they conducted banking operations: "While you don't have to do any of the work yourself, you are responsible for its correctness."[117]

Local staff contributed much of the labor that enabled US banks to operate overseas; however, bank records often masked or erased their contributions. For example, local workers were often excluded from the official pictures of branch staff. And when local staff were pictured, their names were typically not noted in captions or accompanying text, nor were their names recorded in New York staffing records (see figures 7.5, 7.6, and 7.7).[118]

However, by the early 1930s, bank policy shifted to increase the visibility and participation of local staff. National City appointed its first Japanese manager of a Japanese branch in Kobe in 1929. The success of that appointment prompted more local promotions, which engendered good will locally. Another benefit was that promoting locals decreased costs for headquarters. Cutting the number of US staff overseas from two hundred to less than one hundred by 1933 reduced the bank's staffing expenses and improved "the *espirit de corps* of our employees throughout the Orient," remembered one executive.[119]

FIGURE 7.5. Branch Photo with No Local Staff—Kobe, Japan. *Image source:* "Around the World with the I.B.C." *No. 8* 20, no. 5 (May 1925): 18.

FIGURE 7.6. Branch Photo with No Local Staff—Harbin, China. *Image source:* "Around the World with the I.B.C." *No. 8* 20, no. 5 (May 1925): 18.

At times, emphasizing National City Bank's "Americanness" and connection to US interests helped the bank, and bankers actively encouraged the linkage. For example, in China in the 1920s, National City executives debated ideas for how to rename former IBC branches in transitioning to National City's brand. When IBC had first entered China, it acquired the local nickname of "Flowery Flag" bank or "Flowering Flag Silver Shop," because of the flowers IBC printed on its banknotes.[120] As National City Bank sought to change the image of its China branches, one option they considered was *Mei Ta Yin Hang*, or "Big American Bank," according to the bank's sinology

FIGURE 7.7. Branch Photo with Unnamed Local Staff—Beijing, China. *Image source:* "The Last of the I.B.C. Groups," *No. 8* 21, no. 3 (March 1926): 10.

consultant.[121] The strategy of celebrating its connections to US power had worked well for National City Bank in many locations in the 1920s, when the United States helped fund postwar reconstruction efforts around the world and US politicians and military forces exerted new forms of control throughout the Western Hemisphere. However, resistance in the Caribbean highlighted the potential pitfalls of aligning the bank with US imperialism. Local hiring and rebranding strategies offered the bank tools to manage the political pressures, like heightened nationalism and antagonism to US power in some parts of the world.

Another strategy National City Bank used to downplay its US ties involved returning to the curiously powerful charter of IBC. Throughout the interwar period, National City Bank used IBC to maximize regulatory flexibility, expand its client base, and minimize governments' oversight by using IBC as a kind of "shadow" brand in overseas banking.[122] At the time, the bank desperately needed new strategies, given that, after the Depression, the role of providing a concierge service for traveling US salesmen no longer made economic sense, as international trade fell 60 percent from 1929 to 1932.[123] The volume of acceptances that National City Bank generated for customers dropped by nearly half from 1931 to 1932 alone, falling from more than $120 million to $66 million.[124] The 1930s were a time when many US multinationals shuttered overseas branches and canceled expansion plans.[125] In this context, IBC's legal structure and brand allowed National City Bank to avoid onerous regulations and dodge political pressure while maximizing its operational reach.

Throughout the 1920s and 1930s, the bank shape-shifted by adopting the form of National City or the International Banking Corporation—or both—depending on jurisdictional convenience and the potential for profits. This strategy was not the original intention of National City executives in seeking to acquire IBC in 1915.[126] Indeed, National City's acquisition of IBC proceeded slowly due to an early logistical hiccup that blocked a complete consolidation of IBC. The acquisition story is nearly as bizarre as IBC's origin story itself: when National City Bank gained a controlling interest in IBC, a portion of IBC shares were held by the estate of deceased King Leopold of Belgium, a leader known for brutal colonial violence that killed up to ten million people in the Congo. The king was an initial investor in IBC, but upon his death in 1909, stocks of the "Belgian Group" were transferred to a baroness whose village was occupied by the Germans during World War I. The king's shares were sent to the London vaults of the Bank of England for safekeeping and could not be touched until after the war. The fluke vestige of European empire meant that National City Bank could not gain full control of IBC until 1919 and faced challenges in consolidating ownership and dissolving IBC.[127] In the interim period of coexistence, IBC demonstrated its utility to National City as a separate brand, with a different legal framework and different overseas relationships.[128]

A major advantage of IBC as a financial entity was its unique Connecticut charter, which National City executives deemed "too valuable to lose."[129] The charter granted IBC the "wide powers of an English bank," according to National City Bank's assessment. In the early 1900s, IBC gained special permission from the Bank of England to deal in sterling-denominated acceptances on the British market. According to internal bank records, this special exception came about because IBC established its London office "before the British Treasury and the Bank of England tightened the reins on operations in England by foreign banks."[130] The authorization enabled the combined IBC-National City Bank behemoth to access both the dollar-denominated bankers' acceptance market—which was heavily supported by the Federal Reserve—and the more established London acceptance market. It is unclear, exactly, how the sterling acceptance business affected the bank's finances; nonetheless, bank executives were sufficiently concerned about losing access to the market that National City Bank rallied behind the preservation of IBC. Sterling acceptances "have run as high as £4,000,000—and as the National City Bank cannot perform this function, our name [IBC] will continue to appear as acceptors in the London market."[131] Ceding access to this market was not a choice that National City executives wanted to make.

The IBC brand also appealed to a different customer base than that of National City Bank, which gave the merged bank access to even more potential clients. For example, in the 1920s, National City Bank opened a branch in London, even though IBC had operated a London office since 1902.[132] Bank executives explained in an internal memo that a branch under the National City banner would "attract more of their own clients' London business than the I.B.C. has been able to do," given National City Bank's broader name recognition and more established reputation.[133] Strikingly, both banks—National City Bank and IBC—used the same manager to oversee the two London branches, but executives believed that continuing IBC as an independent brand would allow the bank to conduct "any special business that they or we might particularly want to do but which may not be suitable for a national bank to do," executives explained.[134] The memo did not specify what activities might "not be suitable for a national bank," but records from other IBC branches offer some clues.

The bank's regulatory maneuvers in China, Colombia, and Spain exemplify how IBC could serve as a shadow entity for National City to conduct business beyond the legal or reputational boundaries of its flagship brand. Regulations in Hong Kong restricted bank lending against real estate, but IBC faced no such restriction. In fact, National City Bank lawyers noted that IBC had "unusually favorable facilities for taking mortgages of leasehold property as security for advances."[135] Bank attorneys proposed a system that would allow National City Bank and IBC to combine their strengths and negate their weaknesses. Under the scheme, a Hong Kong borrower could mortgage property to IBC while applying for credit at National City Bank. Once IBC had legal claim to the property, IBC would give "National City Bank a guarantee for the due repayment by a customer."[136] The structure effectively used IBC as a pass-through to authorize lending against real estate. The bank's lawyers recommended notifying the Hong Kong government of the proposed workaround: "If they discovered the true position at a later date they might conceivably feel that a trick had been played upon them."[137] The lawyers argued that the legal structure and historical relationships of IBC could "materially enlarg[e] the powers" of National City Bank's charter.[138] The records do not clarify whether or not National City Bank followed this course of action, but the following year, the colonial secretary of Hong Kong notified the IBC branch of its continued authorization to lend against mortgages.[139]

Another value-add of the IBC brand was its relative obscurity in sovereign lending. National City became known for its ability to provide large loans to foreign governments, in Latin America in particular. When National City Bank considered opening a branch in Medellin, Colombia, in 1916, advisers suggested branding it under the IBC banner so the Colombian government

would be less inclined to request loans. "The International Banking Corporation would not be subject to the same pressure from the Government of
Colombia for loans and government financing that The National City Bank
probably would be." By casting itself as an IBC branch, the bank "could confine
its activities to commercial banking and modest exchange operations."[140]
Thus, IBC could provide a cover by allowing National City Bank to access
foreign markets without the political and financial expectations that might
accompany a brand-named branch.

Taxation policies posed a challenge to National City Bank's attempts to
access Spanish markets in the 1920s. Again, the entwined structure of IBC and
National City allowed the bank to maximize its opportunities and minimize
costs. In 1929, National City Bank wanted to restructure its Spanish operations
by converting all IBC branches to National City's brand. However, Spanish
law required banks to calculate their tax liability based in part on global deposits and profits. At the time, National City Bank's total deposits were nearly fifty
times that of IBC's. Thus, the different positions of the two banks had steep
tax implications.[141] A lawyer proposed that National City continue working
"through our correspondent, the International Banking Corporation," rather
than open a branch directly because of the tax implications.[142] Even though
the lawyer's description of IBC as a "correspondent" of National City mischar-
acterizes the relationship structure between the two entities, the dubious depiction did not stop National City Bank from receiving authorization from
both Spanish regulators and Federal Reserve officials to proceed.[143] The workaround reveals the ways that the bank could shape-shift depending on the
jurisdiction.

As National City Bank hopscotched branding issues and jurisdictional
challenges to maximize access to foreign markets, US regulators struggled to
determine the proper ways to oversee foreign bank branches. Several administrative divisions claimed jurisdiction over aspects of overseas branches'
work; however, throughout much of the 1910s and 1920s, no branch of the US
government regulated the day-to-day work of overseas bankers. US consular
officials around the world monitored the US branches operating in their regions and reported back to Washington on their activities and missteps, but
the reports tended to be piecemeal and anecdotal. A consular official in Colombia observed that National City Bank's branch in Bogotá had angered locals because it charged "an unfair rate of exchange on bills received by it . . .
and insist[ed] upon the immediate payment of these obligations during a financial crisis."[144] Meanwhile, the US Consulate in Maracaibo, Venezuela,
warned State Department officials that National City Bank planned to shutter
its local branch—a move that would leave the US business community
stranded: "I consider it of great importance to American interests that the

Maracaibo branch of National City Bank be continued."[145] The correspondence reveals the conviction among State Department staff that US banks overseas mattered to national policy objectives, but it demonstrates little in the way of proactive, structured oversight.

US regulators debated whether the federal government could or should increase its oversight of foreign branch operations. In 1926, a National City official reported on a conversation with a State Department official who wanted to examine IBC's overseas branches. The State Department official ultimately decided the work was not feasible "without spending a year on the task and doing the work himself. This necessitated his abandoning the examination," the bank official reported to his colleagues.[146] The comptroller of the currency published the financial statements for the foreign branches of US national banks in its annual reports, starting in 1915. But the publications suggest little in the way of regular monitoring.[147]

The Federal Reserve's supervision of overseas branches was similarly light-handed and tended more toward collaboration than oversight. IBC executives seized opportunities to establish collegial, peer-based relationships with would-be regulators at the Federal Reserve Board. In 1917, IBC executives offered to help the Federal Reserve Board by acting as the board's agent in negotiations in India and China, though ultimately Fed officials did not accept the invitation.[148] The Federal Reserve Board's early attempts at regulation often ended with compromise and diluted recommendations rather than strict prohibitions and rules. In 1918, the board announced that overseas branches would have to maintain 15 percent cash reserve requirements to safeguard their deposits. Two months later, regulators rescinded the requirement and told IBC to "exercise its own discretion as to the amount of reserve to be carried." Federal Reserve officials added that IBC should provide notification "from time to time" about the standing of branches.[149] Bankers and regulators corresponded about policy and met both informally and formally, such as in a conference convened by the Federal Reserve Board in 1919 designed to give regulators "a better understanding of the business of American corporations engaged principally in foreign business."[150] For much of the 1920s, most of the regulatory "oversight" involved IBC's notifications to the Federal Reserve about the opening and closing of branches.[151]

The dynamics of limited regulation, the use of subsidiary agencies, and the lava-lamp formulations of the bank's different legal structures prefigure some of the hallmark features of multinational corporations' operations in the twentieth century. In the post–World War II era, the use of tax havens and offshoring became commonplace features of multinational businesses. National City Bank's reliance on IBC shares many of the features of "archipelago capitalism" that characterized mid- to late-twentieth-century globalized capitalism.[152]

However, in this early-twentieth-century moment, regulatory evasion took shape less as a corporate grand strategy plotted in New York boardrooms, and more as small pivots in bank policies and last-minute improvisations by National City Bank executives and on-the-ground workers.

The strategies helped National City Bank withstand the economic upheaval of the 1930s. Certainly, the Depression prompted National City to curb its aggressive international expansion—and even contract its branch network. In the early 1930s, National City Bank closed thirty branches, including twelve in Cuba, and it wrote off $33 million in assets from foreign branches.[153] Nonetheless, overseas branches served as a relative bright spot amid the 1930s contractions. In the bank's shareholder meetings in both 1931 and 1932, President Charles Mitchell commented that overseas branches had performed relatively well, despite "depressed" conditions around the world in 1931. "[T]he operations of the foreign branches show approximately the same profit as in the record figures of last year," he noted.[154] By the following year, the earnings of foreign branches had declined, but they "nevertheless produced gratifying net profits" exceeding $5 million, Mitchell reported.[155] By 1934, overseas branches once again became highly profitable, and by 1939, the overseas division constituted almost half of the bank's total deposits—$530 million out of a total $1.1 billion.[156]

One of the most striking aspects of National City Bank's experience with internationalization involves the branches' resilience and endurance. US bankers had first plowed into overseas branching in 1901, with the institutional backing of US imperial expansion, and then again in 1913, with the backing of the Federal Reserve Act. However, their ambitions were often poorly defined and inward looking. First, with IBC, the goal had been to work "hand in hand with Uncle Sam." Then, with National City, the goal was to serve US exporters with credit information, trade support, and even local train schedules.

Yet quickly, the flat, commercial expanse of the "foreign field" fragmented into enclaves within local communities that contained their own internal hierarchies and business norms. Variation created space for regulatory evasion and experimentation with new strategies to minimize governmental oversight and taxation. In this contoured landscape, bankers not only endured but deepened their staying power. Indeed, when international markets failed to deliver on the expected increases in trade, US bankers operating overseas could turn to local markets to sustain business. As one US banker in China observed in 1933, National City Bank's best hope for reviving profits was to appeal not to the dwindling number of US traders or insular British businesses, but instead to cater to Chinese businesspeople, who represented the bank's "chief prospects for the future."[157]

The multinational banking project that began as a side hustle for Gilded Age tycoons had evolved into a network of overseas outposts that sent young graduates of US colleges out to pound the pavement to enlist Cuban farm laborers and Filipino clerks in US banking services. It was likely not the vision of banking that JP Morgan had in mind when he testified before US Congress in 1912 that the foundation of banking credit was "character." Nonetheless, US banks helped expand the circuitry of US foreign financial power by creating new junctions and by smoothing points of resistance. In the new hardwiring, personal connections and patterns of elite privilege intermingled to create a new infrastructure of US financial power. Overlaid on that foundation, bankers institutionalized new practices of rationalized credit and financialized forms of US influence.

Conclusion

TRADITIONAL HISTORIES of US economic power in the twentieth century describe US overseas banks as significant international players only after the 1950s.[1] Before then, most US banks confined themselves to operating branches inside the nation's borders. In 1960, more than thirteen thousand commercial banks operated within the United States; only eight had overseas branches. The assets of foreign branches constituted only about 1 percent of banks' total assets.[2]

Such statistics belie an important dimension of US influence overseas by ignoring the way foreign branches created an infrastructure for expanding US financial power. Foreign branches established systems for gathering information, broadening US commercial contacts, and advancing the global uptake of the US dollar. They offered an institutional foothold in communities around the world that enabled bankers to collect information, facilitate trade, and expand the dollar's reach. Moreover, those institutional footholds could adapt. Branches could pivot from being bastions of elite power to peddlers of retail bank services, depending on the economic conditions and social climate of the place and time. In other words, the infrastructure that bankers built was sturdy—it persisted amid downturns and crises—as well as malleable, as bankers working on the ground could change the scripts and recalibrate their distributional impacts.

As the US government diversified its methods for projecting power overseas in the early twentieth century—from military operations to economic advising—US bankers likewise expanded their repertoires for operating on a multinational scale. They collaborated with local elites. They sought entry into prestigious social clubs. And they organized thrift campaigns. Their branches provided data and personal connections for assuring US clients that the world of international trade was knowable and reliable. Thousands of credit files, maintained in New York, put far-flung businesses on a level playing field of analysis. Branch banks rendered that field accessible and comprehensible to US businesses interested in international opportunities.

Dollars and Dominion began its investigation of US international power by offering two approaches to understanding the nation's transformation in the early twentieth century. The personalist version began with a sweaty banker in Buenos Aires, Fred, who offered a human face to the rise of US foreign power. The institutionalist account focused on imperial powerbrokers—the military, banks, and the state. *Dollars and Dominion* has married key insights from both approaches to offer a different framing: it sees US overseas banking as a type of infrastructure. Bankers' credit files, social connections, data networks, and standardization practices provide a framework for shaping US power, albeit one that scholars often overlook, because it masquerades as the on-the-ground minutiae of banking. However, understanding the early architecture of this system reveals the uneven ways in which US power touched down and took root, as well as the way in which US influence adapted itself in the face of economic crises, political opposition, and other challenges.

One upside of an infrastructural account is its emphasis on fixity and the durability of relationships and systems. To understand how this financial infrastructure evolved, it's worth considering what became of several first movers of this apparatus. Their fates gesture at the geopolitical significance and, simultaneously, the banality of early-twentieth-century globalizing capitalism.

What Became of Them?

The International Banking Corporation pioneered US multinational banking in the early 1900s, but by midcentury its name was little more than a catch-all subsidiary for a hodgepodge of National City Bank's international assets. IBC provided a holding vehicle to collect shares in a French construction venture, bank investments in the Bahamas, and part-ownership of a financial institution in Monrovia, among other assets.[3]

In 1959, executives saw an opportunity to revive the IBC brand and give it a new life. The opportunity was likely not one that IBC founder Marcellus Hartley of Remington Arms would have foreseen. New York City had opened a new airport—Idlewild, known today as JFK—and National City Bank wanted a presence in the new international arrivals building. The bank would open a booth to help travelers with foreign exchange: a money-changing kiosk, where deplaning passengers could get US dollars, and outbound travelers could obtain foreign money. Executives branded the airport booth the International Banking Corporation.[4]

At the time, the bank's executives likely saw IBC as a relic of an earlier financial era—an era eclipsed by modernized bureaucracies and quantitative analysis. And yet, IBC accomplished one of the most sophisticated corporate sleights of hand possible: it fused itself to one of the biggest banks in the world.

IBC seeded its staff, clients, and operating practices into its larger banking parent. Resurrecting that history shows the coevolution of the institutional structures of IBC and National City Bank. Their entanglement increased the bank's overall profit potential while minimizing tax burdens and avoiding political pressure. The analysis also reveals the improvisation and unlikely endurance of a ramshackle project to piggyback on US empire. That rickety project embedded itself into one of the largest and most powerful financial institutions of the early twentieth century. Airport moneychanger was not the most triumphant testament to its legacy, but IBC's true staying power was to make itself both invisible and enduring within its corporate parent, Citigroup.

And what of Guaranty Trust, the onetime competitor of National City Bank in acceptances and trade finance? In the early 1900s, Guaranty Trust seemed positioned to become a cornerstone of JP Morgan and Company's ongoing international expansion. Its operations primarily served US and European clients, and the bank rivaled National City in its acceptance business in the 1920s. However, its growth languished by the 1950s, and the institution became "sleepy, stodgy [and] risk-fearing."[5] Guaranty Trust merged with JP Morgan and Company in 1959 to become Morgan Guaranty Trust Company of New York. In so doing, Guaranty Trust did not simply fade with a whimper. It provided some of the financial connective tissue that anchored the dollar's centrality to the global economy, though in ways that might have surprised the internationalists of the 1920s.

After the turbulent late 1920s, Guaranty Trust shifted from specializing in cotton trade to providing the financial circuitry that made Saudi oil a global commodity traded in US dollars. It did so largely because of a historical fluke. Guaranty Trust served the right clients—the Standard Oil Company of California (Socal)—at the right time. It was Socal's banker when Saudi leaders granted vast oil concessions to US business interests. In that moment in 1933, US companies displaced long-standing British dominance in the Gulf by securing rights to explore and extract Saudi Arabia's oil. Guaranty Trust provided banking services for Socal at the time when Socal negotiators were nearing an agreement with King Ibn Sa'ud after months of protracted talks. Both sides were nearly ready to sign a deal granting Socal a sixty-year oil concession, when President Franklin Roosevelt announced a prohibition against the export of gold from the United States.

Roosevelt's gold ban presented more than a logistical hiccup for Socal's oil aspirations. Saudi negotiators had insisted on gold as the financial format required to make Socal's initial payment to Saudi Arabia for the concession. Paper money did not circulate as legal tender in Saudi Arabia at the time, so Socal applied for a permit from the US Treasury to ship gold as an exemption from the nation's ban. As the deadline for paying the Saudi government approached, approvals from US regulators had not been secured. In the interim, Socal made alternative arrangements. It ordered the London branch of its bank—Guaranty Trust—to ship gold sovereigns on a British steamer to Jeddah.

The arrangement transpired in a legal gray zone, as the Treasury Department soon denied Socal's request for the shipment of US gold. Nonetheless, Socal's gold from the London Guaranty Trust office arrived, and the deal was inked.[6] When Saudi officials asked the US negotiators what to do with the gold, a Socal representative suggested that the Saudi officials work with Guaranty Trust.[7] The firm became banker to Aramco, the Saudi Arabian oil giant, and ultimately a conduit that linked JP Morgan to Saudi Arabia. The bank became known as "the kingdom's bank," according to the Wall Street Journal, given the decades-long relationship.[8] Certainly, dozens of other geopolitical events secured the dollar's role as the currency of global oil trade. The role of Guaranty Trust—later Morgan Guaranty Trust, then JP Morgan and Company, known today as JPMorgan Chase and Company—as banker for US oil concessions likely did not hurt.

And what of the onetime credit instrument on which key components of the scaffolding of US foreign banking depended—the humble bankers' acceptance? The fate of the acceptance market provides a less colorful, more intricate story of institutional shape-shifting. After the financial crisis of the early 1930s, public backing for export financing became tucked into a new entity that was less tethered to the Federal Reserve System. The US government created the Export-Import Bank to provide credit and loans to global buyers of US exports. The Ex-Im Bank was created by President Roosevelt in 1934, and the bank worked to enhance US global trade, much as the acceptance market had once aspired to do. In its early work, the Ex-Im Bank facilitated sales of locomotives to Chile and the marketing of US tobacco in Spain, among other projects.[9]

The Ex-Im Bank continues such work today, alongside the export-credit agencies of dozens of other nations, by subsidizing trade and improving the competitiveness of the nation's businesses. The Ex-Im Bank's activities are not limited to bankers' acceptances; instead, its support often takes shape in different financing formats, such as providing advances on airline construction or negotiating favorable terms for trading technology products.[10] Acceptances have persisted as a credit instrument despite their decline during the Great Depression and World War II, but technological advances in trade and communications have made them less useful to mainstream traders. Bills on London or New York no longer represent the most convenient way to arrange trade financing for most companies. Instead, the appeal of acceptances grew out of specific market conditions, such as demand in Japan for short-term credit instruments after World War II.[11] Today, bankers' acceptances have become even more obscure, and recent use cases include financing real-estate speculation in China in the 2010s and 2020s and being touted by the Central Bank of Nigeria as a promising tool for short-term credit.[12]

Meanwhile, the fate of the flagship piece of this financial architecture—the overseas branch bank—is once again in flux as new pressures, from technological change to "reshoring," upend global trade patterns. Both Citigroup and HSBC, as the Hongkong and Shanghai Banking Corporation is now known, have begun shedding their global network of branches. In 2022, Citigroup announced it was unwinding its global consumer banking services in Australia, China, Mexico, and the Middle East.[13] HSBC has sold off parts of its business in Europe and the Americas and has closed more than a hundred branches in Britain.[14]

This contraction represents a new era for a financial infrastructure forged in the early twentieth century. The brick-and-mortar network of overseas branches provided a physical reminder of international financial connections, such as when Citi helped popularize automatic teller machines, ATMs, in global branches in the late 1970s and 1980s. Eight months after unveiling ATMs in New York, Citi installed them in Hong Kong.[15] The bank adopted the slogan: "Citi never sleeps" because of this global presence.[16] Yet, following the 2008 financial crisis and postpandemic retrenchment in many markets, that global model faltered. Citigroup retreated from global consumer banking to refocus on serving established firms and affluent clients through commercial banking and wealth management, much like its model prior to the Federal Reserve Act.[17] Alongside the overhaul of US global retail banking, many vestiges of the twentieth-century architecture of US financial power seem once again in flux.

With the current shift in the financial infrastructures, many of the core themes in *Dollars and Dominion* have once again become ripe topics for debate, such as the proper role of the Federal Reserve and the government's role in maintaining the financial infrastructure of trade.

The rise of Chinese global power and of Chinese financial technologies has raised numerous questions about how states and financial institutions collaborate to dictate the terms of economic engagement. Chinese state-backed banks and firms have committed trillions to constructing infrastructure around the world. Roughly two-thirds of Chinese state loans to Africa were dedicated to infrastructure from 2000 to 2020.[18] As many policymakers anticipate a new era of great-power rivalry over infrastructure statecraft, the terms that shaped the last century of global growth warrant reexamination.

Understanding banking as an infrastructure of power helps us move away from short-term cycles of economic booms and busts and refocus our attention on the longer-term accretion of financial systems and relationships. It also allows space for seeing on-the-ground pivots and ad hoc solutions that gained traction in one place and became incorporated into larger, transnational systems. Financial missionaries parachuted into metropolitan centers to propose reforms, and private bankers convened to deliver large sovereign loans. Historians have long acknowledged these features of the rise of US power in the twentieth century as impacting its role in the global political economy.

Beneath, amid, and between these peripatetic movements of financiers, policymakers, and advisers, branch banks were conducting the long-term, face-to-face work of building institutions, making connections, and forging relationships that linked US business to global trading partners and enabling greater access to the US dollar. And when economic winds changed, this infrastructure endured and proved amenable to reinvention, depending on the profit potentials and political pressures of the moment. This historical examination of infrastructure building can help us better understand the stakes of today's debates.

Banking and Infrastructural Power

Assessing this earlier period of US ascendance provides a new way to understand the interplay between state and banks, between public and private sectors, in asserting infrastructural power.[19] *Dollars and Dominion* analyzes this history less from the perspective of the US state looking outward—from the framing of the promotional state, for example—and more through the lens of US multinational banks making sense of their foreign contexts.[20] From this perspective, the book demonstrates the way in which overseas banks developed the machinery of US empire, as well as the ways in which bankers' work at times undercut or muddied the aspirations of US government officials.

The financial infrastructure enabled numerous configurations depending on context, with different degrees of imperial power. In Russia, for example, US power was more aspirational than realized as US bankers found their branches seized and assets nationalized. In the Philippines, by contrast, US bankers held government deposits and advocated a stronger US colonial presence despite growing calls for Filipino independence. Along this imperial continuum, US banks reshaped themselves to fit the needs of their context. In the early 1900s in the Caribbean, that meant deal-making with corrupt, US-backed regimes and looking to the US military for protection when the conditions deteriorated.[21] By contrast, the script for working in China involved securing a local go-between to access business opportunities and, when necessary, dialing up or down the Americanness of the institution.

In many contexts, US banks promoted imperial inequality, but what that meant, who benefited, and how coercive that power was varied considerably among different points of touchdown. For example, in the Philippines, IBC was clearly an imperial entity. However, a careful analysis of its loan portfolio reveals that the economic opportunities it conveyed had little to do with the

United States—at least initially. Instead, its early banking work perpetuated imperial inequalities created under Spanish rule by strengthening the economic power of existing European and Chinese businesses.

US bankers' work in Argentina offers a different picture. While British businesses had dominated Argentine economic activity throughout the late nineteenth century, the United States struggled to rival British prominence. US citizens who moved to Buenos Aires often referred to themselves as members of the "American Colony," a close-knit group of expats who convened in the American Club for events, socializing, and nightly dinners.[22] When National City Bank opened an opulent new building in Buenos Aires in 1929—complete with Italian marble and Swedish granite—fittingly, the American Club moved into the building's top three floors, above the US bank.[23] In its local disposition, the Buenos Aires bank became practically synonymous with the "American Colony" and US commercial power.

In this framing, the Federal Reserve System provides a central fixture in the promotional state's operation. Traditional histories of US banking have recognized that the 1913 Federal Reserve Act introduced new possibilities for multinational work. But they have overlooked or downplayed how the bankers' acceptance market affected the work of private banks on the ground. This oversight has obscured the long history of US overseas bankers' reliance on public resources and state power to sustain it, and the way in which the acceptance market functioned as a bulwark against some of the risks of operating internationally. Moreover, the networks that US bankers established took on outsized importance as the United States emerged as the world's leading creditor nation following World War I. The personnel, offices, and connections of US banks shaped the way in which US global power took root and encountered local communities.

Once established in their new locations, overseas bank branches could experiment with new ways to make money. While banking had traditionally been a bastion of elite privilege throughout the nineteenth century, the changing economic terrain of the 1920s prompted many US financial institutions to launch new retail services, from thrift campaigns to small loan programs. National City Bank was the US financial institution best positioned to deploy these programs on a broadly multinational scale. Suddenly, its overseas employees began enticing nonelites—Cuban sugar workers, Burmese laborers, and Filipino clerks, among others—to open deposit accounts. Many of the programs were short-lived, and only a small portion offered access to credit. Further research can help identify what effects they had on local financial practices and business cultures where US bankers inserted themselves. Nonetheless, in terms of understanding the US financial infrastructure, it is striking that a project forged in Gilded Age, railroad-tycoon affluence had shifted within a few decades to a flexible financial project that broadened US power through pavement-pounding campaigns to sell banking services to the unbanked.

Structural Legacy

The guidelines and structures that guide banking and credit affect how the gains from economic development are distributed. They shape the allocation of social power and public resources. Recent economic upheaval has served as a stark reminder that the financial system's rules affect society's winners and losers. The 2008 financial crisis and the COVID-19 pandemic prompted unprecedented changes in how the Federal Reserve operates and how the US government allows the public to access money and credit. Which investments get special protections in an economic crisis? What assets is the Fed allowed to own and on what terms?

These questions have called our attention to the distributional politics of central banking and economic governance. Throughout US history, public- and private-sector entities have collaborated to control financial infrastructures. Their balance of power and the terms of that collaboration affect who can access money, and under what terms. Recent financial upheaval has also laid bare the invisible rules and understandings that shape people's experiences with financial systems. While the approval or rejection of a single credit application might look like an "objective" assessment of a borrower's eligibility, the ultimate decision depends on social values, previous generations' decisions about allocating power and capital, and the distribution of infrastructural power.

Emerging technologies and financial trends, like peer-to-peer lending and shadow banking, have raised questions about the foundations of the financial system that guided twentieth-century growth. A major question involves the biases and blind spots built into credit practices. Turn-of-the-century bankers debated the value of financial statements in assessing a single borrower. Today's credit algorithms can draw from spending patterns, social media, employment history, and other sources to develop metrics that promise to assess credit risks. Yet both systems can perpetuate inequalities of the past because the architecture of these credit systems—whether based on AI algorithms or relationship banking—are rigged in favor of some demographics over others. Those who already hold assets receive higher ratings and preferential consideration. Faring worse are the people who have lacked legal protections or been denied opportunities—either directly or through historical disenfranchisement—to accumulate the assets that the financial system prioritizes, be it a bankers' acceptance or a home mortgage. Credit histories depend on patterns of wealth accumulation and infrastructural power. Thus, they inevitably perpetuate past patterns of inequality.[24] If our credit futures continue to rely on our credit past, our financial systems will continue carrying these inequalities forward.

Dollars and Dominion focuses on a critical period of the early twentieth century, when different approaches to credit and trust came into contact overseas, as the United States built new systems to gain commercial power abroad. Following the work of overseas banks in building this apparatus shows how social privilege was interwoven with state power to create a system that gave a scientific gloss to relationship patterns, while in fact it relied on elitism and insider access. Analyzing these connections and structures gives us a foundation for understanding the entanglement between banks and the US state in expanding US power in the early twentieth century, as well as the hierarchies of privilege and inequality that accompanied that rise.

In 1956, fifty former US bankers met at the Sleepy Hollow Country Club in New York to celebrate the fortieth anniversary of the first graduation of National City Bank's college training program. Over mock turtle soup and sirloin steak, the men reminisced about their work. They read letters they had sent each other from the "foreign field" in the 1920s. They remembered the "high cost of outfitting" to purchase neckties, suits, and handkerchiefs. And they recalled the difficulties of their language training.[25] Fred, the fictional sweaty banker in a wool suit who touched down in Buenos Aires in 1916, would have given an impassioned toast at such an event.

In the decades since their overseas deployment, many of the men had returned to the United States for careers in banking and US business.[26] Some found work with the US government as military advisers, foreign service officials, and trade liaisons.[27] Many went on to become leaders at National City Bank and its competitors.[28] One became President Dwight Eisenhower's budget director—the man who charted financial designs for the military-industrial complex.[29] A *Time* magazine story about one such reunion of National City Bank's early global bankers described them as "the nucleus of a new professional class," who presided over a dramatic change in international political economy—and the US role in that order—between the first and second world wars.[30]

One banker described the period of US bank expansion as "almost as exciting as the tale of the Arabian Nights," with foreign adventures and discovery.[31] But the temptation to focus on individual stories and exploits can obscure how the bankers, working in tandem and in conjunction with institutions such as the Federal Reserve System, shaped the development of US commercial expansion in the early twentieth century. Their work enabled new US systems for "knowing" overseas trading partners and securing markets for US goods.

It was in the financial statements, ledger histories, and discounted acceptances that the staying power of twentieth-century US financial power took shape.

If implementation is policy, then overseas bankers ranked among the chief designers of US foreign engagement. The financial systems they built were not just one-off matters of office protocols. Instead, they created an infrastructure of US influence that was deeply entangled with the US government in terms of foreign policy objectives, trade promotion, and economic growth.

Dollars and Dominion has tracked the coevolution of US global power and the daily practices of US banking. Initially, these threads seem unrelated: histories of US global power tend to focus on imperial incursions in the Caribbean, colonial governance in the Philippines, and the construction of the Panama Canal, for example. Meanwhile, banking histories often highlight themes such as management practices, financialization, and the rise of retail banking. The two through-lines of imperial power and banking practices are entangled and mutually enforcing, and together, they allow us to understand the uneven foundation of economic opportunity that undergirds the expansion of US commercial power in the early twentieth century.

Moreover, as the financial infrastructure of economic development is once again in flux, many of the core questions about the design parameters of the financial system are once again open. How should the Fed oversee the shadow banking system—or *should* it at all? What about opening direct accounts for US savers? These questions are not just about the technocratic operation of our financial system or about changing digits in account holders' balances. They are questions about equality, the politics of distribution, and what type of economic activities we prioritize as a nation. How much does sustainability matter? How do we distribute access to credit more fairly? Revisiting this earlier moment, when US banks function as the pile drivers of support for a new era of US-led capitalism, can help us see how its foundation always relied on continuities and hierarchies of the past. It also sheds light on how that system might be reformatted for different outcomes in the future.

ACKNOWLEDGMENTS

IT IS ONLY fitting for a book about the history of banking to end by acknowl-
edging accumulated debts. In researching and writing *Dollars and Dominion*,
I have acquired many. The project began at Vanderbilt University, where Sarah
Igo, Paul Kramer, and Jeff Cowie helped me frame the ideas and shape the raw
material. Naomi Lamoreaux added expert perspective on banking, as well as
generous mentorship at every juncture, and I am so grateful for her
generosity.

Along the way, scholars and mentors at numerous institutions—particularly
at Yale University and Johns Hopkins School of Advanced International
Studies—have guided the project. Among the key leaders in these institutions
who shared both scholarly insight and professional support are Arne Westad,
Frank Gavin, Mike Brenes, and Brian Balogh. In addition, numerous scholars
have contributed feedback, insights, and inspiration. They read drafts. They
endured video calls. They suggested articles and archives. And they contributed
their brain power and expertise to help me understand different aspects of the
project. I owe particular thanks to Marc Adam, Manuel A. Bautista-González,
Mark Carlson, Andrew Ehrhardt, David Engerman, Kate Epstein, Jonathan
Esty, Marc Flandreau, Henry Gorman, John Handel, Daniel Immerwahr,
Harold James, Richard John, Noam Maggor, Rory Miller, Jamieson Myles,
Gianandrea Nodari, Nadav Orian Peer, Mary O'Sullivan, Atiba Pertilla, Peter
Rousseau, Jay Sexton, Sarah Snyder, Paula Vedoveli, Nicholas Wong, partici-
pants in Princeton's Economic History Workshop, and members of the
US Political Economy Lab. Nic Johnson provided brilliant feedback, ideas,
and edits. And Michael Falcone—editor, friend, and ally in airports and life
pivots—thank you.

Several institutions provided funding and research support for the project.
In particular, Johns Hopkins School of Advanced International Studies, the
Ax:son Johnson Institute for Statecraft and Diplomacy, the International Security Studies program at Yale University, and Vanderbilt University funded
vital pieces of research and enabled writing time. Additional funding came
from the Jefferson Scholars Foundation, the Bentley Library at the University

of Michigan, Harvard Business School, the History Project, the Joint Centre for History and Economics, and the Institute for New Economic Thinking.

As a child of an archivist and a librarian, I must acknowledge my enormous debt to the knowledgeable, generous professionals who helped guide my archival research. I am also grateful to institutions that support researchers and facilitate access to their records. Thank you especially to Kerri Anne Burke and Liz Alleva. In addition, staff at numerous institutions helped me maximize my research time. I owe particular thanks to the interlibrary loan department at Vanderbilt University, research librarians at Yale University, library staff at SAIS, as well as the Heritage Collection at Citi, JP Morgan & Chase, the Morgan Library, the Newberry Library, Harvard's Baker Library, the East Texas Research Center, and the Bentley Library.

In the process of finalizing this book, Priya Nelson provided vital input and editorial vision, and I also appreciate the feedback of two anonymous readers. Audra Wolfe provided masterful insights and recommendations on the structure. And Emma Wagh, Leah Caldwell, and the art department at Princeton University Press have also contributed key pieces to moving the project forward.

I would never have had the time or mental clarity to focus on this project if not for the work of dedicated caregivers who supported my family. Much of this book took shape in the pressure cooker of pandemic lockdowns and school closures, and working on it would not have been possible without the patience and care that Annabelle, Eleonora, Laura, Ari, Karen, Irma, and Angelica gave my family and me.

I have leaned on numerous friends in this journey, and their input and support kept me afloat. Thank you especially to Paul Smyke, Sara Elsayed, Emilie Jacobs, Rowan Finnegan, Max Smith, and Allison Waters. Josh Segall, thank you always for best-friendship for the last many decades. Let's keep up our streak.

I owe the biggest thanks to my family. To Nuclear—and especially Mom and Dad—words are failing me to explain how grateful I am. You gave us the superpower of unconditional love. Orange juice was a scarce commodity; love was not. Sarah and Abby, your friendship, your support, and your examples inspire me daily. Thank you for being the best sisters a middle child could have.

And to Louisa and Edwin, you give me new purpose. Thank you for giving me new motivation to become a better human and parent. And most of all, Bill, guardian of daily hugs, you've been with this project as long as I have, and your love and support have made it possible. Thank you.

NOTES

Introduction

1. Claire Lui, "A Manila Envelope: The Inspiration behind an Exhibition's Graphic Identity," 2021, accessed July 3, 2023, https://www.guggenheim.org/blogs/checklist/a-manila-envelope -the-inspiration-behind-an-exhibitions-graphic-identity; Jonathan M. Katz, *Gangsters of Capitalism: Smedley Butler, the Marines, and the Making and Breaking of America's Empire* (New York: St. Martin's Press, 2022).

2. Craig Robertson, *The Filing Cabinet: A Vertical History of Information* (Minneapolis: University of Minnesota Press, 2021), ebook.

3. Katherine C. Epstein, "The Conundrum of American Power in the Age of World War I," *Modern American History* 2, no. 3 (November 2019): 345–65.

4. The literature on US imperialism in the Caribbean and beyond is vast. A selection of recent works includes: Peter James Hudson, *Bankers and Empire: How Wall Street Colonized the Caribbean* (Chicago: University of Chicago Press, 2017); Katz, *Gangsters of Capitalism*; David Healy, *Drive to Hegemony: The United States in the Caribbean, 1898–1917* (Madison: University of Wisconsin Press, 1988); Ivan Musicant, *The Banana Wars: A History of United States Military Intervention in Latin America from the Spanish-American War to the Invasion of Panama* (New York: Macmillan, 1990); Mary A. Renda, *Taking Haiti: Military Occupation and the Culture of U.S. Imperialism, 1915–1940* (Chapel Hill: University of North Carolina Press, 2001). For a more complete bibliography on US imperialism, see also Paul A. Kramer, "How Not to Write the History of U.S. Empire," *Diplomatic History* 42, no. 5 (2018).

5. Hudson, *Bankers and Empire.*

6. For histories of US military basing, see Rebecca Herman, *Cooperating with the Colossus: A Social and Political History of US Military Bases in World War II Latin America* (New York: Oxford University Press, 2022); David Vine, *Island of Shame: The Secret History of the U.S. Military Base on Diego Garcia* (Princeton, NJ: Princeton University Press, 2009); Jana K. Lipman, *Guantánamo: A Working-Class History between Empire and Revolution, American Crossroads* (Berkeley: University of California Press, 2009); Daniel Immerwahr, *How to Hide an Empire: A History of the Greater United States* (New York: Farrar, Straus and Giroux, 2019); Paul A. Kramer, "A Useful Corner of the World: Guantánamo," *New Yorker*, July 30, 2013.

7. A similar dynamic about the varieties of US imperial forms plays out in: Megan Black, *The Global Interior: Mineral Frontiers and American Power* (Cambridge, MA: Harvard University Press, 2018), 7–12. See also: Emily S. Rosenberg, *Financial Missionaries to the World: The Politics and Culture of Dollar Diplomacy, 1900–1930* (Durham: Duke University Press, 2003 [1999]), 71–77. For more analysis of how investment interests interacted with and amplified the imperial

visions of US policymakers, see also Peter James Hudson, "The National City Bank of New York and Haiti, 1909–1922," *Radical History Review* 2013, no. 115 (2013); John M. Hart, *Empire and Revolution: The Americans in Mexico since the Civil War* (Berkeley: University of California Press, 2002); Cyrus Veeser, *A World Safe for Capitalism: Dollar Diplomacy and America's Rise to Global Power* (New York: Columbia University Press, 2002); Hudson, *Bankers and Empire*; Thomas McCormick, "From Old Empire to New: The Changing Dynamics and Tactics of American Empire," in *Colonial Crucible: Empire in the Making of the Modern American State*, eds. Alfred W. McCoy and Francisco A. Scarano (Madison: University of Wisconsin Press, 2009).

8. Vanessa Ogle, "'Funk Money': The End of Empires, the Expansion of Tax Havens, and Decolonization as an Economic and Financial Event," *Past and Present* (2020).

9. According to the World Bank, the US GDP constituted roughly 25 percent of the world's total in 2022 ($25.5 trillion of a total $101 trillion). By contrast, its share in the 1960s was closer to 35–40 percent. See, for example, The World Bank, "GDP (Current US$)," 2023, accessed July 5, 2023, https://data.worldbank.org/indicator/NY.GDP.MKTP.CD; Govind Bhutada, "The U.S. Share of the Global Economy over Time," 2021, https://www.visualcapitalist.com/u-s-share-of-global-economy-over-time/.

10. See, for example, Serkan Arslanalp, Barry Eichengreen, and Chima Simpson-Bell, "The Stealth Erosion of Dollar Dominance and the Rise of Nontraditional Reserve Currencies," *Journal of International Economics* 138 (2022).

11. See, for example, Barry Eichengreen, "Is De-Dollarisation Happening?" CEPR, 2023, https://cepr.org/voxeu/columns/de-dollarisation-happening; Tyler Cohen, "What De-Dollarization? The Dollar Rules the World," *Bloomberg*, April 23, 2023; Diego Lasarte, "Putin Is Strengthening the Yuan's Role as Russia's Foreign Currency of Choice," *Quartz*, March 21, 2023.

12. "Total Assets of the Federal Reserve, Recent Balance Sheet Trends," Board of Governors of the Federal Reserve System, March 22, 2023, https://www.federalreserve.gov/monetarypolicy/bst_recenttrends.htm.

13. See, for example, "China's Belt and Road Initiative," *The Economist*, February 6, 2020.

14. "China's Overseas Development Finance Database," Boston University, 2023, July 4, 2023, https://www.bu.edu/gdp/chinas-overseas-development-finance/; "China's Latest Attempt to Rally the World against Western Values," *The Economist*, April 27, 2023.

15. Hyman P. Minsky, "Central Banking and Money Market Changes," *Quarterly Journal of Economics* 71, no. 2 (1957); Charles P. Kindleberger, *A Financial History of Western Europe* (Routledge, 2015). I owe thanks to Nic Johnson for development of this argument.

16. For recent analysis of the role of the Federal Reserve in response to crisis, see Lev Menand, *The Fed Unbound: Central Banking in a Time of Crisis* (New York: Columbia Global Reports, 2022); Jenna Smialek, *Limitless: The Federal Reserve Takes on a New Age of Crisis* (New York: Knopf, 2023); Leon Wansleben, *The Rise of Central Banks: State Power in Financial Capitalism* (Cambridge: Harvard University Press, 2023); Christine Desan, "How to Spend a Trillion Dollars: Our Monetary Hardwiring, Why It Matters, and What to Do About It," *SSRN* (2022); Christine Desan and Nadav Orian Peer. "The Constitution and the Fed after the Covid-19 Crisis," JustMoney.org, 2020, https://justmoney.org/the-constitution-and-the-fed-after-the-covid-19-crisis-2/.

17. Excellent accounts of different dimensions of IBC's history appear in: Hudson, *Bankers and Empire*, 55–79; Hart, *Empire and Revolution*, 91–103.

18. See, for example, future analysis of the dataset referenced in Sebastian Alvarez and Gianandrea Nodari, "Argentina Banking System in the Interwar Period: Stylized Facts in the Light of a New Database, 1925–1935," (Asociación Española de Historia Económica, 2023).

19. Morgan Ricks, "Money as Infrastructure," *Columbia Business Law Review* 3 (2018): 757–851.

20. See, for example, Theodore M. Porter, *Trust in Numbers: The Pursuit of Objectivity in Science and Public Life* (Princeton, NJ: Princeton University Press, 1996); Bruno Latour, *Science in Action: How to Follow Scientists and Engineers through Society* (Cambridge, MA: Harvard University Press, 1987); Sheila Jasanoff, "Ordering Knowledge, Ordering Society," in *States of Knowledge: The Co-Production of Science and Social Order*, ed. Sheila Jasanoff (London; New York: Routledge, 2004); Bruno Latour, *Reassembling the Social: An Introduction to Actor-Network-Theory* (Oxford: Oxford University Press, 2005); Mary S. Morgan, "Travelling Facts," in *How Well Do Facts Travel? The Dissemination of Reliable Knowledge*, eds. Peter Howlett and Mary S. Morgan (Cambridge, UK: Cambridge University Press, 2011).

21. Both Perry Mehrling and Christine Desan make powerful use of the term "alchemy" in their insightful analyses of banking. See, for example, Perry G. Mehrling, "Retrospectives: Economists and the Fed: Beginnings," *Journal of Economic Perspectives* 16, no. 4 (2002): 210; Christine Desan, "Coin Reconsidered: The Political Alchemy of Commodity Money," *Theoretical Inquiries in Law* 11, no. 1 (2010): 361.

22. Mehrling, "Retrospectives," 210.

23. For more on the chief features of an infrastructural analysis, see Mary Bridges, "The Infrastructural Turn in Historical Scholarship," *Modern American History* (2023): 1–18.

24. On the quasi-invisibility and taken-for-granted-ness of infrastructures, see David Pinzur, "Infrastructural Power: Discretion and the Dynamics of Infrastructure in Action," *Journal of Cultural Economy* 14, no. 6 (2021): 644–61; Keller Easterling, "Histories of Things That Don't Happen and Shouldn't Always Work," *Social Research* 83, no. 3 (2016): 625–44; Susan Leigh Star and Geoffrey C. Bowker, "How to Infrastructure," in *Handbook of New Media: Social Shaping and Consequences of ICTs*, eds. Leah A. Lievrouw and Sonia Livingstone (London: SAGE Publications, Ltd, 2002), 151–62.

25. Patrick Joyce, *The Rule of Freedom: Liberalism and the Modern City* (London: Verso, 2003), 12.

26. For scholarship in this tradition, see Andrew J. Bacevich, "Tragedy Renewed: William Appleman Williams," *World Affairs* 171, no. 3 (2009); Paul A. Kramer, "Embedding Capital: Political-Economic History, the United States, and the World," *Journal of the Gilded Age and Progressive Era* 15 (2016). Foundational texts linked to the "Wisconsin School" of US foreign relations include: William Appleman Williams, *The Tragedy of American Diplomacy* (Cleveland: World Publishing Company, 1959); Lloyd C. Gardner and William Appleman Williams, eds., *Redefining the Past: Essays in Diplomatic History in Honor of William Appleman Williams* (Corvallis: Oregon State University Press, 1986); Walter LaFeber, *The New Empire: An Interpretation of American Expansion, 1860–1898* (Ithaca, NY: Cornell University Press, 1963). Articulation of the promotional state appears powerfully in: Emily S. Rosenberg, *Spreading the American Dream: American Economic and Cultural Expansion, 1890–1945*, American Century Series (New York: Hill and Wang, 1982); *Financial Missionaries to the World: The Politics and Culture of Dollar Diplomacy, 1900–1930* (Durham, NC: Duke University Press, 2003 [1999]); Burton Ira Kaufman,

Efficiency and Expansion: Foreign Trade Organization in the Wilson Administration, 1913–1921, Contributions in American History (Westport, CT: Greenwood Press, 1974).

27. As quoted in: Martin J. Sklar, "Dollar Diplomacy according to Dollar Diplomats: American Development and World Development," in *The United States as a Developing Country: Studies in U.S. History in the Progressive Era and the 1920s,* ed. Martin J. Sklar (Cambridge, UK: University of Cambridge, 1992), 82.

28. Veeser, *A World Safe for Capitalism*; Hudson, *Bankers and Empire.*

29. Rebca Gomez Betancourt, "The Political Economy of a Modern Missionary: E. W. Kemmerer in the Philippines," *History of Political Economy* 53, no. 3 (2022); Emily S. Rosenberg, "Foundations of United States International Financial Power: Gold Standard Diplomacy, 1900–1905," *Business History Review* 59, no. 2 (1985); Paul W. Drake, *The Money Doctor in the Andes: The Kemmerer Missions, 1923–1933* (Durham, NC: Duke University Press, 1989); Carl Parrini, "Charles A. Conant, Economic Crises and Foreign Policy, 1896–1903," in *Behind the Throne: Servants of Power to Imperial Presidents, 1898–1968,* edited by Thomas J. McCormick and Walter LaFeber (Madison: University of Wisconsin Press, 1993), 35–66; Carl P. Parrini and Martin J. Sklar, "New Thinking about the Market, 1896–1904: Some American Economists on Investment and the Theory of Surplus Capital," *Journal of Economic History* 43, no. 3 (1983): 559–78.

30. Rosenberg, *Spreading the American Dream: American Economic and Cultural Expansion, 1890–1945,* 89–105; Emily S. Rosenberg and Norman L. Rosenberg, "From Colonialism to Professionalism: The Public-Private Dynamic in United States Foreign Financial Advising, 1898–1929," *Journal of American History* 74, no. 1 (1987). See also Black; Jenifer Van Vleck, *Empire of the Air: Aviation and the American Ascendancy* (Cambridge, MA: Harvard University Press, 2013); Stephen A. Schuker, "Money Doctors between the Wars: The Competition between Central Banks, Private Financial Advisers, and Multilateral Agencies, 1919–39," in *Money Doctors: The Experience of International Financial Advising, 1850–2000,* ed. Marc Flandreau (London; New York: Routledge, 2003).

31. Edward S. Fertik, "Steel and Sovereignty: The United States, Nationalism, and the Transformation of World Order, 1898–1941" (PhD diss., Yale University, 2018); Adam Tooze and Ted Fertik, "The World Economy and the Great War," *Geschichte und Gesellschaft* 40, no. 2 (2014); Barry Eichengreen, "The U.S. Capital Market and Foreign Lending, 1920–1955," in *Developing Country Debt and Economic Performance, Volume 1: The International Financial System,* ed. Jeffrey D. Sachs (Chicago: University of Chicago Press, 1991); Trevin Stratton, "Mammon Unbound: The International Financial Architecture of Wall Street Banks, 1915–1925," in *The Impact of the First World War on International Business,* eds. Andrew Smith, Kevin Tennent, and Simon Mollan (New York: Routledge, 2016; reprint, Published on Academia.edu).

32. The twelve regional Federal Reserve Banks are themselves chartered as private corporations; however, the book largely focuses on the work of the Federal Reserve Board, which is a federal government agency that reports to Congress. Moreover, it focuses on regulations around eligible assets, which is determined by Congress and interpreted by the board. Thus, the functionality that is central to this project involved its state-based obligation to "furnish an elastic currency, to afford means of rediscounting commercial paper, to establish a more effective supervision of banking in the United States," per the 1913 Federal Reserve Act. US Congress. *Federal Reserve Act: Public Law 63–43, 63d Congress, H.R. 7837: An Act to Provide for the Establishment of Federal Reserve Banks, to Furnish an Elastic Currency, to Afford Means of Rediscounting Commercial Paper, to Establish a More Effective Supervision of Banking in the United States, and for Other Purposes.* 1913. See also

"Who Owns the Federal Reserve?" Board of Governors of the Federal Reserve System, nd., accessed March 22, 2023, https://www.federalreserve.gov/faqs/about_14986.htm.

33. Others have highlighted this gap between metropolitan intentions and lived realities. See, for example, Veeser, *A World Safe for Capitalism.*

34. See, for example, Hudson, *Bankers and Empire*; Yoshiko Nagano, *State and Finance in the Philippines, 1898–1941: The Mismanagement of an American Colony* (Singapore: NUS Press, 2015); Allan Lumba, *Monetary Authorities: Capitalism and Decolonization in the American Colonial Philippines* (Durham, NC: Duke University Press, 2022); Hudson, "The National City Bank of New York and Haiti, 1909–1922."

35. As Adam Tooze has described, prior to 1914, "America was less relevant than Serbia." See Tooze, "The Rise and Fall and Rise (and Fall) of the U.S. Financial Empire," *Foreign Policy,* January 15, 2021; J. Adam Tooze, *The Deluge: The Great War, America and the Remaking of the Global Order, 1916–1931* (New York: Viking, 2015), 6–7. As noted in a presentation by Nic Johnson to the Understanding Political Economy Lab workshop series, online, March 2023.

36. Several recent works exploring interwar internationalism have emphasized economic affairs as fertile terrain for deploying new expertise, political arrangements, and understandings of sovereignty. See, for example, Nicholas Mulder, *The Economic Weapon: The Rise of Sanctions as a Tool of Modern War* (New Haven, CT: Yale University Press, 2022); Jamie Martin, *The Meddlers: Sovereignty, Empire, and the Birth of Global Economic Governance* (Cambridge, MA: Harvard University Press, 2022); "Globalizing the History of the First World War: Economic Approaches," *The Historical Journal* 65, no. 3 (2022); Katherine C. Epstein, "The Conundrum of American Power in the Age of World War I," *Modern American History* 2, no. 3 (2019).

37. Analyses of exceptionalism and its staying power in historical debate abound. See, for example, David C. Engerman, "Empires, Visible and Invisible," *Modern Intellectual History* 18, no. 1 (2021); Daniel Rodgers, "Exceptionalism," in *Imagined Histories: American Historians Interpret Their Past,* eds. Anthony Molho and Gordon S. Wood (Princeton, NJ: Princeton University Press, 1998); Kramer, "Embedding Capital"; "Power and Connection: Imperial Histories of the United States in the World," 116 (2011); Daniel Rodgers, "American Exceptionalism Revisited," *Raritan* 24, no. 2 (2004); Ian Tyrrell, "American Exceptionalism in an Age of International History," *American Historical Review* 96, no. 4 (1991).

38. For different versions of this debate, see, for example, "H-Diplo Teaching Roundtable Xxi-20 on Teaching the American Empire Debate," H-Net, 2019, accessed April 13, 2023, https://hdiplo.org/to/RT21-20; Tyrone Groh and James Lockhart, "Is America an Empire?" *War on the Rocks,* August 27, 2015; Engerman, "Empires, Visible and Invisible"; Kramer, "Power and Connection: Imperial Histories of the United States in the World."

39. International Banking Corporation: Charter, 1901, Item #631, IBC, Charter, Heritage Collection at Citi (hereafter Citi).

40. Dirk De Young, Yankee Finance on the Seven Seas, 1925, RG 7, Yankee Finance. Citi.

41. Hudson, *Bankers and Empire,* 54–80; Hart, *Empire and Revolution,* 91–103.

42. On the geopolitical implications of bankers' acceptances, see Nicholas A. Lambert, *Planning Armageddon: British Economic Warfare and the First World War* (Cambridge, MA: Harvard University Press, 2012), 111–16, 169–74; Harold James, "The Warburgs and Yesterday's Financial Deterrent," in *People, Nations and Traditions in a Comparative Frame: Thinking about the Past with Jonathan Steinberg,* edited by D'Maris Coffman, Harold James, Nicholas Di Liberto, and Georg Kreis, 59–70.

43. The rules for what counted as a bankers' acceptance changed over the course of the 1910s and 1920s. Initially, bankers' acceptances were trade acceptances between buyers and sellers that had been guaranteed by a bank. Because international trade presented greater challenges related to time required to ship goods and information about the creditworthiness of a buyer—among other obstacles—bankers' acceptances represented a way to substitute the credit of the bank, which typically had greater prestige and name recognition, for the credit of individual firms. Such a substitution lowered the barriers to international trade. By 1916, the eligibility guidelines for acceptances were expanded to include domestic transactions as well, but their usage for such functions continued to be rather limited, as chapters 3 and 4 discuss. For a helpful explanation of the theory of acceptances, see Benjamin Haggott Beckhart, *The New York Money Market, Vol. 3: Uses of Funds* (New York: AMS Press, 1971 [1932]), 256–68.

44. Barry Eichengreen and Marc Flandreau, "The Federal Reserve, the Bank of England, and the Rise of the Dollar as an International Currency, 1914–1939," *Open Economies Review* 23, no. 1 (2012): 73.

45. Susie Pak, *Gentlemen Bankers: The World of J.P. Morgan* (Cambridge, MA: Harvard University Press, 2013); P. J. Cain and A. G. Hopkins, "Gentlemanly Capitalism and British Expansion Overseas II: New Imperialism, 1850–1945," *Economic History Review* 40, no. 1 (1987); Mark Brayshay, Mark Cleary, and John Selwood, "Social Networks and the Transnational Reach of the Corporate Class in the Early-Twentieth Century," *Journal of Historical Geography* 33, no. 1 (2007).

46. For context on the expansiveness of Bretton Woods, see Barry Eichengreen, *Global Imbalances and the Lessons of Bretton Woods* (Cambridge, MA: MIT Press, 2010); Jeffry Frieden, "The Political Economy of the Bretton Woods Agreements: Together with Scholarly Commentaries and Essential Historical Documents," in *Bretton Woods Agreements*, eds. Naomi Lamoreaux and Ian Shapiro (New Haven, CT: Yale University Press, 2019); Eric Helleiner, *States and the Re-Emergence of Global Finance: From Bretton Woods to the 1990s* (Ithaca, NY: Cornell University Press, 1994); Barry Eichengreen, *Globalizing Capital: A History of the International Monetary System* (Princeton, NJ: Princeton University Press, 1996); Vanessa Ogle, "Global Capitalist Infrastructure and U.S. Power," in *The Cambridge History of America and the World: Volume 4: 1945 to the Present*, eds. David C. Engerman, Max Paul Friedman, and Melani McAlister (Cambridge, UK: Cambridge University Press, 2022); Martin, *The Meddlers: Sovereignty, Empire, and the Birth of Global Economic Governance*.

47. "1977 Focus Shifts to Retail Banking." Citigroup, nd., April 7, 2023, https://www.citigroup.com/global/about-us/heritage/1977/focus-shifts-to-retail-banking.

Chapter 1: The Empire Needs a Banker

1. Paul D. Hutchcroft, "Colonial Masters, National Politicos, and Provincial Lords: Central Authority and Local Autonomy in the American Philippines, 1900–1913," *Journal of Asian Studies* 59, no. 2 (2000): 283–87.

2. Peter Hudson also highlights the role of "rogue" bankers in enabling the early work of US multinational banking: Hudson, *Bankers and Empire*, 13. On the work of rogue agents and capitalism's "gangsters," see also, Katz, *Gangsters of Capitalism*.

3. Hudson's work tracks a similar dynamic whereby a motley assemblage of US bankers operating in the Caribbean enacted, extended, and reframed racialized hierarchies that were

central to the functioning of US capitalism: "The question of racism here is not merely one of individual beliefs but one of institutional policy, not simply one of personal sentiment but one of political-economic structure." See Hudson, *Bankers and Empire*, 14.

4. Vincent P. Carosso, *The Morgans: Private International Bankers, 1854–1913* (Cambridge, MA: Harvard University Press, 1987), 173–218.

5. Zachary Karabell, *Inside Money: Brown Brothers Harriman and the American Way of Power* (New York: Penguin, 2021); Edwin J. Perkins, *Financing Anglo-American Trade: The House of Brown, 1800–1880* (Cambridge, MA: Harvard University Press, 1975).

6. Ron Chernow, *The House of Morgan: An American Banking Dynasty and the Rise of the Modern Finance* (New York: Atlantic Monthly Press, 1990), 35–38.

7. For more about the agent networks of preeminent multinational banks, see Rainer Liedtke, "Agents for the Rothschilds," in *Mobility and Biography*, ed. Sarah Panter (Berlin: De Gruyter Oldenbourg, 2016); Manuel Llorca-Jaña, "Huth & Co's Credit Strategies: A Global Merchant-Banker's Risk Management, C. 1810–1850," *Estudios de Economía* 42, no. 2 (2015); Emily Buchnea, "Bridges and Bonds: The Role of British Merchant Bank Intermediaries in Latin American Trade and Finance Networks, 1825–1850," *Enterprise & Society* 21, no. 2 (2020).

8. Charles W. Calomiris and Stephen H. Haber, *Fragile by Design: The Political Origins of Banking Crises and Scarce Credit* (Princeton, NJ: Princeton University Press, 2014), 153–95; Eugene Nelson White, "The Political Economy of Banking Regulation, 1864–1933," *Journal of Economic History* 42, no. 1 (1982). The rule specified that "usual business be transacted at an office or banking house located in the place specified in its organizational certificate," and regulators interpreted the language to preclude the operation of both foreign and domestic branches. As cited by: J. Lawrence Broz, *The International Origins of the Federal Reserve System* (Ithaca, NY: Cornell University Press, 1997), 21.

9. Geoffrey Jones, "Competitive Advantages in British Multinational Banking since 1890," in *Banks as Multinationals*, ed. Geoffrey Jones (London; New York: Routledge), 31.

10. A.S.J. Baster, *The International Banks* (New York: Arno Press, 1977 [1935]), 40.

11. See, for example, Carosso, *The Morgans: Private International Bankers*, 148, 218, 458–59; Chernow, *The House of Morgan*, 46–48.

12. The literature on the nineteenth-century gold standard is vast. See, in particular, Steven Bryan, *The Gold Standard at the Turn of the Twentieth Century: Rising Powers, Global Money, and the Age of Empire* (New York: Columbia University Press, 2010); Eichengreen, *Globalizing Capital: A History of the International Monetary System*; Barry J. Eichengreen and Marc Flandreau, *The Gold Standard in Theory and History* (London: Routledge, 1997); Marcello De Cecco, *The International Gold Standard: Money and Empire*, 2nd ed. (London: F. Pinter, 1984).

13. Eugene Agger, "Correspondence Course in Foreign Exchange and International Banking," ed. National City Bank of New York (1917), Division 2, Paper 1.

14. Bryan, *The Gold Standard at the Turn of the Twentieth Century*, 49.

15. H. A. Shannon, "Evolution of the Colonial Sterling Exchange Standard," *Staff Papers (International Monetary Fund)* 1 (1950): 334–54.

16. Parrini and Sklar, "New Thinking about the Market"; Parrini, "Charles A. Conant"; Rosenberg, "Foundations of United States International Financial Power"; Nicholas P. Johnson, "The Inter-Imperial and Pan-American Origins of the Federal Reserve Act of 1913, and the Birth of the Global Dollar System" (University of Chicago, 2018).

17. Mulder, *The Economic Weapon*, 33.

18. Nicholas A. Lambert, *Planning Armageddon: British Economic Warfare and the First World War* (Cambridge, MA: Harvard University Press, 2012), 67.

19. Mulder, *The Economic Weapon*, 34.

20. Rosenberg, "Foundations of United States International Financial Power," 170.

21. Paul Philip Abrahams, *The Foreign Expansion of American Finance and Its Relationship to the Foreign Economic Policies of the United States, 1907–1921* (New York: Arno Press, 1976), Reprint of author's thesis, University of Wisconsin, 8.

22. Clyde William Phelps, *The Foreign Expansion of American Banks: American Branch Banking Abroad* (New York: Ronald Press Co., 1927), 48.

23. Department of Commerce, *Sources of Foreign Credit Information*, A. S. Hillyer, Washington, DC: Government Printing Office, 1924, 10.

24. Frank H. H. King, David J. S. King, and Catherine E. King, *The History of the Hongkong Bank in Late Imperial China, 1864–1902: On an Even Keel*, 4 vols., vol. 1, The History of the Hongkong and Shanghai Banking Corporation (Cambridge, UK: Cambridge University Press, 1987).

25. King, *The History of the Hongkong Bank in Late Imperial China, 1864–1902*, 87.

26. Frank H. H. King, *The Hongkong Bank in the Period of Imperialism and War, 1895–1918* (1988), 153–74.

27. See, for example, Alfred T. Mahan, *The Influence of Sea Power upon History, 1660–1805* (Novato, CA: Presidio Press, 1987 [1890]); Frederick Jackson Turner, *The Significance of the Frontier in American History* (London: Penguin, 2008 [1893]). For interpretations of these thinkers' influence, see Walter LaFeber, "A Note on the "Mercantilistic Imperialism" of Alfred Thayer Mahan," *Mississippi Valley Historical Review* 48, no. 4 (1962); Frederick Jackson Turner and John Mack Faragher, *Rereading Frederick Jackson Turner: "The Significance of the Frontier in American History" and Other Essays* (New Haven, CT; London: Yale University Press, 1999).

28. See, for example, Rosenberg, "Foundations of United States International Financial Power," 170; Shannon, "Evolution of the Colonial Sterling Exchange Standard."

29. Rosenberg, "Foundations of United States International Financial Power." See also Rosenberg, *Financial Missionaries*.

30. Roy Ybanez, "The Hongkong Bank in the Philippines, 1899–1941," in *Eastern Banking: Essays in the History of the Hongkong and Shanghai Banking Corporation*, ed. Frank H. H. King (London: Athlone Press, 1983), 237–39.

31. Marcellus Hartley, *A Brief Memoir* (New York: Privately Printed, 1903).

32. Roscoe Carlyle Buley, *The Equitable Life Assurance Society of the United States: One Hundredth Anniversary History, 1859–1959* (New York: Appleton-Century-Crofts, 1959).

33. Under the original charter, the bank's name was the "International Corporation," but the bank changed its name several months after its founding. See "International Banking Corporation: Charter," 1901.

34. Hartley, *A Brief Memoir*, 52.

35. Originally the charter listed the bank's name as the International Company: "International Banking Corporation: Charter," 1901.

36. "A Few Gratuitous Privileges," *Hartford Courant*, January 6, 1902. See also "Many Branch Banks to Be Established," *New York Times*, January 2, 1902; "Moyer Succeeds Snyder," *New York Tribune*, November 22, 1902.

37. William L. Higgins, Letter to the International Banking Corporation, September 2, 1931, Board Shareholders Files 1, Item 79 State of Connecticut—Secretary's Office, Citi; C. O. Moore, [Letter to Hon. William L. Higgins, Secretary of State of Connecticut], September 5, 1931, Board Shareholders Files 1, Item 79 State of Connecticut—Secretary's Office, Citi.

38. Henry N. Butler, "Nineteenth-Century Jurisdictional Competition in the Granting of Corporate Privileges," *Journal of Legal Studies* 14, no. 1 (1985): 149.

39. Naomi R. Lamoreaux and John Joseph Wallis, "Economic Crisis, General Laws, and the Mid-Nineteenth-Century Transformation of American Political Economy," *Journal of the Early Republic* 41, no. 3 (2021).

40. Christopher Collier, "New England Specter: Town and State in Connecticut History, Law and Myth," *Connecticut Historical Society Bulletin* 3–4 (1995). For more about Connecticut's "town-rule" legislature, see Clarence Deming, "Town Rule in Connecticut," *Political Science Quarterly* 4, no. 3 (1889).

41. Meeting of the Directors of the International Banking Corporation, December 20, 1901, 7, Annual Directors Meeting Minutes, Citi.

42. Media reports suggest that Paige was involved in Connecticut bank chartering activities: "State Whipping Post," *Hartford Courant*, March 1, 1901.

43. Hart, *Empire and Revolution*, 93.

44. Mitchell C. Harrison, *New York State's Prominent and Progressive Men, Vol. 1* (New York: New York Tribune, 1902), 60–61.

45. "Retirement of Henry S. Manning," *Iron Trade Review*, January 19, 1905.

46. "International Banking Concern," *New York Tribune*, December 13, 1903.

47. A graduate of Bowdoin College, Hubbard became a major booster for the school, and he insisted on hiring many Bowdoin graduates to work at IBC. Hubbard endowed the school's library, which is still known as Hubbard Hall. Henry S. See Burrage, *Thomas Hamlin Hubbard: Bvt. Brigadier General U.S. Vols* (Portland, 1923); "Gen. T. H. Hubbard, Financier, Dead," *New York Times*, May 20, 1915; "Campus and Buildings," Bowdoin College, March 29, 2023, https://www.bowdoin.edu/about/campus-location/facilities/campus-and-buildings.html.

48. Richard White, *Railroaded: The Transcontinentals and the Making of Modern America* (New York: W. W. Norton & Co., 2012).

49. Data sources for infographic: Patricia Beard, *After the Ball: Gilded Age Secrets, Boardroom Betrayals, and the Party That Ignited the Great Wall Street Scandal of 1905*, New York: HarperCollins, 2003; "Equitable Fight Is Hot," *New York Tribune*, April 5 1905, 1; Mitchell C. Harrison, *New York State's Prominent and Progressive Men, Vol 1*, New York: New York Tribune, 1902, 3–4, 60–61; "Juan M. Ceballos Dies in His Office," *New York Times*, February 2 1913, 11; Richard White, *Railroaded: The Transcontinentals and the Making of Modern America*, New York: W. W. Norton & Co., 2012; William B. McCash and June Hall McCash, *The Jekyll Island Club: Southern Haven for America's Millionaires*, Athens: University of Georgia Press, 1989, 107–9; Sven Beckert, *The Monied Metropolis: New York City and the Consolidation of the American Bourgeoisie, 1850–1896*, Cambridge, UK: Cambridge University Press, 2001; "Mr. Carnegie Sheps Out," *Chicago Daily Tribune*, May, 6 1899, 1; John M. Hart *Empire and Revolution: The Americans in Mexico since the Civil War*, Berkeley: University of California Press, 2002, 95–99. Images: IBC Board List: "International Banking Corporation [Advertisement]," *The Straits Times*, October 3, 1902. (1) James W. Alexander: Harrison, *New York State's Prominent and Progressive Men*, p. 3.

(2) Juan M. Ceballos: ibid., 60. (3) Henry Clay Frick: Henry C. Frick, nd., George Grantham Bain Collection, LC-DIG-ggbain-07131, Library of Congress, Prints and Photographs Division. (4) Edwin Gould: Edwin Gould, Portrait Bust, nd., George Grantham Bain Collection, LC-DIG-ggbain-00795, Library of Congress, Prints and Photographs Division. (5) James Hazen Hyde: James Hazen Hyde, Three-Quarter Length Portrait, Seated, Facing Right, c1904, LCPP003B-43051, Library of Congress, Prints and Photographs Division. (6) Alfred Gwynne Vanderbilt: Alman & Co, [Alfred Gwynne Vanderbilt, Three-Quarter Length Portrait, Standing, Facing Front, Wearing Top Hat and Holding Gloves], 1907, Alfred Gwynne Vanderbilt, LC-USZ62–118342, Prints & Photographs Division, Library of Congress.

50. Subscription Agreement, December 20, 1901, RG 7, Annual Directors Meeting Minutes, Citi; Hart, *Empire and Revolution*, 96.

51. Buley, *The Equitable Life Assurance Society of the United States*,106.

52. Cochran, "The International Banking Corporation during the Chairmanship of Thomas H. Hubbard 1901–1915."

53. Equitable leaders James W. Alexander, James H. Hyde, and William H. McIntyre all served on IBC's board through 1904 but discontinued their involvement the following year. *Moody's Manual of Railroads and Corporation Securities* (New York: Moody Manual Co., 1904); *Moody's Manual of Railroads and Corporation Securities*, (New York: Moody Publishing Co., 1905).

54. IBC bears similarities in this overlap between railroad interests and banking with the Western National Bank, which also invested in railroad development in the US West. General Thomas Hubbard had board seats on both IBC and Western National, as did at least six members of Western's and IBC's boards. Equitable was so enmeshed with Western National's work that IBC seems almost like the international outgrowth of their thicket of entangled Gilded Age elites, many of whom commanded extensive political power. See "Two Banks Consolidate: The Western National Absorbs the United States National," *New York Tribune*, November 20, 1897; Hart, *Empire and Revolution*, 93; "Western National Bank Meeting," *New York Tribune*, January 30, 1903; James W. Alexander, Juan M. Ceballos, Marcellus Hartley, Thomas H. Hubbard, James H. Hyde, and Valentine P. Snyder are the key interlocks. See "Elections of the Banks: Few Changes Made in the Directorates of National and State Institutions," *New York Times*, January 10, 1900; "The International Bank: Secretary Gage Not Chosen to Succeed Marcellus Hartley," *New York Times*, January 23, 1902; "Many Branch Banks to Be Established." "Western National Bank Meeting." Notably, future Secretary of State Elihu Root also sat on Western's board, but it's unclear if the relationships he would have developed with future IBC board members affected IBC's future selection as a government fiscal agent.

55. Benjamin O. Fordham, "Protectionist Empire: Trade, Tariffs, and United States Foreign Policy, 1890–1914," *Studies in American Political Development* 31, no. 2 (2017): 179; Rosenberg, "Foundations of United States International Financial Power."

56. James M. Morgan, *Recollections of a Rebel Reefer* (Boston: Houghton Mifflin, 1917), 475.

57. Bishop had developed a close relationship to Theodore Roosevelt when Roosevelt was New York City's police commissioner and Bishop served as editor of New York's *Evening Post*. See Charles O. Bishop, *The Lion and the Journalist: The Unlikely Friendship of Theodore Roosevelt and Joseph Bucklin Bishop* (Guilford, CT: Lyons Press, 2012), vi.

58. Bishop, *The Lion and the Journalist*, vi. See also Joseph Bucklin Bishop, Letter to Theodore Roosevelt, January 21, 1904, Theodore Roosevelt Papers, http://www.theodorerooseveltcenter .org/Research/Digital-Library/Record.aspx?libID=043800. Library of Congress Manuscript

Division, Theodore Roosevelt Digital Library; Theodore Roosevelt, Letter to Joseph Bucklin Bishop, January 22, 1904, Theodore Roosevelt Digital Library, http://www.theodoreroosevelt center.org/Research/Digital-Library/Record.aspx?libID=o187162, Library of Congress Manuscript Division; Letter to Joseph Bucklin Bishop, October 30, 1903, Theodore Roosevelt Digital Library, http://www.theodorerooseveltcenter.org/Research/Digital-Library/Record.aspx?libID =o186328, Library of Congress Manuscript Division.

59. "Plans of New Oriental Bank: International Corporation to Develop the Trade of Far East," *San Francisco Chronicle*, January 3, 1902; "About People and Social Incidents: At the White House," *New York Tribune*, December 17, 1901; "The White House Dinner: Prince Entertained in Great East Room by the President," *New York Times*, February 25, 1902.

60. "Fiscal Agents in Orient: An American Corporation Will Supplant the English Bankers," *Washington Post*, January 1, 1902.

61. W. Murray Crane, [Letter to My Dear Mr. President], December 22, 1901, Theodore Roosevelt Papers, Reel 23, Library of Congress.

62. [Letter to My Dear Mr. President], August 23, 1902, Theodore Roosevelt Papers, Reel 29, Library of Congress; "[Letter to My Dear Mr. President]," 1901, Theodore Roosevelt Papers, Reel 29, Library of Congress.

63. John J. McCook, [Letter to Hon. Theodore Roosevelt], November 2, 1901, Theodore Roosevelt Papers, Reel 20, Library of Congress.

64. [Letter to Mr. President], August 19, 1904, Theodore Roosevelt Papers, Reel 46, Library of Congress.

65. "The Connecticut Muddle," *New York Tribune*, March 9, 1891; "State Whipping Post."

66. IBC Executive Committee, Executive Committee Meeting Minutes, 1902–1905, Item #335–1, Citi, February 7, 1902.

67. Guy Cary, Comments [Letter to G. S. Rentschler], August 24, 1943, RG 7, History of IBC - Cochran (1943–1965). Citi; "Hankow" also appears as "Hankou" in some writings and translations.

68. IBC Executive Committee, 1902–1905, February 27, 1903.

69. "Many Branch Banks to Be Established."

70. De Young, Yankee Finance on the Seven Seas, 1925.

71. Hudson, *Bankers and Empire*, 70.

72. IBC Executive Committee, 1902–1905, March 24, 1902.

73. See, for example, Josephus Daniels, Letter to the Secretary of the Treausury, June 5, 1915, RG 80, Folder 14708–11, National Archive.

74. Another US bank, Guaranty Trust of New York, was also initially named a fiscal agent in Manila, and the bank briefly operated a branch in Manila. However, Guaranty Trust closed its branches in Asia after several months and transferred the "goodwill of the Guaranty Trust Company's business" to IBC in places where it formerly operated. See Balance of Funds, Manila, March 31, 1903, RG 350, Box 418, Folder 5500, National Archive; Guaranty Trust Company of New York, [Announcement of Withdrawal], February 4, 1904, RG 350, Box 418, Folder 5500, National Archive.

75. Philippine Banks: Abstraction of Reports of Philippine Banks, December 31, 1903, 101, PC46–28, Philippines, National Archives.

76. Youssef Cassis, *City Bankers, 1890–1914* (Cambridge, UK: Cambridge University Press, 1994), 185–95. See, for example, Charles Jones, "The Transfer of Banking Techniques from

Britain to Argentina, 1862–1914," *Revue internationale d'histoire de la banque* 26 (1983); David Joslin, *A Century of Banking in Latin America—to Commemorate the Centenary in 1962 of the Bank of London & South America Limited* (London; New York: Oxford University Press, 1963), 42.

77. Compton Mackenzie, *Realms of Silver: One Hundred Years of Banking in the East* (London: Routledge, 1954), 192.

78. Marc-William Palen characterizes this drive as the "imperialism of economic nationalism." See Palen, "The Imperialism of Economic Nationalism, 1890–1913," *Diplomatic History* 39, no. 1 (2014).

79. Clarence R. Edwards, Memorandum for the Secretary of War, in the Matter of Securities for Deposits with the International Banking Corporation, May 24, 1910, RG 350, Box 799, Folder 17959, National Archive.

80. Elihu Root, Letter to the International Banking Corporation, June 21, 1902, RG 350, Box 418, Folder 5500, National Archive.

81. See, for example, International Banking Corporation, [Multiple Letters to War Department, Bureau of Insular Affairs], 1904, RG 350, Box 418, Folder 5500, National Archive; Clarence R. Edwards, Lettter to J. S. Tait, International Banking Corporation, December 9, 1904, RG 350, Box 418, Folder 5500, National Archive.

82. Memorandum for Major McIntyre, May 10, 1909, RG 350, Box 799, Folder 17959, National Archive; Jacob Dickinson, Letter to Gen. Hubbard, International Banking Corporation, June 1, 1910, RG 350, Box 799, Folder 17959, National Archive; "Memorandum for Major McIntyre," 1909; F. C. Boggs, Letter to the International Banking Corporation, April 24, 1915, RG 7, IBC, Citi; Frank McIntyre. Letter to H.T.S. Green. 1917, RG 350, Box 890, Folder 17959–137, National Archive; Clarence R. Edwards, Memorandum for the Secretary of War, April 24, 1911, RG 350, Box 799, Folder 17959, National Archive.

83. "Memorandum for the Secretary of War, in the Matter of Securities for Deposits with the International Banking Corporation," 1910.

84. "Memorandum for Major McIntyre," 1909.

85. Charles Vevier, *The United States and China, 1906–1913: A Study of Finance and Diplomacy* (New Brunswick, NJ: Rutgers University Press, 1969), 106–09; Hudson, *Bankers and Empire*, 72–73.

86. "The American Group," *Far Eastern Review* 6 (1910); "Hankow-Szechuan Railroad Loan and the State Department," *Wall Street Journal*, February 16, 1910.

87. Ian James Bickerton, "Bankers, Businessmen, and the Open Door Policy, 1899–1911" (PhD diss., Claremont Graduate University, 1974), 245.

88. L. A. Doherty, Fourth Brief for the International Banking Corporation on the Subject of the Transfer from Shanghai to the United States of the Chinese Indemnity, March 18, 1914, Safekeeping Documents 1 (1904–1926), Item #335: 1911–1915, Citi.

89. Frank H. H. King, "The Boxer Indemnity: 'Nothing but Bad,'" *Modern Asian Studies* 40, no. 3 (2006): 671–73.

90. IBC Executive Committee, Executive Committee Meeting Minutes, 1914–1918, Item #355–3, IBC, Citi, June 10, 1915.

91. IBC Executive Committee, Executive Committee Meeting Minutes, 1914–1918, Item #355–3, IBC, Citi, Oct. 3.

92. IBC Executive Committee, Executive Committee Meeting Minutes, 1914–1918, Item #355–3, IBC, Citi, Oct. 3.

93. Bureau of Insular Affairs, Confidential Office Memorandum, May 9, 1908, RG 350, Box 799, Folder 17959, National Archive.

94. James M. Morgan, [Letter to Helie], December 23, 1903, #524 James Morris Morgan Papers, Folder 4, The Wilson Library, University of North Carolina at Chapel Hill.

Chapter 2: Protocols and Penmanship

1. Daniel De Menocal, Memoirs of Daniel De Menocal, 1961, RG 12, Folder: De Menocal, Citi, 13.

2. De Menocal, Memoirs of Daniel De Menocal, 13; "Seventy Years in Asia," *Overseas Citibanker* 2 (1972). On IBC's involvement with opium trade, see Selwin Tait, Letter to Honorable Robert Bacon, Acting Secretary of State, December 3, 1908, 59, M862, Reel 106 - 774 / 487, National Archives; IBC Executive Committee, Executive Committee Meeting Minutes, 1905–1914, Item #335–2, Citi.

3. De Menocal, Memoirs of Daniel De Menocal, 1961.

4. For more context on the role of clerical work in making turn-of-the-century capitalism, see Michael Zakim, "Bookkeeping as Ideology," *Common-place* 6, no. 3 (2006); "Paperwork," *Raritan* 33, no. 4 (2014); *Accounting for Capitalism: The World the Clerk Made* (Chicago: University of Chicago Press, 2018); Caitlin Rosenthal, "Balancing the Books: Convergence and Diversity of Accounting in Massachusetts, 1875–1895," *Journal of Economic History* 80, no. 3 (2020). See also "Penmanship," *No. 8* 11, no. 3 (1916).

5. For additional literature about the interimperial origins of US foreign power, see Stephen Tuffnell, "Engineering Inter-Imperialism: American Miners and the Transformation of Global Mining, 1871–1910," *Journal of Global History* 10, no. 1 (2015); Paul A. Kramer, "Empires, Exceptions, and Anglo-Saxons: Race and Rule between the British and United States Empires, 1880–1910," *Journal of American History* (2002); Allan Lumba, "Empire, Expansion, and Its Consequence," in *A Companion to the Gilded Age and Progressive Era*, eds. Christopher M. Nichols and Nancy C. Unger, Wiley Blackwell Companions to American History (West Sussex: Wiley-Blackwell, 2017).

6. For the overarching contours of British multinational banking, see Baster, *The International Banks*, 153; Jones, "Banks as Multinationals"; "Competitive Advantages in British Multinational Banking since 1890." US contemporaries also took Britain to be the model of international banking. See, for example, Marc Flandreau and Stefano Ugolini, "Where It All Began: Lending of Last Resort and the Bank of England during the Overend, Gurney Panic of 1866," in *The Origins, History, and Future of the Federal Reserve: A Return to Jekyll Island*, eds. Michael D. Bordo and William Roberds (New York: Cambridge University Press, 2013), 115.

7. Stanley Chapman, *The Rise of Merchant Banking* (London: Routledge, 2006 [1984]), 11. On the expansion and diversification of British merchant banks in Latin America, see also Rory Miller, "The London Capital Market and Latin American Public Debt, 1860–1930," in *La Deuda Publica En America Latina En Perspectiva Historica*, ed. Reinhard Liehr (Frankfurt, Madrid: Vervuert, 1995), 101.

8. For more on the nineteenth-century British merchant and overseas banking, see Geoffrey Jones, *British Multinational Banking, 1830–1990* (Oxford: Oxford University Press, 1995); Joslin, *A Century of Banking in Latin America*; Jones, "Banks as Multinationals," 3; Chapman, *The Rise of Merchant Banking*; Llorca-Jaña, "Huth & Co's Credit Strategies."

9. Joslin, *A Century of Banking in Latin America*, 36–42.

10. See, for example, Charles A. Jones, "British Financial Institutions in Argentina, 1860–1914" (University of Cambridge, 1973), 35. On the conservative reputation of British banks, see also Department of Commerce, *Banking Opportunities in South America*, William H. Lough, Washington: Government Printing Office, 1915, 30–41.

11. As Lamoreaux notes, prioritizing liquid assets was not just a norm of British bankers. Increasingly in the late nineteenth century, East Coast US banks began abiding by the "50 percent rule," which held that a borrower's liabilities should not exceed 50 percent of his quick assets. See Naomi R. Lamoreaux, *Insider Lending: Banks, Personal Connections, and Economic Development in Industrial New England* (Cambridge, UK: Cambridge University Press, 1997), 103.

12. Joslin, *A Century of Banking in Latin America*, 36–42.

13. Charles Jones, "The Transfer of Banking Techniques," 257.

14. I am indebted to Rory Miller for detailed explanations of these mechanics. See, for example, Robert Greenhill and Rory Miller, "British Trading Companies in South America after 1914," in *The Multinational Traders*, ed. Geoffrey Jones (London: Routledge, 1998); Jones, *British Multinational Banking*.

15. King, *The Hongkong Bank in the Period of Imperialism and War, 1895–1918*, 73.

16. On their conservative reputation, see, for example, Lough, [Department of Commerce], "Banking Opportunities in South America," 32; Baster, *The International Banks*, 152–55.

17. Jones, *British Multinational Banking*, 374.

18. Perkins, *Financing Anglo-American Trade*, 130.

19. Chapman, *The Rise of Merchant Banking*, 70–71.

20. Some British banks maintained a practice of keeping "character books" wherein managers and bank staff recorded direct experience with clients as well as local news items, reports from peers, and other locally sourced information. See Lucy Newton, "Trust and Virtue in Banking: The Assessment of Borrowers by Bank Managements at the Turn of the Twentieth Century," *Financial History Review* 7, no. 2 (2000): 178; Neil C. Quigley, "Bank Credit and the Structure of the Canadian Space Economy C. 1890–1935" (PhD diss., University of Toronto, 1986), 252.

21. For more on reputational banking in the British system, see also Olivier Accominotti, Delio Lucena, and Stefano Ugolini, "The Origination and Distribution of Money Market Instruments: Sterling Bills of Exchange during the First Globalisation," *Economic History Review* 74, no. 4 (2021): 907–18;; Francesco L. Galassi and Lucy Newton, "My Word Is My Bond: Reputation as Collateral in Nineteenth Century English Provincial Banking," (University of Warwick, Department of Economics, 2001).

22. P. L. Cottrell, "Great Britain," in *International Banking, 1870–1914*, eds. Rondo Cameron et al. (New York: Oxford University Press, 1992), 42. On intermarriage in London banking more generally, see also Cassis, *City Bankers*; Brayshay, Cleary, and Selwood, "Social Networks and the Transnational Reach of the Corporate Class in the Early-Twentieth Century."

23. Cottrell, "Great Britain," 26.

24. Charles Jones, "The Transfer of Banking Techniques," 260.

25. James M. Barker, Letter to Mr. Trafford, January 30, 1923, James M. Barker Papers, Box 52, Folder 1174, Newberry Library, Special Collections.

26. See, for example, Rory Miller, "British Investment in Latin America, 1850–1950: A Reappraisal," *Itinerario* 19, no. 3 (1995): 38.

27. For contemporaries' accounts on the limited role of formal education in banking, see, for example, "Training Its Men to Do the Work," *Nation's Business*, September 1916; "Mobilizing Trained Minds for Commercial Preparedness," *The Americas* 2, no. 8 (1916). On the history of commercial and business education in the early twentieth century, see also Cristina V. Groeger, "A 'Good Mixer': University Placement in Corporate America, 1890–1940," *History of Education Quarterly* 58, no. 1 (2018); Carter A. Daniel, *MBA: The First Century* (Lewisburg, PA: Bucknell University Press, 1998); Rakesh Khurana, *From Higher Aims to Hired Hands: The Social Transformation of American Business Schools and the Unfulfilled Promise of Management as a Profession* (Princeton, NJ; Woodstock: Princeton University Press, 2010).

28. P. G. Wodehouse, *Psmith in the City* (London: A. & C. Black, 1910), 176.

29. King et al., *The History of the Hongkong Bank in Late Imperial China*, 1 and 219.

30. Wodehouse, *Psmith in the City*, 34.

31. Wodehouse, 38.

32. King, *The Hongkong Bank in the Period of Imperialism and War, 1895–1918*, 173.

33. King, *The Hongkong Bank in the Period of Imperialism and War, 1895–1918*, 174–75.

34. Cassis, *City Bankers*, 311.

35. Joseph Durrell, History of Foreign Branches of American Banks and Overseas Division, NCB, 1940, Citi; "Report of the President, Bowdoin College, 1914–1915," (Brunswick, Maine: Bowdoin College, 1915); Burrage, *Thomas Hamlin Hubbard*; "Seventy Years in Asia"; "Campus and Buildings."

36. "Special Training Classes Conducted by the Bank, City Company and I.B.C.," *No. 8* 14, no. 7 (1919); "I.B.C.'S Training Divided between New York and London Offices," *No. 8* 14, no. 6 (1919).

37. Citicorp, *Citicorp in China: A Colorful, Very Presonal History since 1902* (Citicorp [Citibank], 1989), 32.

38. W. M. Simmons. Those "Good Old Days," July 25, 1972, RG 7, History of International Banking Corporation—Employee Memoirs. Citi.

39. Citicorp, *Citicorp in China*, 32.

40. George S. Moore, *The Banker's Life* (New York: W. W. Norton, 1987), 176.

41. Cochran, "The International Banking Corporation during the Chairmanship of Thomas H. Hubbard 1901–1915," 16.

42. De Menocal, Memoirs of Daniel De Menocal, 1961.

43. Peter Starr, *Citibank: A Century in Asia* (Singapore: Editions Didier Millet, 2002), 29–30.

44. Bureau of Insular Affairs Confidential Office Memorandum. May 9, 1908. RG 350, Box 799, Folder 17959. National Archive.

45. "Sobriety" and "mode of life" were both listed as conditions of IBC's hiring contract. See The International Banking Corporation Terms of Engagement, March 10, 1920, Series 2: Hall Family Collection, East Texas Research Center, R. W. Steen Library, Stephen F. Austin University. Bankers' papers suggest that colleagues' behavior and lifestyles, from health constraints to frequent alcohol consumption, at times complicated banking operations. See Cochran, "The International Banking Corporation during the Chairmanship of Thomas H. Hubbard

1901–1915," 17; De Menocal, Memoirs of Daniel De Menocal, 16. This challenge was not specific to IBC. See also [American Consul in Para - Brazil], Closing of the American Mercantile Bank of Brazil Inc., January 16, 1922, 59, 7592, 811.51632, National Archives; James M. Barker, Letter to Mr. Trafford, March 15, 1927, James M. Barker Papers, Box 52, Folder 1175, Newberry Library, Special Collections.

46. See, for example, G. Martel Hall. [Letter to Mother and Father], January 13, 1924, Series 1: Hall Family Collection, 7, 7, East Texas Research Center, R. W. Steen Library, Stephen F. Austin University; Memorandum for Executive Committee: International Banking Corporation, January 10, 1917, RG 7, IBC, Correspondence, Memoranda and Organizational Documents of Harry Green—C, Citi.

47. De Young, Yankee Finance on the Seven Seas, 1925. See also Cochran, "The International Banking Corporation during the Chairmanship of Thomas H. Hubbard 1901–1915." On the high proportion of British staff, see also Starr, Citibank: A Century in Asia, 30.

48. Jones, Charles. "The Transfer of Banking Techniques from Britain to Argentina, 1862–1914." Revue internationale d'histoire de la banque 26 (1983): 257.

49. Chapman, The Rise of Merchant Banking, 70.

50. Memorandum in Reference to International Banking Corporation. June 20, 1945. Citi, RG 7, History of IBC - Cochran (1943–1965).

51. Lamoreaux, Insider Lending, 5.

52. Lamoreaux, Insider Lending, 4.

53. Lamoreaux, Insider Lending, 102.

54. Starr, Citibank: A Century in Asia, 54.

55. For example, in 1920, the committee approved an advance of $540,000 for the Pacific Commercial Co. to refinance dishonored drafts for the financing of sugar shipments from Manila. Meanwhile, when Calamba Sugar Estates Co. had requested an advance of $500,000, the request was denied, "unless satisfactorily secured or otherwise suitably guaranteed." The minutes do not provide any greater detail about the basis for approving one and rejecting the other. See International Banking Corporation, Executive Committee Meetings 1918–1921, Citi, Item #355, IBC.

56. Starr, Citibank: A Century in Asia, 54.

57. IBC Executive Committee, "Executive Committee Meeting Minutes," 1902–1905, June 3, 1904. See also H. E. Westcott, International Banking Corporation: Report on Manila Branch and Consolidated Balance Sheet of the Corporation as of December 30th, 1905, May 4, 1907, RG 350, Box 420, Folder 5500, National Archive.

58. IBC Executive Committee, "Executive Committee Meeting Minutes," 1902–1905, August 22, 1904; International Banking Corporation, "The Philippine Islands" (New York: Brown, Lent & Pett, 1908); Percival Fansler, "New Railways in the Philippine Islands," Cassier's Magazine 30, no. 2 (June 1906).

59. IBC Executive Committee, "Executive Committee Meeting Minutes," 1905–1914, April 11, 1912; "International Banking Corporation," Wall Street Journal, October 6, 1903.

60. IBC Executive Committee, "Executive Committee Meeting Minutes," 1902–1905, April 16, 1902.

61. "Executive Committee Meeting Minutes," 1905–1914, 141.

62. Yen-p'ing Hao, "A 'New Class' in China's Treaty Ports: The Rise of the Comprador-Merchants," Business History Review 44, no. 4 (1970).

63. Starr, *Citibank: A Century in Asia*, 32.

64. Reprinted in "The Comprador: A Great Factor in Chinese Trade," *Bulletin of the National Association of Credit Men* 5, no. 12 (1905).

65. Ghassan Moazzin, "Sino-Foreign Business Networks: Foreign and Chinese Banks in the Chinese Banking Sector, 1890–1911," *Modern Asian Studies* (2019).

66. King, *The Hongkong Bank in the Period of Imperialism and War, 1895–1918*, 75.

67. Chongyi Shou and Leying Shou, "Wai Shang Yin Hang Zai Zhongguo [Foreign Banks in China]," (Beijing: Zhongguo wen shi chu ban she, 1996).

68. Moazzin, "Sino-Foreign Business Networks: Foreign and Chinese Banks in the Chinese Banking Sector, 1890–1911," *Modern Asian Studies*, 2019.

69. Kaori Abe, *Chinese Middlemen in Hong Kong's Colonial Economy, 1830–1890* (London: Routledge, 2018), 5.

70. Ghassan Moazzin, *Foreign Banks and Global Finance in Modern China: Banking on the Chinese Frontier, 1870–1919* (Cambridge, UK: Cambridge University Press, 2022), 78–93; "Sino-Foreign Business Networks: Foreign and Chinese Banks in the Chinese Banking Sector, 1890–1911."

71. Shou and Shou, "Wai Shang Yin Hang Zai Zhongguo [Foreign Banks in China]."

72. As quoted by Starr, *Citibank: A Century in Asia*, 32.

73. Starr, *Citibank: A Century in Asia*, 33.

74. Starr, *Citibank: A Century in Asia*, 32; Candido Emilio Ozorio, A Brief History of the Shanghai Branch of the National City Bank of New York, 1900–1932, 1940, RG 12/ Bank Histories, A Brief History of the National City Bank of New York—Shanghai Branch, Citi.

75. As quoted by Starr, Starr, *Citibank: A Century in Asia*, 32.

76. De Menocal, Memoirs of Daniel De Menocal, 50.

77. De Menocal, Memoirs of Daniel De Menocal, 15.

78. "The Currents of Merchandising in the Orient and the South Pacific," *The Americas*, December 1918, 14.

79. Bankers' private papers are littered with such references to dinners at social clubs and at the homes of European and US elites. See, for example, Kermit Roosevelt, Diary, 1915, Kermit Roosevelt and Belle Roosevelt Papers, Box 2, Library of Congress; W. Cameron Forbes, W. Cameron Forbes Papers, 1921–1924, 1921, II, Houghton Library, Harvard University, 506; James M. Barker, Autobiography, 1954, James M. Barker Papers, Box 85, Folder 1588, Newberry Library, Special Collections, 68; G. Martel Hall, [Letter to Mother and Father], October 15, 1922, Series 1: Hall Family Collection, 6, 31, East Texas Research Center, R. W. Steen Library, Stephen F. Austin University; De Menocal, Memoirs of Daniel De Menocal, 1961.

80. For more on the racialized hierarchies and social worlds of US businesspeople and families working in China, see Nan Enstad, *Cigarettes, Inc.: An Intimate History of Corporate Imperialism* (Chicago: University of Chicago Press, 2018), 86–119.

81. King, *The Hongkong Bank in the Period of Imperialism and War, 1895–1918*, 103; Nagano, *State and Finance in the Philippines, 1898–1941*, 9; Ybanez, The Hongkong Bank in the Philippines, 1899–1941."

82. Thiravet Pramuanratkarn, "The Hongkong Bank in Thailand: A Case of a Pioneering Bank," 421; H.L.D. Selvaratnam, "The Guarantee Shroffs, the Chettiars, and the Hongkong Bank in Ceylon," 409; "Delmege: History," 2017, April 16, 2020, https://delmege.com/history/.

83. Moazzin, *Foreign Banks and Global Finance in Modern China: Banking on the Chinese Frontier, 1870–1919*, 24–52.

84. Cassis, *City Bankers*, 315.

85. Edwin J. Perkins, "Financing Antebellum Importers: The Role of Brown Bros. & Co. in Baltimore," *Business History Review* 45, no. 4 (1971).

86. Liedtke, "Agents for the Rothschilds." For more on British merchant banking intermediaries, see Buchnea, "Bridges and Bonds"; Manuel Llorca-Jaña, "Connections and Networks in Spain of a London Merchant-Banker, 1800–1850," *Revista de Historia Económica* 31, no. 3 (2013).

87. Foreign Branches, [nd], RG IBC, Box 496, Foreign Branch, Citi.

88. Moazzin, *Foreign Banks and Global Finance in Modern China: Banking on the Chinese Frontier, 1870–1919*, 109–49.

89. Bickerton, "Bankers, Businessmen, and the Open Door Policy, 1899–1911," 245.

90. One exception was IBC involvement in railway financing in the Philippines, as the next chapter argues.

91. "Seventy Years in Asia," 7.

92. Citicorp, *Citicorp in China*, 32.

93. "Seventy Years in Asia," 8; Cochran, "The International Banking Corporation during the Chairmanship of Thomas H. Hubbard 1901–1915."

94. The bank's official staffing records do not list local hires in the early years. See, for example, List of 770 Employees in the Service of International Banking Corporation, November 1, 1920, Safekeeping Documents 2 (1902–1927), Item #335: 1918–1922, Citi; Harold van Cleveland and Thomas F. Huertas, *Citibank, 1812–1970* (Cambridge, MA: Harvard University Press, 1985), 89. Yet bankers' papers reveal the dominant role that local staff had in shaping branch operations. As one IBC banker in China noted, the ratio of Chinese staff to US and European hires was forty to three. See G. Martel Hall, [Letter to Mother and Father], August 29, 1919, Series 1: Hall Family Collection, 6, 8, East Texas Research Center, R. W. Steen Library, Stephen F. Austin University. See also "With the Old Guard," January–February 1917, RG 2 / NCBNY, Aspersions, Citi.

95. De Menocal, Memoirs of Daniel De Menocal, 15.

96. This account comes from a banker for Guaranty Trust, which entered Chinese ports later than IBC. Nonetheless, the movement of silver and the complexity of settling local bank debts accords with more generalized impressions of IBC bankers regarding the complex movement of silver. See William C. Lane, "China and the United States," *The Guaranty News* 8, no. 3 (1919): 80–81.

97. Cassis calculates profits as a ratio of net profit to paid-up capital. See Cassis, *City Bankers*: "This enables us to measure the efficiency of the capital originally brought to the business" (187).

98. Karen Weise, "Amazon Reports Almost No Profit and Slowing Growth," *New York Times*, February 2, 2023; Tripp Mickle, Karen Weise, and Nico Grant, "Tech's Biggest Companies Discover Austerity, to the Relief of Investors," *New York Times*, February 2, 2023.

99. For analysis of turn-of-the-century challenges in corporate accounting and banking, see also A. J. Arnold, "Should Historians Trust Late Nineteenth-Century Company Financial Statements?" *Business History* 38, no. 2 (1996); Lamoreaux, *Insider Lending*, 96.

100. See, for example, Simmons, 1972; Starr, *Citibank: A Century in Asia*, 31.

101. Jones, *British Multinational Banking*, 479.

102. Bureau of Insular Affairs, Confidential Office Memorandum, 1908, RG 350, Box 799, Folder 17959, May 9, National Archive.

103. Cochran, "The International Banking Corporation during the Chairmanship of Thomas H. Hubbard 1901–1915."

104. IBC Executive Committee, "Executive Committee Meeting Minutes." 1902–1905.

105. IBC Executive Committee, "Executive Committee Meeting Minutes." 1902–1905.

106. Partial data is available for the first decade. In particular, statements for 1905 are not available and only half-year statements are available for 1906–9. However, complementary accounts come from IBC's internal records. See International Banking Corporation, Semi-Annual Statement of International Banking Corporation, 1904–1913, RG 350, Box 418, Folder 5500, National Archives, Cochran, [1945].

107. James H. Rodgers, Directors' Minutes, September 7, 1906, 7, Annual Directors Meeting Minutes, Citi.

108. Cassis, *City Bankers*, 189.

109. De Menocal, Memoirs of Daniel De Menocal, 58–73.

Chapter 3: Imperial Banking on the Ground

1. Different sources disagree as to the exact opening dates. Contemporary news sources report an opening date of June 9, 1902, while National City Bank's internal records suggest an opening in July. "The International Banking Corporation," *Journal of the American Asiatic Association* 3, no. 1 (1903); "Manila's First American Bank: Wall Street Enterprise Just Opening in the Philippines," *New York Times*, June 15, 1902; Joan Orendain, *Citibank: The Philippine Century (1902–2002)* (Manila, Philippines: Citibank, 2002).

2. "Fight Close to Manila," *Chicago Daily Tribune*, August 19, 1902; Christopher J. Einolf, *America in the Philippines, 1899–1902: The First Torture Scandal* (New York: Palgrave Macmillan, 2014), chapter 6.

3. "Gloomy View: Locusts Attack Crops in the Philippines," *Boston Daily Globe* October 27, 1902; Daniel F. Doeppers, *Feeding Manila in Peace and War, 1850–1945*, New Perspectives in Southeast Asian Studies (Madison: University of Wisconsin Press, 2016).

4. Lewis E. Gleeck, *The Manila Americans (1901–1964)* (Manila, Philippines: Carmelo & Bauermann, 1977). Map, p. 33.

5. IBC's Manila branch reported 4.1 million pesos of government deposits, out of a total of 4.9 million deposits in January 1903. In 1904 and 1905, government deposits constituted roughly a third to a fourth of the branch's total deposit base. See Comparative Statement of the Financial Condition of the Manila Branch of the International Banking Corporation, January 21, 1903, RG 250, Box 418, 5500, National Archives II; "Balance of Funds, Manila," 1903. See also "Comparative Statements" for December 31, 1903, and 1904, as well as June 30, 1905.

6. Charles H. Darling. Special Order No. 33, December 22, 1902, RG 80, Box E19A, Folder 10424, National Archive.

7. "International Banking Corporation: Charter," 1901.

8. In doing so, it draws on recent scholarship on issues of US rule, resistance, and colonization in the Philippines. See, for example, Sarah Steinbock-Pratt, *Educating the Empire: American Teachers and Contested Colonization in the Philippines*, Cambridge Studies in US Foreign

Relations (Cambridge, UK: Cambridge University Press, 2019); Alvita Akiboh, "Pocket-Sized Imperialism: U.S. Designs on Colonial Currency," *Diplomatic History* 41, no. 5 (2017); Theresa Marie Ventura, "From Small Farms to Progressive Plantations: The Trajectory of Land Reform in the American Colonial Philippines, 1900–1916," *Agricultural History* 90, no. 4 (2016); Lumba, *Monetary Authorities: Capitalism and Decolonization in the American Colonial Philippines*; Lumba, "Imperial Standards: Colonial Currencies, Racial Capacities, and Economic Knowledge During the Philippine-American War," *Diplomatic History* 39, no. 4 (2015). More traditional works on resistance movements include: Motoe Terami-Wada, "The Sakdal Movement, 1930–34," *Philippine Studies* 36, no. 2 (1988); Milagros Camayon Guerrero, "Luzon at War: Contradictions in Philippine Society, 1898–1902" (PhD diss., University of Michigan, 1977). For a bibliography of recent histories of US colonial rule in the Philippines and of Filipino resistance, see Kramer, "How Not to Write the History of U.S. Empire."

9. John A. Larkin, *Sugar and the Origins of Modern Philippine Society* (Berkeley: University of California Press, 1993); Norman G. Owen, *Prosperity without Progress: Manila Hemp and Material Life in the Colonial Philippines* (Berkeley: University of California Press, 1984); Doeppers, *Feeding Manila in Peace and War, 1850–1945*.

10. Smith Bell and Company, *Under Four Flags: The Story of Smith, Bell, & Company in the Philippines* (Bristol, England: J. W. Arrowsmith, Ltd., 1972), 2.

11. Nagano, *State and Finance in the Philippines, 1898–1941*, 55–60.

12. Lewis E. Gleeck, *American Business and Philippine Economic Development* (Manila: Carmelo & Bauermann, 1975), 88; Bureau of Labor. *Labor Conditions in the Philippines*; Victor S. Clark, Washington, DC: Government Printing Office, 1905.

13. Owen, *Prosperity without Progress*, 190–92; Clark, Washington, DC: Government Printing Office, 1905.

14. See, for example, Justin F. Jackson, "'A Military Necessity Which Must Be Pressed': The U.S. Army and Forced Road Labor in Early American Colonial Philippines," in *On Coerced Labor: Work and Compulsion after Chattel Slavery*, eds. Marcel van der Linden and Magaly Rodriguez Garcia (London: Brill, 2016), 54–63; Harlan R. Crippen, "Philippine Agrarian Unrest: Historical Backgrounds," *Science & Society* 10, no. 4 (1946): 338; James S. Allen, "Agrarian Tendencies in the Philippines," *Pacific Affairs* 11, no. 1 (1938).

15. Ybanez, "The Hongkong Bank in the Philippines, 1899–1941," 440.

16. Ybanez, "The Hongkong Bank in the Philippines, 1899–1941," 438–40.

17. Epstein, "The Conundrum of American Power in the Age of World War I"; Rosenberg, *Spreading the American Dream: American Economic and Cultural Expansion, 1890–1945*; Carl P. Parrini, *Heir to Empire: United States Economic Diplomacy, 1916–1923* (Pittsburgh, PA: University of Pittsburgh Press, 1991 [1969]).

18. Veeser, *A World Safe for Capitalism*.

19. Colin D. Moore, "State Building through Partnership: Delegation, Public-Private Partnerships, and the Political Development of American Imperialism, 1898–1916," *Studies in American Political Development* 25, no. 1 (2011): 40.

20. Dean C. Worcester, *Coconut Growing in the Philippine Islands: Cost of Production and Profits, Copra Making* (War Department, Bureau of Insular Affairs, 1911), 1.

21. Edwards, "Memorandum for the Secretary of War, in the Matter of Securities for Deposits with the International Banking Corporation," 1910.

22. Image: International Banking Corporation, "The Philippine Islands."

23. Burrage, *Thomas Hamlin Hubbard*, 23–44.

24. Edwards, "Memorandum for the Secretary of War, in the Matter of Securities for Deposits with the International Banking Corporation," 1910.

25. Gleeck, *The Manila Americans (1901–1964)*, 66.

26. Henry Hooker Van Meter, *The Truth About the Philippines, from Official Records and Authentic Sources . . . A Reference Review* (Chicago: Liberty League, 1900); James H. Rodgers, Directors' Minutes, May 21, 1908, RG 7, Annual Directors Meeting Minutes, Citi.

27. IBC Executive Committee, "Executive Committee Meeting Minutes," 1902–1905; "Col. Charles D. Palmer," *New York Times*, October 5, 1940.

28. Gleeck, *American Business and Philippine Economic Development*, 119; *The Philippine Club*, (Boston: The Merrymont Press, 1930); Philip G. Eastwick, [Letter to Martin Egan], December 2, 1925, Martin Egan Papers, 14, Eastwick, Philip G. Pierpont Morgan Library.

29. For more about colonial education policies in the Philippines, see Steinbock-Pratt, *Educating the Empire*; Adrianne Marie Francisco, "From Subjects to Citizens: American Colonial Education and Philippine Nation-Making, 1900–1934" (PhD diss., University of California, Berkeley, 2015).

30. Hugo Miller, The Teaching of Business Methods in the Public Schools of the Philippine Islands, [1914], Walter W. Marquardt papers, Box 5, Volume: Special Files, Bentley Historical Library, University of Michigan.

31. Theresa Marie Ventura, "American Empire, Agrarian Reform and the Problem of Tropical Nature in the Philippines, 1898–1916" (PhD diss., Columbia University, 2009), chapter 4. For more about postal savings banks, see also R. Daniel Wadhwani, "The Institutional Foundations of Personal Finance: Innovation in U.S. Savings Banks, 1880s–1920s," *Business History Review* 85, no. Autumn (2011).

32. Walter W. Marquardt, The Encouragement of Thrift by the Bureau of Education, 1914, Walter W. Marquardt papers, 6, Volume: Bureau of Education: Activities, 1914, Bentley Historical Library, University of Michigan.

33. Nagano, *State and Finance in the Philippines, 1898–1941*, 23–24.

34. Betancourt, "The Political Economy of a Modern Missionary: E. W. Kemmerer in the Philippines"; Johnson, "The Inter-Imperial and Pan-American Origins of the Federal Reserve Act of 1913, and the Birth of the Global Dollar System"; Lumba, *Monetary Authorities: Capitalism and Decolonization in the American Colonial Philippines*.

35. Shannon, "Evolution of the Colonial Sterling Exchange Standard"; Rosenberg, "Foundations of United States International Financial Power."

36. Nagano, *State and Finance in the Philippines, 1898–1941*, 25.

37. Ybanez, "The Hongkong Bank in the Philippines, 1899–1941," 461.

38. Yoshiko Nagano, "Philippine 'Colonial Banking' during the American Period," *Philippine Review of Economics and Business* 36, no. 1 (1999).

39. See also Nagano, "The Agricultural Bank of the Philippine Government, 1908–1916," *Journal of Southeast Asian Studies* 28, no. 2 (1997); Nagano, "Philippine 'Colonial Banking' during the American Period"; Nagano, *State and Finance*; Allan Lumba, "Monetary Authorities: Market Knowledge and Imperial Government in the Colonial Philippines, 1892–1942" (PhD diss., University of Washington, 2013); Lumba, "Imperial Standards"; Ventura, "American

Empire, Agrarian Reform and the Problem of Tropical Nature in the Philippines, 1898–1916," chapter 4.

40. Nagano, "The Agricultural Bank of the Philippine Government, 1908–1916," 318.

41. *Annual Report of the Treasurer of the Philippine Islands* (Manila: Bureau of Printing, 1910), 16.

42. Ventura, "From Small Farms to Progressive Plantations," 459–83.

43. Ventura, "From Small Farms to Progressive Plantations," 473; Glenn Anthony May, *Social Engineering in the Philippines: The Aims, Execution, and Impact of American Colonial Policy, 1900–1913* (Quezon City: New Day Publishing, 1984), 172–74.

44. Ventura, "From Small Farms to Progressive Plantations," 464.

45. Gleeck, *American Business and Philippine Economic Development*, 120.

46. H. E. Westcott, International Banking Corporation: Report on Manila Branch and Consolidated Balance Sheet of the Corporation as of December 30, 1905. May 4, 1907, RG 350, Box 420, Folder 5500, National Archives.

47. Ybanez, "The Hongkong Bank in the Philippines, 1899–1941," 436; United States Commission to the Philippine Islands Department of State, *Report of the Philippine Commission to the President, Vol. 2*, Charles Denby et al. (Washington: Government Printing Office, 1900), 182.

48. Statement Showing the Condition of the Manila Branch of the International Banking Corporation . . . November 21, 190, RG 350, Box 419, 5, National Archives; B.H.H. Report of an Examination of the Financial Condition of the International Banking Corporation, Manila Branch, August 22, 1910, RG 350, Box 418, National Archives.

49. The final category of "other" borrowers includes US citizens who established business interests in the Philippines in the late nineteenth century, predating the US colonial regime, by working with British firms. Because the chapter's interest is understanding IBC's impact on the goals associated with the US colonial administration, such hybrid cases do not fall conveniently in the categories used here. Examples of such hybrid cases are rare, so for the coarse level of assessment conducted here, the four categories adequately describe the economic dynamics under review.

50. See, for example, Kwok-chu Wong, *The Chinese in the Philippine Economy, 1898–1941* (Quezon City, Philippines: Ateneo De Manila University Press, 1994). For more on the elaborate racial stratification under Spanish rule, see Paul A. Kramer, *The Blood of Government: Race, Empire, the United States, & the Philippines* (Chapel Hill: University of North Carolina Press, 2006), 43–44; Richard T. Chu, "'Catholic,' 'Mestizo,' 'Sangley': Negotiating 'Chinese' Identities in Manila 1870–1905" (PhD diss., University of Southern California, 2003); "The 'Chinese' and the 'Mestizos' of the Philippines: Towards a New Interpretation," *Philippine Studies* 50, no. 3 (2002): 327–70.

51. For context on the establishment of British business interests in the Philippines, see Frank R. Golay, "'Manila Americans' and the Philippine Policy: The Voice of American Business," in *The Philippine Economy and the United States in Past and Present Interactions*, ed. Norman G. Owen (Ann Arbor: Center for South and Southeast Asian Studies, University of Michigan, 1983), 1–35; Smith Bell and Company, *Under Four Flags*; Kramer, "Empires, Exceptions, and Anglo-Saxons: Race and Rule between the British and United States Empires, 1880–1910," 1315–53.

52. Thomas H. Hubbard, Subject: Security for Deposits of Philippine Government Money, May 13, 1910, 350, 799, 17959, National Archive.

53. Data Sources: H., B. H. Report of an Examination of the Financial Condition of the International Banking Corporation, Manila Branch, 1910, RG 350, Box 418, August 22, National Archives; Kwok-chu Wong, *The Chinese in the Philippine Economy, 1898–1941*, Quezon City, Philippines: Ateneo De Manila University Press, 1994, 39; "Americans in the Philippine Islands: Walter E. Olsen," *Journal of the American Chamber of Commerce in the Philippines* 1 (August 1921): 5; "Sanitary Steam Laundry Company's Installation," *Far Eastern Review*, March 1909, 354; "Helping the World to Be Better Shod," *Boot and Shoe Recorder* 72 (December 7, 1917): 33; Richard T. Chu, "'Catholic,' 'Mestizo,' 'Sangley': Negotiating 'Chinese' Identities in Manila 1870–1905," PhD diss., University of Southern California, 2003, 70; Gleeck, Lewis E. *The Manila Americans (1901–1964)*, Manila, Philippines: Carmelo & Bauermann, 1977, 53; Roy Ybanez, "The Hongkong Bank in the Philippines, 1899–1941," in *Eastern Banking: Essays in the History of the Hongkong and Shanghai Banking Corporation*, edited by Frank H. H. King, London: Athlone Press, 1983, 456; *Commercial Directory of Manila*. Manila, Philippines, 1901, 104; Peter W. Stanley, *A Nation in the Making: The Philippines and the United States, 1899–1921*, Cambridge, MA: Harvard University Press, 1974, 81. Image Sources: Fort Mills, courtesy of the National Museum of the United States Air Force.

54. "San Nicolas Iron Works," *Far East Review* (1906): 99; Norman G. Owen, *Prosperity without Progress*.

55. Smith Bell and Company, *Under Four Flags*.

56. Data Source: H., 1910. Roughly half of the bank's total loan portfolio in 1910 went to three entities, one of which was a Smith, Bell-linked consortium Analysis refers to the portfolio of secured loans. Collectively, Luzon Rice Mills Company; Gsell, Carlos; and Yu Biao Sontua borrowed $220,000 of the total $450,400 in loans inventoried. See Doeppers, *Feeding Manila in Peace and War, 1850–1945*, 55; Smith Bell and Company, *Under Four Flags*, 22.

57. *The Chronicle & Directory for China, Corea, Japan, the Philippines, Cochin-China, Annam, Tonquin, Siam, Borneo, Straits Settlements, Malay States, &C.*, (Hongkong: Daily Press Office, 1912), 1465.

58. Wong, *The Chinese in the Philippine Economy*, 39.

59. IBC loaned $2,250 to the North American Trading Company, a supply company considered to be part of the United States' "'commercial invasion' of the Orient." See "Point of View," *Western Christian Advocate*, March 5, 1902. See also Charles Ballentine, *As It Is in the Philippines* (New York: Lewis, Scribner & Co., 1902), 198.

60. "Americans in the Philippine Islands: Walter E. Olsen," *Journal of the American Chamber of Commerce in the Philippines* 1 (1921): 5.

61. "Sanitary Steam Laundry Company's Installation," *Far Eastern Review*, March 1909, 354.

62. Daniel R. Williams, *The Odyssey of the Philippine Commission* (Chicago: A. C. McClurg & Co., 1913); Gleeck, *The Manila Americans (1901–1964)*, 53.

63. Data source: H., 1910.

64. For example, San Nicolas Iron Works constructed ships for the US Navy, among its other work. The Philippine Tobacco Trust Company—which received a $12,000 loan—represented a consortium of tobacco growers and might have included US investors and interests. The firm was organized "under the auspices of the Rothschilds" in London, which suggests a preponderance of European and likely British interests. See "Philippine Tobacco Trust," *Hartford Courant*, December 6, 1901. The "Bell" in Smith, Bell & Company was New England-born Lawrence Bell

who became a partner in the British-Philippine firm in the 1850s; however, he left in 1862. The firm hired other US citizens, but its management was largely British. See Smith Bell and Company, *Under Four Flags*.

65. See also Lou Gopal, "Brias Roxas Story," *Manila Nostalgia*, 2014, June 24, 2020, http:// www.lougopal.com/manila/?p=2276. Nigel Gooding, "Philippine Business Firms: Hand-stamp Markings & Privately Printed Covers," 2019, May 3, 2020, https://www.nigelgooding.co .uk/Spanish/Business%20Firms/Adolfo%20Roensch%20&%20Co/AdolfoRoensch.pdf; *The Chronicle & Directory for China, Corea, Japan, the Philippines, Cochin-China, Annam, Tonquin, Siam, Borneo, Straits Settlements, Malay States, & C.*, (Hongkong: Daily Press Office, 1910), 1471.

66. Yoshihiro Chiba, "The 1919 and 1935 Rice Crises in the Philippines: The Rice Market and Starvation in American Colonial Times," *Philippine Studies* 58, no. 4 (2010): 527–31.

67. Wong, *The Chinese in the Philippine Economy*, 36–39.

68. IBC loaned a total of P62,411 to "Sy Chung Chim" and Siuliong & Co. "Sy Chung Chim" was most likely a misspelling of Siy Chong Lin (alias of Tomas Siy Cong Bieng), son of well-established Chinese businessman Benito Siy Cong Bieng. The family was involved in rice and abaca trade at the time, and fittingly, the security provided for the loan was rice. Siuliong & Co was an import-export partnership backed by Guillermo A. Cu Unjieng, one of Manila's most prominent businessmen. The firm was also listed as "most valued customer" of HSBC. See *Commercial Directory of Manila* (Manila, Philippines 1901); Wong, *The Chinese in the Philippine Economy*, 41–42.

69. The interests of Yu Biao Sontua constituted P90,000 ($45,000) in loans.

70. On bankers' observations of table manners in China, see De Menocal, Memoirs of Daniel De Menocal, 50.

71. Nagano, *State and Finance in the Philippines, 1898–1941*, 59. See also Hudson, *Bankers and Empire*, 68.

72. Lumba, "Monetary Authorities," 55–57.

73. Wong, *The Chinese in the Philippine Economy*, 41–42.

74. Treasury Department, *Annual Report of the Comptroller of the Currency*, Washington: Government Printing Office, 1905, 375; H. A. Cartwright, *Twentieth Century Impressions of British Malaya* (London: Lloyd's Great Britain Publishing Company, 1908), 143.

75. Gleeck, *American Business and Philippine Economic Development*, 118; Comparative Statement of the Financial Condition of the Manila Branch of the International Banking Corporation, January 21, 1904, RG 250, Box 418, 5500, National Archives II.

76. Westcott, H. E. International Banking Corporation: Report on Manila Branch and Consolidated Balance Sheet of the Corporation as of December 30th; IBC Executive Committee, "Executive Committee Meeting Minutes." 1902–1905.

77. Smith Bell and Company, *Under Four Flags*, 21.

78. Seung Woo Park, "Agrarian Transformation and Colonialism in the Context of Capitalist Development: An Historical-Comparative Study of Korea and the Philippines" (PhD diss., University of Georgia, 1991), 101–4; James S. Allen, "Agrarian Tendencies in the Philippines," *Pacific Affairs* 11, no. 1 (1938): 52–65; Rigoberto Tiglao, *The Philippine Coconut Industry: Looking into Coconuts* (Manila: Arc Publication, 1981).

79. See, for example, Allen, 61–63; Crippen, "Philippine Agrarian Unrest: Historical Backgrounds," 340–42.

80. Joan Orendain, *Citibank: The Philippine Century (1902–2002)* (Manila: Citibank, 2002), 51.

81. Barry Eichengreen et al., "Public Debt through the Ages," *IMF Working Paper* 2019 / 006 (2019): 10–15.

82. Marc Flandreau and Juan H. Flores, "Bonds and Brands: Foundations of Sovereign Debt Markets, 1820–1830," *Journal of Economic History* 69, no. 3 (2009).

83. Carosso, *The Morgans: Private International Bankers*, 615; International Banking Corporation, To the Stockholders, April 15, 1905, RG 350, Box 418, Folder 5500, National Archive.

84. Carosso, *The Morgans: Private International Bankers*, 111, 27–28, 428–32.

85. Ching-Chun Wang, "The Hankow-Szechuan Railway Loan," *American Journal of International Law* 5, no. 3 (1911).

86. "Claim to China Loan," *Washington Post*, July 24, 1909.

87. De Menocal, Memoirs of Daniel De Menocal, 36.

88. "The American Group," 523.

89. Data source for Figure 3: International Banking Corporation: Board of Directors, 1903, RG 350, Container #418, 5500–21, National Archives; *The Manual of Statistics: Railroads, Grain and Produce*, vol. 22, The Manual of Statistics (New York: Financial News Association, 1901).

90. By 1906, several of the bank's railroad-affiliated founders had left the board, including Edwin Gould and Alfred Vanderbilt. Nonetheless, more than one-third of the bank's 1906 board members held prominent leadership positions in railway lines. See *Moody's Manual of Corporation Securities*, Moody's Manual of Corporation Securities (New York: John Moody & Co., 1906).

91. Frank McIntyre, "Railroads in the Philippine Islands," *The Annals of the American Academy of Political and Social Science* 30 (1907).

92. May, *Social Engineering in the Philippines*, 163–66; The Philippine Railway Company—Board of Directors, June 29, 1907, RG 350, Box 726, Folder 15058. National Archive.

93. To Colin Moore, public-private partnerships on such infrastructure projects represent an "alternative means of state development." Peter Hudson characterizes IBC's participation in the syndicate as a "project of US colonial control in the Philippines." See Moore, "State Building through Partnership," 31; Hudson, *Bankers and Empire*, 69.

94. On the racialized foundations of US colonial rule in the Philippines, see Lumba, *Monetary Authorities: Capitalism and Decolonization in the American Colonial Philippines*; Ventura, "From Small Farms to Progressive Plantations"; Nagano, *State and Finance*; Kramer, *The Blood of Government Race, Empire, the United States, & the Philippines*; Lumba, "Monetary Authorities"; Paul A. Kramer, "Race-Making and Colonial Violence in the U.S. Empire: The Philippine-American War as Race War," *Diplomatic History* 30, no. 2 (2006).

95. "Philippine Railroad Building with Filipino Builders," *Railroad Gazette* 43, no. 11 (1907): 300.

96. "Philippine Railroad Building with Filipino Builders," 299.

97. "Philippine Railroad Building with Filipino Builders," 299.

98. May, *Social Engineering in the Philippines*, 164.

99. Frank McIntyre, Letter to Hon. J. Hampton Moore, Representative in Congress, January 24, 1914, RG 350, Box 711, Folder 14221, National Archive.

100. Letter to Hon. Frances Burton Harrison, Governor-General of the Philippine Islands, March 13, 1914, RG 350, Box 711, Folder 14221, National Archive.

101. Letter to Hon. Frances Burton Harrison, Governor-General of the Philippine Islands, March 13, 1914, RG 350, Box 711, Folder 14221, National Archive.

102. A. L. Flint, Letter to the International Banking Corporation, April 24, 1915, Safekeeping Documents 1 (1904–1926), Item #335: Panama Canal Zone (1910–1926), Citi; Boggs, Letter to the International Banking Corporation, 1915.

103. H.T.S. Green, Letter to Chief of Office, the Panama Canal, April 26, 1915, Safekeeping Documents 1 (1904–1926), Item #335: Panama Canal Zone (1910–1926), Citi; Certificate of Deposit of Bonds by the International Banking Corporation, June 5, 1918, #335, Safekeeping Documents, Panama Canal, 1910–1926, Citi; Certificate of Deposit of Bonds by the International Banking Corporation, May 5, 1915, #335, Safekeeping Documents, Panama Canal, 1910–1926, Citi. In a similar case several years later, IBC had to provide security for serving as a government depository in London in 1917, for disbursing funds to the army and navy. The bank borrowed $1 million in Treasury certificates from National City Bank—which had, at the time, acquired the majority share of IBC—in order to deposit the security with the Federal Reserve Bank of New York. See IBC Executive Committee, "Executive Committee Meeting Minutes," 1914–1918.

104. Assistant Cashier, [Letter to] the National City Bank of New York, December 31, 1926, Item #337, IBC, F.E.D.—General (1926–1930), Citi; "Philippine Railway Faces Receivership: Manila Government Is Reported Planning to Force Insolvency as Bonds Mature, Unpaid," *New York Times*, July 1, 1937.

105. "The Philippine Railway Company—Board of Directors," 1907.

106. Gleeck, *The Manila Americans (1901–1964)*, 66–67.

107. Gleeck, *The Manila Americans (1901–1964)*, 63. See also Lou Gopal, "Los Tamaraos Polo Club," 2015, April 17, 2019, http://www.lougopal.com/manila/?p=3000.

108. Kramer, "Empires, Exceptions, and Anglo-Saxons: Race and Rule between the British and United States Empires, 1880–1910," 1346.

109. "The New Manila Hotel," *Far Eastern Review* 6, no. 2 (1909): 185; William Cameron Forbes, *The Philippine Islands, Vol 2* (Boston: Houghton Mifflin, 1928).

110. "The New Manila Hotel," Committee on Insular Affairs. House of Representatives, *Administration of Philippine Lands, Part 2: Report by the Committee on Insular Affairs of the House of Representatives of Its Investigation of the Interior Department of the Philippine Government Touching the Administration of Philippine Lands and All Matters of Fact and Law Pertaining Therto, in Pursuance of House Resolution No. 795*, Government Printing Office, 1911.

111. Gleeck, *The Manila Americans (1901–1964)*, 85.

112. Gleeck, *The Manila Americans (1901–1964)*, 91; Manuel Luis Quezon III, "The Glory Days," *Philippine Tatler* (2007).

113. Ventura, "From Small Farms to Progressive Plantations," 466; José P. Apostol, *The Economic Policy of the Philippine Government: Ownership and Operation of Business* (Manila: University of the Philippines, 1927), 8.

114. Ventura, "From Small Farms to Progressive Plantations," 467–71.

115. The Mindoro Company: Charles J. Welch and Horace Havemeyer First Mortgage, April 24, 1914, #335, Safekeeping Documents, Rothschild, Archie Wilson, et al., Citi; Frank Hindman Golay, *Face of Empire: United States - Philippine Relations, 1898–1946* (Madison: University of Wisconsin-Madison, Center for Southeast Asian Studies, 1998), 134.

116. Larkin, *Sugar and the Origins of Modern Philippine Society*, 57.

117. "Last Payment to Friars," *Boston Daily Globe*, October 21, 1905.

118. "The Mindoro Company: Charles J. Welch and Horace Havemeyer First Mortgage," 1914.

119. Peter W. Stanley, *A Nation in the Making: The Philippines and the United States, 1899–1921* (Cambridge, MA: Harvard University Press, 1974), chapter 6.

120. As quoted in Stanley, *A Nation in the Making*, 151.

121. Volker Schult, "The San Jose Sugar Hacienda," *Philippine Studies* 39, no. 4 (1991): 461–62.

122. Stanley, *A Nation in the Making*, 158.

123. Golay, *Face of Empire*, 137–38.

124. H., B. H. Report of an Examination of the Financial Condition of the International Banking Corporation, Manila Branch, 1910, RG 350, Box 418, August 22, National Archives; Golay, *Face of Empire*, 138–39.

125. "Administration of Philippine Lands, Part 2: Report by the Committee on Insular Affairs of the House of Representatives of Its Investigation of the Interior Department of the Philippine Government Touching the Administration of Philippine Lands and All Matters of Fact and Law Pertaining Therto, in Pursuance of House Resolution No. 795," 1286.

126. For more on the pro-imperial stance on the US business community in Manila, see Stanley, *A Nation in the Making*, 189–210; Gleeck, *The Manila Americans (1901–1964)*, 103–7.

127. Kramer, *The Blood of Government Race, Empire, the United States, & the Philippines*, chapter 6.

128. "American-Philippine Company [Prospectus, Report #1, Report #2]," (New York: American-Philippine Company, 1912).

129. The Vegetable Oil Corporation, June 6, 1918, Manuel Luis Quezon papers, Reel 8, Bentley Historical Library, University of Michigan; "American-Philippine Co. To Get Dean C. Worcester's Aid," *Wall Street Journal*, February 5, 1914.

Chapter 4: US Imperial Power and the Fed

1. Office of the Comptroller of the Currency, *Annual Report of the Comptroller of the Currency, Vol 1*, Washington: Government Printing Office, 1918, 51–53.

2. Jennifer Pahlka, *Recoding America: Why Government Is Failing in the Digital Age and How We Can Do Better* (New York: Metropolitan Books, 2023), 202.

3. For more on banks and infrastructural power, see Benjamin Braun and Daniela Gabor, "Central Banking, Shadow Banking, and Infrastructural Power," (SocArXiv, 2019); Benjamin Braun and Kai Koddenbrock, "The Three Phases of Financial Power: Leverage, Infrastructure, and Enforcement," in *Capital Claims: Power and Global Finance*, eds. Benjamin Braun and Kai Koddenbrock (London: Routledge, 2022), 1–30; Wansleben; Bridges, "The Infrastructural Turn in Historical Scholarship."

4. Francesca Trivellato, *The Promise and Peril of Credit: What a Forgotten Legend about Jews and Finance Tells Us about the Making of European Commercial Society* (Princeton, NJ: Princeton University Press, 2019); Olivier Accominotti and Stefano Ugolini, "International Trade Finance from the Origins to the Present: Market Structures, Regulation, and Governance," in *The Oxford Handbook of Institutions of International Economic Governance and Market Regulation*, eds. Eric Brousseau, Jean-Michel Glachant, and Jérôme Sgard (New York: Oxford University Press, 2019).

5. Barry J. Eichengreen, Arnaud Mehl, and Livia Chiṭu, *How Global Currencies Work: Past, Present, and Future* (Princeton, NJ: Princeton University Press, 2018), 58.

6. Accominotti and Ugolini, "International Trade Finance"; Olivier Accominotti, Delio Lucena-Piquero, and Stefano Ugolini, "The Origination and Distribution of Money Market Instruments," *Economic History Review* 74, no. 4 (2021).

7. Under the 1863 and 1864 National Banking Acts, national banks were not allowed to engage in "selling their name," which courts and regulators interpreted as a ban on acceptances. See Marc Flandreau and Gabriel Geisler Mesevage, "The Separation of Information and Lending and the Rise of Rating Agencies in the USA (1841–1907)," *Scandinavian Economic History Review* 62, no. 3 (2014): 29.

8. Data sources for infographic: Jamieson Myles, "Steering the Wheels of Commerce: State and Enterprise in International Trade Finance, 1914–1929," University of Geneva, 2021, 59; Olivier Accominotti, Delio Lucena-Piquero, and Stefano Ugolini, "The Origination and Distribution of Money Market Instruments: Sterling Bills of Exchange During the First Globalization," *Economic History Review* 74, no. 4 (2021): 897; J. Gaspar, "Financing International Trade," Texas A&M University, Mays Business School, 2016, January 28, 2022, http://mays.tamu.edu /center-for-international-business-studies/wp-content/uploads/sites/14/2016/02/Chapter -19-Compatibility-Mode.pdf.

9. Accominotti and Ugolini, "International Trade Finance"; Trivellato, *The Promise and Peril of Credit.*

10. "The Mechanism of Exchange," *The Americas* 4, no. 2 (1917).

11. William Cronon, *Nature's Metropolis: Chicago and the Great West* (New York: W. W. Norton, 1991), 97–131.

12. For more on the political economy of negotiability, see also Samuel Segura Cobos, "Making Money Amnesiac: The 1882 Making of Modern Negotiability in the United Kingdom," *Capitalism: A Journal of History and Economics* 3, no. 1 (2022); Accominotti and Ugolini, "International Trade Finance," 5–10.

13. This was not the first US experience with bankers' acceptances. Acceptances had also existed in the antebellum United States; however, currency volatility during the Civil War caused merchants to insist on cash payments rather than selling on credit, and regulators barred banks entirely from dealing in the paper. See Jon R. Moen and Ellis W. Tallman, "The Call Loan Market in the U.S. Financial System Prior to the Federal Reserve System," *Federal Reserve Bank of Atlanta Working Papers*, no. 2003–43 (2003); Broz, *The International Origins of the Federal Reserve System*, 40–43.

14. Flandreau and Ugolini, "Where It All Began."

15. Accominotti, Lucena, and Ugolini, "The Origination and Distribution of Money Market Instruments," 21–27.

16. William Notz, "Export Trade Problems and an American Foreign Trade Policy," *Journal of Political Economy* 26, no. 2 (1918): 112; Mary O'Sullivan, "Past Meets Present in Policymaking: The Federal Reserve Act and the U.S. Moneymarket, 1913–1929," *UPIER Working Papers* 6, no. 18/4 (2018): 14.

17. The major exception involved the Manila branch and Philippine-related operations, which also used pesos and US dollars to dominate transactions. See IBC Executive Committee, "Executive Committee Meeting Minutes," 1905–1914.

18. John E. Rovensky, "The Development of Dollar Exchange," *Bulletin of the National Association of Credit Men* 17 (1917): 998.

19. Eichengreen, Mehl, and Chiţu, *How Global Currencies Work*, 61.

20. Agger, "Correspondence Course in Foreign Exchange and International Banking," Topic 1, page 5. Referenced by Jamieson Myles, "Steering the Wheels of Commerce: State and Enterprise in International Trade Finance, 1914–1929" (University of Geneva, 2021).

21. The value of annual exports of US merchandise from 1911–15 ranged between $2.1 billion and $2.7 billion. See *Historical Statistics of the United States, Colonial Times to 1970*, Bureau of the Census, Washington, DC: U.S. Dept. of Commerce, Bureau of the Census, 1975, 884.

22. Phelps, *The Foreign Expansion of American Banks*, 48. See also John E. Gardin, American Branch Banks Abroad, April 1919, 208.

23. Epstein, "The Conundrum of American Power in the Age of World War I," 345.

24. Benjamin J. Cohen, *Currency Statecraft: Monetary Rivalry and Geopolitical Ambition* (Chicago: University of Chicago Press, 2019). See also David M. Andrews, *International Monetary Power* (Ithaca, NY: Cornell University Press, 2012).

25. See, for example, Adam Tooze, "The Rise and Fall and Rise (and Fall) of the U.S. Financial Empire"; Cohen, *Currency Statecraft*.

26. On US economic advising to promote global uptake of the dollar, see, for example, Rosenberg, "Foundations of United States International Financial Power"; Nic Johnson, "The Imperial Fed," *Phenomenal World*, March 30, 2023.

27. Vincent P. Carosso and Richard Sylla, "U.S. Banks in International Finance," in *International Banking, 1870–1914*, eds. Rondo Cameron et al. (New York: Oxford University Press, 1992), 48.

28. Nadav Orian Peer, "Negotiating the Lender-of-Last-Resort: The 1913 Fed Act as a Debate over Credit Distribution," *NYU Journal of Law & Business* 15 (2019): 371.

29. See, for example, National Monetary Commission, Senate, *The Discount System in Europe*, Paul Moritz Warburg, Washington: Government Printing Office, 1910; Senate, *Interviews on the Banking and Currency Systems of England, Scotland, France, Germany, Switzerland, and Italy*, National Monetary Commission, US Government Printing Office, 1910; Barry Eichengreen, "Comments on 'Where It All Began: Lending of Last Resort and Bank of England Monitoring during the Overend, Gurney Panic of 1866,'" in *The Origins, History, and Future of the Federal Reserve: A Return to Jekyll Island*, eds. Michael D. Bordo and William Roberds (New York: Cambridge University Press, 2013), 162.

30. Flandreau and Ugolini, "Where It All Began," 115.

31. Perry G. Mehrling, *The New Lombard Street: How the Fed Became the Dealer of Last Resort* (Princeton, NJ: Princeton University Press, 2011), 33–34.

32. The rhetoric differentiated between productive and speculative credit in accordance with the "real bills" doctrine. See Ann-Marie Meulendyke, *U.S. Monetary Policy and Financial Markets* (Federal Reserve Bank of New York, 1998), 24; David Marshall, "Origins of the Use of Treasury Debt in Open Market Operations: Lessons for the Present," *Economic Perspective (Federal Reserve Bank of Chicago)* 26, no. 1 (2002): 45–48; Allan H. Meltzer, *A History of the Federal Reserve: Volume 1, 1913–1951* (Chicago: University of Chicago Press, 2003), 70–73. For more context on the real bills doctrine, see also Mehrling, "Retrospectives: Economists and the Fed: Beginnings"; Milton Friedman and Anna Jacobson Schwartz, *A Monetary History of the United States: 1867–1960* (Princeton, NJ: Princeton University Press, 1971), 279–80.

33. See, for example, Robert M. O'Hara, "Creating and Marketing of Bankers Acceptances," *Acceptance Bulletin* 7, no. 11 (1925); Paul M. Warburg, *The Federal Reserve System, Its Origin and Growth; Reflections and Recollections, Vol 2* (New York: Macmillan Co., 1930), 191–212.

34. Initially, some agrarian reformers objected to acceptances as too short-term to finance their goods. However, a series of debates and compromises helped assuage these interests and assure rural interests that a more comprehensive package of financial reforms—of which acceptances were a small piece—would address their concerns. See M. Elizabeth Sanders, *Roots of Reform: Farmers, Workers, and the American State, 1877–1917*, American Politics and Political Economy (Chicago: University of Chicago Press, 1999), 245–50.

35. Several scholars have examined the way in which bankers, Warburg, and exporters advocated for different dimensions of the Federal Reserve System, and they have debated the degree to which international prestige matters to Fed framers' lobbying, as compared to domestic interests, such as economic stability. See, for example, Mary O'Sullivan, *Dividends of Development: Securities Markets in the History of U.S. Capitalism, 1866–1922* (Oxford: Oxford University Press, 2016), 242–67; Broz, *The International Origins of the Federal Reserve System*, 18–51; Peer, "Negotiating the Lender-of-Last-Resort," 10–13. For a range of perspectives on the political debates that informed the founding of the Fed and its central credit mechanisms, see, in particular, Sanders, *Roots of Reform*; James Livingston, *Origins of the Federal Reserve System: Money, Class, and Corporate Capitalism, 1890–1913* (Ithaca, NY: Cornell University Press, 1986).

36. Paul Warburg, "Defects and Needs of Our Banking System," *New York Times*, January 6, 1907.

37. "Federal Reserve Act: Public Law 63–43, 63d Congress, H.R. 7837: An Act to Provide for the Establishment of Federal Reserve Banks, to Furnish an Elastic Currency, to Afford Means of Rediscounting Commercial Paper, to Establish a More Effective Supervision of Banking in the United States, and for Other Purposes," Sect. 13.

38. Broz, *The International Origins of the Federal Reserve System*, 46.

39. W. Randolph Burgess, *The Reserve Banks and the Money Market* (New York; London: Harper & Brothers, 1946 [1927]), 157. See also Broz, *The International Origins of the Federal Reserve System*, 132.

40. For more on the hierarchy of money, see also, Mehrling, *The New Lombard Street*.

41. Data sources: Mark Carlson and Burcu Duygan-Bump, "The Tools and Transmission of Federal Reserve Monetary Policy in the 1920s," in FEDS Notes (Washington: Board of Governors of the Federal Reserve System, 2016); Bureau of the Census, "Historical Statistics of the United States, Colonial Times to 1970," in *Historical Statistics of the United States, Colonial Times to 1970*, Washington, DC: U.S. Dept. of Commerce, 1975, 1042.

42. Marshall, "Origins of the Use of Treasury Debt in Open Market Operations," 45.

43. The classic work on this approach is Walter Bagehot, *Lombard Street* (Homewood, IL: Richard D. Irwin, 1962 [1873]).

44. Kenneth D. Garbade, *Birth of a Market: The U.S. Treasury Securities Market from the Great War to the Great Depression* (Cambridge, MA: MIT Press, 2012), 49.

45. Marshall, "Origins of the Use of Treasury Debt in Open Market Operations," 49–51.

46. On the Federal Reserve's shift from commercial debt to Treasury debt, see Mehrling, *The New Lombard Street*, 31–37.

47. Barry Eichengreen and Marc Flandreau, "The Rise and Fall of the Dollar (or When Did the Dollar Replace Sterling as the Leading Reserve Currency?)," *European Review of Economic History* 13, no. 3 (2009); "The Federal Reserve, the Bank of England . . ."

48. Eichengreen and Flandreau, "The Rise and Fall of the Dollar," 379; "The Federal Reserve, the Bank of England . . ." 58.

49. "The Federal Reserve, the Bank of England . . ." 63–66.

50. For a history of National City Bank, see Cleveland and Huertas, *Citibank, 1812–1970*.

51. Carosso and Sylla, "U.S. Banks in International Finance," 68; Mira Wilkins, *The Maturing of Multinational Enterprise: American Business Abroad from 1914 to 1970* (Cambridge, MA: Harvard University Press, 1974), 21.

52. Joseph W. Rebovich, "Frank A. Vanderlip and the National City Bank" (PhD diss., New York University, Graduate School of Business Administration, 1972), 84.

53. Srinivas B. Prasad, "The Metamorphosis of City and Chase as Multinational Banks," *Business and Economic History* 28, no. 2 (1999): 204; Carosso and Sylla, "U.S. Banks in International Finance," 68.

54. Hudson, *Bankers and Empire*, chapters 3–4.

55. Rebovich, "Frank A. Vanderlip and the National City Bank," 109–16; Kaufman, *Efficiency and Expansion*, 145–47.

56. Peer, "Negotiating the Lender-of-Last-Resort," 52.

57. "Report of the Condition of the National City Bank of New York," *New York Times*, December 4, 1912; International Banking Corporation, Statement of Condition, 1902–1946, HS 231, Item #1034 IBC, Citi.

58. Bickerton, "Bankers, Businessmen, and the Open Door Policy, 1899–1911," 271.

59. Bickerton, "Bankers, Businessmen, and the Open Door Policy, 1899–1911," 271.

60. See, for example, Eichengreen and Flandreau, "The Federal Reserve, the Bank of England . . ." 72.

61. "Tying the World to New York," *New York Tribune*, January 12, 1919; "NCB Will Get You a Haircut in Buenos Aires," *No. 8* 15, no. 9 (1920).

62. Stenographic Report of Meeting: Wednesday, January 3, 1917, RG 7, Correspondence, Memoranda and Organizational Documents of Harry T. S. Green—S, Citi.

63. "We practically make no attempt to restrict the volume of bills of very short maturities," noted E. R. Kenzel, deputy governor of the Federal Reserve Bank of New York. See E. R. Kenzel, Letter to Charles Peple, Deputy Governor, Federal Reserve Bank of Richmond, February 27, 1929, Box 171546, Folder 440—Acceptances 1927–1929, Federal Reserve Bank of New York. See, for example, W. Randolph Burgess, Open Market Operations of the Federal Reserve System, Address before the American Acceptance Council, December 11, 1928, 128154, 740-A: W. R. Burgess 1921–1944, Federal Reserve Bank of New York; Bankers' Acceptances: Role of Bankers' Acceptances, June 9, 1954. Box 616550, Folder 440L: Acceptances 1962–1918, Federal Reserve Bank of New York, 14–16.

64. Kaufman, *Efficiency and Expansion*, 132.

65. Rovensky, "The Development of Dollar Exchange," 999.

66. Accominotti and Ugolini, "International Trade Finance," 11.

67. Categories included "Letters of credit and Acceptances (19116–1928); "Letters of credit and Acceptances executed by reporting bank" (1922–1928); "Customers' Liability on Account of Acceptances" (1929–1934); "Acceptances of Other Banks and Foreign Bills of Exchange or Drafts Sold with Indorsement of this Bank" (1927–1928). See, for example, Office of the Comptroller of the Currency, *Annual Report of the Comptroller of the Currency, Vol 1*, Washington: Government Printing Office, 1917, and future years.

68. District 2 Federal Reserve, *Report of Condition—the National City Bank of New York*, New York: 1929.

69. Industry averages tended to be 1 percent as a standard rate. See "Editorial Comment: Commission Rates on Bankers Acceptance Credits," *Acceptance Bulletin* 9, no. 5 (1927). One account from 1925 suggested higher rates of up to 2 percent. See "American Bankers Acceptance an Important Factor in Financing Foreign Trade," *Acceptance Bulletin* 7, no. 10 (1925). But a larger number of sources support the 1927 report that rates averaged 1 percent. See, for example, "Address of President Paul M. Warburg," *Acceptance Bulletin of the American Acceptance Council* 5, no. 12 (1923); E. R. Kenzel, Letter to Hon. W. J. Bailey, Governor, Federal Reserve Bank of Kansas City, August 24, 1929, Box 171546, Folder 440—Acceptances 1927–1929, Federal Reserve Bank of New York.

70. O'Sullivan, "Past Meets Present," 31; "The Problem of Bill Distribution," *Acceptance Bulletin* 11, no. 5 (1929): 2; "Bankers' Acceptances: Role of Bankers' Acceptances," 1954.

71. Data sources: Acceptance liabilities taken from Proquest Annual Reports, Moody's Manual of Investments, and Harvard Baker Library Special Collections, as well as supplemental sources where needed. National bank data comes from Annual Reports of the Office of the Comptroller. See Office of the Comptroller of the Currency, *Annual Report of the Comptroller of the Currency, Vol 1*, Washington: Government Printing Office, 1914, and subsequent years.

72. Guaranty Trust grew out of the interests of Metropolitan Life Insurance, while IBC was founded by Equitable Life Assurance executives. IBC's board was dominated by leaders of Equitable Life Assurance, while Guaranty Trust was held by interests associated with Mutual Life Insurance. Moreover, Guaranty Trust vied for the designation of US agent to collect the Boxer Indemnity payment, but it ultimately lost to IBC. See Guaranty Trust Company of New York, *One Hundred Years of Banking Service, 1839–1939* (New York: Guaranty Trust, 1939), 24; "Banking News of New York City," *New York Financier*, January 6, 1902.

73. "Guaranty Trust in Front Ranks," *Wall Street Journal*, July 16, 1927.

74. Jean Strouse, *Morgan: American Financier* (New York: Random House, 1999), 603; Ron Chernow, *The House of Morgan: An American Banking Dynasty and the Rise of the Modern Finance* (New York: Atlantic Monthly Press, 1990), 152. J. P. Morgan and Guaranty Trust merged formally in 1959.

75. Chernow, *The House of Morgan*, 152–53.

76. Chernow, *The House of Morgan*, 188; Tooze, *The Deluge*, 38. Total US exports of merchandise, gold, and silver in 1915 amounted to $2.97 billion; total exports of merchandise constituted $2.77 billion. See Bureau of the Census, 885.

77. Guaranty Trust Company of New York, *One Hundred Years of Banking Service, 1839–1939*, 26, 33–34; "Big New York Banks Active in Foreign Field," *Wall Street Journal*, June 10, 1921.

78. Guaranty Trust Company of New York, *One Hundred Years of Banking Service, 1839–1939*, 34.

79. Guaranty Trust Company of New York, *One Hundred Years of Banking Service, 1839–1939*, 34.

80. Challen R. Parker, "Department of Banks and Bankers," *The Guaranty News* 8, no. 12 (1920).

81. See, for example, Guaranty Trust Company of New York, *Acceptances* ([New York]: Guaranty Trust Company of New York, 1919); *Banking Service for Foreign Trade* (New York: Guaranty Trust Company of New York, 1919); *How Business with Foreign Countries Is Financed* (New York: Guaranty Trust Company of New York, 1916).

82. Image Credit: International Acceptance Bank, *Report of the International Acceptance Bank Incorporated to the Stock Holders at the Annual Meeting, 1925–1928* (New York, 1925–1928).

83. Olivier Accominotti, "International Banking and Transmission of the 1931 Financial Crisis," *Economic History Review* 72, no. 1 (2019): 268–69.

84. "Warburg a Leader in Banking Reform," *New York Times,* January 25, 1932.

85. Ron Chernow, *The Warburgs: The Twentieth-Century Odyssey of a Remarkable Jewish Family* (New York: Vintage, 2016), 221–32.

86. "International Acceptance Bank," *Wall Street Journal,* November 30, 1921; "Warburgs Found Firm in Holland," *New York Times,* September 4, 1929.

87. Minutes of the Credit and Investment Committee, 1922, RG 3 Chase Manhattan Bank Collection, 17B6, 7, JPMorgan Chase Corporate History Collection, September 21.

88. See, for example, Minutes of the Credit and Investment Committee, 1924, RG 3 Chase Manhattan Bank Collection, 17B6, 9, JPMorgan Chase Corporate History Collection; Examination Record [IAB], June 16, 1927, RG 3 Chase Manhattan Bank Collection, 17B11, 3, JPMorgan Chase Corporate History Collection.

89. Eichengreen and Flandreau, "The Rise and Fall of the Dollar," 385.

90. Eichengreen and Flandreau, "The Rise and Fall of the Dollar," 386.

91. O'Sullivan, "Past Meets Present," 25, 37.

92. See also "Bankers' Acceptances: Role of Bankers' Acceptances," 1954, 17.

93. O'Sullivan, "Past Meets Present," 36–38.

94. Bureau of the Census, 885. Total paid-in capital and surplus of US national banks as of October 3, 1928, constituted $3.1 billion. Acceptance liabilities are listed in three categories: first, "Acceptances of other banks and foreign bills of exchange or drafts sold with indorsement"; second, "Acceptances executed for customers"; and third, "Acceptances executed by other banks." The total of these categories is $669 million. See Office of the Comptroller of the Currency, *Annual Report of the Comptroller of the Currency,* Washington: Government Printing Office, 1929.

95. Beckhart, *The New York Money Market,* 262.

96. American Acceptance Council, *Bankers Acceptances, Principles and Practices, Second Edition* (New York: American Acceptance Council, 1929), 21. Italics in original.

97. Stewart McKee, "The Movement of a Bill in London," *Acceptance Bulletin* 10, no. 8 (1928): 5.

98. Sir Ernest Maes Harvey, "Battle Royale between 'Dollar' and 'Sterling,'" *Acceptance Bulletin* 7, no. 6 (1925).

99. McKee, "The Movement of a Bill in London," 7.

100. Harvey, "Battle Royale between 'Dollar' and 'Sterling,'" 6.

101. O'Sullivan, "Past Meets Present," 36–40. Eichengreen and Flandreau also note that the Fed allocated funds from foreign central banks—and particularly the Bank of France—toward the acceptance market. See Eichengreen and Flandreau, "The Federal Reserve, the Bank of England . . ." 78.

102. Data sources: Mark Carlson and Burcu Duygan-Bump, "The Tools and Transmission of Federal Reserve Monetary Policy in the 1920s," in *FEDS Notes,* Washington: Board of Governors of the Federal Reserve System, 2016; Bureau of the Census, "Historical Statistics of the United States, Colonial Times to 1970," in *Historical Statistics of the United States, Colonial Times to 1970,* Washington, DC: U.S. Dept. of Commerce, 1975, 1042; Benjamin Haggott Beckhart, *The New York Money Market, Vol. 3: Uses of Funds,* New York: AMS Press, 1971 [1932]; "The Monthly Review," *Acceptance Bulletin* 13, no. 12 (December 1931): 14.

103. Marshall, "Origins of the Use of Treasury Debt in Open Market Operations," 51.

Chapter 5: Information and the Routines of Empire

1. Cleveland and Huertas, *Citibank, 1812–1970*, 81.

2. John Fuller, Journal—Russia. 1917–1919, John L. H. Fuller Papers, Box 1, Folder 8, Indiana Historical Society.

3. Letter to Hector Fuller, December 29, 1917, John L. H. Fuller Papers, Box 1, Folder 2, Indiana Historical Society.

4. "Circular," ed. National City Bank of New York Petrograd Branch (1918).

5. Jones, "Banks as Multinationals," 1.

6. For a rich literature on the creation of information practice and statistics, see also Porter, *Trust in Numbers*; Morgan, "Travelling Facts"; Poovey, *A History of the Modern Fact*; Bouk, *How Our Days Became Numbered*.

7. [Letter to James Stillman], June 5, Frank A. Vanderlip papers, B-1-5, Columbia University Rare Book and Manuscript Library (hereafter Columbia RBML).

8. Vanderlip as quoted by Thomas F. Huertas, "U.S. Multinational Banking: History and Prospects," in *Banks as Multinationals*, ed. Geoffrey Jones (London; New York: Routledge, 1990), 250–51.

9. F. Charles Schwedtman, The Financial Situation in Relation to Foreign Service, May 1922, RG 5, 27, Citi.

10. Cleveland and Huertas, *Citibank, 1812–1970*, 77; Abrahams, *The Foreign Expansion of American Finance*, 23; Frank Vanderlip, [Letter to James Stillman], 1914, Frank A. Vanderlip papers, B-1-5, June 5, Columbia RBML.

11. "American Bank Going into the Latin American Field," *Bankers' Magazine* 89, no. 2 (1914).

12. *Practical Bank Operation* (New York: Ronald Press Company), 240.

13. "The Creation of Acceptance Credits–Part II," *Acceptance Bulletin of the American Acceptance Council* 4, no. 10.

14. "The Question of Whether Credit Insurance Would Pay for Itself," *The Americas* 5, no. 8.

15. "The Question of Whether Credit Insurance Would Pay for Itself," *The Americas* 5, no. 8.

16. "The Development of Our Export Trade," *Bankers Home Magazine* 12, no. 1; Suggestions as to Organization & Scope of Foreign Services; Frank A. Vanderlip papers, Box E-39, Folder: Foreign Trade Department. Columbia RBML; "A New Era in Banking," *No. 8* 9, no. 7–10.

17. Austin began working in the Bureau of Statistics when it was housed within the Treasury Department. The position later became part of the Department of Commerce and Labor. See "Oscar Phelps Austin," *No. 8* 12, no. 2 (1917).

18. Bureau of Statistics Treasury Department, *Colonial Administration, 1800–1900: Methods of Government and Development Adopted by the Principal Colonizing Nations in Their Control of Tropical and Other Colonies and Dependencies*, Oscar P. Austin, Washington: Government Printing Office, 1901.

19. "Oscar P. Austin Dies at 85 Years," *New York Times*, January 8, 1933.

20. "The Foreign Branch Service," *The Americas* 1, no. 1; Ames Higgins, "A New Era in Banking," *No. 8* 9, no. 7–10 (1914): 1–7.

21. Memorandum, 1916, Box E-39, Folder: Foreign Trade Department, Columbia RBML.

22. Memorandum.,1916, Box E-39, Folder: Foreign Trade Department, Columbia RBML.

23. "Suggestions as to Organization & Scope of Foreign Services."

24. "What Has Been Done in a Year," *The Americas* 1, no. 11 (1915).

25. "The Foreign Trade Bureau," *Bankers Home Magazine* 12, no. 8.

26. Guaranty Trust Company of New York, *Essentials of Trading with Latin America* (New York: Guaranty Trust Company of New York, 1920).

27. *Acceptances* (New York: Guaranty Trust Company of New York, 1920).

28. *Acceptances* (New York: Guaranty Trust Company of New York, 1918).

29. Phelps, *The Foreign Expansion of American Banks*, 43.

30. Phelps, *The Foreign Expansion of American Banks*, 51.

31. See, for example, Tobias Rötheli, "Innovations in US Banking Practices and the Credit Boom of the 1920s," *Business History Review* 87, no. 2 (2013): 310–14.

32. Rowena Olegario, *A Culture of Credit: Embedding Trust and Transparency in American Business* (Cambridge, MA: Harvard University Press, 2006), 176.

33. David Sellers Smith, "The Elimination of the Unworthy: Credit Men and Small Retailers in Progressive Era Capitalism," *Journal of the Gilded Age and Progressive Era* 9, no. 2 (2010): 199.

34. Josh Lauer, "The Good Consumer: Credit Reporting and the Invention of Financial Identity in the United States, 1840–1940" (PhD diss., University of Pennsylvania, 2008), 120; Lauer, *Creditworthy: A History of Consumer Surveillance and Financial Identity in America* (New York: Columbia University Press, 2017), 88–91.

35. Bruce G. Carruthers, "From Uncertainty toward Risk: The Case of Credit Ratings," *Socio-Economic Review* 11 (2013): 537.

36. Marc Flandreau, Norbert Gaillard, and Frank Packer, "To Err Is Human: US Rating Agencies and the Interwar Foreign Government Debt Crisis," *European Review of Economic History* 15, no. 3 (2011).

37. Flandreau and Mesevage, "The Separation of Information and Lending and the Rise of Rating Agencies in the USA," 217.

38. Chapman, *The Rise of Merchant Banking*, 70.

39. Flandreau and Mesevage, "The Separation of Information and Lending and the Rise of Rating Agencies in the USA," 217. See, for example, "His Credit A1," *Bulletin of the National Association of Credit Men* 13, no. 7 (1913).

40. Carruthers, "From Uncertainty toward Risk: The Case of Credit Ratings," 543.

41. Wilson Newman, J. Facts About Dun & Bradstreet, Inc. 1956, Dun & Bradstreet Records—Series IV(A), Box 23, Folder 9, Harvard Business School; Rowena Olegario, "Credit Reporting Agencies: A Historical Perspective," in *Credit Reporting Systems and the International Economy*, ed. Margaret J. Miller (Cambridge, MA: MIT Press, 2003), 139.

42. See, for example, Volumes 15–20 from the Harvard Business School collection of Letterbooks in the Dun & Bradstreet Corporation Records, Series II (A).

43. R. G. Dun & Co., Letter to Messrs R. G. Dun & Co., New Orleans, La., March 16, 1897, Dun & Bradstreet Corporation Records II(A), v. 19 Letterbook, Harvard Business School.

44. See, for example, R. G. Dun. Letter to Joseph Packard, Esq., Baltimore, Md., January 18, 1912, Dun & Bradstreet Corporation Records II(A), v. 12 Letterbook, Harvard Business School; [Letter to Banco Del Callao, Lima, Peru], August 13, 1896, Dun & Bradstreet Corporation Records II(A), v. 11 Letterbook, Harvard Business School.

45. Olegario, *A Culture of Credit*, 190.

46. Hartmut Berghoff, "Civilizing Capitalism? The Beginnings of Credit Rating in the United States and Germany," *Bulletin of the German Historical Institute* 45 (2009): 23.

47. A. D. Whiteside, [Memo], May 19, 1933, Dun & Bradstreet Records—Series IV(B), Box 37, Folder 1, Harvard Business School.

48. See, for example, Frank Mortimer, "Some Elements of Credit," *No. 8* 8, no. 7 (1918): 19.

49. Rötheli, "Innovations in US Banking Practices and the Credit Boom of the 1920s," 315.

50. Robert Morris Associates, *A Short Descriptive History of the Robert Morris Associates: A National Organization of Bank Loaning Executives* (Lansdowne, PA: The Associates, 1928), 4.

51. William Martin, "The Improvement of Credit Department Methods in Member and Reserve Banks," *Bulletin of the National Association of Credit Men* 16, no. 4 (1916): 285.

52. Russell Prudden, *The Bank Credit Investigator* (New York: The Bankers Publishing Company, 1922), 98–100; Alexander Wall, *Credit Barometrics* (Washington, DC: Federal Reserve Board, Division of Analysis and Research, 1922); "The Genesis of Financial Statements," *The Credit Monthly* 32, no. 9 (1930); Robert Morris Associates, *The Robert Morris Associates: A Brief History and Description of the Accomplishments, Aims and Principles of This Organization of Bank Credit Executives*, Robert Morris Associates: A Short Explanatory History of the Aims and Accomplishments (Lansdowne, PA, 1924).

53. William H. Kniffin, "Deductions of a Credit Man in Analyzing Business Statements," *Journal of the American Bankers Association* 7, no. 8 (1915): 625.

54. James Matthews, "How to Approach the Questions Involved in Doing a South American Business," *Bulletin of the National Association of Credit Men* 17 (1917).

55. "English and American Mercantile Agency Methods [Response]," *Bulletin of the National Association of Credit Men* 11, no. 5 (1911): 306.

56. George William Edwards, *International Trade Finance* (New York: H. Holt and Company, 1924), 210.

57. Olegario, *A Culture of Credit*, 78; Berghoff, "Civilizing Capitalism?" 24.

58. Olegario, "Credit Information, Institutions, and International Trade: The United Kingdom, United States, and Germany, 1850–1930," 63.

59. Berghoff, "Civilizing Capitalism?" 16.

60. Berghoff, "Civilizing Capitalism?" 16. Similar pressures of high immigration and mobile populations shaped Argentina's credit information practices. Much like the United States, Argentina saw the development of privatized credit services in the nineteenth century before the expansion of R. G. Dun into Argentina. See Andrea Lluch, "Las Agencias De Informes Crediticios En La Argentina: Una Aproximación Al Funcionamiento De Los Mecanismos Informativos En El Mercado Crediticio (1892-C.1935)," *Investigaciones de historia económica: revista de la Asociación Española de Historia Económica*, no. 12 (2008).

61. Additional debates have focused on US and European courts' interpretations of "Qualified Privilege," a tradition that protects an entity from libel if information disclosures were provided in the public interest. See, for example, Flandreau and Mesevage, "The Separation of Information and Lending and the Rise of Rating Agencies in the USA"; Flandreau and Mesevage, "The Untold History of Transparency: Mercantile Agencies, the Law, and the Lawyers," *Enterprise & Society* 15, no. 2 (2014).

62. This terminology echoes a call from Flandreau and Mesevage to understand the "information architecture" around finance. See Flandrea and Mesevage, "The Separation of Information and Lending and the Rise of Rating Agencies in the USA," 215.

63. Galassi and Newton, "My Word Is My Bond."

64. Newton, "Trust and Virtue in Banking," 184–85.

65. Newton, "Trust and Virtue in Banking," 188, 97.

66. Leonard Minty, "Where American Banks Lead," *No. 8* 17, no. 7–8 (1922).

67. For a longer history of the role of information intermediaries in British merchant banks, see Liedtke, "Agents for the Rothschilds"; Llorca-Jaña, "Connections and Networks in Spain of a London Merchant-Banker, 1800–1850"; Perkins, "Financing Antebellum Importers: The Role of Brown Bros. & Co. in Baltimore."

68. Jones, "Competitive Advantages in British Multinational Banking since 1890," 46. Cottrell, "Great Britain," 26.

69. Jones, *British Multinational Banking*, 374.

70. Flandreau and Mesevage, "The Separation of Information and Lending and the Rise of Rating Agencies in the USA," 218.

71. See, for example, IBC Executive Committee, "Executive Committee Meeting Minutes." 1914–1918.

72. Flandreau and Mesevage, "The Separation of Information and Lending and the Rise of Rating Agencies in the USA," 226.

73. On the information functions of discount houses, see Accominotti, Lucena-Piquero, and Ugolini, "The Origination and Distribution of Money Market Instruments."

74. Flandreau and Mesevage, "The Separation of Information and Lending and the Rise of Rating Agencies in the USA," 226.

75. Department of Commerce U.S. Bureau of Foreign and Domestic Commerce, *Financing Agricultural Exports from the United States*, George William Edwards. Washington: Government Printing Office, 1924, 10.

76. The US-oriented scholarship often focuses on explaining the exceptional development of mercantile agencies in the United States. This framing, by contrast, asks why *Britain's* system was exceptional in British banks' development of sophisticated practices for information authentication. See Flandreau and Mesevage, "The Separation of Information and Lending and the Rise of Rating Agencies in the USA."

77. US Congress, *Federal Reserve Act*, Government Printing Office, 1913, 263, Section 13.

78. "Interpretation of Regulation B as to Borrower's Statements," *Federal Reserve Bulletin* (1915); Federal Reserve Board, *Circulars and Regulations*, Washington: Government Printing Office, 1916; Martin, "The Improvement of Credit Department Methods in Member and Reserve Banks."

79. Federal Reserve Board, *Informal Rulings of the Board: Responsibility on Acceptances*, Washington: Government Printing Office, 1916; "Circulars and Regulations," 15–16.

80. "Informal Rulings of the Board: Responsibility on Acceptances."

81. Charles O. Hardy, *Credit Policies of the Federal Reserve System* (Washington, DC: Brookings Institution, 1932), 267–68.

82. Martin, "The Improvement of Credit Department Methods in Member and Reserve Banks," 282.

83. See, for example, Federal Reserve Board, *Foreign Credit Information*, Washington: Government Printing Office, 1922.

84. Federal Reserve Board, *Foreign Credit Information*, Washington: Government Printing Office, 1922, 796.

85. Federal Reserve Board, *Informal Rulings of the Board*, Washington: Government Printing Office, 1922, 111.

86. Tooze, *The Deluge*, 3–30.

87. Rosenberg, *Financial Missionaries*, 97; Eichengreen, "U.S. Capital Market," 110.

88. Eichengreen and Flandreau, "The Rise and Fall of the Dollar," 379.

89. See, for example, Tooze, *The Deluge*; Fertik, "Steel and Sovereignty"; Tooze and Fertik, "The World Economy and the Great War"; Frank Costigliola, *Awkward Dominion: American Political, Economic, and Cultural Relations with Europe, 1919–1933* (Ithaca, NY: Cornell University Press, 1984).

90. Eichengreen, "U.S. Capital Market," 122; Fertik, "Steel and Sovereignty," 126.

91. The publication launched its first issue in December 1928.

92. Wilbur Carr, Facilities Offered by American Banks for Financing International Trade, March 8, 1916, RG 59, Box 7592, Folder 811.516 / 431, National Archives.

93. Secretary of State, Special Instructions No. 505—field for American Banks, February 16, 1917, RG 59, Box 7590, Folder 811.516, National Archive.

94. Bureau of Foreign and Domestic Commerce, [Misc. Letters and Reports], 1924, RG 59, Box 7593, Folder 811.51675-811.51699, National Archives.

95. F. R. Eldridge, Letter to Mr. Carr, Assistant Secretary of State, November 17, 1924, RG 59, Box 7592, Folder 811.51644 / 1, National Archives. For a similar exchange regarding banking in Nassau, see S. H. Cross, Letter to Mr. Carr, Assistant Secretary of State, November 17, 1925, RG 59, Box 7592, Folder 811.51644 / 1, National Archives.

96. For more on the dynamics of the promotional state, see Rosenberg, *Spreading the American Dream: American Economic and Cultural Expansion, 1890–1945*; Kaufman, *Efficiency and Expansion*.

97. Kaufman, *Efficiency and Expansion*, 121–22.

98. Data Source: Office of the Comptroller of the Currency, *Annual Report of the Comptroller of the Currency, Vol 1*, Washington: Government Printing Office, 1916, and subsequent years, 1916–1933.

99. For context on Petrograd, see Lars T. Lih, *Bread and Authority in Russia, 1914–1921* (Berkeley: University of California Press eScholarship Editions, 1990), 125.

100. Fuller, "Journal—Russia." 1917–1919.

101. On commensurability as a practice, see Wendy Nelson Espeland, "Commensuration as a Social Process," *Annual Review of Sociology* 24 (1988).

Chapter 6: The Human Infrastructure of Foreign Finance

1. National City Bank of New York, *No. 8, Educational Edition*, vol. 11 (1916).

2. "Oscar Phelps Austin."

3. "Commercial Geography: The Examination," *No. 8* 11, no. 3 (1916). Descriptions of the 1916 class come from the 1916 "Educational Edition" of National City Bank's in-house magazine, *No. 8*, vol. 11, no. 3. Specific contents of Oscar Austin's Commercial Geography course come from Oscar P. Austin, *Commercial Geography: History of World Commerce* (New York: National City Bank, 1916).

4. "City Bank Students Get Rigid Training," *New York Times*, August 15, 1915.

5. James H. Carter, "South America as a Field for Young Men," *No. 8* 10, no. 5–7 (1915).

6. Ferdinand C. Schwedtman, "The Making of Better Trained Men," *The Americas* 2, no. 2 (1915): 8.

7. Destin Jenkins, *The Bonds of Inequality: Debt and the Making of the American City* (Chicago: University of Chicago Press, 2021); Destin Jenkins and Justin Leroy, "Introduction: The Old History of Capitalism," in *Histories of Racial Capitalism*, eds. Destin Jenkins and Justin Leroy (New York: Columbia University Press, 2021); Hudson, "The National City Bank of New York and Haiti, 1909–1922."; Hudson, *Bankers and Empire*; Pak, *Gentlemen Bankers*.

8. For example, in China, US and European merchants tended to be more nuanced and less essentializing in their writings about Chinese business practices than their government and missionary counterparts, who often used Orientalist framings to explain Chinese social and business dynamics. See Miriam Kaminishi and Andrew David Smith, "Western Debates about Chinese Entrepreneurship in the Treaty Port Period, 1842–1911," *Enterprise & Society* 21, no. 1 (2020).

9. Important works on racial capitalism include: Jenkins, *The Bonds of Inequality*; Hudson, *Bankers and Empire*; Cedric J. Robinson, *Black Marxism: The Making of the Black Radical Tradition* (London: Zed Press, 1983); Destin Jenkins and Justin Leroy, eds., *Histories of Racial Capitalism* (New York: Columbia University Press, 2021); Jodi Melamed, "Racial Capitalism," *Critical Ethnic Studies* 1, no. 1 (2015); Kris Manjapra, "Plantation Dispossessions: The Global Travel of Agricultural Racial Capitalism," in *American Capitalism: New Histories*, eds. Sven Beckert and Christine Desan (New York: Columbia University Press, 2018); Paige Glotzer, *How the Suburbs Were Segregated: Developers and the Business of Exclusionary Housing, 1890–1960*, Columbia Studies in the History of U.S. Capitalism (New York: Columbia University Press, 2020).

10. Daniel, *MBA: The First Century*, 20–21.

11. Lars Engwall, "Business Schools and Consultancies: The Blurring of Boundaries," in *The Oxford Handbook of Management Consulting*, eds. Matthias Kipping and Timothy Clark (Oxford: Oxford University Press, 2012), 365–67.

12. Marion Fourcade and Rakesh Khurana, "From Social Control to Financial Economics: The Linked Ecologies of Economics and Business in Twentieth Century America," *Theory and Society* 42, no. 2 (2013): 131.

13. "Progress of the Educational Work of the City Bank Club," *No. 8* 9, no. 5–6 (1914); "A Sketch of the Educational Activities of the National City Bank," *No. 8* 11, no. 3 (1916).

14. A Plan for Practical Co-Operation between the Universities and Colleges of the United States and the National City Bank of New York, 1916, SJ Papers, Francis A. Barnum, Box 7, Folder 11, Georgetown University Library Booth Family Center for Special Collections.

15. The College Training Class, 1921, RG 2, NCBNY, College Training Class, Citi; Schwedtman, "A Plan for Practical Co-Operation between the Universities and Colleges of the United States and the National City Bank of New York," 1916.

16. "Training Its Men to Do the Work."

17. Frank Vanderlip, [Letter to James Stillman], January 22, 1916, Frank A. Vanderlip papers, B-1-7, Columbia RBML.

18. J. A. Carter, [Speech at Plaza Hotel], November 21, 1919, RG 12, NCBNY, Dinner Given by Mr. Vanderlip, Citi.

19. Pak, *Gentlemen Bankers*, chapter 2.

20. Photograph: "The 1916 College Class [Photograph]," *No. 8* 11, no. 3 (1916): 113.

21. Jerome Karabel, *The Chosen: The Hidden History of Admission and Exclusion at Harvard, Yale, and Princeton* (Boston: Houghton Mifflin, 2005), 22–23.

22. Karabel, *The Chosen*, 23.

23. Karabel, *The Chosen*, 74–85.

24. Karabel, *The Chosen*, 23.

25. Groeger, "A 'Good Mixer': University Placement in Corporate America, 1890–1940," 43.

26. "A 'Good Mixer': University Placement in Corporate America, 1890–1940," 53.

27. National City Bank of New York, 11.

28. Austin, *Commercial Geography: History of World Commerce*.

29. Austin, *Commercial Geography: History of World Commerce*, Lecture 20, p. 9.

30. For more about the educational context of commercial or "economic geography," see Mona Domosh, "Geoeconomic Imaginations and Economic Geography in the Early Twentieth Century," *Annals of the Association of American Geographers* 103, no. 4 (2013); Trevor J. Barnes, "Inventing Anglo-American Economic Geography, 1889–1960," in *A Companion to Economic Geography*, eds. Eric Sheppard and Trevor J. Barnes (Blackwell Publishing, 2002).

31. Austin, *Commercial Geography: History of World Commerce*, Lecture 17, p. 3.

32. Ventura, "American Empire, Agrarian Reform and the Problem of Tropical Nature in the Philippines, 1898–1916."

33. David John Arnold, *The Tropics and the Traveling Gaze: India, Landscape, and Science, 1800–1856* (Seattle: University of Washington Press, 2015), 111; Rob Aitken, "'Numberless Little Risks': 'Tropical Exposure' in Globalizing Actuarial Discourse, 1852–1947," *Enterprise & Society* (2022).

34. Several academic trends deserve mentioning, as they complicate some of the core tenets of commercial geography. The field of anthropology, for example, offered different approaches to explaining economic exchange in different societies and diverse explanations for why primitive people failed to behave like *homo economicus*. Explanations ranged from factors such as innate mental dysfunction to evolutionary conditions. For more on comparable moves in related disciplines, see Heath Pearson, "Homo Economicus Goes Native, 1859–1945: The Rise and Fall of Primitive Economics," *History of Political Economy* 32, no. 4 (2000); Thomas C. Leonard, "Eugenics and Economics in the Progressive Era," *Journal of Economic Perspectives* 19, no. 4 (2005); Leonard, *Illiberal Reformers: Race, Eugenics, and American Economics in the Progressive Era* (Princeton, NJ: Princeton University Press, 2016).

35. Domosh, "Geoeconomic Imaginations and Economic Geography in the Early Twentieth Century," 948.

36. "The Luncheon Classes," *No. 8* 11, no. 3 (1916); "The Teachers," *No. 8* 11, no. 3 (1916).

37. "The Training of Men for Foreign Service," *No. 8* 11 no. 3 (1916): 447.

38. "The Training of Men for Foreign Service," *No. 8* 11 no. 3 (1916): 447.

39. "List of Students Enrolled in the Classes of the National City Bank at the Close of the Year 1915–1916," *No. 8* 11, no. 3 (1916); "With the Old Guard," 1917.

40. Hall, "[Letter to Mother and Father]," 1919.

41. "From the Firing Line," June 1916, RG 2 / NCBNY, Aspersions, Citi; "List of Students Enrolled in the Classes of the National City Bank at the Close of the Year 1915–1916."

42. Hudson, *Bankers and Empire*, 14–17.

43. "Progress of the Educational Work of the City Bank Club," 22; Hudson, *Bankers and Empire*, 14–17.

44. "Nineteen-Fourteen Outing," *No. 8* 9, no. 5–6 (1914): 15, 20.

45. Hudson, *Bankers and Empire*, 15. See, for example, "Guaranty Club to Give a Minstrel Show," *The Guaranty News* 8, no. 11 (1920).

46. Schwedtman, "The Making of Better Trained Men," 8.

47. The films have not been preserved; however, students' accounts appear in a few sources, such as Timothy Fettin, "An Old Silver Mine in Peru," *No. 8* 11, no. 3 (1916).

48. Timothy Fettin, "An Old Silver Mine in Peru," *No. 8* 11, no. 3 (1916).

49. "Training Its Men to Do the Work."

50. Photo source: "City Bank Club House," *No. 8* 11, no. 3 (1916): 117.

51. "The Training of Men for Foreign Service," 118.

52. "The Training of Men for Foreign Service," 118.

53. "On to Russia," January–February 1917, RG 2 / NCBNY, Aspersions, Citi, 8.

54. "Japanese Snapshots," January–February 1917, RG 2 / NCBNY, Aspersions, Citi, 15.

55. William B. Richardson, The High Cost of Outfitting, 1917, John L. H. Fuller Papers, Box 2, Folder 4, Indiana Historical Society.

56. "A Vexed Question: Should a Man Marry on Less Than a Thousand a Year?" *Los Angeles Times*, March 9, 1904.

57. "Shall Bank Clerks Marry?" *Brooklyn Daily Eagle*, February 23, 1904. This citation was referenced and eloquently contextualized in Atiba Pertilla, "'Shall Bank Clerks Marry?': Gender, Labor, and the Wall Street Workforce, 1890–1915," in *Social Science History Association Conference* (Baltimore, MD, 2015).

58. Lawrence Merton Jacobs, "Talk to the College Training Class," *No. 8* 13, no. 9 (1918).

59. King, *The Hongkong Bank in the Period of Imperialism and War, 1895–1918*, 153.

60. Jacobs, Talk to the College Training Class, 10.

61. Starr, *Citibank: A Century in Asia*, 57.

62. Starr, *Citibank: A Century in Asia*, 57.

63. Citicorp, *Citicorp in China*, 23.

64. Barker, "Letter to Mr. Trafford," 1923.

65. "Following Our Example in South American Trade," *The Americas* 2, no. 7 (1916): 9.

66. Louis Goldstein and A. H. Boette, "A Study of Foreign Business, Especially from the Credit Side," *Bulletin of the National Association of Credit Men* 15, no. 3 (1915): 167–68.

67. James Matthews, Credit Conditions in South American Countries: An Address before the Members of Banking IV Class, the National City Bank of New York, 1917, RG 10, Address before Members of the Banking IV Class. Citi.

68. Lluch, "Las Agencias De Informes Crediticios En La Argentina."

69. Jack E. Hodges, "Credit Granting in Mexico," *The Credit Monthly* 27, no. 10 (1925): 9.

70. R. Boomer, "Mexican Credit Characteristics," *The Credit Monthly*, 1921, 10.

71. Matthews, "How to Approach the Questions Involved in Doing a South American Business," 219.

72. Nearly every issue of *The Americas* throughout the late 1910s and early 1920s featured a spotlight article on a foreign country or region. Not all focused on locations where National City Bank had opened branches, but many did. Peter Hudson has documented the white

supremacist rhetoric that frequently characterized bankers' accounts in National City Bank's inhouse newsletter, *No. 8*. Its client-facing publications, such as *The Americas*, focused less on people and culture and more on commodity production and infrastructure. Many of the accounts gestured to generalizations about the supposed innate characteristics of different populations, such as the Turkish inhabitants of Smyrna versus the Greek, or the clever Cantonese merchant class versus the less trustworthy "boat population." See, for example, Ernest L. Harris, "Smyrna, Gateway of a Rich Country in Asia," *The Americas* 3, no. 3 (1916); M. Drew Carrel, "Tucuman and the Sugar Industry of Argentina," *The Americas* 2, no. 7; S. R. Brown, "Canton, Industrial Center of the New South China," *The Americas* 3, no. 8 (1917); Ernest L. Harris, "Commercial Growth of Norway," *The Americas* 3, no. 6 (1916). See also Hudson, *Bankers and Empire*, chapter 4. For anti-Black rhetoric in the bank's internal publications, such as *No. 8*, see Harriet G. Brown, "Havana," *No. 8* 8, no. 4 (1918); Irving Barnard, "Five Years in Jungle Land," *No. 8* 12 (1917).

73. Goldstein and Boette, "A Study of Foreign Business, Especially from the Credit Side," 167.

74. J. F. Rivera, "Banking in Cuba," *No. 8* 14, no. 10 (1919): 17.

75. C. O. Weber, "Race Psychology and Industry," *The Credit Monthly* 27, no. 9 (1925).

76. Matthews, "How to Approach the Questions Involved in Doing a South American Business," 221.

77. Guaranty Trust Company of New York, *Essentials of Trading with Latin America*, #2432.

78. James H. Perkins, "South American Trade and Establishment of Dollar Credits," *Journal of the American Bankers Association* 8, no. 1 (1915).

79. John Backer, "Business-Getting in South America," *The Americas* 1, no. 12 (1915).

80. William E. Aughinbaugh, *Selling Latin America: A Problem in International Salesmanship What to Sell and How to Sell It* (Boston: Small Maynard and Company, 1915), 242.

81. J. G. South, Letter to the Secretary of State, April 16, 1929, RG 59, Box 7592, Folder 811.51619 / 1, National Archives.

82. Barker, "Autobiography," 1954.

83. According to branch manager James Barker, the Bank of Boston employed a teller who was accused of local crimes, but the bank retained the employee at the personal request of the interior minister. "We were doing business in the Argentine, not in the United States," Barker noted in his unpublished memoir. Working in foreign countries required "a certain flexibility of mind." See Barker, "Autobiography," 69–70.

84. Shou and Shou, "Wai Shang Yin Hang Zai Zhongguo [Foreign Banks in China]."

85. Hall, "[Letter to Mother and Father]," August 29, 1919.

86. Hall, "[Letter to Mother and Father]," March 19, 1922.

87. Hall, "[Letter to Mother and Father]," March 19, 1922.

88. Gastão Chaves, "Social Life in Brazil," *No. 8* 12, no. 5 (1917): 42; Barker, "Autobiography," 1954, 68.

89. A.L.M. Gottschalk, Concerning the Local Branch of the National City; Letter to the Secretary of State, June 22, 1915, RG 59, Box 7590, Folder 811.516, National Archive.

90. Barker, "Letter to Mr. Trafford," 1923.

91. Kermit Roosevelt, Diary, 1915.

92. Stefan Link and Noam Maggor, "The United States as a Developing Nation: Revisiting the Peculiarities of American History," *Past & Present* 246, no. 1 (2020): 282–83.

93. See, for example, Oliver Howard Wolfe, *Elementary Banking* (New York: Correspondence Chapter, Inc., American Institute of Banking, 1915), 71–72. Mortimer.

94. "Foreign Credit Information," 798.

95. "Foreign Credit Information," 797–98.

96. "Our Legacy in South America," Caterpillar, 2021, January 7, 2022, https://www
.caterpillar.com/en/news/caterpillarNews/2021/legacy-south-america.html.

97. Credit Report No. 499: Casteran Hnos & Cia. n.d., Frank A. Vanderlip papers, E-29,
Columbia University Rare Books & Manuscript Library, 13.

98. Barker, "Autobiography," 56.

99. See, for example, "A Frank Word Concerning Slip-Shod Export Methods," *The Americas* 2,
no. 12 (1916); "Why Exports to South America's West Coast Must Be Well Packed," *The Americas*
6, no. 8 (1920). "A United States Manufacturer Explains," *The Americas* 3, no. 3 (1916).

100. *Our South American Trade and Its Financing: How to Develop, How to Finance, and How
to Hold Trade with South America*, Foreign Commerce Series (New York: National City Bank
of New York), 38–41.

101. "The Argentine Industrial Union and North American Traders," *Pan American
Magazine*, 23.

102. "The Argentine Industrial Union and North American Traders," *Pan American
Magazine*, 23.

103. "A Frank Word Concerning Slip-Shod Export Methods."

104. "Tying the World to New York," Carter, 1919.

105. Ruy Lowndes, Plan for Reorganization of Commercial Department, February 27, 1919,
Item #249, Foreign Branches - Rio de Janeiro - Confidential Letters, April–December 1920,
Citi.

Chapter 7: Getting Local

1. "General News," April 1916, 2/NCBNY, Aspersions, Citi.

2. Fuller, "Journal—Russia," 1917–1919.

3. Hall, "[Letter to Mother and Father]," 1919.

4. James H. Carter, "South America as a Field for Young Men," *No. 8* 10, no. 5–7 (1915).

5. "From the Firing Line," 1916.

6. "Exports from the United States before and after the Outbreak of the War," *Federal Reserve
Bulletin* (October 1919): 955. See also: Kaufman, *Efficiency and Expansion*, 132.

7. Office of the Comptroller of the Currency, *Annual Report of the Comptroller of the Currency, Vol 1*, Washington: Government Printing Office, 1919, 93.

8. IBC operated twenty-three overseas branches in 1918, and nearly two-thirds were in Asia.
The bank also operated a branch in London, two in Panama, one in Colombia, and four in the
Dominican Republic. See "Foreign Business of the National City Bank of New York," *Federal
Reserve Bulletin* (1918).

9. The cost of this analytical approach is that it does not sufficiently interrogate the transnational dimensions of many places where US banks operated and instead focuses primarily on
US actors, institutions, and financial instruments. This emphasis aligns with the book's overall
goal of understanding the evolution of US global power and its reliance on financial intermediaries. In adopting this focus, it opens the door for future work that will more thoroughly interrogate the dynamics of place. Peter Hudson's work highlights the specific and important dynamics of US banking and imperialism in the Caribbean, and similarly nuanced analysis is needed

to understand similarities and differences in China, Argentina, and France, for example. See Hudson, *Bankers and Empire*. For more about transnationalism and the risks of reproducing Western hegemonic discourses, see Mae M. Ngai, "Transnationalism and the Transformation of the 'Other': Response to the Presidential Address," *American Quarterly* 57, no. 1 (2005): 59–65.

10. Parrini, *Heir to Empire*, 114–17.

11. "Seventy Years in Asia," 8.

12. Boies C. Hart, Banker at Large [Unpublished Memoir], 2007, RG12–History, Sub-group Oral Histories and Employee Memoirs, Box 3, Citi, 109.

13. Prices reached a high of $0.225 in May 1920, as compared to prewar prices around $0.05 per pound. See Bureau of the Census.

14. Hudson, *Bankers and Empire*, chapter 4. As historian Mary Speck has argued, differentiating Cuban from non-Cuban control within the sugar industry is a challenging proposition. Cuban sugar was already a multinational industry before World War I. Many mills combined European and US capital with "local" investment. In addition, mill owners often had hybrid nationalities including Spanish, local, US, and other European parentage and life experiences. See Mary Speck, "Prosperity, Progress, and Wealth: Cuban Enterprise During the Early Republic, 1902–1927," *Cuban Studies* 36 (2005).

15. Cleveland and Huertas, *Citibank, 1812–1970*, 106.

16. Moore, "State Building through Partnership," 172.

17. See, for example, Assistant Comptroller, [Letter to] the Manager, January 12, 1927, Item #337, IBC, F.E.D.—General (1926–1930), Citi; Citicorp, 28–32; Cochran, "The International Banking Corporation during the Chairmanship of Thomas H. Hubbard 1901–1915"; Starr, *Citibank: A Century in Asia*, 43–48.

18. H. S. Knapp, Military Government of Santo Domingo, Executive Order No. 42, March 17, 1917, 7, Item 335, Safekeeping Documents - Dominican Republic. Citi; Hudson, *Bankers and Empire*, 133–34. For the earlier history of Michelena Bank's entanglement with the US State Department and National City Bank, see Hudson, *Bankers and Empire*, 48–51.

19. Knapp, Military Government of Santo Domingo, 1917; "Acquires New Branch in Santo Domingo," *New York Tribune*, April 2, 1917; Hudson, *Bankers and Empire*, 44–48; Veeser, *A World Safe for Capitalism*.

20. Durrell, History of Foreign Branches of American Banks and Overseas Division, 1940, 141.

21. Memorandum for Mr. G. E. Mitchell, President Re: Dominican Branches of the International Banking Corporation. Dec. 22, 1925. Item #337—Transfer of Dominican Branches to NCB. Citi; Santo Domingo: Bad & Doubtful Debts Written Down to $1.00. 1926. Item 337 / IBC, Dominican Branches. Citi. This memorandum calculates write-downs at roughly $3 million. Given the likelihood that subsequent accounting revealed more losses, the figure of $5.7 million cited by Durrell in 1940 is likely more accurate: Durrell, History of Foreign Branches of American Banks and Overseas Division.

22. Doubtful Accounts—Reserves, Santo Domingo, March 24, 1924, Item 337 / IBC, Dominican Branches, Citi.

23. Doubtful Accounts—Reserves, Santo Domingo, March 24, 1924, Item 337 / IBC, Dominican Branches, Citi.

24. James C. Baker and Miles Gerald Bradford, *American Banks Abroad: Edge Act Companies and Multinational Banking* (New York: Praeger, 1975), 58; Hudson, *Bankers and Empire*, 152–76.

Hudson characterizes MBA's work in the Caribbean and South America as following a pattern of "concentration, cartelization, coordination, and collusion" (152).

25. D.G.M. Mercantile Bank of the Americas, July 17, 1920, RG 59, Box 7592, Folder 811.516 / 313, National Archives.

26. Parrini, *Heir to Empire*, 114.

27. Durrell, History of Foreign Branches of American Banks and Overseas Division, 45; Hudson, *Bankers and Empire*, 152–76.

28. D.G.M. Mercantile Bank of the Americas, July 17, 1920, RG 59, Box 7592, Folder 811.516 / 313, National Archives.

29. Hudson, *Bankers and Empire*, 170–75.

30. "Mercantile Bank of Americas Gets Credit Aid," *Journal of Commerce*, Augist 13, 1921; "Bank Needs Met, Says Morgan Firm," *New York Times*, August 13, 1921.

31. Hudson, *Bankers and Empire*, 173.

32. Durrell, History of Foreign Branches of American Banks and Overseas Division, 45. Hudson reports that the official losses to investors were $20 million, but some people estimated the losses to be as high as $80 million. See Hudson, *Bankers and Empire*, 175.

33. Vanderlip had lobbied heavily for the expansion of branches into Russia, but after the branches were nationalized amid the civil war, National City Bank faced losses of up to $33 million in liabilities to depositors and Russian assets it owned. The fiasco prompted infighting among bank leaders, and Vanderlip was asked to resign in 1918. See Cleveland and Huertas, *Citibank, 1812–1970*, 101–12.

34. Cleveland and Huertas, *Citibank, 1812–1970*, 110–12.

35. See, for example, Minutes—Bank Branch Committee: July 24, 1916, E, E-38, Bank Branch Committee, Columbia RBML.

36. Minutes—Bank Branch Committee: September 7, 1916, Frank A. Vanderlip papers, E-38, Bank Branch Committee, Columbia RBML.

37. Minutes—Bank Branch Committee: August 25, 1916, Frank A. Vanderlip papers, E-38, Bank Branch Committee, Columbia RBML.

38. See, for example, To the Men in the Foreign Field, 1916, John L. H. Fuller Papers, 2, 3, Indiana Historical Society; Frank Vanderlip, [Letter to James Stillman], May 14, 1915, Frank A. Vanderlip papers, B-1-5, Columbia RBML.

39. Durrell, History of Foreign Branches of American Banks and Overseas Division, 98.

40. Laurence F. Schmeckebier and Gustavus Adolphus Weber, *The Bureau of Foreign and Domestic Commerce*, Institute for Government Research (Baltimore, MD: Johns Hopkins Press, 1924), 41.

41. Ellen B. Lewis, "The Foreign Trade Bureau," *The Guaranty News* 9, no. 8 (1920).

42. Durrell, History of Foreign Branches of American Banks and Overseas Division, 98.

43. See, for example, John H. Allen, [Letter to Mr. H. H. Hollingshead, Manager, the National City Bank of New York, Bahia, Brazil], March 19, 1920, Item #248; Letters to Mr. Allen - S. America - Bahia, 1920, Citi.

44. A. V. Edwards, [Letter to the Manager, the National City Bank of New York, Rio De Janeiro, Brazil], May 21, 1920, Item #249, Foreign Branches - Rio de Janeiro - Confidential Letters, 1920, Citi.

45. Leopoldo Casas, *Branch Management* (Havana, Cuba: National City Bank of New York, 1933), 11.

46. Casas, *Branch Management*, 26, 70–71.

47. Eichengreen, "U.S. Capital Market," 110.

48. Chernow, *The House of Morgan*, 243–53.

49. The literature on sovereign lending by US banks in the interwar period is vast in economic, cultural, and diplomatic terms. Examples include: Eichengreen, "U.S. Capital Market"; Barbara Stallings, *Banker to the Third World: U.S. Portfolio Investment in Latin America, 1900–1986* (Berkeley: University of California Press, 1987); Rosenberg, *Spreading the American Dream: American Economic and Cultural Expansion, 1890–1945*; Rosenberg, *Financial Missionaries*; Cleona Lewis and Karl T. Schlotterbeck, *America's Stake in International Investments* (Washington, DC: Brookings Institution, 1938).

50. Chernow, *The House of Morgan*, 243; Fertik, "Steel and Sovereignty," 130.

51. Rosenberg, *Spreading the American Dream*.

52. John Foster Dulles, "Our Foreign Loan Policy," *Foreign Affairs* 5 (1926); Rosenberg, *Spreading the American Dream*, 146–47; Rosenberg, *Financial Missionaries*, 106–7.

53. Stallings, 142. Rosenberg, *Spreading the American Dream*; Rosenberg, *Financial Missionaries*.

54. Dulles, "Our Foreign Loan Policy," 33–34.

55. Eichengreen, "U.S. Capital Market," 108.

56. Chernow, *The House of Morgan*, 243.

57. On the diversification of domestic agencies offering international credit information, see William A. Prendergast and William Howard Steiner, *Credit and Its Uses* (New York: D. Appleton and Company, 1931), 492–509; John Edward Sellstrom, "The Credit Interchange and Adjustment Work of the National Association of Credit Men" (MBA, University of Texas, 1937); Olegario, "Credit Information," 69–71.

58. Parrini, *Heir to Empire*, 121. See also "Foreign Business of the National City Bank of New York," 943.

59. Hart, *Empire and Revolution*, 117.

60. Hart, *Empire and Revolution*, 118.

61. Hart, *Empire and Revolution*, 156.

62. Data sources: "Brazil-U.S. Body Pushed," *New York Times*, December 11, 1937, 3; "U.S. Brazil Trade Studied," *New York Times*, November 3, 1944, 11; "Foreign Relations of the United States: Diplomatic Papers, the American Republics," edited by Department of State, Washington: Government Printing Office, 1938 [1956], 402; "Franklin H. Baker," *New York Times*, April 4, 1941, 21; Field, Glore & Co., International Acceptance Bank, Baker, Kellogg & Co., and Ulen & Company to the Secretary of State, *Papers Relating to the Foreign Relations of the United States* 1928, Folder: 832.51 Sa 6 / 128, July 17, https://history.state.gov/historicaldocuments/frus1928v01/d830. Randall, Stephen James; "Colombia, the United States, and Interamerican Aviation Rivalry, 1927–1940," *Journal of Interamerican Studies and World Affairs* 14, no. 3 (1972): 322; Chamber of Commerce of the United States of America in the Argentine Republic, *Comments on Argentine Trade* 16, no. 1 (August 1936), 74; "Growth of the Foreign Credit Corporation," *Bankers' Magazine* 102, no. 2 (February 1921): 291; "Devendorf with Founders Trust," *New York Times*, October 23, 1927, 1; "To Widen Appeal of Am. Founders," *Wall Street Journal*, August 10, 1928, 9; "Gets Half Control of Credit Company," *New York Times*, June 14, 1929, 38; Julia C. Ott, *When Wall Street Met Main Street: The Quest for an Investors' Democracy*, Cambridge, MA:

Harvard University Press, 2011, 176; "Moves to Meet South American Rail Maturity," *New York Herald Tribune*, July 17, 1932, 1; "Cuba Co. Elects," *Wall Street Journal*, October 2, 1933, 2; "Department of Commerce: Bureau of Foreign and Domestic Affairs," *Commerce Reports* 15 (April 12, 1926): 128, "Memorandum by Mr. Richard F. O'Toole of the Division of Brazilian Affairs to the Chief of That Division (Dawson)," *Foreign Relations of the United States*, Washington, DC: Government Printing Office, 1947: 832.6584 / 3–347; Burton Crane, "Stronger State Department Stand on Foreign Debt Service Demanded," *New York Times*, November 19, 1944, 2; "Says Debt in Brazil Ran up Unchecked," *New York Times*, January 22, 1933, 1; "Baker, Kellogg Segregation," *Wall Street Journal*, May 1, 1934, 15; Kenneth Apollonio; Letter from Buenos Aires, Argentina, 1916, John L. H. Fuller Papers, 2, 3, Indiana Historical Society; "Alumni Notes," *Harvard Alumni Bulletin* 23, no. 15 (1920): 351; "The Chamber of Commerce of the United States of America in the Argentine Republic," *Comments on Argentine Trade* 1 (August 1921–1922), "Bankers Representing $50,448,500 Bonds Authorized to Enter C. & N. W. Rail Case," *New York Times*, September 5, 1936, 19.

63. "College Men in Foreign Service," *No. 8* 11, no. 3 (1916).

64. "Baker, Kellogg Combine with Amer. Intl. Corpn," *New York Tribune*, July 9, 1923; Minutes of the Credit and Investment Committee, January–June 1926, RG 3, Chase Manhattan Bank Collection, 17B6, 12, JPMorgan Chase Corporate History Collection; "Says Debt in Brazil Ran Up Unchecked," *New York Times*, January 22, 1933.

65. The careers of James C. Luitweiler and Ermond L. Sylvester follow this arc. See, for example, "New Bond Brokers Make Bow," *Los Angeles Times*, May 1, 1934; "Growth of the Foreign Credit Corporation," *Bankers' Magazine* 102, no. 2 (1921). Kenneth Appolonio went on to found an importing business in Buenos Aires: "Alumni Notes," *Harvard Alumni Bulletin* 29, no. 28 (1927). Henry Pearson Melzer went on to a leadership role in the foreign department of the First National Bank of Boston. See *Twenty-Fifth Reunion Record of the Class of 1915*, (University of Pennsylvania, 1941), 52.

66. Julia C. Ott, *When Wall Street Met Main Street: The Quest for an Investors' Democracy* (Cambridge, MA: Harvard University Press, 2011), 2.

67. Ott, *When Wall Street Met Main Street*, 44.

68. Ott, *When Wall Street Met Main Street*, 62–63.

69. Ott, *When Wall Street Met Main Street*, 62–63.

70. For an explanation of the Federal Reserve's role in the process of habituating US consumers to investing in securities during and after World War I, see also O'Sullivan, *Dividends of Development: Securities Markets in the History of U.S. Capitalism, 1866–1922*, 351.

71. "Committee on Americanization," *Journal of the American Bankers Association* 12, no. 5 (1919).

72. Alexander J. Hemphill, "The Banker's Part in Americanization," *The Guaranty News* 8, no. 1 (1919).

73. "Savings Bank Section: Americanization," *Journal of the American Bankers Association* 11, no. 10 (1919): 564. See also "Experiences in Selling Certain Classes of Immigrants," *Bulletin of the National Association of Credit Men* 16, no. 4 (1916).

74. Hemphill, "The Banker's Part in Americanization."

75. On savings banks, postal savings banks, and small-saver reform efforts, see also Wadhwani, "The Institutional Foundations of Personal Finance," 504–12; Jeffrey Fear and R. Daniel

Wadhwani, "Populism and Political Entrepreneurship: The Universalization of German Savings Banks and the Decline of American Savings Banks, 1907–1934," in *Business in the Age of Extremes: Essays in Modern German and Austrian Economic History*, eds. Hartmut Berghoff, Jürgen Kocka, and Dieter Ziegler (Cambridge, UK: Cambridge University Press, 2013); Nicholas Osborne, "Little Capitalists: The Social Economy of Saving in the United States, 1816–1914" (PhD diss., Columbia University, 2014).

76. Alexander Robinson, "The Budget System in the American Home," *Journal of the American Bankers Association* 13, no. 5 (1920): 327–28; Mrs. Clarence Renshaw, "The Home Service Department," *Journal of the American Bankers Association* 12, no. 7.

77. Leo Day Woodworth, "New Phase in Savings Banking," *Journal of the American Bankers Association* 12, no. 8: 443; "Banking for Women Develops Friendly Service," *No. 8* 16, no. 9 (1921): 8; John E. Gardin, Liberty Bonds for the Business Woman, June 8, 1917, Economic & Trade Conditions: Pamphlets, Harvard Business School.

78. "In the Women's Department at Forty-Second Street," *No. 8* 20, no. 4 (1925).

79. Durrell, History of Foreign Branches of American Banks and Overseas Division, 183; "New Budget Plan for C.I.D. Depositors," *No. 8* 22, no. 4 (1927); National City Bank of New York, Remarks of the President at the Annual Meeting of Shareholders, January 10, 1928.

80. Hudson, *Bankers and Empire*, 209–10.

81. Hudson, *Bankers and Empire*, 182.

82. "Cuba and Porto Rico Set a World Record in Savings Contest," *No. 8* 21, no. 1 (1926).

83. "Rangoon Savings Contest Winners," *No. 8* 25, no. 4 (1930).

84. "Rangoon Savings Contest Winners."

85. See, for example, "Cuba's Brilliant Record," *No. 8* 23, no. 8 (1928): 27.

86. "Cuba and Porto Rico Set a World Record in Savings Contest."

87. "World Contest Tops All Records with $10,226,884 in 74,082 Accounts," *No. 8* 23, no. 8 (1928): 5. For an account of these contests in the Caribbean and Cuba in particular, see also Hudson, *Bankers and Empire*, 209–11.

88. "Rangoon Savings Contest Winners"; "Woman Wins First Prize in Manila Savings Essay Contest," *No. 8* 22, no. 4 (1927).

89. Hart, *Empire and Revolution*, 181.

90. "World Contest Tops All Records with $10,226,884 in 74,082 Accounts."

91. Durrell, History of Foreign Branches of American Banks and Overseas Division, 1940.

92. National City Bank of New York, "Remarks of the President at the Annual Meeting of Shareholders," 1928.

93. Schwedtman, "The Financial Situation in Relation to Foreign Service."

94. [Timeline], nd., RG12, Citibank Book, Argentina–History, 1812–1978, Citi; John Walker Harrington, "Big Banks and Small Personal Loans," *Bankers Magazine* 116, no. 6 (1928): 895; "In Two Years Personal Loan Dept Has Aided 134,294 Families," *No. 8* 25, no. 5 (1930); "Personal Loan Facilities Are Broadened," *No. 8* 23, no. 6–7 (1928).

95. "Banking in 21 Languages a Specialty at Our New Branch in B.A.," *No. 8*, Dece,ber 1930.

96. See, for example, "This Is Very Much the Same as Usual," March–April 1917, RG 2 / NCBNY, Aspersions, Citi; Hudson, *Bankers and Empire*, 71.

97. Vanderlip, "[Letter to James Stillman]," 1915; Peter O'Shea, "A Talk with an International Banker," *Magazine of Wall Street* 29, no. 3 (1921): 152.

98. Photograph: Oscar P. Austin, "Our 1916 Trade with the Neutral World," *The Americas* 3, no. 6 (1917): 36.

99. Cleveland and Huertas, *Citibank, 1812–1970*, 77–79.

100. John Durland, Letter to Frank Vanderlip, April 6, 1917, Frank A. Vanderlip Papers, Box F-1, Chile, Columbia RBML.

101. Drake, *The Money Doctor in the Andes*, 86.

102. Rosenberg, *Financial Missionaries*, 161.

103. "Chilean Staffs Score High in First Bond Selling Contest," *No. 8* 24, no. 3–4 (1929).

104. Drake, *The Money Doctor in the Andes*, 115.

105. Durrell, History of Foreign Branches of American Banks and Overseas Division, 1940.

106. National City Bank of New York, Facilidades Bancarias, 1926, RG 2, 2A, Facilidades Bancarias, Citi.

107. National City Company, Valores De Inversión, 1927, RG 7, 2, Valores de Inversión, Citi.

108. National City Company, Valores De Inversión, 1927, RG 7, 2, Valores de Inversión, Citi.

109. Transfer Securities Record, 1909–1918, RG 7, Item #324, Citi.

110. IBC Secretary, Directors' Minutes, November 14, 1918, 7, Annual Directors Meeting Minutes, Citi.

111. Mary O'Sullivan makes this argument in terms of past analysis of bankers' acceptances vis-à-vis Federal Reserve policies: O'Sullivan, "Past Meets Present." And indeed, excellent scholarship has unearthed the way in which financial practices of the 1920s contributed to turbulence in international markets. See, for example, Marc Christopher Adam, "Liquidating Bankers' Acceptances: International Crisis, Doctrinal Conflict and American Exceptionalism in the Federal Reserve 1913–1932," in *Diskussionsbeiträge* (Free University Berlin, School of Business & Economics, 2020); Matthew Jaremski and David C. Wheelock, "The Founding of the Federal Reserve, the Great Depression, and the Evolution of the U.S. Interbank Network," *Journal of Economic History* 80, no. 1 (2020); Barry J. Eichengreen, *Golden Fetters: The Gold Standard and the Great Depression, 1919–1939* (New York: Oxford University Press, 1992).

112. Marc Flandreau, Norbert Gaillard, and Ugo Panizza, "Conflicts of Interest, Reputation, and the Interwar Debt Crisis: Banksters or Bad Luck?" ed. Geneva Graduate Institute (2010), 3.

113. A. Guerra Trigueros, The National City Bank of New York and Our Freedom, April 16, 1929, RG 59, Box 7592, Folder 811.51616 / 2, National Archives.

114. Hudson, "The National City Bank of New York and Haiti, 1909–1922," 91–114.

115. Cables from South American Branches, November 21, 1917–1918, Item #230, NCB of NY, South American Branches—Cables sent to Main Office (important), 1917–1918, Citi.

116. Hall, "[Letter to Mother and Father]," September 6, 1919.

117. [Letter to Mother and Father], January 18, 1920, Series 1: Hall Family Collection, 6, 11, East Texas Research Center, R. W. Steen Library, Stephen F. Austin University.

118. Image: "The Last of the I.B.C. Groups," *No. 8* 21, no. 3 (1926): 10.

119. "Seventy Years in Asia," 12; Hart, *Empire and Revolution*, 167.

120. Hall, "Letter to Mother and Father," 1919; "Seventy Years in Asia," 11.

121. Letter to Charles Rich, July 19, 1920, Item #337, Folder: Peking, Citi.

122. Former IBC banker Alexander Calhoun used the term "shadow branch" to describe IBC's ongoing work in China even as National City Bank opened offices. I believe this term fits

a larger strategy of opportunistic uses of IBC. See "Seventy Years in Asia," 11. In addition, Peter Hudson has noted a similar dynamic in National City Bank's work in Haiti: its acquisition of Banque Nationale de la République d'Haïti: Hudson, "The National City Bank of New York and Haiti, 1909–1922." The present research builds upon these insights and expands their geographic and political scope.

123. Wilkins, *The Maturing of Multinational Enterprise,* 169.

124. Decrease refers to "acceptance liabilities for customers." See *Moody's Manual of Investments, American and Foreign: Banks - Insurance Companies - Investment Trusts - Real Estate - Finance and Credit Companies,* ed. John Sherman Porter (New York: Moody's Investor Services, 1933), 1961–62.

125. Wilkins, *The Maturing of Multinational Enterprise,* chapter 3.

126. Cochran, "The International Banking Corporation during the Chairmanship of Thomas H. Hubbard," [1945]. 21.

127. Starr, *Citibank: A Century in Asia,* 43.

128. When National City purchased the controlling interest in IBC in October 1915, it did so through its overseas investing arm, the National City Company. National City Company was a National City Bank affiliate, incorporated under the laws of New York in 1911. In its early years, NCC served as a holding company for the bank's interest in other financial institutions, such as state-chartered banks and trust companies. Bank executives had long been in the practice of holding interests in other financial institutions, but NCC allowed the bank to institutionalize the relationships. After the passage of the Federal Reserve Act, National City Bank itself could have purchased IBC, but observers speculated that NCC acted first as the bank awaited approval from the Federal Reserve to acquire the international branches. When and how that approval was finalized remains unclear, but by 1924, IBC was listed as a line item on National City Bank's statement of condition, and the two institutions functioned much like a merged entity without any visible presence of National City Company. See Cleveland and Huertas, *Citibank, 1812–1970,* 62–65; "Bache Sells Bank to National City Co," *New York Times,* October 29, 1915; "National City Bank Extends Sway to Orient," *New York Tribune,* October 29, 1915; National City Bank of New York, Statement of Condition, December 31, 1924.

129. Lawrence Merton Jacobs, What Shall We Do with the International Banking Corporation? May 23, 1916, Frank A. Vanderlip papers, E-27 International Banking Corporation, Rare Book and Manuscript Library, Columbia University Library.

130. "Memorandum in Reference to International Banking Corporation," 1945.

131. London Branch, July 6, 1920, Item #337, Folder: Lyons, Citi.

132. "Foreign Branches," [nd].

133. "London Branch," 1920.

134. "London Branch," 1920.

135. Wilkinson & Grist, Re: International Banking Corporation and National City Bank of New York, December 21, 1926, Item #337, IBC, F.E.D.—General (1926–1930), Citi.

136. Wilkinson & Grist, Re: International Banking Corporation and National City Bank of New York, December 21, 1926, Item #337, IBC, F.E.D.—General (1926–1930), Citi.

137. Wilkinson & Grist, Re: International Banking Corporation and National City Bank of New York, December 21, 1926, Item #337, IBC, F.E.D.—General (1926–1930), Citi.

138. Wilkinson & Grist, Re: International Banking Corporation and National City Bank of New York, December 21, 1926, Item #337, IBC, F.E.D.—General (1926–1930), Citi.

139. E. W. Hamilton, Letter to George Hogg, Manager, International Banking Corporation, Hongkong, January 7, 1927, Item #337, IBC, F.E.D.—General (1926–1930), Citi.

140. Memo, March 14, 1916, Frank A. Vanderlip Papers, Box E-39, Foreign Trade Department, Columbia RBML.

141. Whereas IBC's total deposits were around $35 million in 1929, those of National City Bank were $1.7 billion. See G. K. Weeks, Copy of Letter from International Banking Corporation Madrid, October 25, 1929, Item #337, IBC, Reorganization of Spanish Branches, Citi.

142. Memorandum Re Tax Situation—Spain, October 24, 1929, Item #337, IBC, Reorganization of Spanish Branches, Citi.

143. Letter to W.P.G. Harding, Governor, Federal Reserve Board, July 15, 1920, 7, Item 79, Federal Reserve Board Reports, Citi.

144. Letter to Secretary of State, November 6, 1920, RG 59, Box 7592, Folder 811.516 / 324. ,National Archives.

145. Dudley Dwyre, Letter to John C. Wiley, Chargé d'Affaires, American Legation, Caracas, December 9, 1920, RG 59, Box 7592, Folder 811.516 / 330. ,National Archives.

146. W.W.L., Re: I.B.C. Transfer to N.C.B., November 12, 1926, Item #337, F.E.D.—General (1926–1930), Citi.

147. See, for example, Office of the Comptroller of the Currency. *Annual Report of the Comptroller of the Currency, Vol 1*, Washington: Government Printing Office, 1915. 75–76. On the evidence of a surprise visit by a US regulator to foreign branches, see Hart, *Empire and Revolution*, 2007. 115.

148. IBC Executive Committee, "Executive Committee Meeting Minutes," 1914–1918.

149. Executive Committee Meeting Minutes, 1918–1921, Item #335–4, Citi.

150. W. Harding, Letter to the International Banking Corporation, June 5, 1919, Box: Board Shareholders Files 1, Item 79 - Federal Reserve Board Reports, Citi.

151. IBC Executive Committee, "Executive Committee Meeting Minutes," 1918–1921.

152. Vanessa Ogle, "Archipelago Capitalism: Tax Havens, Offshore Money, and the State, 1950s–1970s," *American Historical Review* 122, no. 5 (2017); "'Funk Money': The End of Empires, the Expansion of Tax Havens, and Decolonization as an Economic and Financial Event."

153. Cleveland and Huertas, *Citibank, 1812–1970*, 205–6.

154. National City Bank of New York, "Remarks of C. E. Mitchell, Chairman at the Annual Meeting of Shareholders," (New York: National City Bank of New York, 1931).

155. "Remarks of C. E. Mitchell, Chairman at the Annual Meeting of Shareholders," (New York: National City Bank of New York, 1932).

156. Durrell, History of Foreign Branches of American Banks and Overseas Division, 249. Data from Cleveland and Huertas, *Citibank, 1812–1970* (p. 207) suggests that international deposits were lower for 1939, constituting roughly $470 million, but the difference in figures is likely due to differences in dating between comptroller's reports and the bank's internal accounting reported by Durrell.

157. G. Martel Hall, Problems in Hongkong, December 12, 1933, Series 2: Hall Family Collection, 18, 39, East Texas Research Center, R. W. Steen Library, Stephen F. Austin University.

Conclusion

1. Huertas, *Citibank, 1812–1970*, 253.

2. Huertas, *Citibank, 1812–1970*, 252.

3. I.B.C.: Fiftieth Anniversary of Citibank's Giant Step, October 1965, Citi, RG 7, History of IBC; Clarence Wasson, International Banking Corporation: File in Cashier's Administration, November 2, 1978, 7, 2, History of IBC, Citi; Minutes of the Board of Directors, 1965–1978, RG 7, 1, Minutes of the Board of Directors, Citi.

4. Folder Contents,1950–1960, Board Shareholders Files 1, Item 79 Miscellaneous, Citi.

5. Chernow, *The House of Morgan*.

6. Wallace Stegner, *Discovery!: The Search for Arabian Oil* (Lebanon: Middle East Export Press, 1971), chapter 2.

7. Chernow, *The House of Morgan*, 605.

8. Maureen Farrell and Nicolas Parasie, "In Aramco IPO, a Bonanza for Banks," *Wall Street Journal*, Jun 10, 2016.e

9. Department of State, *The Export-Import Bank of Washington, the First Ten Years*, Eleanor Lansing Dulles, Washington: Government Printing Office, 1944, 8; William H. Becker, *The Market, the State, and the Export-Import Bank of the United States, 1934–2000*, ed. William M. McClenahan (Cambridge, UK: Cambridge University Press, 2003), 34.

10. "Exim Board Votes to Renew Finance Facility for Boeing, Supporting Small Business Suppliers across America," Export-Import Bank of the United States, 2023, https://www.exim .gov/news/exim-board-votes-renew-finance-facility-for-boeing-supporting-small-business -suppliers-across; "Export-Import Bank of the United States Signs Co-Financing Agreement with EKN of Sweden," Export-Import Bank of the United States, 2023, https://www.exim.gov /news/export-import-bank-united-states-signs-co-financing-agreement-ekn-sweden.

11. Ralph T. Helfrich, "Trading in Bankers' Acceptances: A View from the Acceptance Desk of the Federal Reserve Bank of New York," *Monthly Review (Federal Reserve Bank of New York)* (1976): 51.

12. Matthew Lowenstein, "China's Shadow Currency," *The Diplomat*, December 12, 2013; Pete Sweeney, "China Shadow Bankers Pray to Be Systemically Risky," Reuters, August 23, 2022; Omodele Adigun, "How to Finance Your Trade with Banker's Acceptance," *The Sun (Nigeria)*, February 28, 2017.

13. "Citigroup Is Disposing of Its International Retail Network," *The Economist*, February 19, 2022; Xie Yu, "Citi to Wind Down Consumer Banking in China, Affecting About 1,200 Staff," Reuters, December 15, 2022.

14. Tom Espiner, "HSBC to Close 114 UK Branches as More People Bank Online," BBC, November 30, 2022; Lawrence White, "Exclusive: HSBC Puts Global Footprint under Fresh Scrutiny, Considers Dozen Exits," Reuters, May 24, 2023.

15. Noel Tichy and Ram Charan, "Citicorp Faces the World: An Interview with John Reed," *Harvard Business Review*, November–December 1990.

16. "1977 Focus Shifts to Retail Banking."

17. "Citigroup Is Disposing of Its International Retail Network."

18. "Chinese Loans and Investment in Infrastructure Have Been Huge," *The Economist*, May 20, 2022.

19. For more context on infrastructural power, see, for example, Pinzur, "Infrastructural Power"; Benjamin Braun, "Central Banking and the Infrastructural Power of Finance: The Case of ECB Support for Repo and Securitization Markets," *Socio-Economic Review* 18, no. 2 (2020). For the relevance of this concept to historians, see also Bridges, "The Infrastructural Turn."

20. Rosenberg, *Spreading the American Dream*, 38–86.

21. Hudson, "The National City Bank of New York and Haiti, 1909–1922"; Hudson, *Bankers and Empire*.

22. See, for example, James M. Barker, American Club Luncheon Speech, September 28, 1928, James M. Barker Papers, Box 93, Folder 1662, Newberry Library, Special Collections.

23. "Bank Opens Its New Branch Building in Buenos Aires," *No. 8* 24, no. 12 (1929).

24. This conceptualization appears eloquently in Sarah L. Quinn, *American Bonds: How Credit Markets Shaped a Nation* (Princeton, NJ: Princeton University Press, 2019), 18.

25. Fortieth-Plus Anniversary Review, 1957–1959, John L. H. Fuller Papers, 2, 1st National Bank Training Class Reunion, Indiana Historical Society.

26. See, for example, "Deaths: Thomas C. Boushall Richmond Banker," *Washington Post*, May 13, 1992; "Rites for Developer of Palos Verdes Conducted," *Los Angeles Times*, September 6, 1977.

27. See, for example, "Foreign Trade Groups Unite for Efficiency," *New York Herald Tribune*, September 11, 1933; "Chinese Bandits Capture U. S. Captain in Yunnan: T. J. Betts, Army Officer, Was Attached to American Legation; Served since 1917," *New York Herald*, May 20, 1926.

28. Hart, *Empire and Revolution*, 12; Moore, "State Building through Partnership," 186–87; "Arthur Mccain Named Chase Bank President," *Wall Street Journal*, April 25, 1946.

29. "The Logical Man," *Time Magazine* 67, no. 4 (1956).

30. "A U.S. Foreign Legion," *Time* 37, no. 26 (1941).

31. De Young, Yankee Finance on the Seven Seas, 1925.

WORKS CITED

"The 1916 College Class [Photograph]." *No. 8* 11, no. 3 (September 1916): 113.

"1977 Focus Shifts to Retail Banking." Citigroup, nd. April 7, 2023. https://www.citigroup.com /global/about-us/heritage/1977/focus-shifts-to-retail-banking.

Abe, Kaori. *Chinese Middlemen in Hong Kong's Colonial Economy, 1830–1890.* London: Routledge, 2018.

"About People and Social Incidents: At the White House." *New York Tribune,* December 17, 1901, 6.

Abrahams, Paul Philip. *The Foreign Expansion of American Finance and Its Relationship to the Foreign Economic Policies of the United States, 1907–1921.* New York: Arno Press, 1976. Reprint of author's thesis, University of Wisconsin, 1967.

Accominotti, Olivier. "International Banking and Transmission of the 1931 Financial Crisis." *Economic History Review* 72, no. 1 (February 2019): 260–85.

Accominotti, Olivier, Delio Lucena-Piquero, and Stefano Ugolini. "The Origination and Distribution of Money Market Instruments: Sterling Bills of Exchange during the First Globalization." *Economic History Review* 74, no. 4 (2021): 892–921.

Accominotti, Olivier, and Stefano Ugolini. "International Trade Finance from the Origins to the Present: Market Structures, Regulation, and Governance." In *The Oxford Handbook of Institutions of International Economic Governance and Market Regulation,* edited by Eric Brousseau, Jean-Michel Glachant, and Jérôme Sgard. New York: Oxford University Press, 2019.

"Acquires New Branch in Santo Domingo." *New York Tribune,* April 2, 1917, 10.

Adam, Marc Christopher. "Liquidating Bankers' Acceptances: International Crisis, Doctrinal Conflict and American Exceptionalism in the Federal Reserve 1913–1932." In *Diskussionsbeiträge:* Free University Berlin, School of Business & Economics, 2020.

"Address of President Paul M. Warburg." *Acceptance Bulletin of the American Acceptance Council* 5, no. 12 (December 1923): 4–8.

Adigun, Omodele. "How to Finance Your Trade with Banker's Acceptance." *The Sun (Nigeria),* February 28, 2017.

Agger, Eugene. "Correspondence Course in Foreign Exchange and International Banking," edited by National City Bank of New York, 1917.

Aitken, Rob. "'Numberless Little Risks': 'Tropical Exposure' in Globalizing Actuarial Discourse, 1852–1947." *Enterprise & Society* (2022): 1–43.

Akiboh, Alvita. "Pocket-Sized Imperialism: U.S. Designs on Colonial Currency." *Diplomatic History* 41, no. 5 (2017): 874–902.

Allen, James S. "Agrarian Tendencies in the Philippines." *Pacific Affairs* 11, no. 1 (1938): 52–65.

Allen, John H. [Letter to Mr. H. H. Hollingshead, Manager, the National City Bank of New York, Bahia, Brazil]. Mar 19, 1920. Item #248, Letters to Mr. Allen - S. America - Bahia, 1920. Heritage Collection at Citi.

Alman & Co. [Alfred Gwynne Vanderbilt, Three-Quarter Length Portrait, Standing, Facing Front, Wearing Top Hat and Holding Gloves]. 1907. Alfred Gwynne Vanderbilt, LC-USZ62–118342, Prints & Photographs Division, Library of Congress.

"Alumni Notes." *Harvard Alumni Bulletin* 29, no. 28 (1927).

Alvarez, Sebastian, and Gianandrea Nodari. "Argentina Banking System in the Interwar Period: Stylized Facts in the Light of a New Database, 1925–1935." Asociación Española de Historia Económica, 2023.

American Acceptance Council. *Bankers Acceptances, Principles and Practices, Second Edition.* New York: American Acceptance Council, 1929.

"American Bank Going into the Latin American Field." *Bankers' Magazine* 89, no. 2 (August 1914): 115.

"American Bankers Acceptance an Important Factor in Financing Foreign Trade." *Acceptance Bulletin* 7, no. 10 (October 1925): 7–8.

[American Consul in Para - Brazil]. Closing of the American Mercantile Bank of Brazil Inc. January 16, 1922. 59, 7592, 811.51632. National Archives.

"The American Group." *Far Eastern Review* 6 (April 1910): 523–26.

"American-Philippine Co. to Get Dean C. Worcester's Aid." *Wall Street Journal*, February 5, 1914, 5.

"American-Philippine Company [Prospectus, Report #1, Report #2]." New York: American-Philippine Company, 1912.

"Americans in the Philippine Islands: Walter E. Olsen." *Journal of the American Chamber of Commerce in the Philippines* 1 (August 1921): 5.

Andrews, David M. *International Monetary Power.* Ithaca, NY: Cornell University Press, 2012.

Annual Report of the Treasurer of the Philippine Islands. Manila: Bureau of Printing, 1910.

Apostol, José P. *The Economic Policy of the Philippine Government: Ownership and Operation of Business.* Manila: University of the Philippines, 1927.

"The Argentine Industrial Union and North American Traders." *Pan American Magazine* 23 (1916): 341–46.

Arnold, A. J. "Should Historians Trust Late Nineteenth-Century Company Financial Statements?" *Business History* 38, no. 2 (1996): 40–54.

Arnold, David John. *The Tropics and the Traveling Gaze: India, Landscape, and Science, 1800–1856.* Seattle: University of Washington Press, 2015.

Arslanalp, Serkan, Barry Eichengreen, and Chima Simpson-Bell. "The Stealth Erosion of Dollar Dominance and the Rise of Nontraditional Reserve Currencies." *Journal of International Economics* 138 (September 1 2022): 1–23.

"Arthur Mccain Named Chase Bank President." *Wall Street Journal*, April 25, 1946, 4.

Assistant Cashier. [Letter to] the National City Bank of New York. December 31, 1926. Item #337, IBC, F.E.D.—General (1926–1930). Heritage Collection at Citi.

Assistant Comptroller. [Letter to] the Manager. January 12, 1927. Item #337, IBC, F.E.D.—General (1926–1930). Heritage Collection at Citi.

Aughinbaugh, William E. *Selling Latin America: A Problem in International Salesmanship What to Sell and How to Sell It.* Boston: Small Maynard and Company, 1915.

Bacevich, Andrew J. "Tragedy Renewed: William Appleman Williams." *World Affairs* 171, no. 3 (2009): 62–72.

"Bache Sells Bank to National City Co." *New York Times*, October 29, 1915, 1.

Backer, John. "Business-Getting in South America." *The Americas* 1, no. 12 (September 1915): 25.

Bagehot, Walter. *Lombard Street.* Homewood, IL: Richard D. Irwin, 1962 [1873].

Baker, James C., and Miles Gerald Bradford. *American Banks Abroad: Edge Act Companies and Multinational Banking.* New York: Praeger, 1975.

"Baker, Kellogg Combine with Amer. Intl. Corpn." *New York Tribune,* July 9, 1923, 15.

Balance of Funds, Manila. March 31, 1903. RG 350, Box 418, Folder 5500. National Archive.

Baldwin, A. H. "The Foreign Trade Bureau." *Bankers Home Magazine* 12, no. 8 (July 1919): 38–40.

Ballentine, Charles. *As It Is in the Philippines.* New York: Lewis, Scribner & Co., 1902.

"Bank Needs Met, Says Morgan Firm." *New York Times,* August 13, 1921.

"Bank Opens Its New Branch Building in Buenos Aires." *No. 8* 24, no. 12 (December 1929): 3–4.

"Bankers' Acceptances: Role of Bankers' Acceptances." June 9, 1954. Box 616550, Folder 440L: Acceptances 1962–1918. Federal Reserve Bank of New York.

"Banking for Women Develops Friendly Service." *No. 8* 16, no. 9 (September 1921): 8.

"Banking in 21 Languages a Specialty at Our New Branch in B. A." *No. 8,* December 1930, 9.

"Banking News of New York City." *New York Financier,* January 6, 1902, 35.

Barker, James M. American Club Luncheon Speech. September 28, 1928. James M. Barker Papers, Box 93, Folder 1662. Newberry Library, Special Collections.

———. Autobiography. 1954. James M. Barker Papers, Box 85, Folder 1588. Newberry Library, Special Collections.

———. Letter to Mr. Trafford. March 15, 1927. James M. Barker Papers, Box 52, Folder 1175. Newberry Library, Special Collections.

———. Letter to Mr. Trafford. January 30, 1923. James M. Barker Papers, Box 52, Folder 1174. Newberry Library, Special Collections.

Barnard, Irving. "Five Years in Jungle Land." *No. 8* 12, no. 4 (April 1917): 12–27.

Barnes, Trevor J. "Inventing Anglo-American Economic Geography, 1889–1960." In *A Companion to Economic Geography,* edited by Eric Sheppard and Trevor J. Barnes. Hoboken, NJ: Blackwell Publishing, 2002.

Baster, A.S.J. *The International Banks.* New York: Arno Press, 1977 [1935].

Becker, William H., and William M. McClenahan, eds. *The Market, the State, and the Export-Import Bank of the United States, 1934–2000.* Cambridge, UK: Cambridge University Press, 2003.

Beckhart, Benjamin Haggott. *The New York Money Market, Vol. 3: Uses of Funds.* New York: AMS Press, 1971 [1932].

Berghoff, Hartmut. "Civilizing Capitalism? The Beginnings of Credit Rating in the United States and Germany." *Bulletin of the German Historical Institute* 45 (2009): 9–28.

Betancourt, Rebca Gomez. "The Political Economy of a Modern Missionary: E. W. Kemmerer in the Philippines." *History of Political Economy* 53, no. 3 (2022): 483–505.

Bhutada, Govind. "The U.S. Share of the Global Economy over Time." 2021. https://www.visualcapitalist.com/u-s-share-of-global-economy-over-time/.

Bickerton, Ian James. "Bankers, Businessmen, and the Open Door Policy, 1899–1911." PhD diss., Claremont Graduate University, 1974.

"Big New York Banks Active in Foreign Field." *Wall Street Journal*, June 10, 1921, 6.

Bishop, Charles O. *The Lion and the Journalist: The Unlikely Friendship of Theodore Roosevelt and Joseph Bucklin Bishop*. Guilford, CT: Lyons Press, 2012.

Bishop, Joseph Bucklin. Letter to Theodore Roosevelt. January 21, 1904. Theodore Roosevelt Papers, http://www.theodorerooseveltcenter.org/Research/Digital-Library/Record.aspx?libID=043800. Library of Congress Manuscript Division, Theodore Roosevelt Digital Library.

Black, Megan. *The Global Interior: Mineral Frontiers and American Power*. Cambridge, MA: Harvard University Press, 2018.

Boggs, F. C. Letter to the International Banking Corporation. April 24, 1915. RG 7, IBC, Heritage Collection at Citi.

Boomer, R. "Mexican Credit Characteristics." *The Credit Monthly*, October 1921, 9–10.

Bouk, Daniel. *How Our Days Became Numbered: Risk and the Rise of the Statistical Individual*. Chicago: University of Chicago Press, 2015.

Braun, Benjamin. "Central Banking and the Infrastructural Power of Finance: The Case of ECB Support for Repo and Securitization Markets." *Socio-Economic Review* 18, no. 2 (2020): 395–418.

Braun, Benjamin, and Daniela Gabor. "Central Banking, Shadow Banking, and Infrastructural Power." SocArXiv, 2019.

Braun, Benjamin, and Kai Koddenbrock. "The Three Phases of Financial Power: Leverage, Infrastructure, and Enforcement." In *Capital Claims: Power and Global Finance*, edited by Benjamin Braun and Kai Koddenbrock, 1–30. London: Routledge, 2022.

Brayshay, Mark, Mark Cleary, and John Selwood. "Social Networks and the Transnational Reach of the Corporate Class in the Early-Twentieth Century." *Journal of Historical Geography* 33, no. 1 (2007): 144–67.

Bridges, Mary. "The Infrastructural Turn in Historical Scholarship." *Modern American History* (2023): 1–18.

Brown, Harriet G. "Havana." *No. 8* 8, no. 4 (April 1918): 3–9.

Brown, S. R. "Canton, Industrial Center of the New South China." *The Americas* 3, no. 8 (May 1917): 10–17.

Broz, J. Lawrence. *The International Origins of the Federal Reserve System*. Ithaca, NY: Cornell University Press, 1997.

Bryan, Steven. *The Gold Standard at the Turn of the Twentieth Century: Rising Powers, Global Money, and the Age of Empire*. New York: Columbia University Press, 2010.

Buchnea, Emily. "Bridges and Bonds: The Role of British Merchant Bank Intermediaries in Latin American Trade and Finance Networks, 1825–1850." *Enterprise & Society* 21, no. 2 (2020): 453–93.

Buley, Roscoe Carlyle. *The Equitable Life Assurance Society of the United States: One Hundredth Anniversary History, 1859–1959*. New York: Appleton-Century-Crofts, 1959.

Bureau of Foreign and Domestic Commerce. [Misc. Letters and Reports]. 1924. RG 59, Box 7593, Folder 811.51675-811.51699. National Archives.

Bureau of Insular Affairs. Confidential Office Memorandum. May 9, 1908. RG 350, Box 799, Folder 17959. National Archive.

Bureau of Labor. Labor Conditions in the Philippines. Clark, Victor S. Washington, DC: Government Printing Office, 1905.

Bureau of Statistics Treasury Department. *Colonial Administration, 1800–1900: Methods of Government and Development Adopted by the Principal Colonizing Nations in Their Control of Tropical and Other Colonies and Dependencies.* Austin, Oscar P. Washington: Government Printing Office, 1901.

——. *Commercial Geography: History of World Commerce.* New York: National City Bank, 1916.

——. "Our 1916 Trade with the Neutral World." *The Americas* 3, no. 6 (March 1917): 33–36.

Burgess, W. Randolph. Open Market Operations of the Federal Reserve System, Address before the American Acceptance Council. Dec. 11, 1928. 128154, 740-A: W. R. Burgess 1921–1944. Federal Reserve Bank of New York.

——. *The Reserve Banks and the Money Market.* New York: Harper & Brothers, 1946 [1927].

Burrage, Henry S. *Thomas Hamlin Hubbard: Bvt. Brigadier General U.S. Vols.* Portland, 1923.

Butler, Henry N. "Nineteenth-Century Jurisdictional Competition in the Granting of Corporate Privileges." *Journal of Legal Studies* 14, no. 1 (January 1985): 129–66.

Cables from South American Branches. November 21, 1917–1918. Item #230, NCB of NY, South American Branches—Cables sent to Main Office (important), 1917–1918. Heritage Collection at Citi.

Cain, P. J., and A. G. Hopkins. "Gentlemanly Capitalism and British Expansion Overseas II: New Imperialism, 1850–1945." *Economic History Review* 40, no. 1 (1987): 1–26.

Calomiris, Charles W., and Stephen H. Haber. *Fragile by Design: The Political Origins of Banking Crises and Scarce Credit.* Princeton, NJ: Princeton University Press, 2014.

"Campus and Buildings." Bowdoin College, March 29, 2023. https://www.bowdoin.edu/about/campus-location/facilities/campus-and-buildings.html.

Carosso, Vincent P. *The Morgans: Private International Bankers, 1854–1913.* Cambridge, MA: Harvard University Press, 1987.

Carosso, Vincent P., and Richard Sylla. "U.S. Banks in International Finance." In *International Banking, 1870–1914,* edited by Rondo Cameron, V. I. Bovykin, Boris V. Anan'ich, A. A. Fursenko, Richard Sylla, and Mira Wilkins, 48–71. New York: Oxford University Press, 1992.

Carr, Wilbur. Facilities Offered by American Banks for Financing International Trade. March 8, 1916. RG 59, Box 7592, Folder 811.516 / 431. National Archives.

Carrel, M. Drew. "Tucuman and the Sugar Industry of Argentina." *The Americas* 2, no. 7 (1916): 21–27.

Carruthers, Bruce G. "From Uncertainty toward Risk: The Case of Credit Ratings." *Socio-Economic Review* 11 (2013): 525–51.

Carter, J. A. Speech at Plaza Hotel. November 21, 1919. RG 12, NCBNY, Dinner Given by Mr. Vanderlip. Heritage Collection at Citi.

Carter, James H. "South America as a Field for Young Men." *No. 8* 10, no. 5–7 (1915): 25–32.

Cartwright, H. A. *Twentieth Century Impressions of British Malaya.* London: Lloyd's Great Britain Publishing Company, 1908.

Cary, Guy. Comments [Letter to G. S. Rentschler]. August 24, 1943. RG 7, History of IBC - Cochran (1943–1965). Heritage Collection at Citi.

Casas, Leopoldo. *Branch Management.* Havana, Cuba: The National City Bank of New York, 1933.

Cassis, Youssef. *City Bankers, 1890–1914.* Cambridge, UK: Cambridge University Press, 1994.

Certificate of Deposit of Bonds by the International Banking Corporation. May 5, 1915. #335, Safekeeping Documents, Panama Canal, 1910–1926. Heritage Collection at Citi.

Certificate of Deposit of Bonds by the International Banking Corporation. June 5, 1918. #335, Safekeeping Documents, Panama Canal, 1910–1926. Heritage Collection at Citi.

Chapman, Stanley. *The Rise of Merchant Banking*. London: Routledge, 2006 [1984].

Chaves, Gastão. "Social Life in Brazil." *No. 8* 12, no. 5 (1917): 40–42.

Chernow, Ron. *The House of Morgan: An American Banking Dynasty and the Rise of the Modern Finance*. New York: Atlantic Monthly Press, 1990.

———. *The Warburgs: The Twentieth-Century Odyssey of a Remarkable Jewish Family*. New York: Vintage, 2016.

Chiba, Yoshihiro. "The 1919 and 1935 Rice Crises in the Philippines: The Rice Market and Starvation in American Colonial Times." *Philippine Studies* 58, no. 4 (2010): 523–56.

"Chilean Staffs Score High in First Bond Selling Contest." *No. 8* 24, no. 3–4 (March–April 1929): 11.

"China's Belt and Road Initiative." *The Economist*, February 6, 2020.

"China's Latest Attempt to Rally the World against Western Values." *The Economist*, April 27, 2023.

"China's Overseas Development Finance Database." Boston University, 2023. July 4, 2023. https://www.bu.edu/gdp/chinas-overseas-development-finance/.

"Chinese Bandits Capture U.S. Captain in Yunnan: T. J. Betts, Army Officer, Was Attached to American Legation; Served since 1917." *New York Herald*, May 20, 1926, 1.

"Chinese Loans and Investment in Infrastructure Have Been Huge." *The Economist*, May 20, 2022.

The Chronicle & Directory for China, Corea, Japan, the Philippines, Cochin-China, Annam, Tonquin, Siam, Borneo, Straits Settlements, Malay States, &C. Hongkong: Daily Press Office, 1912.

The Chronicle & Directory for China, Corea, Japan, the Philippines, Cochin-China, Annam, Tonquin, Siam, Borneo, Straits Settlements, Malay States, &C. Hongkong: Daily Press Office, 1910.

Chu, Richard T. "'Catholic,' 'Mestizo,' 'Sangley': Negotiating 'Chinese' Identities in Manila 1870–1905." PhD diss., University of Southern California, 2003.

———. "The 'Chinese' and the 'Mestizos' of the Philippines: Towards a New Interpretation." *Philippine Studies* 50, no. 3 (2002): 327–70.

"Circular." Edited by National City Bank of New York Petrograd Branch, 1918.

Citicorp. *Citicorp in China: A Colorful, Very Personal History since 1902*. Citicorp [Citibank], 1989.

"Citigroup Is Disposing of Its International Retail Network." *The Economist*, February 19, 2022.

"City Bank Club House." *No. 8* 11, no. 3 (September 1916): 116–18.

"City Bank Students Get Rigid Training." *New York Times*, August 15, 1915, 1.

"Claim to China Loan." *Washington Post*, July 24, 1909, 2.

Cleveland, Harold van, and Thomas F. Huertas. *Citibank, 1812–1970*. Cambridge, MA: Harvard University Press, 1985.

Cobos, Samuel Segura. "Making Money Amnesiac: The 1882 Making of Modern Negotiability in the United Kingdom." *Capitalism: A Journal of History and Economics* 3, no. 1 (2022): 160–90.

Cochran, Thomas. "The International Banking Corporation during the Chairmanship of Thomas H. Hubbard 1901–1915." [1945]. RG 7, History of IBC - Cochran (1943–1965), Heritage Collection at Citi.

Cohen, Benjamin J. *Currency Statecraft: Monetary Rivalry and Geopolitical Ambition*. Chicago: University of Chicago Press, 2019.

Cohen, Tyler. "What De-Dollarization? The Dollar Rules the World." *Bloomberg*, April 23, 2023.

"College Men in Foreign Service." *No. 8* 11, no. 3 (September 1916): 108–10.

The College Training Class. 1921. RG 2, NCBNY, College Training Class. Heritage Collection at Citi.

Collier, Christopher. "New England Specter: Town and State in Connecticut History, Law and Myth." *Connecticut Historical Society Bulletin* 3–4 (Summer 1995): 137–92.

Commercial Directory of Manila. Manila, Philippines, 1901.

"Commercial Geography: The Examination." *No. 8* 11, no. 3 (1916): 71–3.

"Committee on Americanization." *Journal of the American Bankers Association* 12, no. 5 (December 1919): 325.

Committee on Insular Affairs. House of Representatives. *Administration of Philippine Lands, Part 2: Report by the Committee on Insular Affairs of the House of Representatives of Its Investigation of the Interior Department of the Philippine Government Touching the Administration of Philippine Lands and All Matters of Fact and Law Pertaining Therto, in Pursuance of House Resolution No. 795.* Government Printing Office, 1911.

Comparative Statement of the Financial Condition of the Manila Branch of the International Banking Corporation. January 21, 1903. RG 250, Box 418, 5500. National Archives II.

Comparative Statement of the Financial Condition of the Manila Branch of the International Banking Corporation. January 21, 1904. RG 250, Box 418, 5500. National Archives II.

"The Comprador: A Great Factor in Chinese Trade." *Bulletin of the National Association of Credit Men* 5, no. 12 (December 15 1905): 24.

"The Connecticut Muddle." *New York Tribune*, March 9, 1891, 3.

Costigliola, Frank. *Awkward Dominion: American Political, Economic, and Cultural Relations with Europe, 1919–1933.* Ithaca, NY: Cornell University Press, 1984.

Cottrell, P. L. "Great Britain." In *International Banking, 1870–1914*, edited by Rondo Cameron, V. I. Bovykin, Boris V. Anan'ich, A. A. Fursenko, Richard Sylla, and Mira Wilkins, 25–47. New York: Oxford University Press, 1992.

Crane, W. Murray. [Letter to My Dear Mr. President]. December 22, 1901. Theodore Roosevelt Papers, Reel 23, Library of Congress.

———. [Letter to My Dear Mr. President]. August 23, 1902. Theodore Roosevelt Papers, Reel 29, Library of Congress.

Credit Report No. 499: Casteran Hnos & Cia. n.d. Frank A. Vanderlip papers, E-29, Columbia University Rare Books & Manuscript Library.

Crippen, Harlan R. "Philippine Agrarian Unrest: Historical Backgrounds." *Science & Society* 10, no. 4 (1946): 337–60.

Cronon, William. *Nature's Metropolis: Chicago and the Great West* (New York: W. W. Norton, 1991).

Cross, S. H. Letter to Mr. Carr, Assistant Secretary of State. November 17, 1925. RG 59, Box 7592, Folder 811.51644 / 1. National Archives.

"Cuba and Porto Rico Set a World Record in Savings Contest." *No. 8* 21, no. 1 (January 1926): 5–11.

"Cuba's Brilliant Record." *No. 8* 23, no. 8 (August 1928): 4–6, 23–27.

"The Currents of Merchandising in the Orient and the South Pacific." *The Americas*, December 1918, 10–16.

Daniel, Carter A. *MBA: The First Century.* Lewisburg, PA: Bucknell University Press, 1998.

Daniels, Josephus. Letter to the Secretary of the Treasury. June 5, 1915. RG 80, Folder 14708–11. National Archive.

Darling, Charles H. Special Order No. 33. December 22, 1902. RG 80, Box E19A, Folder 10424. National Archive.

De Cecco, Marcello. *The International Gold Standard: Money and Empire*. 2nd ed. London: F. Pinter, 1984.

De Menocal, Daniel. Memoirs of Daniel De Menocal. 1961. RG 12, Folder: De Menocal. Heritage Collection at Citi.

De Young, Dirk. Yankee Finance on the Seven Seas. 1925. RG 7, Yankee Finance. Heritage Collection at Citi.

"Deaths: Thomas C. Boushall Richmond Banker." *Washington Post*, May 13, 1992, D5.

"Delmege: History." 2017. April16, 2020. https://delmege.com/history/.

Deming, Clarence. "Town Rule in Connecticut." *Political Science Quarterly* 4, no. 3 (1889): 408–32.

Desan, Christine. "Coin Reconsidered: The Political Alchemy of Commodity Money." *Theoretical Inquiries in Law* 11, no. 1 (2010): 361–409.

———. "How to Spend a Trillion Dollars: Our Monetary Hardwiring, Why It Matters, and What to Do About It." *SSRN* (March 12 2022).

Desan, Christine, and Nadav Orian Peer. "The Constitution and the Fed after the Covid-19 Crisis." JustMoney.org, 2020. https://justmoney.org/the-constitution-and-the-fed-after-the -covid-19-crisis-2/.

Dickinson, Jacob. Letter to Gen. Hubbard, International Banking Corporation. June 1, 1910. RG 350, Box 799, Folder 17959. National Archive.

District 2 Federal Reserve. Report of Condition—the National City Bank of New York. New York: 1929.

Doeppers, Daniel F. *Feeding Manila in Peace and War, 1850–1945*. New Perspectives in Southeast Asian Studies. Madison: University of Wisconsin Press, 2016.

Doherty, L. A. Fourth Brief for the International Banking Corporation on the Subject of the Transfer from Shanghai to the United States of the Chinese Indemnity. March 18, 1914. Safekeeping Documents 1 (1904–1926), Item #335: 1911–1915. Heritage Collection at Citi.

Domosh, Mona. "Geoeconomic Imaginations and Economic Geography in the Early Twentieth Century." *Annals of the Association of American Geographers* 103, no. 4 (2013): 944–66.

Doubtful Accounts—Reserves; Santo Domingo. March 24, 1924. Item 337 / IBC, Dominican Branches. Heritage Collection at Citi.

Drake, Paul W. *The Money Doctor in the Andes: The Kemmerer Missions, 1923–1933*. Durham: Duke University Press, 1989.

Dulles, Eleanor Lansing. Department of State. The Export-Import Bank of Washington, the First Ten Years. Washington: Government Printing Office, 1944.

Dulles, John Foster. "Our Foreign Loan Policy." *Foreign Affairs* 5 (October 1, 1926): 33–48.

Dun, R. G. [Letter to Banco Del Callao, Lima, Peru]. August 13, 1896. Dun & Bradstreet Corporation Records II(A), v. 11 Letterbook. Harvard Business School.

———. Letter to Joseph Packard, Esq., Baltimore, Md. January 18, 1912. Dun & Bradstreet Corporation Records II(A), v. 12 Letterbook. Harvard Business School.

Durland, John. Letter to Frank Vanderlip. April 6, 1917. Frank A. Vanderlip Papers, Box F-1, Chile. Columbia RBML.

Durrell, Joseph. History of Foreign Branches of American Banks and Overseas Division, NCB. 1940. Heritage Collection at Citi.

Dwyre, Dudley. Letter to John C. Wiley, Chargé d'Affaires, American Legation, Caracas. December 9, 1920. RG 59, Box 7592, Folder 811.516 / 330. National Archives.

Easterling, Keller. "Histories of Things That Don't Happen and Shouldn't Always Work." *Social Research* 83, no. 3 (Fall 2016): 625–44.

Eastwick, Philip G. [Letter to Martin Egan]. December 2, 1925. Martin Egan Papers, 14, Eastwick, Philip G. Pierpont Morgan Library.

"Editorial Comment: Commission Rates on Bankers Acceptance Credits." *Acceptance Bulletin* 9, no. 5 (May 31, 1927): 3–5.

Edwards, A. V. [Letter to the Manager, the National City Bank of New York, Rio De Janeiro, Brazil]. May 21, 1920. Item #249, Foreign Branches - Rio de Janeiro - Confidential Letters, 1920. Heritage Collection at Citi.

Edwards, Clarence R. Lettter to J. S. Tait, International Banking Corporation. December 9, 1904. RG 350, Box 418, Folder 5500. National Archive.

———. Memorandum for the Secretary of War. April 24, 1911. RG 350, Box 799, Folder 17959. National Archive.

———. Memorandum for the Secretary of War, in the Matter of Securities for Deposits with the International Banking Corporation. May 24, 1910. RG 350, Box 799, Folder 17959. National Archive.

Edwards, George William. Department of Commerce. US Bureau of Foreign and Domestic Commerce. Financing Agricultural Exports from the United States. Washington: Government Printing Office, 1924.

———. *International Trade Finance*. New York: H. Holt and Company, 1924.

Edwin Gould, Portrait Bust. nd. George Grantham Bain Collection, LC-DIG-ggbain-00795, Library of Congress, Prints and Photographs Division.

Eichengreen, Barry. "Comments on 'Where It All Began: Lending of Last Resort and Bank of England Monitoring during the Overend, Gurney Panic of 1866.'" In *The Origins, History, and Future of the Federal Reserve: A Return to Jekyll Island*, edited by Michael D. Bordo and William Roberds, 162–65. New York: Cambridge University Press, 2013.

———. *Global Imbalances and the Lessons of Bretton Woods*. Cambridge, MA: MIT Press, 2010.

———. *Globalizing Capital: A History of the International Monetary System*. Princeton, NJ: Princeton University Press, 1996.

———. *Golden Fetters: The Gold Standard and the Great Depression, 1919–1939*. New York: Oxford University Press, 1992.

———. "Is De-Dollarisation Happening?" CEPR, 2023. https://cepr.org/voxeu/columns/de-dollarisation-happening.

———. "The U.S. Capital Market and Foreign Lending, 1920–1955." In *Developing Country Debt and Economic Performance, Volume 1: The International Financial System*, edited by Jeffrey D. Sachs, 107–55. Chicago: University of Chicago Press, 1991.

Eichengreen, Barry, Asmaa El-Ganainy, Rui Pedro Esteves, and Kris James Mitchener. "Public Debt through the Ages." *IMF Working Paper* 2019 / 006 (January 2019).

Eichengreen, Barry, and Marc Flandreau. "The Federal Reserve, the Bank of England, and the Rise of the Dollar as an International Currency, 1914–1939." *Open Economies Review* 23, no. 1 (2012): 57–87.

———. "The Rise and Fall of the Dollar (or When Did the Dollar Replace Sterling as the Leading Reserve Currency?)" *European Review of Economic History* 13, no. 3 (2009): 377–411.

———. *The Gold Standard in Theory and History*. London: Routledge, 1997.

Eichengreen, Barry, Arnaud Mehl, and Livia Chiţu. *How Global Currencies Work: Past, Present, and Future*. Princeton, NJ: Princeton University Press, 2018.

Einolf, Christopher J. *America in the Philippines, 1899–1902: The First Torture Scandal*. New York: Palgrave Macmillan, 2014.

Eldridge, F. R. Letter to Mr. Carr, Assistant Secretary of State. November 17, 1924. RG 59, Box 7592, Folder 811.51644 / 1. National Archives.

"Elections of the Banks: Few Changes Made in the Directorates of National and State Institutions." *New York Times*, January 10, 1900, 9.

Engerman, David C. "Empires, Visible and Invisible." *Modern Intellectual History* 18, no. 1 (2021): 288–97.

"English and American Mercantile Agency Methods [Response]." *Bulletin of the National Association of Credit Men* 11, no. 5 (May 15, 1911): 306.

Engwall, Lars. "Business Schools and Consultancies: The Blurring of Boundaries." In *The Oxford Handbook of Management Consulting*, edited by Matthias Kipping and Timothy Clark, 365–87. Oxford: Oxford University Press, 2012.

Enstad, Nan. *Cigarettes, Inc.: An Intimate History of Corporate Imperialism*. Chicago: University of Chicago Press, 2018.

Epstein, Katherine C. "The Conundrum of American Power in the Age of World War I." *Modern American History* 2, no. 3 (November 2019): 345–65.

Espeland, Wendy Nelson. "Commensuration as a Social Process." *Annual Review of Sociology* 24 (August 1988): 313–43.

Espiner, Tom. "HSBC to Close 114 UK Branches as More People Bank Online." BBC, November 30, 2022.

Examination Record [IAB]. June 16, 1927. RG 3 Chase Manhattan Bank Collection, 17B11, 3. JPMorgan Chase Corporate History Collection.

"Exim Board Votes to Renew Finance Facility for Boeing, Supporting Small Business Suppliers across America." Export-Import Bank of the United States, 2023. https://www.exim.gov /news/exim-board-votes-renew-finance-facility-for-boeing-supporting-small-business -suppliers-across.

"Experiences in Selling Certain Classes of Immigrants." *Bulletin of the National Association of Credit Men* 16, no. 4 (April 1916): 373–74.

"Export-Import Bank of the United States Signs Co-Financing Agreement with EKN of Sweden." Export-Import Bank of the United States, 2023. https://www.exim.gov/news/export -import-bank-united-states-signs-co-financing-agreement-ekn-sweden.

Fansler, Percival. "New Railways in the Philippine Islands," *Cassier's Magazine* 30, no. 2 (June 1906): 161–74.

Farrell, Maureen, and Nicolas Parasie. "In Aramco IPO, a Bonanza for Banks." *Wall Street Journal*, June 10, 2016.

Fear, Jeffrey, and R. Daniel Wadhwani. "Populism and Political Entrepreneurship: The Universalization of German Savings Banks and the Decline of American Savings Banks, 1907–1934." In *Business in the Age of Extremes: Essays in Modern German and Austrian*

Economic History, edited by Hartmut Berghoff, Jürgen Kocka, and Dieter Ziegler. Cambridge, UK: Cambridge University Press, 2013.

Federal Reserve Board. Circulars and Regulations. Washington: Government Printing Office, 1916.

———. Foreign Credit Information. Washington: Government Printing Office, 1922.

———. Informal Rulings of the Board. Washington: Government Printing Office, 1922.

———. Informal Rulings of the Board: Responsibility on Acceptances. Washington: Government Printing Office, 1916.

Fertik, Edward S. "Steel and Sovereignty: The United States, Nationalism, and the Transformation of World Order, 1898–1941." PhD diss., Yale University, 2018.

Fettin, Timothy. "An Old Silver Mine in Peru." *No. 8* 11, no. 3 (September 1916): 99.

"A Few Gratuitous Privileges." *Hartford Courant*, January 6, 1902, 10.

"Fight Close to Manila." *Chicago Daily Tribune*, August 19, 1902, 5.

"Fiscal Agents in Orient: An American Corporation Will Supplant the English Bankers." *Washington Post*, January 1, 1902, 3.

Flandreau, Marc, and Juan H. Flores. "Bonds and Brands: Foundations of Sovereign Debt Markets, 1820–1830." *Journal of Economic History* 69, no. 3 (2009): 646–84.

Flandreau, Marc, Norbert Gaillard, and Frank Packer. "To Err Is Human: US Rating Agencies and the Interwar Foreign Government Debt Crisis." *European Review of Economic History* 15, no. 3 (2011): 495–538.

Flandreau, Marc, Norbert Gaillard, and Ugo Panizza. "Conflicts of Interest, Reputation, and the Interwar Debt Crisis: Banksters or Bad Luck?" edited by Geneva Graduate Institute, 2010.

Flandreau, Marc, and Gabriel Geisler Mesevage. "The Separation of Information and Lending and the Rise of Rating Agencies in the USA (1841–1907)." *Scandinavian Economic History Review* 62, no. 3 (2014): 213–42.

———. "The Untold History of Transparency: Mercantile Agencies, the Law, and the Lawyers." *Enterprise & Society* 15, no. 2 (June 2014): 214–51.

Flandreau, Marc, and Stefano Ugolini. "Where It All Began: Lending of Last Resort and the Bank of England during the Overend, Gurney Panic of 1866." In *The Origins, History, and Future of the Federal Reserve: A Return to Jekyll Island*, edited by Michael D. Bordo and William Roberds, 113–61. New York: Cambridge University Press, 2013.

Flint, A. L. Letter to the International Banking Corporation. April 24, 1915. Safekeeping Documents 1 (1904–1926), Item #335: Panama Canal Zone (1910–1926). Heritage Collection at Citi.

Folder Contents. 1950–1960. Board Shareholders Files 1, Item 79 Miscellaneous. Heritage Collection at Citi.

"Following Our Example in South American Trade." *The Americas* 2, no. 7 (1916): 9–10.

Forbes, William Cameron. W. Cameron Forbes Papers, 1921–1924. 1921. II, Houghton Library, Harvard University.

———. *The Philippine Islands, Vol 2*. Boston: Houghton Mifflin, 1928.

Fordham, Benjamin O. "Protectionist Empire: Trade, Tariffs, and United States Foreign Policy, 1890–1914." *Studies in American Political Development* 31, no. 2 (2017): 170–92.

"The Foreign Branch Service." *The Americas* 1, no. 1 (1914): 11–13.

Foreign Branches. [nd]. RG IBC, Box 496, Foreign Branch. Heritage Collection at Citi.

"Foreign Business of the National City Bank of New York." *Federal Reserve Bulletin* (October 1 1918): 942–48.

"Foreign Trade Groups Unite for Efficiency." *New York Herald Tribune*, September 11, 1933, 29.

Fortieth-Plus Anniversary Review. 1957–1959. John L. H. Fuller Papers, 2, 1st National Bank Training Class Reunion. Indiana Historical Society.

Fourcade, Marion, and Rakesh Khurana. "From Social Control to Financial Economics: The Linked Ecologies of Economics and Business in Twentieth Century America." *Theory and Society* 42, no. 2 (March 2013): 121–59.

Francisco, Adrianne Marie. "From Subjects to Citizens: American Colonial Education and Philippine Nation-Making, 1900–1934." PhD diss., University of California-Berkeley, 2015.

"A Frank Word Concerning Slip-Shod Export Methods." *The Americas* 2, no. 12 (September 1916): 1–5.

Frieden, Jeffry. "The Political Economy of the Bretton Woods Agreements: Together with Scholarly Commentaries and Essential Historical Documents." In *Bretton Woods Agreements*, edited by Naomi Lamoreaux and Ian Shapiro, 21–37. New Haven, CT: Yale University Press, 2019.

Friedman, Milton, and Anna Jacobson Schwartz. *A Monetary History of the United States: 1867–1960*. Princeton, NJ: Princeton University Press, 1971.

"From the Firing Line." June 1916. RG 2 / NCBNY, Aspersions. Heritage Collection at Citi.

Fuller, John. Journal - Russia. 1917–1919. John L. H. Fuller Papers, Box 1, Folder 8. Indiana Historical Society.

———. Letter to Hector Fuller. December 29, 1917. John L. H. Fuller Papers, Box 1, Folder 2. Indiana Historical Society.

Galassi, Francesco L., and Lucy Newton. "My Word Is My Bond: Reputation as Collateral in Nineteenth Century English Provincial Banking." University of Warwick, Department of Economics, 2001.

Garbade, Kenneth D. *Birth of a Market: The U.S. Treasury Securities Market from the Great War to the Great Depression*. Cambridge, MA: MIT Press, 2012.

Gardin, John E. American Branch Banks Abroad. April 1919.

———. Liberty Bonds for the Business Woman. June 8, 1917. Economic & Trade Conditions: Pamphlets, Harvard Business School.

Gardner, Lloyd C., and William Appleman Williams, eds. *Redefining the Past: Essays in Diplomatic History in Honor of William Appleman Williams*. Corvallis: Oregon State University Press, 1986.

"Gen. T. H. Hubbard, Financier, Dead." *New York Times*, May 20, 1915, 11.

"General News". April 1916. 2 /NCBNY, Aspersions. Heritage Collection at Citi.

Gleeck, Lewis E. *American Business and Philippine Economic Development*. Manila: Carmelo & Bauermann, 1975.

———. *The Manila Americans (1901–1964)*. Manila: Carmelo & Bauermann, 1977.

"Gloomy View: Locusts Attack Crops in the Philippines." *Boston Daily Globe*, October 27, 1902, 9.

Glotzer, Paige. *How the Suburbs Were Segregated: Developers and the Business of Exclusionary Housing, 1890–1960*. Columbia Studies in the History of US Capitalism. New York: Columbia University Press, 2020.

Golay, Frank Hindman. *Face of Empire: United States-Philippine Relations, 1898–1946*. Madison: University of Wisconsin-Madison, Center for Southeast Asian Studies, 1998.

Golay, Frank R. "'Manila Americans' and the Philippine Policy: The Voice of American Business." In *The Philippine Economy and the United States in Past and Present Interactions*, edited by Norman G. Owen, 1–35. Ann Arbor: Center for South and Southeast Asian Studies, University of Michigan, 1983.

Goldstein, Louis, and A. H. Boette. "A Study of Foreign Business, Especially from the Credit Side." *Bulletin of the National Association of Credit Men* 15, no. 3 (March 1915): 166.

Gooding, Nigel. "Philippine Business Firms: Handstamp Markings & Privately Printed Covers." 2019. May 3, 2020. https://www.nigelgooding.co.uk/Spanish/Business%20Firms/Adolfo%20Roensch%20&%20Co/AdolfoRoensch.pdf.

Gopal, Lou. "Brias Roxas Story," *Manila Nostalgia.* 2014. June 24, 2020. http://www.lougopal.com/manila/?p=2276.

———. "Los Tamaraos Polo Club." 2015. April 17, 2019. http://www.lougopal.com/manila/?p=3000.

Gottschalk, A.L.M. Concerning the Local Branch of the National City; Letter to the Secretary of State. June 22, 1915. RG 59, Box 7590, Folder 811.516. National Archive.

Green, H.T.S. Letter to Chief of Office, the Panama Canal. April 26, 1915. Safekeeping Documents 1 (1904–1926), Item #335: Panama Canal Zone (1910–1926). Heritage Collection at Citi.

Greenhill, Robert, and Rory Miller. "British Trading Companies in South America after 1914." In *The Multinational Traders,* edited by Geoffrey Jones. London: Routledge, 1998.

Groeger, Cristina V. "A 'Good Mixer': University Placement in Corporate America, 1890–1940." *History of Education Quarterly* 58, no. 1 (February 2018): 33–64.

Groh, Tyrone, and James Lockhart. "Is America an Empire?" *War on the Rocks,* August 27, 2015.

"Growth of the Foreign Credit Corporation." *Bankers' Magazine* 102, no. 2 (February 1921): 291.

"Guaranty Club to Give a Minstrel Show." *The Guaranty News* 8, no. 11 (January 1920): 356.

Guaranty Trust Company of New York. *Acceptances.* [New York]: Guaranty Trust Company of New York, 1919.

———. *Acceptances.* New York: Guaranty Trust Company of New York, 1920.

———. *Acceptances.* New York: Guaranty Trust Company of New York, 1918.

———. [Announcement of Withdrawal]. February 4, 1904. RG 350, Box 418, Folder 5500. National Archive.

———. *Banking Service for Foreign Trade.* New York: Guaranty Trust Company of New York, 1919.

———. *Essentials of Trading with Latin America.* New York: Guaranty Trust Company of New York, 1920.

———. *How Business with Foreign Countries Is Financed.* New York: Guaranty Trust Company of New York, 1916.

———. *One Hundred Years of Banking Service, 1839–1939.* New York: Guaranty Trust, 1939.

"Guaranty Trust in Front Ranks." *Wall Street Journal,* July 16, 1927, 8.

Guerrero, Milagros Camayon. "Luzon at War: Contradictions in Philippine Society, 1898–1902." PhD diss., University of Michigan, 1977.

"H-Diplo Teaching Roundtable Xxi-20 on Teaching the American Empire Debate." H-Net, 2019. April 13, 2023. https://hdiplo.org/to/RT21-20.

H., B. H. Report of an Examination of the Financial Condition of the International Banking Corporation, Manila Branch. Aug 22, 1910. RG 350, Box 418, National Archives.

Hall, G. Martel. [Letter to Mother and Father]. January 18, 1920. Series 1: Hall Family Collection, 6, 11. East Texas Research Center, R. W. Steen Library, Stephen F. Austin University.

———. [Letter to Mother and Father]. January 13, 1924. Series 1: Hall Family Collection, 7, 7. East Texas Research Center, R. W. Steen Library, Stephen F. Austin University.

Hall, G. Martel. [Letter to Mother and Father]. August 29, 1919. Series 1: Hall Family Collection, 6, 8. East Texas Research Center, R. W. Steen Library, Stephen F. Austin University.

———. [Letter to Mother and Father]. October 15, 1922. Series 1: Hall Family Collection, 6, 31. East Texas Research Center, R. W. Steen Library, Stephen F. Austin University.

———. Problems in Hongkong. December 12, 1933. Series 2: Hall Family Collection, 18, 39. East Texas Research Center, R. W. Steen Library, Stephen F. Austin University.

Hamilton, E. W. Letter to George Hogg, Manager, International Banking Corporation, Hongkong. January 7, 1927. Item #337, IBC, F.E.D.—General (1926–1930). Heritage Collection at Citi.

"Hankow-Szechuan Railroad Loan and the State Department." Wall Street Journal, February 16, 1910, 2.

Hao, Yen-p'ing. "A 'New Class' in China's Treaty Ports: The Rise of the Comprador-Merchants." The Business History Review 44, no. 4 (Winter 1970): 446–59.

Harding, W. Letter to the International Banking Corporation. June 5, 1919. Box: Board Shareholders Files 1, Item 79 - Federal Reserve Board Reports. Heritage Collection at Citi.

Hardy, Charles O. Credit Policies of the Federal Reserve System. Washington, DC: Brookings Institution, 1932.

Harrington, John Walker. "Big Banks and Small Personal Loans." The Bankers Magazine 116, no. 6 (1928): 895.

Harris, Ernest L. "Commercial Growth of Norway." The Americas 3, no. 6 (March 1916): 26–29.

———. "Smyrna, Gateway of a Rich Country in Asia." The Americas 3, no. 3 (December 1916): 21–27.

Harrison, Mitchell C. New York State's Prominent and Progressive Men, Vol. 1. New York: New York Tribune, 1902.

Hart, Boies C. Banker at Large [Unpublished Memoir]. 2007. RG12–History, Sub-group Oral Histories and Employee Memoirs, Box 3, Heritage Collection at Citi.

Hart, John M. Empire and Revolution: The Americans in Mexico since the Civil War. Berkeley: University of California Press, 2002.

Hartley, Marcellus. A Brief Memoir. New York: Privately Printed, 1903.

Harvey, Sir Ernest Maes. "Battle Royale between 'Dollar' and 'Sterling.'" Acceptance Bulletin 7, no. 6 (June 1925): 5–6.

Healy, David. Drive to Hegemony: The United States in the Caribbean, 1898–1917. Madison: University of Wisconsin Press, 1988.

Helfrich, Ralph T. "Trading in Bankers' Acceptances: A View from the Acceptance Desk of the Federal Reserve Bank of New York." Monthly Review (Federal Reserve Bank of New York), February 1976, 51–57.

Helleiner, Eric. States and the Re-Emergence of Global Finance: From Bretton Woods to the 1990s. Ithaca, NY: Cornell University Press, 1994.

Hemphill, Alexander J. "The Banker's Part in Americanization." The Guaranty News 8, no. 1 (March 1919): 1–6.

Henry C. Frick. nd. George Grantham Bain Collection, LC-DIG-ggbain-07131. Library of Congress, Prints and Photographs Division.

Herman, Rebecca. Cooperating with the Colossus: A Social and Political History of US Military Bases in World War II Latin America. New York: Oxford University Press, 2022.

Higgins, Ames. "A New Era in Banking." No. 8 9, no. 7–10 (1914): 1–7.

Higgins, William L. Letter to the International Banking Corporation. September 2, 1931. Board Shareholders Files 1, Item 79 State of Connecticut—Secretary's Office. Heritage Collection at Citi.

Hillyer, A. S. Department of Commerce. Sources of Foreign Credit Information. Washington, DC: Government Printing Office, 1924.

"His Credit A1." Bulletin of the National Association of Credit Men 13, no. 7 (July 15 1913): 439.

Historical Statistics of the United States, Colonial Times to 1970. Bureau of the Census. Washington, DC: U.S. Dept. of Commerce, Bureau of the Census, 1975.

Hodges, Jack E. "Credit Granting in Mexico." The Credit Monthly 27, no. 10 (October 1925): 7–9.

Hubbard, Thomas H. Subject: Security for Deposits of Philippine Government Money. May 13, 1910. 350, 799, 17959. National Archive.

Hudson, Peter James. Bankers and Empire: How Wall Street Colonized the Caribbean. Chicago: University of Chicago Press, 2017.

———. "The National City Bank of New York and Haiti, 1909–1922." Radical History Review 2013, no. 115 (2013): 91–114.

Huertas, Thomas F. "U.S. Multinational Banking: History and Prospects." In Banks as Multinationals, edited by Geoffrey Jones. London; New York: Routledge, 1990.

Hutchcroft, Paul D. "Colonial Masters, National Politicos, and Provincial Lords: Central Authority and Local Autonomy in the American Philippines, 1900–1913." Journal of Asian Studies 59, no. 2 (2000): 277–306.

IBC: Fiftieth Anniversary of Citibank's Giant Step. October 1965. Citi, RG 7, History of IBC.

"IBC's Training Divided between New York and London Offices." No. 8 14, no. 6 (June 1919): 25–26.

IBC Executive Committee. Executive Committee Meeting Minutes. 1902–1905. Item #335–1. Heritage Collection at Citi.

———. Executive Committee Meeting Minutes. 1905–1914. Item #335–2. Heritage Collection at Citi.

———. Executive Committee Meeting Minutes. 1914–1918. Item #355–3, IBC. Heritage Collection at Citi.

———. Executive Committee Meeting Minutes. 1918–1921. Item #335–4. Heritage Collection at Citi.

IBC Secretary. Directors' Minutes. November 14, 1918. 7, Annual Directors Meeting Minutes. Heritage Collection at Citi.

Immerwahr, Daniel. How to Hide an Empire: A History of the Greater United States. New York: Farrar, Straus and Giroux, 2019.

"In the Women's Department at Forty-Second Street." No. 8 20, no. 4 (April 1925): 13.

"In Two Years Personal Loan Dept Has Aided 134,294 Families." No. 8 25, no. 5 (May 1930): 8.

"International Acceptance Bank." Wall Street Journal, November 30, 1921, 4.

International Acceptance Bank. Report of the International Acceptance Bank Incorporated to the Stock Holders at the Annual Meeting, 1925–1928. New York, 1925–1928.

"The International Bank: Secretary Gage Not Chosen to Succeed Marcellus Hartley." New York Times, January 23, 1902, 16.

"International Banking Concern." New York Tribune, December 13, 1903, 6.

"The International Banking Corporation." Journal of the American Asiatic Association 3, no. 1 (February 1, 1903): 25.

"International Banking Corporation." *Wall Street Journal*, October 6, 1903, 2.

International Banking Corporation. Executive Committee Meetings 1918–1921. Citi, Item #355, IBC.

———. [Multiple Letters to War Department, Bureau of Insular Affairs]. 1904. RG 350, Box 418, Folder 5500. National Archive.

———. "The Philippine Islands." New York: Brown, Lent & Pett, 1908.

———. Semi-Annual Statement of International Banking Corporation. 1904–1913. RG 350, Box 418, Folder 5500. National Archives.

———. Statement of Condition. 1902–1946. HS 231, Item #1034 IBC. Heritage Collection at Citi.

———. To the Stockholders. April 15, 1905. RG 350, Box 418, Folder 5500. National Archive.

"International Banking Corporation [Advertisement]." *The Straits Times*, October 3, 1902.

The International Banking Corporation Terms of Engagement. March 10, 1920. Series 2: Hall Family Collection, East Texas Research Center, R. W. Steen Library, Stephen F. Austin University.

International Banking Corporation: Board of Directors. 1903. RG 350, Container #418, 5500–21. National Archives.

International Banking Corporation: Charter. 1901. Item #631, IBC, Charter. Heritage Collection at Citi.

"Interpretation of Regulation B as to Borrower's Statements." *Federal Reserve Bulletin* (August 1915): 213.

Jackson, Justin F. "'A Military Necessity Which Must Be Pressed': The U.S. Army and Forced Road Labor in Early American Colonial Philippines." In *On Coerced Labor: Work and Compulsion after Chattel Slavery*, edited by Marcel van der Linden and Magaly Rodriguez Garcia, 127–58. London: Brill, 2016.

Jacobs, Lawrence Merton. "Talk to the College Training Class." *No. 8* 13, no. 9 (September 1918): 3–8.

———. What Shall We Do with the International Banking Corporation? May 23, 1916. Frank A. Vanderlip papers, E-27 International Banking Corporation. Rare Book and Manuscript Library, Columbia University Library.

James Hazen Hyde, Three-Quarter Length Portrait, Seated, Facing Right. c1904. LCPP003B-43051. Library of Congress, Prints and Photographs Division.

"Japanese Snapshots." January–February 1917. RG 2/NCBNY, Aspersions. Heritage Collection at Citi.

Jaremski, Matthew, and David C. Wheelock. "The Founding of the Federal Reserve, the Great Depression, and the Evolution of the U.S. Interbank Network." *Journal of Economic History* 80, no. 1 (2020): 69–99.

Jasanoff, Sheila. "Ordering Knowledge, Ordering Society." In *States of Knowledge: The Co-Production of Science and Social Order*, edited by Sheila Jasanoff. London; New York: Routledge, 2004.

Jenkins, Destin. *The Bonds of Inequality: Debt and the Making of the American City*. Chicago: University of Chicago Press, 2021.

Jenkins, Destin, and Justin Leroy, eds. *Histories of Racial Capitalism*. New York: Columbia University Press, 2021.

———. "Introduction: The Old History of Capitalism." In *Histories of Racial Capitalism*, edited by Destin Jenkins and Justin Leroy. New York: Columbia University Press, 2021.

Johnson, Nic. "The Imperial Fed." *Phenomenal World*, March 30, 2023.

Johnson, Nicholas P. "The Inter-Imperial and Pan-American Origins of the Federal Reserve Act of 1913, and the Birth of the Global Dollar System." University of Chicago, 2018.

Jones, Charles. "The Transfer of Banking Techniques from Britain to Argentina, 1862–1914." *Revue internationale d'histoire de la banque* 26 (1983): 252–64.

Jones, Charles A. "British Financial Institutions in Argentina, 1860–1914." University of Cambridge, 1973.

Jones, Geoffrey. "Banks as Multinationals." In *Banks as Multinationals*, edited by Geoffrey Jones. London; New York: Routledge, 1990.

———. *British Multinational Banking, 1830–1990*. Oxford: Oxford University Press, 1995.

———. "Competitive Advantages in British Multinational Banking since 1890." In *Banks as Multinationals*, edited by Geoffrey Jones, 30–61. London; New York: Routledge, 1990.

Joslin, David. *A Century of Banking in Latin America—to Commemorate the Centenary in 1962 of the Bank of London & South America Limited*. London; New York: Oxford University Press, 1963.

Joyce, Patrick. *The Rule of Freedom: Liberalism and the Modern City*. London: Verso, 2003.

Kaminishi, Miriam, and Andrew David Smith. "Western Debates about Chinese Entrepreneurship in the Treaty Port Period, 1842–1911." *Enterprise & Society* 21, no. 1 (2020): 134–69.

Karabel, Jerome. *The Chosen: The Hidden History of Admission and Exclusion at Harvard, Yale, and Princeton*. Boston: Houghton Mifflin, 2005.

Karabell, Zachary. *Inside Money: Brown Brothers Harriman and the American Way of Power*. New York: Penguin, 2021.

Katz, Jonathan M. *Gangsters of Capitalism: Smedley Butler, the Marines, and the Making and Breaking of America's Empire*. New York: St. Martin's Press, 2022.

Kaufman, Burton Ira. *Efficiency and Expansion: Foreign Trade Organization in the Wilson Administration, 1913–1921*. Contributions in American History. Westport, CT: Greenwood Press, 1974.

Kenzel, E. R. Letter to Charles Peple, Deputy Governor, Federal Reserve Bank of Richmond. February 27, 1929. Box 171546, Folder 440 - Acceptances 1927–1929. Federal Reserve Bank of New York.

———. Letter to Hon. W. J. Bailey, Governor, Federal Reserve Bank of Kansas City. August 24, 1929. Box 171546, Folder 440 - Acceptances 1927–1929. Federal Reserve Bank of New York.

Khurana, Rakesh. *From Higher Aims to Hired Hands: The Social Transformation of American Business Schools and the Unfulfilled Promise of Management as a Profession*. Princeton, NJ; Woodstock: Princeton University Press, 2010.

Kies, William S. "The Development of Our Export Trade." *Bankers Home Magazine* 12, no. 1 (October 1917): 14–23.

Kindleberger, Charles P. *A Financial History of Western Europe*. New York: Routledge, 2015.

King, Frank H. H. "The Boxer Indemnity: 'Nothing but Bad.'" *Modern Asian Studies* 40, no. 3 (2006): 663–89.

———. *The Hongkong Bank in the Period of Imperialism and War, 1895–1918*. The History of the Hongkong and Shanghai Banking Corporation. Cambridge, UK: Cambridge University Press, 1988.

King, Frank H. H., David J. S. King, and Catherine E. King. *The History of the Hongkong Bank in Late Imperial China, 1864–1902: On an Even Keel*. The History of the Hongkong and Shanghai Banking Corporation. 4 vols. Vol. 1, Cambridge, UK: Cambridge University Press, 1987.

Knapp, H. S. Military Government of Santo Domingo, Executive Order No. 42. March 17, 1917. 7, Item 335, Safekeeping Documents - Dominican Republic. Heritage Collection at Citi.

Kniffin, William H. "Deductions of a Credit Man in Analyzing Business Statements." *Journal of the American Bankers Association* 7, no. 8 (February 1915): 623–25.

Kramer, Paul A. *The Blood of Government: Race, Empire, the United States, & the Philippines.* Chapel Hill: University of North Carolina Press, 2006.

———. "Embedding Capital: Political-Economic History, the United States, and the World." *Journal of the Gilded Age and Progressive Era* 15 (2016): 331–62.

———. "Empires, Exceptions, and Anglo-Saxons: Race and Rule between the British and United States Empires, 1880–1910." *Journal of American History* (March 2002): 1315–53.

———. "How Not to Write the History of U.S. Empire." *Diplomatic History* 42, no. 5 (November 2018): 911–31.

———. "Power and Connection: Imperial Histories of the United States in the World." *American Historical Review* 116 (2011): 1348–92.

———. "Race-Making and Colonial Violence in the U.S. Empire: The Philippine-American War as Race War." *Diplomatic History* 30, no. 2 (2006): 169–210.

———. "A Useful Corner of the World: Guantánamo." *New Yorker,* July 30, 2013.

LaFeber, Walter. *The New Empire: An Interpretation of American Expansion, 1860–1898.* Ithaca, NY: Cornell University Press, 1963.

———. "A Note on the 'Mercantilistic Imperialism' of Alfred Thayer Mahan." *Mississippi Valley Historical Review* 48, no. 4 (1962): 674–85.

Lambert, Nicholas A. *Planning Armageddon: British Economic Warfare and the First World War.* Cambridge, MA: Harvard University Press, 2012.

Lamoreaux, Naomi R. *Insider Lending: Banks, Personal Connections, and Economic Development in Industrial New England.* Cambridge, UK: Cambridge University Press, 1997.

Lamoreaux, Naomi R., and John Joseph Wallis. "Economic Crisis, General Laws, and the Mid-Nineteenth-Century Transformation of American Political Economy." *Journal of the Early Republic* 41, no. 3 (Fall 2021): 1–32.

Lane, William C. "China and the United States." *The Guaranty News* 8, no. 3 (May 1919): 77–82.

Langston, L. H. *Practical Bank Operation.* New York: Ronald Press Company, 1921.

Larkin, John A. *Sugar and the Origins of Modern Philippine Society.* Berkeley: University of California Press, 1993.

Lasarte, Diego. "Putin Is Strengthening the Yuan's Role as Russia's Foreign Currency of Choice." *Quartz,* March 21, 2023.

"The Last of the IBC Groups." *No. 8* 21, no. 3 (March 1926): 10.

"Last Payment to Friars." *Boston Daily Globe,* October 21, 1905, 6.

Latour, Bruno. *Reassembling the Social: An Introduction to Actor-Network-Theory.* Oxford: Oxford University Press, 2005.

———. *Science in Action: How to Follow Scientists and Engineers through Society.* Cambridge, MA: Harvard University Press, 1987.

Lauer, Josh. *Creditworthy: A History of Consumer Surveillance and Financial Identity in America.* New York: Columbia University Press, 2017.

———. "The Good Consumer: Credit Reporting and the Invention of Financial Identity in the United States, 1840–1940." PhD diss., University of Pennsylvania, 2008.

Leonard, Thomas C. "Eugenics and Economics in the Progressive Era." *Journal of Economic Perspectives* 19, no. 4 (2005): 207–24.

————. *Illiberal Reformers: Race, Eugenics, and American Economics in the Progressive Era*. Princeton, NJ: Princeton University Press, 2016.

Letter to Charles Rich. July 19, 1920. Item #337, Folder: Peking. Heritage Collection at Citi.

Letter to Secretary of State. November 6, 1920. RG 59, Box 7592, Folder 811.516 / 324. National Archives.

Letter to W.P.G. Harding, Governor, Federal Reserve Board. July 15, 1920. 7, Item 79, Federal Reserve Board Reports. Heritage Collection at Citi.

Lewis, Cleona, and Karl T. Schlotterbeck. *America's Stake in International Investments*. Washington, DC: Brookings Institution, 1938.

Lewis, Ellen B. "The Foreign Trade Bureau." *The Guaranty News* 9, no. 8 (October 1920): 245–48.

Liedtke, Rainer. "Agents for the Rothschilds." In *Mobility and Biography*, edited by Sarah Panter, 33–46. Berlin: De Gruyter Oldenbourg, 2016.

Lih, Lars T. *Bread and Authority in Russia, 1914–1921*. Berkeley: University of California Press eScholarship Editions, 1990.

Link, Stefan, and Noam Maggor. "The United States as a Developing Nation: Revisiting the Peculiarities of American History." *Past & Present* 246, no. 1 (2020): 269–306.

Lipman, Jana K. *Guantánamo: A Working-Class History between Empire and Revolution*. American Crossroads. Berkeley: University of California Press, 2009.

List of 770 Employees in the Service of International Banking Corporation. November 1, 1920. Safekeeping Documents 2 (1902–1927), Item #335: 1918–1922. Heritage Collection at Citi.

"List of Students Enrolled in the Classes of the National City Bank at the Close of the Year 1915–1916." *No. 8* 11, no. 3 (September 1916): 121–35.

Livingston, James. *Origins of the Federal Reserve System: Money, Class, and Corporate Capitalism, 1890–1913*. Ithaca, NY: Cornell University Press, 1986.

Llorca-Jaña, Manuel. "Connections and Networks in Spain of a London Merchant-Banker, 1800–1850." *Revista de historia económica* 31, no. 3 (2013): 423–58.

————. "Huth & Co's Credit Strategies: A Global Merchant-Banker's Risk Management, C. 1810–1850." *Estudios de economía* 42, no. 2 (2015).

Lluch, Andrea. "Las Agencias De Informes Crediticios En La Argentina: Una Aproximación Al Funcionamiento De Los Mecanismos Informativos En El Mercado Crediticio (1892-C.1935)." *Investigaciones de historia económica: revista de la Asociación Española de Historia Económica*, no. 12 (2008): 111–40.

"The Logical Man." *Time Magazine* 67, no. 4 (1956): 18–20.

London Branch. July 6, 1920. Item #337, Folder: Lyons. Heritage Collection at Citi.

Lough, William H. Department of Commerce. Banking Opportunities in South America. Washington: Government Printing Office, 1915.

Lowenstein, Matthew. "China's Shadow Currency." *The Diplomat*, December 12, 2013.

Lowndes, Ruy. Plan for Reorganization of Commercial Department. February 27, 1919. Item #249, Foreign Branches - Rio de Janeiro - Confidential Letters, April–December 1920. Heritage Collection at Citi.

Lui, Claire. "A Manila Envelope: The Inspiration behind an Exhibition's Graphic Identity." 2021. July 3, 2023. https://www.guggenheim.org/blogs/checklist/a-manila-envelope-the -inspiration-behind-an-exhibitions-graphic-identity.

Lumba, Allan. "Empire, Expansion, and Its Consequence." In *A Companion to the Gilded Age and Progressive Era*, edited by Christopher M. Nichols and Nancy C. Unger. Wiley Blackwell Companions to American History, 399–410. West Sussex: Wiley-Blackwell, 2017.

———. "Imperial Standards: Colonial Currencies, Racial Capacities, and Economic Knowledge During the Philippine-American War." *Diplomatic History* 39, no. 4 (September 2015): 603–28.

———. *Monetary Authorities: Capitalism and Decolonization in the American Colonial Philippines*. Durham, NC: Duke University Press, 2022.

———. "Monetary Authorities: Market Knowledge and Imperial Government in the Colonial Philippines, 1892–1942." PhD diss., University of Washington, 2013.

"The Luncheon Classes." *No. 8* 11, no. 3 (September 1916): 92.

M., D. G. Mercantile Bank of the Americas. July 17, 1920. RG 59, Box 7592, Folder 811.516 / 313. National Archives.

Mackenzie, Compton. *Realms of Silver: One Hundred Years of Banking in the East*. London: Routledge, 1954.

Mahan, Alfred T. *The Influence of Sea Power upon History, 1660–1805*. Novato, CA: Presidio Press, 1987 [1890].

"Manila's First American Bank: Wall Street Enterprise Just Opening in the Philippines." *New York Times*, June 15, 1902, 33.

Manjapra, Kris. "Plantation Dispossessions: The Global Travel of Agricultural Racial Capitalism." In *American Capitalism: New Histories*, edited by Sven Beckert and Christine Desan, 361–87. New York: Columbia University Press, 2018.

The Manual of Statistics: Railroads, Grain and Produce. The Manual of Statistics. Vol. 22, New York: Financial News Association, 1901.

"Many Branch Banks to Be Established." *New York Times*, January 2, 1902, 6.

Marquardt, Walter W. The Encouragement of Thrift by the Bureau of Education. 1914. Walter W. Marquardt papers, 6, Volume: Bureau of Education: Activities, 1914. Bentley Historical Library, University of Michigan.

Marshall, David. "Origins of the Use of Treasury Debt in Open Market Operations: Lessons for the Present." *Economic Perspective (Federal Reserve Bank of Chicago)* 26, no. 1 (2002): 45–54.

Martin, Jamie. "Globalizing the History of the First World War: Economic Approaches." *The Historical Journal* 65, no. 3 (2022): 838–55.

———. *The Meddlers: Sovereignty, Empire, and the Birth of Global Economic Governance*. Cambridge, MA: Harvard University Press, 2022.

Martin, William. "The Improvement of Credit Department Methods in Member and Reserve Banks." *Bulletin of the National Association of Credit Men* 16, no. 4 (April 1916): 281–88.

Matthews, James. Credit Conditions in South American Countries: An Address before the Members of Banking IV Class, the National City Bank of New York. 1917. RG 10, Address before Members of the Banking IV Class. Heritage Collection at Citi.

———. "How to Approach the Questions Involved in Doing a South American Business." *Bulletin of the National Association of Credit Men* 17 (April 1917): 217–22.

May, Glenn Anthony. *Social Engineering in the Philippines: The Aims, Execution, and Impact of American Colonial Policy, 1900–1913*. Quezon City, Philippines: New Day Publishing, 1984.

McCook, John J. [Letter to Hon. Theodore Roosevelt]. November 2, 1901. Theodore Roosevelt Papers, Reel 20, Library of Congress.

———. [Letter to Mr. President]. August 19, 1904. Theodore Roosevelt Papers, Reel 46, Library of Congress.

McCormick, Thomas. "From Old Empire to New: The Changing Dynamics and Tactics of American Empire." In *Colonial Crucible: Empire in the Making of the Modern American State*, edited by Alfred W. McCoy and Francisco A. Scarano, 63–79. Madison: University of Wisconsin Press, 2009.

McIntyre, Frank. Letter to H.T.S. Green. 1917. RG 350, Box 890, Folder 17959–137. National Archive.

———. Letter to Hon. Frances Burton Harrison, Governor-General of the Philippine Islands. March 13, 1914. RG 350, Box 711, Folder 14221. National Archive.

———. Letter to Hon. J. Hampton Moore, Representative in Congress. January 24, 1914. RG 350, Box 711, Folder 14221. National Archive.

———. "Railroads in the Philippine Islands." *The Annals of the American Academy of Political and Social Science* 30 (1907): 52–61.

McKee, Stewart. "The Movement of a Bill in London." *Acceptance Bulletin* 10, no. 8 (August 31 1928): 5–8.

"The Mechanism of Exchange." *The Americas* 4, no. 2 (November 1917): 4–7.

Meeting of the Directors of the International Banking Corporation. December 20, 1901. 7, Annual Directors Meeting Minutes. Heritage Collection at Citi.

Mehrling, Perry G. *The New Lombard Street: How the Fed Became the Dealer of Last Resort*. Princeton, NJ: Princeton University Press, 2011.

———. "Retrospectives: Economists and the Fed: Beginnings." *Journal of Economic Perspectives* 16, no. 4 (2002): 207–18.

Melamed, Jodi. "Racial Capitalism." *Critical Ethnic Studies* 1, no. 1 (2015): 76–85.

Meltzer, Allan H. *A History of the Federal Reserve: Volume 1, 1913–1951*. Chicago: University of Chicago Press, 2003.

Memo. March 14, 1916. Frank A. Vanderlip Papers, Box E-39, Foreign Trade Department. Columbia RBML.

Memorandum. 1916. Box E-39, Folder: Foreign Trade Department. Columbia RBML.

Memorandum for Executive Committee: International Banking Corporation. January 10, 1917. RG 7, IBC, Correspondence, Memoranda and Organizational Documents of Harry Green—C. Heritage Collection at Citi.

Memorandum for Major McIntyre. May 10, 1909. RG 350, Box 799, Folder 17959. National Archive.

Memorandum for Mr. G. E. Mitchell, President Re: Dominican Branches of the International Banking Corporation. Dec. 22, 1925. Item #337—Transfer of Dominican Branches to NCB. Heritage Collection at Citi.

Memorandum in Reference to International Banking Corporation. June 20, 1945. Citi, RG 7, History of IBC - Cochran (1943–1965).

Menand, Lev. *The Fed Unbound: Central Banking in a Time of Crisis*. New York: Columbia Global Reports, 2022.

"Mercantile Bank of Americas Gets Credit Aid." *Journal of Commerce*, August 13, 1921.

Meulendyke, Ann-Marie. *U.S. Monetary Policy and Financial Markets*. Federal Reserve Bank of New York, 1998.

Mickle, Tripp, Karen Weise, and Nico Grant. "Tech's Biggest Companies Discover Austerity, to the Relief of Investors." *New York Times*, February 2, 2023.

Miller, Hugo. The Teaching of Business Methods in the Public Schools of the Philippine Islands. [1914]. Walter W. Marquardt papers, Box 5, Volume: Special Files. Bentley Historical Library, University of Michigan.

Miller, Rory. "British Investment in Latin America, 1850–1950: A Reappraisal." *Itinerario* 19, no. 3 (1995): 21–52.

———. "The London Capital Market and Latin American Public Debt, 1860–1930." In *La Deuda Publica En America Latina En Perspectiva Historica*, edited by Reinhard Liehr, 91–116. Frankfurt, Madrid: Vervuert, 1995.

The Mindoro Company: Charles J. Welch and Horace Havemeyer First Mortgage. April 24, 1914. #335, Safekeeping Documents, Rothschild, Archie Wilson, et al. Heritage Collection at Citi.

Minsky, Hyman P. "Central Banking and Money Market Changes." *The Quarterly Journal of Economics* 71, no. 2 (1957): 171–87.

Minty, Leonard. "Where American Banks Lead." *No. 8* 17, no. 7–8 (August 1922): 1–3.

Minutes—Bank Branch Committee: August 25, 1916. Frank A. Vanderlip papers, E-38, Bank Branch Committee. Columbia RBML.

Minutes—Bank Branch Committee: July 24, 1916. E, E-38, Bank Branch Committee. Columbia RBML.

Minutes—Bank Branch Committee: September 7, 1916. Frank A. Vanderlip papers, E-38, Bank Branch Committee. Columbia RBML.

Minutes of the Board of Directors. 1965–1978. RG 7, 1, Minutes of the Board of Directors. Heritage Collection at Citi.

Minutes of the Credit and Investment Committee. 1924. RG 3 Chase Manhattan Bank Collection, 17B6, 9. JPMorgan Chase Corporate History Collection.

Minutes of the Credit and Investment Committee. 1922. RG 3 Chase Manhattan Bank Collection, 17B6, 7. JPMorgan Chase Corporate History Collection.

Minutes of the Credit and Investment Committee, Jan–Jun. 1926. RG 3 Chase Manhattan Bank Collection, 17B6, 12. JPMorgan Chase Corporate History Collection.

Moazzin, Ghassan. *Foreign Banks and Global Finance in Modern China: Banking on the Chinese Frontier, 1870–1919*. Cambridge, UK: Cambridge University Press, 2022.

———. "Sino-Foreign Business Networks: Foreign and Chinese Banks in the Chinese Banking Sector, 1890–1911." *Modern Asian Studies* (2019): 1–35.

"Mobilizing Trained Minds for Commercial Preparedness." *The Americas* 2, no. 8 (1916): 1–5.

Moen, Jon R., and Ellis W. Tallman. "The Call Loan Market in the U.S. Financial System Prior to the Federal Reserve System." *Federal Reserve Bank of Atlanta Working Papers*, no. 2003–43 (December 2003).

Moody's Manual of Corporation Securities. Moody's Manual of Corporation Securities. New York: John Moody & Co., 1906.

Moody's Manual of Investments, American and Foreign: Banks - Insurance Companies - Investment Trusts - Real Estate - Finance and Credit Companies. Edited by John Sherman Porter. New York: Moody's Investor Services, 1933.

Moody's Manual of Railroads and Corporation Securities. New York: Moody Publishing Co., 1905.

Moody's Manual of Railroads and Corporation Securities. New York: Moody Manual Co., 1904.

Moore, C. O. [Letter to Hon. William L. Higgins, Secretary of State of Connecticut]. September 5, 1931. Board Shareholders Files 1, Item 79 State of Connecticut—Secretary's Office. Heritage Collection at Citi.

Moore, Colin D. "State Building through Partnership: Delegation, Public-Private Partnerships, and the Political Development of American Imperialism, 1898–1916." *Studies in American Political Development* 25, no. 1 (2011): 27–55.

Moore, George S. *The Banker's Life*. New York: W. W. Norton, 1987.

Morgan, James M. [Letter to Helie]. December 23, 1903. #524 James Morris Morgan Papers, Folder 4. The Wilson Library, University of North Carolina at Chapel Hill.

———. *Recollections of a Rebel Reefer*. Boston: Houghton Mifflin, 1917.

Morgan, Mary S. "Travelling Facts." In *How Well Do Facts Travel? The Dissemination of Reliable Knowledge*, edited by Peter Howlett and Mary S. Morgan, 3–39. Cambridge, UK: Cambridge University Press, 2011.

Mortimer, Frank. "Some Elements of Credit." *No. 8* 8, no. 7 (July 1918): 18–25.

"Moyer Succeeds Snyder." *New York Tribune*, November 22, 1902, 12.

Mulder, Nicholas. *The Economic Weapon: The Rise of Sanctions as a Tool of Modern War*. New Haven, CT: Yale University Press, 2022.

Musicant, Ivan. *The Banana Wars: A History of United States Military Intervention in Latin America from the Spanish-American War to the Invasion of Panama*. New York: Macmillan, 1990.

Myles, Jamieson. "Steering the Wheels of Commerce: State and Enterprise in International Trade Finance, 1914–1929." PhD diss., University of Geneva, 2021.

Nagano, Yoshiko. "The Agricultural Bank of the Philippine Government, 1908–1916." *Journal of Southeast Asian Studies* 28, no. 2 (1997): 301–23.

———. "Philippine 'Colonial Banking' during the American Period." *Philippine Review of Economics and Business* 36, no. 1 (June 1999): 58–81.

———. *State and Finance in the Philippines, 1898–1941: The Mismanagement of an American Colony*. Singapore: NUS Press, 2015.

"National City Bank Extends Sway to Orient." *New York Tribune*, October 29, 1915, 3.

National City Bank of New York. Facilidades Bancarias. 1926. RG 2, 2A, Facilidades Bancarias. Heritage Collection at Citi.

———. *No. 8, Educational Edition*. Vol. 11, 1916.

———. "Remarks of C. E. Mitchell, Chairman at the Annual Meeting of Shareholders." New York: National City Bank of New York, 1931.

———. "Remarks of C. E. Mitchell, Chairman at the Annual Meeting of Shareholders." New York: National City Bank of New York, 1932.

———. Remarks of the President at the Annual Meeting of Shareholders. January 10, 1928.

———. Statement of Condition. December 31, 1924.

National City Company. Valores De Inversión. 1927. RG 7, 2, Valores de Inversión. Heritage Collection at Citi.

Senate. Interviews on the Banking and Currency Systems of England, Scotland, France, Germany, Switzerland, and Italy. National Monetary Commission. US Government Printing Office, 1910.

"NCB Will Get You a Haircut in Buenos Aires." *No. 8* 15, no. 9 (September 1920): 20.

"New Bond Brokers Make Bow." *Los Angeles Times*, May 1, 1934, 14.

"New Budget Plan for C.I.D. Depositors." *No. 8* 22, no. 4 (April 1927): 1–2.

"The New Manila Hotel." *Far Eastern Review* 6, no. 2 (July 1909).

Newman, Wilson, J. Facts About Dun & Bradstreet, Inc. 1956. Dun & Bradstreet Records— Series IV(A), Box 23, Folder 9. Harvard Business School.

Newton, Lucy. "Trust and Virtue in Banking: The Assessment of Borrowers by Bank Managements at the Turn of the Twentieth Century." *Financial History Review* 7, no. 2 (2000): 177–99.

Ngai, Mae M. "Transnationalism and the Transformation of the 'Other': Response to the Presidential Address." *American Quarterly* 57, no. 1 (2005): 59–65.

"Nineteen-Fourteen Outing." *No. 8* 9, no. 5–6 (May–June 1914): 14–20.

Notz, William. "Export Trade Problems and an American Foreign Trade Policy." *Journal of Political Economy* 26, no. 2 (February 1918): 105–24.

O'Malley, Frank. *Our South American Trade and Its Financing: How to Develop, How to Finance, and How to Hold Trade with South America*. Foreign Commerce Series. New York: National City Bank of New York, 1920.

O'Shea, Peter. "A Talk with an International Banker." *Magazine of Wall Street* 29, no. 3 (1921): 152+.

O'Sullivan, Mary. *Dividends of Development: Securities Markets in the History of U.S. Capitalism, 1866–1922*. Oxford: Oxford University Press, 2016.

———. "Past Meets Present in Policymaking: The Federal Reserve Act and the U.S. Money-market, 1913–1929." *UPIER Working Papers* 6, no. 18/4 (2018).

O'Hara, Robert M. "Creating and Marketing of Bankers Acceptances." *Acceptance Bulletin* 7, no. 11 (November 1925): 17–21.

Office of the Comptroller of the Currency. *Annual Report of the Comptroller of the Currency, Vol 1*. Washington: Government Printing Office, 1914 through 1919.

———. *Annual Report of the Comptroller of the Currency*. Washington: Government Printing Office, 1929.

Ogle, Vanessa. "Archipelago Capitalism: Tax Havens, Offshore Money, and the State, 1950s–1970s." *American Historical Review* 122, no. 5 (December 2017): 1431–58.

———. "'Funk Money': The End of Empires, the Expansion of Tax Havens, and Decolonization as an Economic and Financial Event." *Past and Present* (2020).

———. "Global Capitalist Infrastructure and U.S. Power." In *The Cambridge History of America and the World: Volume 4: 1945 to the Present*, edited by David C. Engerman, Max Paul Friedman, and Melani McAlister, 31–54. Cambridge, UK: Cambridge University Press, 2022.

Olegario, Rowena. "Credit Information, Institutions, and International Trade: The United Kingdom, United States, and Germany, 1850–1930." In *The Foundations of Worldwide Economic Integration: Power, Institutions, and Global Markets, 1850–1930*, edited by Christof Dejung and Niels P. Petersson, 60–85. New York: Cambridge University Press, 2013.

———. "Credit Reporting Agencies: A Historical Perspective." In *Credit Reporting Systems and the International Economy*, edited by Margaret J. Miller, 115–60. Cambridge, MA: MIT Press, 2003.

———. *A Culture of Credit: Embedding Trust and Transparency in American Business*. Cambridge, MA: Harvard University Press, 2006.

"On to Russia." January–February 1917. RG 2 / NCBNY, Aspersions. Heritage Collection at Citi.

Orendain, Joan. *Citibank: The Philippine Century (1902–2002)*. Manila: Citibank, 2002.

Osborne, Nicholas. "Little Capitalists: The Social Economy of Saving in the United States, 1816–1914." PhD diss., Columbia University, 2014.

"Oscar P. Austin Dies at 85 Years." *New York Times*, January 8, 1933, 30.

"Oscar Phelps Austin." *No. 8* 12, no. 2 (1917): 26–27.

Ott, Julia C. *When Wall Street Met Main Street: The Quest for an Investors' Democracy*. Cambridge, MA: Harvard University Press, 2011.

"Our Legacy in South America." Caterpillar, 2021. January 7, 2022. https://www.caterpillar.com /en/news/caterpillarNews/2021/legacy-south-america.html.

Owen, Norman G. *Prosperity without Progress: Manila Hemp and Material Life in the Colonial Philippines*. Berkeley: University of California Press, 1984.

Ozorio, Candido Emilio. A Brief History of the Shanghai Branch of the National City Bank of New York, 1900–1932. 1940. RG 12/ Bank Histories, A Brief History of the National City Bank of New York—Shanghai Branch. Heritage Collection at Citi.

Pahlka, Jennifer. *Recoding America: Why Government Is Failing in the Digital Age and How We Can Do Better*. New York: Metropolitan Books, 2023.

Pak, Susie. *Gentlemen Bankers: The World of J. P. Morgan*. Cambridge, MA: Harvard University Press, 2013.

Palen, Marc-William. "The Imperialism of Economic Nationalism, 1890–1913." *Diplomatic History* 39, no. 1 (2014): 157–85.

Park, Seung Woo. "Agrarian Transformation and Colonialism in the Context of Capitalist Development: An Historical-Comparative Study of Korea and the Philippines." PhD diss., University of Georgia, 1991.

Parker, Challen R. "Department of Banks and Bankers." *The Guaranty News* 8, no. 12 (February 1920): 377–81.

Parrini, Carl P. "Charles A. Conant and Foreign Policy, 1896–1903." In *Behind the Throne: Servants of Power to Imperial Presidents*, edited by Thomas J. McCormick and Walter LaFeber, 35–66 (Madison: University of Wisconsin Press, 1993).

———. *Heir to Empire: United States Economic Diplomacy, 1916–1923*. Pittsburgh, PA: University of Pittsburgh Press, 1991 [1969].

Parrini, Carl P. and Martin J. Sklar. "New Thinking about the Market, 1896–1904: Some American Economists on Investment and the Theory of Surplus Capital." *Journal of Economic History* 43, no. 3 (September 1983), 559–578.

Peer, Nadav Orian. "Negotiating the Lender-of-Last-Resort: The 1913 Fed Act as a Debate over Credit Distribution." *NYU Journal of Law & Business* 15 (2019): 367–452.

"Penmanship." *No. 8* 11, no. 3 (September 1916): 50.

Perkins, Edwin J. *Financing Anglo-American Trade: The House of Brown, 1800–1880*. Cambridge, MA: Harvard University Press, 1975.

———. "Financing Antebellum Importers: The Role of Brown Bros. & Co. in Baltimore." *Business History Review* 45, no. 4 (1971): 421–51.

Perkins, James H. "South American Trade and Establishment of Dollar Credits." *Journal of the American Bankers Association* 8, no. 1 (July 1915): 75–76.

"Personal Loan Facilities Are Broadened." *No. 8* 23, no. 6–7 (June–July 1928): 3.

Pertilla, Atiba. "'Shall Bank Clerks Marry?': Gender, Labor, and the Wall Street Workforce, 1890–1915." In *Social Science History Association Conference*. Baltimore, MD, 2015.

Phelps, Clyde William. *The Foreign Expansion of American Banks: American Branch Banking Abroad*. New York: Ronald Press Co., 1927.

Philippine Banks: Abstraction of Reports of Philippine Banks. December 31, 1903. 101, PC46–28, Philippines. National Archives.

The Philippine Club. Boston: The Merrymont Press, 1930.

"Philippine Railroad Building with Filipino Builders." *Railroad Gazette* 43, no. 11 (September 13, 1907): 297–301.

The Philippine Railway Company—Board of Directors. June 29, 1907. RG 350, Box 726, Folder 15058. National Archive.

"Philippine Railway Faces Receivership: Manila Government Is Reported Planning to Force Insolvency as Bonds Mature, Unpaid." *New York Times*, July 1, 1937, 48.

"Philippine Tobacco Trust." *Hartford Courant*, December 6, 1901.

Pinzur, David. "Infrastructural Power: Discretion and the Dynamics of Infrastructure in Action." *Journal of Cultural Economy* 14, no. 6 (2021): 644–61.

A Plan for Practical Co-Operation between the Universities and Colleges of the United States and the National City Bank of New York. 1916. SJ Papers Francis A. Barnum, Box 7, Folder 11. Georgetown University Library Booth Family Center for Special Collections.

"Plans of New Oriental Bank: International Corporation to Develop the Trade of Far East." *San Francisco Chronicle*, January 3, 1902, 2.

"Point of View." *Western Christian Advocate*, March 5, 1902, 4.

Poovey, Mary. *A History of the Modern Fact: Problems of Knowledge in the Sciences of Wealth and Society*. Chicago: University of Chicago Press, 1998.

Porter, Theodore M. *Trust in Numbers: The Pursuit of Objectivity in Science and Public Life*. Princeton, NJ: Princeton University Press, 1996.

Pramuanratkarn, Thiravet. "The Hongkong Bank in Thailand: A Case of a Pioneering Bank." In *Eastern Banking: Essays in the History of the Hongkong and Shanghai Banking Corporation*, edited by Frank H. H. King, 421–34. London: Athlone Press, 1983.

Prasad, Srinivas B. "The Metamorphosis of City and Chase as Multinational Banks." *Business and Economic History* 28, no. 2 (1999): 201–11.

Prendergast, William A., and William Howard Steiner. *Credit and Its Uses*. New York: D. Appleton and Company, 1931.

"The Problem of Bill Distribution." *Acceptance Bulletin* 11, no. 5 (May 31, 1929): 1–3.

"Progress of the Educational Work of the City Bank Club." *No. 8* 9, no. 5–6 (May–June 1914): 21–24.

Prudden, Russell. *The Bank Credit Investigator*. New York: The Bankers Publishing Company, 1922.

"The Question of Whether Credit Insurance Would Pay for Itself." *The Americas* 5, no. 8 (May 1919): 21–24.

Quezon III, Manuel Luis. "The Glory Days." *Philippine Tatler*, November 2007.

Quigley, Neil C. "Bank Credit and the Structure of the Canadian Space Economy C. 1890–1935." PhD diss., University of Toronto, 1986.

Quinn, Sarah L. *American Bonds: How Credit Markets Shaped a Nation*. Princeton, NJ: Princeton University Press, 2019.

R. G. Dun & Co. Letter to Messrs R. G. Dun & Co., New Orleans, LA. March 16, 1897. Dun & Bradstreet Corporation Records II(A), v. 19 Letterbook. Harvard Business School.

"Rangoon Savings Contest Winners." *No. 8* 25, no. 4 (April 1930): 12–13.

Rebovich, Joseph W. "Frank A. Vanderlip and the National City Bank." PhD diss., New York University, Graduate School of Business Administration, 1972.

Renda, Mary A. *Taking Haiti: Military Occupation and the Culture of U.S. Imperialism, 1915–1940.* Chapel Hill: University of North Carolina Press, 2001.

Renshaw, Mrs. Clarence. "The Home Service Department." *Journal of the American Bankers Association* 12, no. 7 (January 1920): 356–57.

"Report of the Condition of the National City Bank of New York." *New York Times*, December 4, 1912, 16.

"Report of the President, Bowdoin College, 1914–1915." Brunswick, Maine: Bowdoin College, 1915.

"Retirement of Henry S. Manning." *Iron Trade Review*, January 19, 1905, 43.

Richardson, William B. The High Cost of Outfitting. 1917. John L. H. Fuller Papers, Box 2, Folder 4. Indiana Historical Society.

Ricks, Morgan. "Money as Infrastructure." *Columbia Business Law Review* 3 (2018): 757–851.

"Rites for Developer of Palos Verdes Conducted." *Los Angeles Times*, September 6, 1977, D5.

Rivera, J. F. "Banking in Cuba." *No. 8* 14, no. 10 (October 1919): 16–18.

Robert Morris Associates. *The Robert Morris Associates: A Brief History and Description of the Accomplishments, Aims and Principles of This Organization of Bank Credit Executives.* Robert Morris Associates: A Short Explanatory History of the Aims and Accomplishments, Lansdowne, PA. 1924.

———. *A Short Descriptive History of the Robert Morris Associates: A National Organization of Bank Loaning Executives.* Lansdowne, PA: The Associates, 1928.

Robertson, Craig. *The Filing Cabinet: A Vertical History of Information.* Minneapolis: University of Minnesota Press, 2021. Ebook.

Robinson, Alexander. "The Budget System in the American Home." *Journal of the American Bankers Association* 13, no. 5 (November 1920): 327–30.

Robinson, Cedric J. *Black Marxism: The Making of the Black Radical Tradition.* London: Zed Press, 1983.

Rodgers, Daniel. "American Exceptionalism Revisited." *Raritan* 24, no. 2 (2004): 21–47.

———. "Exceptionalism." In *Imagined Histories: American Historians Interpret Their Past*, edited by Anthony Molho and Gordon S. Wood, 21–40. Princeton, NJ: Princeton University Press, 1998.

Rodgers, James H. Directors' Minutes. May 21, 1908. RG 7, Annual Directors Meeting Minutes. Heritage Collection at Citi.

———. Directors' Minutes. September 7, 1906. 7, Annual Directors Meeting Minutes. Heritage Collection at Citi.

Roosevelt, Kermit. Diary. 1915. Kermit Roosevelt and Belle Roosevelt Papers, Box 2, Library of Congress.

Roosevelt, Theodore. Letter to Joseph Bucklin Bishop. October 30, 1903. Theodore Roosevelt Digital Library, http://www.theodorerooseveltcenter.org/Research/Digital-Library/Record.aspx?libID=o186328. Library of Congress Manuscript Division.

———. Letter to Joseph Bucklin Bishop. January 22, 1904. Theodore Roosevelt Digital Library, http://www.theodorerooseveltcenter.org/Research/Digital-Library/Record.aspx?libID=o187162. Library of Congress Manuscript Division.

Root, Elihu. Letter to the International Banking Corporation. June 21, 1902. RG 350, Box 418, Folder 5500. National Archive.

Rosenberg, Emily S. *Financial Missionaries to the World: The Politics and Culture of Dollar Diplomacy, 1900–1930*. Durham, NC: Duke University Press, 2003 [1999].

———. "Foundations of United States International Financial Power: Gold Standard Diplomacy, 1900–1905." *Business History Review* 59, no. 2 (1985): 169–202.

———. *Spreading the American Dream: American Economic and Cultural Expansion, 1890–1945*. American Century Series. New York: Hill and Wang, 1982.

Rosenberg, Emily S., and Norman L. Rosenberg. "From Colonialism to Professionalism: The Public-Private Dynamic in United States Foreign Financial Advising, 1898–1929." *The Journal of American History* 74, no. 1 (1987): 59–82.

Rosenthal, Caitlin. "Balancing the Books: Convergence and Diversity of Accounting in Massachusetts, 1875–1895." *Journal of Economic History* 80, no. 3 (September 2020): 782–812.

Rötheli, Tobias. "Innovations in US Banking Practices and the Credit Boom of the 1920s." *Business History Review* 87, no. 2 (2013): 309–27.

Rovensky, John E. "The Development of Dollar Exchange". *Bulletin of the National Association of Credit Men* 17 (October 1917): 997–1000.

"San Nicolas Iron Works." *Far East Review* (August 1906): 99.

Sanders, M. Elizabeth. *Roots of Reform: Farmers, Workers, and the American State, 1877–1917*. American Politics and Political Economy. Chicago: University of Chicago Press, 1999.

"Sanitary Steam Laundry Company's Installation." *The Far Eastern Review*, March 1909, 354.

Santo Domingo: Bad & Doubtful Debts Written Down to $1.00. 1926. Item 337/IBC, Dominican Branches. Heritage Collection at Citi.

"Savings Bank Section: Americanization." *Journal of the American Bankers Association* 11, no. 10 (April 1919): 564–65.

"Says Debt in Brazil Ran Up Unchecked." *New York Times*, January 22, 1933, 1.

Schmeckebier, Laurence F., and Gustavus Adolphus Weber. *The Bureau of Foreign and Domestic Commerce*. Institute for Government Research. Baltimore: Johns Hopkins Press, 1924.

Schuker, Stephen A. "Money Doctors between the Wars: The Competition between Central Banks, Private Financial Advisers, and Multilateral Agencies, 1919–39." In *Money Doctors: The Experience of International Financial Advising, 1850–2000*, edited by Marc Flandreau, 49–77. London; New York: Routledge, 2003.

Schult, Volker. "The San Jose Sugar Hacienda." *Philippine Studies* 39, no. 4 (1991): 458–74.

Schwedtman, F. Charles. The Financial Situation in Relation to Foreign Service. May 1922. RG 5, 27, Heritage Collection at Citi.

Schwedtman, Ferdinand C. "The Making of Better Trained Men." *The Americas* 2, no. 2 (November 1915): 5–8.

Secretary of State. Special Instructions No. 505—field for American Banks. Feb 16, 1917. RG 59, Box 7590, Folder 811.516. National Archive.

Sellstrom, John Edward. "The Credit Interchange and Adjustment Work of the National Association of Credit Men." MBA thesis, University of Texas, 1937.

Selvaratnam, H.L.D. "The Guarantee Shroffs, the Chettiars, and the Hongkong Bank in Ceylon." In *Eastern Banking: Essays in the History of the Hongkong and Shanghai Banking Corporation*, edited by Frank H. H. King, 409–34. London: Athlone Press, 1983.

"Seventy Years in Asia." *Overseas Citibanker* 2 (1972): 5–15.

"Shall Bank Clerks Marry?" *The Brooklyn Daily Eagle*, February 23, 1904.

Shannon, H. A. "Evolution of the Colonial Sterling Exchange Standard." *Staff Papers (International Monetary Fund)* 1 (1950): 334–54.

Shou, Chongyi, and Leying Shou. "Wai Shang Yin Hang Zai Zhongguo [Foreign Banks in China]." Beijing: Zhongguo wen shi chu ban she, 1996.

Simmons, W. M. Those "Good Old Days." July 25, 1972. RG 7, History of International Banking Corporation—Employee Memoirs. Heritage Collection at Citi.

"A Sketch of the Educational Activities of the National City Bank." *No. 8* 11, no. 3 (September 1916): 6–11.

Sklar, Martin J. "Dollar Diplomacy According to Dollar Diplomats: American Development and World Development." In *The United States as a Developing Country: Studies in U.S. History in the Progressive Era and the 1920s*, edited by Martin J. Sklar, 78–101. Cambridge, UK: University of Cambridge, 1992.

Smialek, Jenna. *Limitless: The Federal Reserve Takes on a New Age of Crisis.* New York: Knopf, 2023.

Smith Bell and Company. *Under Four Flags: The Story of Smith, Bell, & Company in the Philippines.* Bristol, England: J. W. Arrowsmith, Ltd., 1972.

Smith, David Sellers. "The Elimination of the Unworthy: Credit Men and Small Retailers in Progressive Era Capitalism." *Journal of the Gilded Age and Progressive Era* 9, no. 2 (2010): 197–220.

South, J. G. Letter to the Secretary of State. April 16, 1929. RG 59, Box 7592, Folder 811.51619 / 1. National Archives.

"Special Training Classes Conducted by the Bank, City Company and I.B.C." *No. 8* 14, no. 7 (July 1919): 22–25.

Speck, Mary. "Prosperity, Progress, and Wealth: Cuban Enterprise during the Early Republic, 1902–1927." *Cuban Studies* 36 (2005): 50–86.

Stallings, Barbara. *Banker to the Third World: U.S. Portfolio Investment in Latin America, 1900–1986.* Berkeley: University of California Press, 1987.

Stanley, Peter W. *A Nation in the Making: The Philippines and the United States, 1899–1921.* Cambridge, MA: Harvard University Press, 1974.

Star, Susan Leigh, and Geoffrey C. Bowker. "How to Infrastructure." In *Handbook of New Media: Social Shaping and Consequences of ICTs*, edited by Leah A. Lievrouw and Sonia Livingstone, 151–62. London: SAGE Publications, Ltd., 2002.

Starr, Peter. *Citibank: A Century in Asia.* Singapore: Editions Didier Millet, 2002.

"State Whipping Post." *Hartford Courant*, March 1, 1901, 12.

Statement Showing the Condition of the Manila Branch of the International Banking Corporation . . . November 21, 1903. RG 350, Box 419, 5. National Archives.

Stegner, Wallace. *Discovery!: The Search for Arabian Oil.* Lebanon: Middle East Export Press, 1971.

Steinbock-Pratt, Sarah. *Educating the Empire: American Teachers and Contested Colonization in the Philippines.* Cambridge Studies in US Foreign Relations. Cambridge, UK: Cambridge University Press, 2019.

Stenographic Report of Meeting: Wednesday, January 3, 1917. RG 7, Correspondence, Memoranda and Organizational Documents of Harry T. S. Green—S. Heritage Collection at Citi.

Stratton, Trevin. "Mammon Unbound: The International Financial Architecture of Wall Street Banks, 1915–1925." In *The Impact of the First World War on International Business*, edited by Andrew Smith, Kevin Tennent and Simon Mollan. New York: Routledge, 2016. Reprint, Published on Academia.edu.

Subscription Agreement. December 20, 1901. RG 7, Annual Directors Meeting Minutes. Heritage Collection at Citi.

Suggestions as to Organization & Scope of Foreign Services. 1916. Frank A. Vanderlip papers, Box E-39, Folder: Foreign Trade Department. Columbia RBML.

Sweeney, Pete. "China Shadow Bankers Pray to Be Systemically Risky." Reuters, August 23, 2022.

Tait, Selwin. Letter to Honorable Robert Bacon, Acting Secretary of State. December 3, 1908. 59, M862, Reel 106 - 774 / 487. National Archives.

"The Teachers." No. 8 11, no. 3 (September 1916): 16.

Terami-Wada, Motoe. "The Sakdal Movement, 1930–34." Philippine Studies 36, no. 2 (1988): 131–50.

The World Bank. "GDP (Current US$)." 2023. July 5, 2023. https://data.worldbank.org/indicator /NY.GDP.MKTP.CD.

"This Is Very Much the Same as Usual." March–April 1917. RG 2 / NCBNY, Aspersions. Heritage Collection at Citi.

Tichy, Noel, and Ram Charan. "Citicorp Faces the World: An Interview with John Reed." Harvard Business Review, November–December 1990.

Tiglao, Rigoberto. The Philippine Coconut Industry: Looking into Coconuts. Manila: Arc Publication, 1981.

[Timeline]. nd. RG12, Citibank Book, Argentina–History, 1812–1978. Heritage Collection at Citi.

To the Men in the Foreign Field. 1916. John L. H. Fuller Papers, 2, 3. Indiana Historical Society.

Tooze, J. Adam. The Deluge: The Great War, America and the Remaking of the Global Order, 1916–1931. New York: Viking, 2015.

———. "The Rise and Fall and Rise (and Fall) of the U.S. Financial Empire." Foreign Policy, January 15, 2021.

Tooze, Adam, and Ted Fertik. "The World Economy and the Great War." Geschichte und Gesellschaft 40, no. 2 (2014): 214–38.

"Total Assets of the Federal Reserve, Recent Balance Sheet Trends." Board of Governors of the Federal Reserve System, 2023. March 22, 2023. https://www.federalreserve.gov/monetary policy/bst_recenttrends.htm.

"Training Its Men to Do the Work." Nation's Business, September 1916, 1.

"The Training of Men for Foreign Service." No. 8 11, no. 3 (September 1916): 107–19.

Transfer Securities Record. 1909–1918. RG 7, Item #324. Heritage Collection at Citi.

Treasury Department. Annual Report of the Comptroller of the Currency. Washington: Government Printing Office, 1905.

Trigueros, A. Guerra. The National City Bank of New York and Our Freedom. April 16, 1929. RG 59, Box 7592, Folder 811.51616 / 2. National Archives.

Trivellato, Francesca. The Promise and Peril of Credit: What a Forgotten Legend about Jews and Finance Tells Us about the Making of European Commercial Society. Princeton, NJ: Princeton University Press, 2019.

Tuffnell, Stephen. "Engineering Inter-Imperialism: American Miners and the Transformation of Global Mining, 1871–1910." Journal of Global History 10, no. 1 (2015): 53–76.

Turner, Frederick Jackson. The Significance of the Frontier in American History. London: Penguin, 2008 [1893].

Turner, Frederick Jackson, and John Mack Faragher. *Rereading Frederick Jackson Turner: "The Significance of the Frontier in American History" and Other Essays.* New Haven; London: Yale University Press, 1999.

Twenty-Fifth Reunion Record of the Class of 1915. University of Pennsylvania, 1941.

"Two Banks Consolidate: The Western National Absorbs the United States National." *New York Tribune,* November 20, 1897, 9.

"Tying the World to New York." *New York Tribune,* January 12, 1919, A2.

Tyrrell, Ian. "American Exceptionalism in an Age of International History." *American Historical Review* 96, no. 4 (1991): 1031–55.

US Commission to the Philippine Islands Department of State. *Report of the Philippine Commission to the President, Vol. 2.* Denby, Charles, John R. MacArthur, J.G. Schurman, George Dewey, and Dean C. Worcester. Washington: Government Printing Office, 1900.

US Congress. Federal Reserve Act. Government Printing Office, 1913.

US Congress. Federal Reserve Act: Public Law 63–43, 63d Congress, H.R. 7837: An Act to Provide for the Establishment of Federal Reserve Banks, to Furnish an Elastic Currency, to Afford Means of Rediscounting Commercial Paper, to Establish a More Effective Supervision of Banking in the United States, and for Other Purposes. 1913.

"A U.S. Foreign Legion." *Time* 37, no. 26 (June 30, 1941): 71.

"A United States Manufacturer Explains." *The Americas* 3, no. 3 (December 1916): 35.

Van Meter, Henry Hooker. *The Truth about the Philippines, from Official Records and Authentic Sources . . . A Reference Review.* Chicago: Liberty League, 1900.

Van Vleck, Jenifer. *Empire of the Air: Aviation and the American Ascendancy.* Cambridge, MA: Harvard University Press, 2013.

Vanderlip, Frank. [Letter to James Stillman]. June 5, 1914. Frank A. Vanderlip papers, B-1-5, Columbia RBML.

———. [Letter to James Stillman]. May 14, 1915. Frank A. Vanderlip papers, B-1-5, Columbia RBML.

———. [Letter to James Stillman]. January 22, 1916. Frank A. Vanderlip papers, B-1-7, Columbia RBML.

Veeser, Cyrus. *A World Safe for Capitalism: Dollar Diplomacy and America's Rise to Global Power.* New York: Columbia University Press, 2002.

The Vegetable Oil Corporation. June 6, 1918. Manuel Luis Quezon papers, Reel 8, Bentley Historical Library, University of Michigan.

Ventura, Theresa Marie. "American Empire, Agrarian Reform and the Problem of Tropical Nature in the Philippines, 1898–1916." PhD diss., Columbia University, 2009.

———. "From Small Farms to Progressive Plantations: The Trajectory of Land Reform in the American Colonial Philippines, 1900–1916." *Agricultural History* 90, no. 4 (2016): 459–83.

Vevier, Charles. *The United States and China, 1906–1913: A Study of Finance and Diplomacy.* New Brunswick, NJ: Rutgers University Press, 1969.

"A Vexed Question: Should a Man Marry on Less Than a Thousand a Year?" *Los Angeles Times,* March 9, 1904, 12.

Vine, David. *Island of Shame: The Secret History of the U.S. Military Base on Diego Garcia.* Princeton, NJ: Princeton University Press, 2009.

W.W.L. Re: I.B.C. Transfer to N.C.B. Nov 12, 1926. Item #337, F.E.D.—General (1926–1930). Heritage Collection at Citi.

Wadhwani, R. Daniel. "The Institutional Foundations of Personal Finance: Innovation in U.S. Savings Banks, 1880s–1920s." *Business History Review* 85, no. Autumn (2011): 499–528.

Wall, Alexander. *Credit Barometrics*. Washington, DC: Federal Reserve Board, Division of Analysis and Research, 1922.

———. "The Genesis of Financial Statements." *The Credit Monthly* 32, no. 9 (September 1930): 17, 40.

Wang, Ching-Chun. "The Hankow-Szechuan Railway Loan." *American Journal of International Law* 5, no. 3 (1911): 653–64.

Wansleben, Leon. *The Rise of Central Banks: State Power in Financial Capitalism*. Cambridge, MA: Harvard University Press, 2023.

"Warburg a Leader in Banking Reform." *New York Times*, January 25, 1932, 5.

Warburg, Paul. "Defects and Needs of Our Banking System." *New York Times*, January 6, 1907, 4.

Warburg, Paul M. *The Federal Reserve System, Its Origin and Growth; Reflections and Recollections, Vol 2*. New York: Macmillan Co., 1930.

National Monetary Commission. Senate. The Discount System in Europe. Warburg, Paul Moritz. Washington: Government Printing Office, 1910.

"Warburgs Found Firm in Holland." *New York Times*, September 4, 1929, 44.

Ward, Wilbert. "The Creation of Acceptance Credits–Part II." *Acceptance Bulletin of the American Acceptance Council* 4, no. 10 (October 1922): 4–6.

Wasson, Clarence. International Banking Corporation: File in Cashier's Administration. November 2, 1978. 7, 2, History of IBC. Heritage Collection at Citi.

Weber, C. O. "Race Psychology and Industry." *The Credit Monthly* 27, no. 9 (September 1925): 12–13.

Weeks, G. K. Copy of Letter from International Banking Corporation Madrid. October 25, 1929. Item #337, IBC, Reorganization of Spanish Branches. Heritage Collection at Citi.

———. Memorandum Re Tax Situation—Spain. October 24, 1929. Item #337, IBC, Reorganization of Spanish Branches. Heritage Collection at Citi.

Weise, Karen. "Amazon Reports Almost No Profit and Slowing Growth." *New York Times*, February 2, 2023.

Westcott, H. E. International Banking Corporation: Report on Manila Branch and Consolidated Balance Sheet of the Corporation as of December 30th, 1905. May 4, 1907. RG 350, Box 420, Folder 5500. National Archive.

"Western National Bank Meeting." *New York Tribune*, January 30, 1903, 12.

"What Has Been Done in a Year." *The Americas* 1, no. 11 (August 1915): 18–19.

White, Eugene Nelson. "The Political Economy of Banking Regulation, 1864–1933." *Journal of Economic History* 42, no. 1 (1982): 33–40.

"The White House Dinner: Prince Entertained in Great East Room by the President." *New York Times*, February 25, 1902, 1.

White, Lawrence. "Exclusive: HSBC Puts Global Footprint under Fresh Scrutiny, Considers Dozen Exits." Reuters, May 24, 2023.

White, Richard. *Railroaded: The Transcontinentals and the Making of Modern America*. New York: W. W. Norton & Co., 2012.

Whiteside, A. D. [Memo]. May 19, 1933. Dun & Bradstreet Records—Series IV(B), Box 37, Folder 1. Harvard Business School.

"Who Owns the Federal Reserve?". Board of Governors of the Federal Reserve System, nd. Accessed March 22, 2023. https://www.federalreserve.gov/faqs/about_14986.htm.

"Why Exports to South America's West Coast Must Be Well Packed." *The Americas* 6, no. 8 (May 1920): 21–25.

Wilkins, Mira. *The Maturing of Multinational Enterprise: American Business Abroad from 1914 to 1970*. Cambridge, MA: Harvard University Press, 1974.

Wilkinson & Grist. Re: International Banking Corporation and National City Bank of New York. December 21, 1926. Item #337, IBC, F.E.D.—General (1926–1930). Heritage Collection at Citi.

Williams, Daniel R. *The Odyssey of the Philippine Commission*. Chicago: A.C. McClurg & Co., 1913.

Williams, William Appleman. *The Tragedy of American Diplomacy*. Cleveland, OH: World Publishing Company, 1959.

"With the Old Guard." January–February 1917. RG 2 / NCBNY, Aspersions. Heritage Collection at Citi.

Wodehouse, P. G. *Psmith in the City*. London: A. & C. Black, 1910.

Wolfe, Oliver Howard. *Elementary Banking*. New York: Correspondence Chapter, inc., American Institute of Banking, 1915.

"Woman Wins First Prize in Manila Savings Essay Contest." *No. 8* 22, no. 4 (April 1927): 19.

Wong, Kwok-chu. *The Chinese in the Philippine Economy, 1898–1941*. Quezon City, Philippines: Ateneo De Manila University Press, 1994.

Woodworth, Leo Day. "New Phase in Savings Banking." *Journal of the American Bankers Association* 12, no. 8 (February 1920): 443–47.

Worcester, Dean C. *Coconut Growing in the Philippine Islands: Cost of Production and Profits, Copra Making*. War Department, Bureau of Insular Affairs, 1911.

"World Contest Tops All Records with $10,226,884 in 74,082 Accounts." *No. 8* 23, no. 8 (August 1928): 1–5+.

Ybanez, Roy. "The Hongkong Bank in the Philippines, 1899–1941." In *Eastern Banking: Essays in the History of the Hongkong and Shanghai Banking Corporation*, edited by Frank H. H. King. London: Athlone Press, 1983.

Yu, Xie. "Citi to Wind Down Consumer Banking in China, Affecting About 1,200 Staff." Reuters, December 15, 2022.

Zakim, Michael. *Accounting for Capitalism: The World the Clerk Made*. Chicago: University of Chicago Press, 2018.

———. "Bookkeeping as Ideology." *Common-place* 6, no. 3 (2006): 1.

———. "Paperwork." *Raritan* 33, no. 4 (Spring 2014): 34–56.

INDEX

acceptances, 15–16, 79–81, 171; and banks' bottom lines, 92–98; and British banks, 113; commission rates on, 207n68; compared to Treasury securities, 94; eligibility guidelines for, 182n43; fate of, 168–69; and Federal Reserve System, 85–89; and financial risks, 105; and Guaranty Trust Company, 107, 108; history and mechanics of, 81–85; IBC's access to British, 159; and National City Bank, 90–91; in 1910s and 1920s, 99–101; and rural interests, 205n33; and US banks, 98–99, 204n12

Adolfo Roensch & Co., 66–67

Agricultural Bank (Philippines), 61

Alexander, James W., 28

Allen, Douglas F., 147

American Bankers Association, 149

"American Colony" (Argentina), 171

American exceptionalism, 14

American International Corporation, 90

Americanization campaigns, 148–49

American-Philippine Company, 77

American Sugar Refining Company, 75–77

Americas, The (magazine), 106–7, 131, 135, 136, 217n72

Anglo-Saxon superiority, 121, 123–25

Apollonio, Kenneth, 147

archipelago capitalism, 162–63

Argentina, 133, 138; banking and infrastructural power in, 171; British banks in, 40; conflict resolution in, 135–36; credit information practices in, 212n60; national

bonds in, 153; small-scale lending programs in, 152

Austin, Oscar, 106, 119–20, 124–25

Bache, Jules, 27

Baker, Franklin H., 146, 147

Bank Branch Committee (National City Bank), 142

Bank of Boston, 132, 218n83

bankers' acceptances. *See* acceptances

banks: and economic opportunity, 9–12, 18; and the Great Depression, 155–56; information practices of (*see* information); during interwar period, 17, 138–39; local staff of, 51, 156–57, 158, 194n94; in Manila, 56–62; public function of, 10; regulatory adaptation by, 158–64; reorganization of, 139–45; retail banking and localization by, 148–55; and US colonial empire, 19–20; and US financial power, 3–6, 12–14, 165, 170–74. *See also* acceptances; British banks; Federal Reserve System; *and specific banks*

Barker, James, 218n83

Belgian Group, 30–31, 159

BFDC (Bureau of Foreign and Domestic Commerce), 142

BIA (Bureau of Insular Affairs), 57, 62–63, 76–77

bills of exchange. *See* acceptances

Bishop, Joseph Bucklin, 29–30

bonds: IBC railway, 72–73; international marketing of, 70, 153–55; retail banking focus on, 148